1ST EDITION

THE ULTIMATE SUMMER PROGRAM GUIDE

FOR *HIGH SCHOOL STUDENTS*

SCIENCE • TECHNOLOGY • ENGINEERING • MATH • BUSINESS
HISTORY • LAW • PRE-MED • AND MORE

The first compilation of pre-collegiate programs to support career exploration and self-discovery. Offering 800+ summer program opportunities to boost academic and college planning success.

JENNIFER WILLIAMS TAYLOR
JOYCE WONG

College Consulting Experts
By Jennifer Williams Taylor
By Joyce Wong
Copyright © 2018 by College Consulting Experts
All Rights Reserved

Printed in the United States of America

Book Design by Victor Hwang

To our families and friends who have journeyed with us
each step of the way in our passion
and commitment to support higher education.

Thank you to Gary for taking this remarkable
journey with me.
This text honors Jonathan, Lindsay, and Matthew who have
become compassionate and accomplished adults; it also
celebrates high school students everywhere
as they aspire to do the same.

With gratitude to Randall for your unwavering
midnight conversations about pursuing
my dreams for young people.
This text honors Kiana, Kayla, and Kaitlyn for the adults we
hope you will become –
dynamic, curious, eager to be a part of something good.

Table of Contents

PREFACE

Introduction To The Purpose Of This Text

WHY SUMMER PROGRAMS

Pre-collegiate summer programs aren't just one of the most exciting components of the college admissions process, but one of the most critical components of adolescent self-development. In fact, the value of summer college programs is so often-overlooked yet so universally beneficial, that we have dedicated an entire book to helping students explore these opportunities.

It's no secret that college costs are only getting higher while admissions rates are dropping lower. Students and parents are faced with growing fears amidst every aspect of the admissions process, perhaps even wondering if all of this will really be 'worth it'. This is where the value of summer programs truly emerges. They provide advantages across virtually every facet of the admissions process, not to mention the self-discovery journey.

Contrary to popular belief, summer programs are not limited to a few select offerings at a few elite institutions. There are nearly 700 pre-collegiate experiences at public and private universities across the United States. As an on-campus, residential immersion program ranging from typically 1-8 weeks, summer programs may present a hands-on preview of the college campus, the chosen field of study and the student-professor dynamic. In addition, they are an authentic (and often first) introduction to living and learning away from home.

Do I really know what my desired major entails? Will I like living away from home as much as I hope I will? Does my desired campus atmosphere support my learning needs? Am I really ready?

One of the only ways to know... is to apply to a summer program and find out. Students whom attend a summer program gain a contextual sampling of college life. In reflection, students may choose to adjust their admissions strategy or college list, validate or change their desired major or take steps to prepare for self-sufficiency. After all, it's far easier to set expectations once you actually know what to expect. The small upfront personal and financial investment can save you tens of thousands of dollars and several (frustrating) semesters of irrelevant coursework down the road.

Furthermore, attending a summer program is a huge college admissions advantage (hint: this is a little-known secret, until now!). Admissions readers appreciate the motivation, willingness and commitment evidenced by the successful completion of a summer program. This distinction demonstrates a pre-disposition to self-examination and scholastic command, attributes highly-desired by admissions officers. When all candidates are created equal, participation in a summer program can offer a decisive advantage within the intense admissions environment.

WHAT YOU WILL FIND

Inside this resource, you will find a truly better way to prepare for one of the largest decisions of your life. *The Ultimate Summer Program Guide For High School Students* is the academic industry's largest, most extensive publication dedicated exclusively to this missing piece of the higher education equation.

As a diverse and relentlessly researched compilation of over 800+ summer program opportunities across the United States, options will appeal to virtually every high school student with every aspiration. Subject areas include but are not limited to: Science, Technology, Math, Engineering, Business, History, Law, Liberal Arts, Pre-Med, free opportunities and much, much more. Programs may accept applicants on qualifications alone or on a first-come, first-serve basis; they may be led by current students, graduate students or taught by faculty; cohorts may consist of dozens, hundreds or thousands of students; some are even designed to allow attendees to start earning college credits.

The information in the pages to follow is intended to provide a two-fold benefit. Students will tread invaluable ground in their journey to self-discovery as they explore all that can be accomplished in a pre-collegiate summer AND attain the contact and application information to get started in this highly constructive and searchable guide.

Whether seeking programs which validate current interests, provide peer support or fine-tune soft-skills, college-bound youth can turn the most powerful summer of their high school years into the most influential instrument in their academic careers.

WHO THIS IS FOR

More often than not, college resources often feel like they are designed for those whom already have a firm sense of direction. In contrast, this guide challenges every student to look beyond what they think they know or predicate what they don't know. It provides a connection to trialing colleges, careers and communities, which in turn aids in self-reflection and educational planning.

Thus, *The Ultimate Summer Program Guide For High School Students* is for the student who has an idea of where he/she wants to go, but no idea how to get there. It's also for the student who knows he/she needs to do something, but isn't sure what or how to start figuring it out. With our utmost appreciation for those invested in youth development, this book is also for the student 'village'. It's for the many well-meaning parents, mentors and dedicated educators who long to support students in finding themselves and their career paths, but struggle with providing real-life opportunities to do so.

The teen who wants to experience his first computer engineering class? The future doctor who wants to meet a pre-med graduate? The creative future liberal arts major who wants to test-drive a small-town campus? The history teacher who wants to find an inspiring program for his most dedicated student? The parent who wants his/her child to see what 'fits'?

YES. This compilation is designed for anyone who wants to be empowered or empower someone in navigating their college and career ambitions.

HOW IT WILL SUPPORT YOU

More than strictly academically beneficial, we've referred to summer program experiences as truly meaningful. As readers prepare to make the time investment of a summer, they are also entering spheres of like-minded peers, granting themselves permission to discover passions, inquiring beyond the book and questioning what the next four years may bring.

We urge students to keep an open mind, to try several programs when torn in multiple directions, to apply themselves in full and to accept when an experience feels right – or not. The hardest climbs lead to the best views; whether these glimpses into college life are open windows or squeaky doors, they hold equal value in mapping the journey.

WHAT YOU NEED TO KNOW

It would be unfair to write a book that helps students develop expectations without also setting a few of our own. While the outcomes of summer programs are vast and highly personal, our experience supporting over 10,000 college applicants has refined what we consider to be the '7 Essential Summer Program Expectations'.

1. Attending A Specific Summer Program Does NOT Guarantee Admission Into A Specific University. While it may be disheartening, it is also true, for instance: getting into an Ivy League summer program does not grant an automatic golden ticket to any college. The experience and achievement will no doubt be academically and fundamentally valuable and will support a solid admissions profile. But it is not an all-encompassing college insurance policy.

2. Costs Will Vary Greatly. If one or two summer programs feel financially unattainable, look further. Some programs offer financial aid or scholarships. Some may be closer to home or shorter in duration which may mitigate overall cost. Don't be afraid to ask if assistance is available, and don't stop looking if it's not. Did we mention summer programs are also a test of perseverance, a practice everyone can appreciate during the admissions process (trust us)?!

3. Teachers & Faculty May Vary. Not all summer programs are led by full-time faculty, nor by every professor from every department. Summer program providers may be the school's world-renowned English professor, or a graduate student. In some cases, third-party providers are brought onto campus to lead the course or experience. None of these are right or wrong, they are just considerations to be aware of as data is gathered and priorities are set.

4. Accept The Unexpected. We've heard of students having a lifelong desire to be a scientist – only to learn they hated being stuck in a lab. There has even been a case or two (or hundreds) where that first-choice UC campus just didn't feel 'right' after staying there. Summer programs are designed to deliver realities – not validate pre-conceived perceptions. This does not mean an obstacle is now blocking the road, it simply means a juncture has been reached.

5. No Credits, No Problem. Many students and parents alike feel that spending a summer at college is only advantageous if credits are accrued. While that is a feature of some, it is not what we consider the biggest benefit. Discounting a program that does not offer course credits could mean missing out on the immeasurable social, emotional and contextual elements that generate the highest non-tangible value.

6. Start Researching ASAP. The earlier students start researching summer programs, the more they will have access to. Many accept high school students at age 14 (there are even some for middle schoolers). If you can make the most of one summer – imagine what you could do with three? Moreover, summer program deadlines vary greatly; waiting to find a program and apply in spring is almost always too late.

7. Strategize With Support. Once high schoolers see how many programs exist, they are often hard-pressed to choose which to apply to. While it's tempting to use cost, location and peer interest as primary factors, this is not academically nor individually favorable. A student's current and desired admissions strengths/weaknesses, as well as his/her actual college list and majors of interest are the components that lead to the most impactful opportunities. Please consult with a college admissions professional to truly maximize this highly-regarded season of time.

OUR HOPE FOR YOU

What we hope for our readers is actually a dichotomy. We hope they find exactly what they are looking for, and exactly what they weren't looking for at all. The diverse and far-reaching offerings enclosed are intended to give students a glimpse into what they think they want, and question what else there might be.

Our hope is that students will gain invaluable experiences through the selection, application and completion of one or more summer programs. Our hope is to evoke curiosity, enhance strengths and identify weaknesses. Our hope is to create the most academically, socially and contextually prepared classes of college graduates in the years to come, such that countless individuals can look back and say that *one summer* truly made all the difference.

Art Programs

Name of College
Academy of Art University

Name of Program
Summer Pre-College Art Experience: Course- Introduction to 3D Modeling and Animation

Academic / Career Interest
Art

Website
https://catalog.academyart.edu/catalog/pre-college/1860?0

Application Timeline
Contact institution for more information.

Eligibility
Students must be entering high school as a sophomore, junior or senior year in the fall. Students staying in campus housing must take three on-campus classes (only available in summer). Additional fees apply. Students must be at least 16 years old to be eligible for housing during the summer program, but 15 year olds interested in campus housing may submit two Letters of Reference from a school teacher and from an employer or a non-profit organization where the high school student has done volunteer work.

Tuition Fees
Estimated Fees: About $917 per unit - 3 units per class

Information about the program:
Students will learn the basic concepts of 3D modeling and animation for the entertainment industry. Production techniques and tool sets of a leading modeling and animation program will be explored. Students will learn to model, animate, and render a student proposed project. The online course requires students have access to Maya 2013 software to take the course, check with institution for current software updates and requirements.

Contact
(800) 544-2787

Name of College
Academy of Art University

Name of Program
Summer Pre-College Art Experience: Fashion Construction

Academic / Career Interest
Art

Website
https://catalog.academyart.edu/catalog/pre-college/1660?1

Application Timeline
Contact institution for more information.

Eligibility
Students must be entering high school as a sophomore, junior or senior year in the fall. Students staying in campus housing must take three on-campus classes (only available in summer). Additional fees apply. Students must be at least 16 years old to be eligible for housing during the summer program, but 15 year olds interested in campus housing may submit two Letters of Reference from a school teacher and from an employer or a non-profit organization where the high school student has done volunteer work.

Tuition Fees
Estimated Fees: $917 per unit - 3 units per class and an additional $80 for supplies

Information about the program:
In this course, students will learn how to operate industrial equipment, source fabrics, deconstruct then reconstruct old garments, create original designs, and cut, construct, and finish designs for three projects. One example of the final project will be an oversized messenger bag.

Contact
(800) 544-2787

Name of College
Adelphi University

Name of Program
Summer Pre-College Program for High School Students

Academic / Career Interest
Art

Website
https://precollege.adelphi.edu/programs/programs-for-credit/musical-theatre-bootcamp/

Application Timeline
Applications are reviewed on a rolling basis and will continue to be accepted until the program is fully enrolled.

Eligibility
Students entering their sophomore, junior or senior year in the fall of each academic year are eligible to apply.

Tuition Fees
Estimated Fees: $3,500

Information about the program:
This two-week intensive program is designed to introduce and strengthen overall performance skills. It will emphasize the various tools an actor must have in seeking a professional career in the theatre and will take advantage of Adelphi's proximity to New York City and the lights of Broadway. Daily workshops in singing, improvisation, theatre games, scene study, monologues, dance movement, make-up, and stage combat will be offered over the two-week period. Students will rehearse in the afternoon and evenings, which will culminate in an original performance that utilizes the skills acquired during their training. Students will work with their instructors in a stress-free environment, collaborating closely with their fellow actors, creating a healthy community of supportive, ensemble actors.

Contact
(516) 877-3410
precollege@adelphi.edu

Name of College
ArtCenter College of Design

Name of Program
Summer Intensives

Academic / Career Interest
Art

Website
https://www.artcenter.edu/teens/summerintensives.jsp

Application Timeline
Registration begins approx. April, classes begin approx. June

Eligibility
Courses in art and design for high school students (grades 9-12)

Tuition Fees
Estimated Fees: $1,700

Information about the program:
ArtCenter for Teens introduces a four-week intensive summer program for students seeking a rigorous in-depth experience in a chosen area of concentration. In addition to studio classes, weekly guest speakers (practicing artists and designers) will share their stories and career paths. Lectures about art and design will familiarize students with design history, cultural icons and design trends. The program will conclude with a final exhibition and celebration of student work open to friends, family and educators. Areas of concentration: Graphic Design/Advertising, Entertainment Design, Industrial Design (Product & Transportation Design).

Contact
(626) 396-2319
teens@artcenter.edu

Name of College
School of the Art Institute of Chicago

Name of Program
Summer Institute Residency Program

Academic / Career Interest
Art

Website
http://www.saic.edu/cs/high_school/summerinstituteresidency-program/

Application Timeline
Contact institution for more information.

Eligibility
Students must be at least 15 years old and not older than 18 years and have completed their sophomore year of high school to enroll in the Early College Program (ECP) Summer Institute.

Tuition Fees
Estimated Fees:

- Two-Week Session: Total for Tuition, Housing, and Meals: $4,181
- Four-Week Session: Total for Tuition, Housing, and Meals: $8,362

Information about the program:
Students will study with School of the Art Institute of Chicago's amazing faculty, passionate teachers and acclaimed practicing artists, designers, and scholars, many of whom teach in the undergraduate program. Students will experience state-of-the-art facilities and resources including the Art Institute of Chicago museum, the third largest collection of art in the world. Students will live in the incomparable student residence halls in the heart of downtown Chicago.

Contact
(312) 629-6170
ecp@saic.edu

Name of College
University of the Arts

Name of Program
Summer Institute: Dance

Academic / Career Interest
Dance

Website
https://www.uarts.edu/academics/pre-college-programs/summer-institute-dance

Application Timeline
Priority application deadline: approx. March
Scholarship application deadline: approx. March

Eligibility
Rising juniors and seniors or international students of equivalent grade level (residential or commuter). Rising sophomores (commuter only).

Tuition Fees
Estimated Fees range from $2,000 - $3,300

Information about the program:
Through daily technique classes and opportunities to choreograph, improvise, and perform repertory, this immersive three-week program stretches students' body, mind, and understanding of dance as an art form, a college major, and a career. With a rotating selection of guest artists in each of the core courses, students will gain an expansive understanding of the facets of ballet, modern, and composition and improvisation. Students will develop both physically and artistically under the guidance of celebrated dancers and choreographers. The program includes electives in over a dozen genres, repertory projects, artist talks, professional dance concerts, museum trips, and open studio space for developing choreography.

Contact
(215) 717-6430
precollege@uarts.edu

Name of College
University of the Arts

Name of Program
Summer Institute: Theater

Academic / Career Interest
Theater

Website
https://www.uarts.edu/academics/pre-college-programs/summer-institute-theater

Application Timeline
Priority application deadline: approx. March
Scholarship application deadline: approx. March

Eligibility
Rising juniors and seniors or international students of equivalent grade level (residential or commuter). Rising sophomores (commuter only)

Tuition Fees
Estimated Fees:

- Residential Program Cost: $5,293
- Commuter Program Cost: $3,700

Information about the program:
Students will experience University of the Arts (UArts) summer program in Center City Philadelphia, one of the nation's largest theater destinations, for four weeks of immersive study. Students will choose one of three tracks: Acting, Musical Theater Performance, or Directing, Playwriting + Production. Modeled after the renowned UArts undergraduate experience, this program trains artists looking for individualized and hybrid opportunities to write, direct, design, and produce in addition to performing. Students will enliven their unique artistry in any direction they choose.

Contact
(215) 717-6430
precollege@uarts.edu

Name of College
University of the Arts

Name of Program
Summer Institute: Music Business

Academic / Career Interest
Music Business

Website
https://www.uarts.edu/academics/pre-college-programs/summer-institute-music-business-entrepreneurship-technology

Application Timeline
Priority application deadline: approx. March
Scholarship application deadline: approx. March

Eligibility
Rising juniors and seniors or international students of equivalent grade level (residential or commuter). Rising sophomores (commuter only)

Tuition Fees
Estimated Fees:

- Residential Program Cost: $4,150
- Commuter Program Cost: $2,875

Information about the program:
The music industry is quickly evolving, and this three-week Music Business program gives students an edge by sharing the latest in technology and business practices. Students will dive into an immersive, real-world curriculum and collaborate with peers and professionals. Through project simulations, students will merge new software skills with their love of music. Students will work with a network of professionals in the music and technology industries, from respected performers to master technicians.

Contact
(215) 717-6430
precollege@uarts.edu

Name of College
University of the Arts

Name of Program
One-Week Commuter Intensives: Street Photography

Academic / Career Interest
Art

Website
https://www.uarts.edu/academics/pre-college-programs/summer-institute-one-week-intensives

Application Timeline
Space permitting, registrations for One-Week Commuter Intensives will be accepted on an on-going basis.

Eligibility
Rising 9th - 12th graders are welcome to apply.

Tuition Fees
Estimated Fees: $560 per class

Information about the program:
Students follow in the footsteps of pioneering street photographers such as Eugène Atget and Henri Cartier-Bresson — and contemporary artists like Vivian Maier, Diane Arbus, and Bill Cunningham — by capturing the city's spirit through their lens. Students will explore camera control along with essential photographic concepts such as "the decisive moment". Students will put these concepts to use on walking trips to local Philadelphia parks, markets, and galleries, where they'll transform the conventional into the exceptional and hone their distinct perspective of the world around them. Previous experience using a camera is preferred for this course.

Contact
(215) 717-6430
precollege@uarts.edu

Name of College
University of the Arts

Name of Program
One-Week Commuter Intensives: Graphic Design

Academic / Career Interest
Art

Website
https://www.uarts.edu/academics/pre-college-programs/summer-institute-one-week-intensives

Application Timeline
Space permitting, registrations for One-Week Commuter Intensives will be accepted on an on-going basis.

Eligibility
Rising 9th - 12th graders are welcome to apply.

Tuition Fees
Estimated Fees: $560 per class

Information about the program:
Design is everywhere in our modern world — posters, publications, album covers, apparel, digital and other media utilize graphic design to convey messages to viewers. Design and popular culture have grown more intertwined through recent history, and this course aims to explore this relationship. Students will focus on the principles and possibilities of visual communication, including graphic form, type design, layout, image treatment, and sequence using the Adobe Creative Suite. Investigate the influence of design on trending topics while mastering the technical skills involved in this relevant profession.

Contact
(215) 717-6430
precollege@uarts.ed

Name of College
University of the Arts

Name of Program
One-Week Commuter Intensives: Portfolio Preparation

Academic / Career Interest
Art

Website
https://www.uarts.edu/academics/pre-college-programs/summer-institute-one-week-intensives

Application Timeline
Space permitting, registrations for One-Week Commuter Intensives will be accepted on an on-going basis.

Eligibility
Rising 9th - 12th graders are welcome to apply.

Tuition Fees
Estimated Fees: $560 per class

Information about the program:
Students critically evaluate their visual arts college application portfolio in this dynamic and useful course. Students work with a variety of 2D media to create four to six works suitable for inclusion in their portfolio, including foundational design projects and observational drawings. Students will discuss strategies for presenting and photographing their work. At the end of the course, students will review their portfolio with a UArts admission counselor to assess its strengths and areas for improvement. This course is open to high school juniors and seniors. Nude figure models will be used in this course.

Contact
(215) 717-6430
precollege@uarts.edu

Name of College
The Art Institute of California in San Diego

Name of Program
College Bound: Concepts & Theories in Culinary with Lab

Academic / Career Interest
Culinary Arts

Website
http://getcreative.artinstitutes.edu/san-diego

Application Timeline
Contact institution for more information.

Eligibility
Open to high school juniors and seniors.

Tuition Fees
Contact institution for more information.

Information about the program:
This 11-week course primarily centers on delivering the foundational knowledge and skills in the fundamental techniques and theories of the culinary arts and in industry practices. But unlike a standard lecture-style theory course, this course will take place in a real, industrial kitchen where hands-on demonstrations and lab assignments will be performed to demonstrate the principles being covered. Through applied coursework and hands-on experiences including preparation of a variety of recipes, participants will have the opportunity to build the necessary skills and abilities needed in the food service industry.

Contact
www.getcreative.artinstitutes.edu/san-diego

Name of College
Boston University

Name of Program
Boston University Summer Theatre Institute (BUSTI)

Academic / Career Interest
Theater

Website
https://www.bu.edu/cfa/busti/

Application Timeline
BUSTI will evaluate applications and admit students on a rolling basis throughout the spring.

Eligibility
Rising sophomores, juniors, and seniors in high school.

Tuition Fees
Estimated Fees: $6,436 - $6,628

Information about the program:
BUSTI is a five-week conservatory experience for highly motivated high school theatre artists. Designed to mirror the freshman BFA experience within the College of Fine Arts School of Theatre at Boston University, the Institute allows all participants the opportunity to test their interests and abilities in a professional training environment. Students earn 4.0 college credits for their coursework in acting, design, voice, singing, and stage combat, as well as master classes, experimental theatre laboratories, and the creation of an original piece of theatre with members of their ensemble. Throughout the five-week program, students engage with Boston University, the professional artistic community in Boston, and the city's historic and cultural offerings. Students graduate from BUSTI having honed their technique, depth of intellectual and artistic questioning, playfulness in collaboration, and ability to tell a dynamic story through the theatrical medium.

Contact
(617) 353-3350
askcfa@bu.edu

Name of College
Boston University

Name of Program
Boston University Tanglewood Institute (BUTI)

Academic / Career Interest
Music

Website
https://www.bu.edu/cfa/tanglewood/

Application Timeline
Applications accepted and reviewed on a space-available basis

Eligibility
Ages 10–20

Tuition Fees
Contact institution for more information.

Information about the program:
52 years and 10,000 alumni strong, BUTI is a leader in the field, a program of Boston University College of Fine Arts and affiliated with the Boston Symphony Orchestra and Tanglewood Music Center. With those resources at their fingertips, students can expect an unforgettable experience, but it goes even deeper than that. For many, the program is a summer of exploration and discovery. And for some, it's a pivotal moment when a student dares to pursue a life in the arts. BUTI students become a part of the Tanglewood continuum—a rich community of artists like no other. From peer musicians in training, to teachers who inspire, to the rock stars in the field, the collective learning and aspirations of every musician are fueled by the synergy of a world-class university and major symphony orchestra. That's what makes BUTI extraordinary. BUTI has programs for all orchestral instruments, voice, piano, and composition, ranging in duration from two to six weeks. Check with institution for more information about program offerings.

Contact
(617) 353-3350
askcfa@bu.edu

Name of College
Brandeis University

Name of Program
Precollege: Vocal Music

Academic / Career Interest
Music

Website
https://www.brandeis.edu/precollege/bima/index.html

Application Timeline
Applications are viewed on a rolling basis until spaces are filled

Eligibility
Students must be rising juniors and seniors.

Tuition Fees
Estimated Fees: $6,400

Information about the program:
The vocal ensemble program is focused on strengthening a student's versatility as a vocalist and musician in a small vocal ensemble setting. Small vocal ensemble work focuses on improving vocal technique, implementing a variety of tones and performance techniques and bringing individual voices together to form one unified powerfully emotional sound. The ensemble works on complex arrangements from a variety of music styles with a Jewish history emphasis, past selections included pieces from the Renaissance, Yiddish Jazz, Ladino, Israeli pop, Acapella, Broadway and Contemporary Classical. Arrangements often focus on 4-7 parts harmony with 1-2 singers on a part. This is a great opportunity for members of a large choir to find their individual voice and contribution in an ensemble, and for solo singers to develop harmonizing, musicianship and teamwork skills.

Contact
(781) 736-8416
precollege@brandeis.edu

Name of College
Brandeis University

Name of Program
Precollege: Visual Arts

Academic / Career Interest
Art

Website
https://www.brandeis.edu/precollege/bima/majors/visual-arts.html

Application Timeline
Applications are viewed on a rolling basis until spaces are filled.

Eligibility
Students must be rising juniors and seniors

Tuition Fees
Estimated Fees: $6,400

Information about the program:
As a BIMA visual artist, students will join their peers and the professional arts faculty to create a vibrant studio community in the Brandeis fine arts studios. Students will be encouraged to experiment as they develop their technical and creative skills with guidance from exhibiting artists. Throughout the summer, students will work in a variety of two- and three-dimensional media, including drawing, painting, sculpture, collage and mixed media. Directed assignments and open-ended questions invite students to test new ideas and techniques, and to develop their visual vocabulary. Students will create a number of individual pieces to add to their portfolio, including a self-directed final project. Students will also have opportunities to work with their peers to create collaborative projects and installations professional gallery settings.

Contact
(781) 736-8416
precollege@brandeis.edu

Name of College
University of California, Los Angeles

Name of Program
Acting and Performance Summer Institute

Academic / Career Interest
Acting

Website
https://summer.ucla.edu/institutes/ActingandPerformance

Application Timeline
Approx. February - April: Summer Scholars Support for California High School Students Application Period

Eligibility
The program is designed for high school students completing grades 9 through 12.

Tuition Fees
Estimated Fees:

- U.S. Visiting Students (Non-UC): $5,798.00
- Fall 2018 UCLA Students: $5,487.32
- Fall 2018 Other UC Students: $5,518.00

Information about the program:
The UCLA Acting and Performance Summer Institute is a three-week, UC credit-bearing, intensive program for high school students in theater arts, encompassing performance training classes, movement-based techniques, a final performance project, guest workshops and field trips.

Contact
(310) 825-4101
info@summer.ucla.edu

Name of College
University of California, Los Angeles

Name of Program
Film and Television Summer Institute

Academic / Career Interest
Film & Television

Website
https://summer.ucla.edu/institutes/FilmandTV

Application Timeline
Contact institution for more information.

Eligibility
Contact institution for more information.

Tuition Fees
Estimated Fees:

- U.S. Visiting Students (Non-UC): $5,798.00
- Fall UCLA Students: $5,487.32
- Fall Other UC Students: $5,518.00

Information about the program:
The University of California, Los Angles (UCLA) Film & Television Summer Institute gives students from across the country and around the globe an unparalleled opportunity to study filmmaking at one of the most prestigious film schools in the world. Applicants can select one of the following concentrations: Creative Producing; Film Producing (offered twice); Traditional Animation; Stop Motion Animation. The UCLA Film & Television Summer Institute shapes the filmmakers of tomorrow right in the heart of Los Angeles, the entertainment capital of the world.

Contact
(310) 825-4101
info@summer.ucla.edu

Name of College
California Institute of the Arts

Name of Program
Discover Animation

Academic / Career Interest
Art

Website
https://extendedstudies.calarts.edu/search/publicCourse-SearchDetails.do?method=load&courseId=202244&selectedProgramAreaId=17977&selectedProgramStreamId=

Application Timeline
Contact institution for more information.

Eligibility
High school students age 14-17 are encouraged to apply.

Tuition Fees
Contact institution for more information.

Information about the program:
Students live and learn at the beautiful Santa Clarita Valley campus located just north of Los Angeles. In addition to working closely with engaging artists and exploring animation, students will have the opportunity to make friends with other artists in the program and participate in a variety of on-campus social activities at Chouinard Hall, the BFA dorms where Discover students will live while attending the program. There will be daily activities such as film screenings, games in the recreation hall, or open swim in the CalArts pool. In addition, students enrolled in the two-week program are eligible to sign up for a field trip to Disneyland for an additional fee.

Contact
(661) 222-2746

Name of College
Culinary Institute of America

Name of Program
Journey for Juniors

Academic / Career Interest
Culinary

Website
https://www.ciachef.edu/journey-for-juniors/

Application Timeline
Contact institution for more information.

Eligibility
To participate in Journey for Juniors, students must:

- Be entering their senior year in high school by Fall, be at least 16 years of age, and be considering a culinary or baking and pastry career.
- Have one parent or legal guardian accompany them. Parent will take part in all aspects of the program, with the exception of the kitchen class on Saturday.

Tuition Fees
Contact institution for more information.

Information about the program:
At Journey for Juniors, students will:

- Take part in an interactive cooking demonstration and tasting, learning from a CIA chef.
- Learn all about the hot career paths and cool CIA majors they can choose
- Get the lowdown on what it's like to be a CIA student from the source, current CIA students
- Walk around campus and imagine themselves as a CIA student in a year or less!

Contact
(845) 451-1509
Ronald.Knoth@culinary.edu

Name of College
Carnegie Mellon University

Name of Program
Summer Pre-College Drama Program

Academic / Career Interest
Drama

Website
http://admission.enrollment.cmu.edu/pages/pre-college-drama

Application Timeline
Admission decision are made on a rolling basis, with consideration given to space available in a particular program.

Eligibility
Students must be in high school, have completed their sophomore year and be 16 to 18 years old.

Tuition Fees
Estimated Fees:

- Resident: $8,691
- Commuter: $6,289

Information about the program:
Pre-College Drama introduces high school students to rigorous, conservatory style challenges. The length and depth of the summer conservatory-style program can lead to a stronger resolve to pursue a career in theater. Pre-College Drama focuses on the audition process rather than a production, which allows students to enter the college application/audition process with a repertoire of monologues and songs, as well as the skills needed to find material appropriate for their age and type. The opportunity for students to hone their pieces with nationally acclaimed faculty and perform a mock audition, for which they receive constructive feedback, gives the students a clear idea of their strengths and weaknesses.

Contact
(412) 268-2082
admission@andrew.cmu.edu

Name of College
Carnegie Mellon University

Name of Program
Summer Pre-College Music Program

Academic / Career Interest
Music

Website
http://music.cmu.edu/pages/pre-college

Application Timeline
Application Deadline: approx. April
Admissions are rolling, applications may be accepted after the deadline pending space in the program.

Eligibility
Designed for rising high school juniors and seniors.

Tuition Fees
Estimated Fees:

- Resident: $8,274
- Commuter: $5,874

Information about the program:
Carnegie Mellon University School of Music educates outstanding musicians in a stimulating conservatory-style environment, inspiring imagination and creativity in music, and in the construction of musical knowledge in all of its diverse forms. Designed for rising high school juniors and seniors, the six-week Summer Pre-College residential program will give students the opportunity to see what college is like in a highly regarded atmosphere. This is not high school, and it is not camp - it is as close to college as a high school student can get. Students get to live on campus, take classes with conservatory professors, rehearse and perform with other students from all over the country, and enjoy the freedom of college life in a safe environment.

Contact
music-precollege@andrew.cmu.edu

Name of College
Chapman University

Name of Program
Summer Film Academy

Academic / Career Interest
Film

Website
https://www.chapman.edu/dodge/summer-programs/summer-film-academy/index.aspx

Application Timeline
Application deadline: approx. March

Eligibility
Students entering high junior or senior year at start of program with at least a 3.0 weighted GPA.

Tuition Fees
Estimated Fees: $3,100 (includes housing)

Information about the program:
For two weeks students are immersed in the world of film through class discussions, film screenings, guest speakers, field trips, and filmmaking in small groups. They live, breathe and eat filmmaking around the clock while being taught by Chapman faculty who are industry professionals and mentored by current Dodge College grad students and alumni. All of this will be shared with their peers as they work in groups to complete projects to create short digital, narrative projects which are showcased to parents and relatives on the final night of the program in the 500-seat Folino Theater.

Contact
(714) 997-6765
summerfilmacad@chapman.edu

Name of College
Cleveland Institute of Art

Name of Program
Pre-College Program

Academic / Career Interest
Journalism

Website
https://www.cia.edu/continuing-education/pre-college

Application Timeline
Contact institution for more information.

Eligibility
High school students entering grades 10–12.

Tuition Fees
Estimated Fees ranges from $2,000 - $4,000

Information about the program:
Students will sharpen their artistic skills, experiment with new media, build their portfolios and focus on their art at Cleveland Institute of Art's Pre-College Program. During this two- or four-week residential program, students will use the tools and processes available only to Cleveland Institute of Art students and experience the life of an art student at a premier college of art and design.

Alongside other students entering grades 10–12, students will:

- Earn college credits
- Experience college life
- Explore new media, while building their portfolio
- Study with professional artists and designers
- Learn about careers in art and design
- Meet with a CIA admissions counselor

Contact
(216) 421-7460

Name of College
Columbus College of Art and Design

Name of Program
Columbus College of Art and Design (CAD) College Preview

Academic / Career Interest
Journalism

Website
https://www.ccad.edu/college-preview

Application Timeline
Registration due: approx. June

Eligibility
High school students in grades 10-12

Tuition Fees
Estimated fees: $3,450 covers three college credits, three weeks of on-campus residence, all meals and all required supplies.

Information about the program:
For high school students in grades 10-12 considering a future in art and design, CCAD College Preview will make their decision clear — and earn them three college credits. Students will be able to experience any CCAD fine arts programs as they participate in classes, workshops and activities all taught by CCAD talented faculty and staff. In and out of the classroom, students will have opportunities to meet and collaborate with other emerging artists and designers from all across the country.

Contact
(614) 222-3236
outreach@ccad.edu

Name of College
University of Connecticut

Name of Program
Pre-College Summer @ UConn: Animation

Academic / Career Interest
Art

Website
https://precollege-summer.uconn.edu/academic-areas/art-animation/

Application Timeline
Applications closed one week prior to each session start date.

Eligibility
PCS participants must be rising juniors or seniors in high school and at least 15 years of age to apply.

Tuition Fees
Estimated fees: $1950 (tuition) and $45.00 (studio/lab fee)

Information about the program:
Students learn how to make an animation based on a character they invent. This course is an exploration of stop-motion animation using traditional and experimental methods. In addition to creating characters and objects that move, participants will learn about character development and visual story telling devices. This course emphasizes creative resolution and experimentation within the realm of animation.

Working with new media artist, John O'Donnell, students will be challenged to imagination to develop a unique character, the character's backstory and environment. Participants will generate their own story line and the final project will be a collaborative exercise in creative story telling. No prior animation experience is required.

Contact
(860) 486-0149
PreCollegeSummer@UConn.edu

Name of College
The Cooper Union

Name of Program
Pre-college Summer Art Program NYC

Academic / Career Interest
Art

Website
http://cooper.edu/academics/outreach-and-pre-college/sum-mer-art-intensive

Application Timeline
Approx. April

Eligibility
The Cooper Union Summer Art Intensive accepts resident and non-resident students, ages 15-18 years, who will be living in New York City or surrounding areas during the course of the summer program. Preference is given to rising Juniors and Seniors.

Tuition Fees
Estimated fees are about $2,700.

Information about the program:
The Cooper Union Summer Art Intensive helps high school students prepare a portfolio for college applications, worthy of top under-graduate programs. Participants choose a two-day studio concentra-tion, devoting the rest of the week to intensive drawing instruction and the study of contemporary art issues. A mix of local, out-of-town and international students will engage with the vast cultural resources of New York City through visits to major museums and gallery districts..The program culminates with a student exhibition, a publication of art and writings, and a public animation screening with a reception in Cooper's Great Hall.

Contact
(212) 353-4202
cusummerart@gmail.com

Name of College
Cornish College of the Arts

Name of Program
Summer at Cornish (S@C): ART+DESIGN

Academic / Career Interest
Art

Website
http://www.cornish.edu/summer/art_design/

Application Timeline
Contact institution for more information.

Eligibility
Open to students ages 14 to 18 years.

Tuition Fees
Estimated fees:

- Pre-College Course Package: $2178
- Per-Afternoon Elective Course: $630
- For Portfolio Development Only: $530

Information about the program:
Summer at Cornish is a four-week pre-college program to prepare students for a first-year art school experience. Students enroll in Art and Design Foundations as well as choose two elective courses they would like to learn and explore. Elective options include Comics, Life Drawing, Digital Photography, Introduction to Graphic Design and Beginning Object Design. Students enrolled in Art and Design Foundations are also automatically enrolled in Portfolio Develop-ment at no additional cost. Portfolio Development can also be taken as a single course for those students solely interested in portfolio development. At the conclusion of the program students will pres-ent a final exhibition of their artwork.

Contact
(800) 726-ARTS

Name of College
DigiPen Institute of Technology

Name of Program
Pre-College Program

Academic / Career Interest
Art

Website
https://projectfun.digipen.edu/summer-programs/pre-college-program/

Application Timeline
Approx. May

Eligibility
Students must have completed their high school sophomore, junior, or senior year in order to enroll in a Pre-College Program.

Tuition Fees
Estimated fees: $2,699

Information about the program:
The program combines college-level coursework in fundamental academic subjects like applied mathematics, computer science, and foundational art with practical production experience in a team environment. Taught by DigiPen faculty level instructors, this extended program provides students with an excellent opportunity to experience what post-secondary education is like. During this month-long college prep technology program, offered at DigiPen's Redmond, WA, campus, students take on the roles of programmers, designers, artists, music and sound designers, and computer engineers. Students choose one of the following tracks: Game Design, Game Programming, Game Art Production, Computer Engineering, Music and Sound Design

Contact
(425) 629-5007
projectfun@digipen.edu

Name of College
Dean College

Name of Program
New England Summer Dance Intensive

Academic / Career Interest
Dance

Website
http://www.dean.edu/summer_dance_intensive.aspx

Application Timeline
Scholarship deadline: approx. July

Eligibility
Open to High school students ages 14-18 years.

Tuition Fees
Estimated fees:

- $1,250 (all-inclusive)
- $950 (commuter)

Information about the program:
High school students ages 14-18 years interested in majoring in dance will train with esteemed faculty from around New England during the New England Summer Dance Intensive at Dean College. Conservatory training in ballet, modern, jazz, tap, choreography and hip-hop techniques taught by renowned New England faculty from schools such as Boston Conservatory, Dean College, College of the Holy Cross, Brown University, Harvard University, and other guest artists. Perform original work as well as work by celebrated guest artists. Workshops in college life, majoring in dance, resume writing, and headshots. Staff-guided residential program with 24-hour supervision. Athletic trainer on-site for injury prevention.

Contact
(508) 541-1606
tlane@dean.edu

Name of College
Drexel University

Name of Program
Fashion Design: Innovation and Transformation

Academic / Career Interest
Fashion

Website
http://drexel.edu/westphal/admissions/precollege/Summer_Programs_FASH/

Application Timeline
Approx. June

Eligibility
Motivated students who are at least 16 years of age and who have completed their high school sophomore or junior year by the start of the program are welcome.

Tuition Fees
Estimated fees: $1,800.00

Information about the program:
For one week, students live on campus and explore "hands-on" the field of Fashion Design. Students will attend a carefully designed curriculum consisting of lectures, demonstrations, studio work, activities, and field trips. Faculty members all have extensive experience in various aspects of the fashion industry. Students will research concepts, develop ideas through sketching, and use innovative technology to produce a variety of sample projects that can help you develop a fashion portfolio. This unique opportunity will immerse students in the world of fashion while offering a true preview of the college experience. During their stay, students will visit local fashion studios and go on field trips to discover cultural attractions in the Philadelphia area.

Contact
(215) 895-1834
westphal.admissions@drexel.edu

Name of College
Emerson College

Name of Program
Pre-College Acting 5-Week Studio Program

Academic / Career Interest
Acting

Website
https://www.emerson.edu/academics/pre-college/acting

Application Timeline
Acting Studio Priority Application Deadline: approx. March
Applications will be accepted through approx. May.

Eligibility
Students in grades 11 and 12 when applying and who will be between the ages of 16 and 18 at the start of the program.

Tuition Fees
Estimated fees:

- Acting Studio Non-credit Tuition: $4701
- Acting Studio Credit Tuition: $5500
- Residential Room and Board Fee: $2975
- Non-refundable program application fee: $60

Information about the program:
Acting Studio introduces students to a pre-professional theater intensive and reflects the training in the Emerson BFA Acting Program. The five-week program, which qualifies for four college credits, offers and introduction to acting training including classes in voice, movement, improvisation, scene study, auditioning technique / monologues, and stage combat. Classes are taught exclusively by Emerson's Acting faculty, with additional specialty master classes offered by local professionals.

Contact
(617) 824-8280
precollege@emerson.edu

Name of College
University of Hartford

Name of Program
Meet the Masters Summer Jazz Workshop

Academic / Career Interest
Jazz

Website
http://www.hartford.edu/hcd/music/summer-music/meet-the-masters.aspx

Application Timeline
Approx. May

Eligibility
For participants in grade 9 through adults

Tuition Fees
Estimated fees are $800

Information about the program:
The University of Hartford's Hartt School Community Division invites jazz instrumentalists and vocalists in grade 9 through adults for Meet the Masters Summer Jazz Workshop. Under the direction of Javon Jackson, chair of the University of Hartford's Jackie McLean Institute of Jazz, this intensive 5-day summer workshop provides students the opportunity to develop their improvisation skills while delving into the historical narrative of our distinctly American art form. Students join together with internationally renowned jazz professionals and educators in an intimate, concentrated workshop to hone their abilities and skills. Through daily sessions in ear training, jazz theory, and improvisational development, students will strengthen their playing to reach the next level in their artistry. Highlights include master classes and Q&A sessions with innovative faculty.

Contact
(860) 768-4451
harttcomm@hartford.edu

Name of College
University of Hartford

Name of Program
Summer Musical Theater Intensive (SMTI)

Academic / Career Interest
Musical Theater

Website
http://www.hartford.edu/hcd/music/summer-music/smti-prepro-fessional.aspx

Application Timeline
Contact institution for more information.

Eligibility
Students aged 14–20 years.

Tuition Fees
Estimated fees:

- Application Fee: $25
- Tuition: $1550 (full 2-week program)
- Optional housing (2 weeks): $2000 (includes excursion)

Information about the program:
The SMTI Preprofessional program provides exceptional opportunities for high school and college-age performers aged 14–20 years to develop and integrate their acting, singing, and dance skills while working closely with NYC industry professionals. The program culminates in an original showcase performance designed specifically by the artistic directors to highlight the skills of the participants.

Contact
(860) 768-4451
harttcomm@hartford.edu

Name of College
University of Hartford

Name of Program
Young Composers Project

Academic / Career Interest
Music composition

Website
http://www.hartford.edu/hcd/music/summer-music/ycp-summer.aspx

Application Timeline
Approx. July

Eligibility
For students in grades 7–12, or homeschool equivalents, including those entering 7th grade and seniors who have just graduated

Tuition Fees
Estimated fees: $775

Information about the program:
The Young Composers Project (YCP) Summer Edition is a five-day intensive workshop for students interested in writing music. Each year focuses on a different musical topic, for example "Composing for the Big Screen." Students will be given instruction on composition techniques, approaches to scoring films, and the use of relevant software to create electronic scores. Participants will work in small groups and one-on-one with YCP Director Jessica Rudman to develop scores for film scenes over the course of the week, and their compositions will be presented in a showcase on the final day.

Contact
(860) 768-4451
Rudman@hartford.edu

Name of College
Indiana University Bloomington

Name of Program
Midsummer Theatre Program

Academic / Career Interest
Theater

Website
https://theatre.indiana.edu/about/high-school-summer-programs/
midsummer-theatre.html

Application Timeline
Applications will be considered through approx. June.

Eligibility
Students who have completed their freshman year of high school
are eligible for the program.

Tuition Fees
Estimated fees: $1,800.

Information about the program:
Indiana University's Midsummer Theatre Program is a dynamic
two-week immersive theatre and drama institute designed especially for young people serious about studying theatre. Classes are
taught by IU faculty, outstanding teaching assistants, and guest
artists. Together, students and theatre professionals share the
common endeavor of building an intensive ensemble. Over the
years, the Midsummer Theatre Program has enjoyed tremendous
success. Dedicated students are accepted from around the country
for challenging and rewarding theatrical training. Students develop
their talents while gaining exposure to one of the richest cultural
landscapes in the country.

Contact
(812) 855-4342

Name of College
Ithaca College

Name of Program
Digital Photography

Academic / Career Interest
Photography

Website
https://www.ithaca.edu/summercollege/mini/coursedescrip-tions/?item=5663

Application Timeline
Application deadline is approx. May.

Eligibility
Students who will be between 15 years and 18 years of age at the time of the summer college program are welcome to apply.

Tuition Fees
Estimated fees: $1,680

Information about the program:
In this course, students get a hands-on introduction to digital photography, including camera use and imaging for art photography. Using their own digital camera images taken during the week, students create new artwork using advanced Photoshop techniques. From their very first semester, students in the program begin their work as makers of the still and moving image, receiving extensive hands-on experience with the tools and techniques of cinema and photography. Whether students are interested in telling a story, imparting information, or conducting an argument, the classes provide students with the necessary analytical, critical, and intellectual skills to be informed and effective image makers.

Contact
(754) 422-4233
rwishna@ithaca.edu

Name of College
International Culinary Center

Name of Program
Summer Cooking School

Academic / Career Interest
Culinary

Website
https://www.internationalculinarycenter.com/culinary-topics/summer-cooking-school/

Application Timeline
Contact institution for more information.

Eligibility
Open to students 13 to 18 years.

Tuition Fees
Contact institution for more information.

Information about the program:
Cooking Camp for Teens will be offered as a total of five weekday sessions – one for Culinary, one for Pastry – learning the art of cooking from one of ICC's experienced chef-instructors. From creating handmade gnocchi to paper-thin crepes and profiteroles, the programs introduce students to the culinary world, giving them the opportunity to develop basic skills that will build the foundation to cook for a lifetime. On the first day of each class, students will be in the kitchen learning and cooking. Beginning with the basics of kitchen safety, students participate in hands-on culinary classes in ICC's professional kitchens, the same facilities used by International Culinary Center students.

Contact
New York Campus
(888) 324-2433

California Campus
(866) 318-2433

Name of College
Johnson & Wales University

Name of Program
Career Explorations: Baking & Pastry Arts

Academic / Career Interest
Baking and pastry arts

Website
https://www.jwu.edu/admissions/cx/home/index.html

Application Timeline
Contact institution for more information.

Eligibility
Open to rising high school juniors and seniors.

Tuition Fees
Estimated fees:

- Drive-In: Baking & Pastry Arts or Culinary Arts (all campuses): $275
- Fly-In: Baking & Pastry Arts or Culinary Arts (all campuses): $550

Information about the program:
Students choose any campus and explore careers in the baking and pastry industry at the university's International Baking & Pastry Institute. Students will learn as they produce pastries and plated desserts at the direction of world-class pastry chefs. (Offered at all JWU campuses.)

Contact
(800 342-5598

Name of College
Juilliard School

Name of Program
Summer Dance Intensive

Academic / Career Interest
Dance

Website
https://www.juilliard.edu/dance/summer-dance-intensive

Application Timeline
Contact institution for more information.

Eligibility
Applicants who are in high school.

Tuition Fees
Estimated fees are about $2,000.

Information about the program:
The Summer Dance Intensive is a three-week program in classical ballet and modern dance for advanced students who are dedicated, disciplined, and dance with a generosity of spirit. The program is limited to dancers who have completed at least one year of high school/secondary school and who will not graduate before the program begins. Generally, this means that dancers in the program are aged 15-17 and have completed grade 9, 10, or 11. International students are welcome to apply. The program is designed to give young dancers a taste of what a Juilliard dance student's life is all about: refining technique and performance, broadening understanding of various dance styles, experiencing New York City, and making lifelong friends. The program takes place at The Juilliard School in New York City, and optional on-campus housing is available.

Contact
(212) 799-5000

Name of College
Marymount Manhattan College

Name of Program
Musical Theatre Precollege Summer Intensive

Academic / Career Interest
Musical Theatre

Website
https://www.mmm.edu/academics/auxiliary-education/pre-col-lege-programs/summer-intensives/musical-theatre-intensive/

Application Timeline
Contact institution for more information.

Eligibility
Applicants must be 16 years of age on or before July in order to participate in the Musical Theatre Intensive.

Tuition Fees
Estimated fees: $3,400

Information about the program:
The Musical Theatre Precollege Summer Intensive Program at Marymount Manhattan College gives high school rising juniors and seniors the opportunity to study in New York City. The program offers training in dance, voice and acting as well as college audition preparation and access to Broadway shows. Students will focus on the fundamentals and process of their craft and will have the opportunity to share their work with friends and family at the end of the program. Faculty from Marymount Manhattan's nationally renowned musical theatre program will lead the intensive, giving students a true college experience. Guest artists from the industry will also be brought in for seminars and special topics.

Contact
IPAS@mmm.edu

Name of College
Maine College of Art

Name of Program
Pre-College

Academic / Career Interest
Art

Website
https://www.meca.edu/academics/pre-college/

Application Timeline
Approx. April

Eligibility
Pre-College is open to students who have completed their sophomore, junior or senior year of high school.

Tuition Fees
Estimated fees: $3,550

Information about the program:
Pre-College is open to students who have completed their high school sophomore, junior or senior year. Students customize their individual Pre-College program by choosing two majors from the following media:

- Children's Book Illustration
- Music: Composition + Collaboration
- B + W Darkroom Photography
- Painting -Commercial Illustration
- Comic + Graphic Novel Illustration
- Ceramics
- Fashion + Textile Design
- Metalsmithing + Jewelry Design
- Printmaking
- Photography
- Woodworking + Furniture Design

Contact
(207) 699-5061

Name of College
Mason Gross School of the Arts

Name of Program
Rutgers Summer Dance Conservatory

Academic / Career Interest
Dance

Website
http://www.masongross.rutgers.edu/extension/rutgers-summer-dance-conservatory

Application Timeline
Session I & Dual Session Registration Deadline: approx. June
Session II Registration Deadline: approx. July

Eligibility
In-person or video audition is required for all students. Dancers entering grade 9 through rising seniors (students entering their first year of college) may apply.

Tuition Fees
Estimated fees range from $1,500 - $3,000

Information about the program:
The Rutgers Summer Dance Conservatory is an intensive, pre-college program for intermediate to advanced dancers who seek to build artistic acuity and technical endurance while learning about options for college study and careers in dance. Dancers attend daily classes in ballet and modern technique and work in intimate repertory groups with professional choreographers. Students gain exposure to a variety of dance forms and topics through a series of master classes and lectures with world class teaching artists and experts in the field. Daily course studies in improvisation allow students to create their own movement and dances, which are performed alongside of repertory pieces in two fully produced, end- of-session showcases. Dancers start each day with instruction in stretching and conditioning in preparation for the intense pace of the Summer Dance Conservatory.

Contact
(848) 932-8618

Name of College
Massachusetts College of Art and Design

Name of Program
Summer Studios

Academic / Career Interest
Art

Website
https://massart.edu/summer-studios

Application Timeline
Payment in full is due approx. June

Eligibility
For students entering grades 11 and 12.

Tuition Fees
Estimated fees: $3,000

Information about the program:
Summer Studios is an intensive four-week program for the young artist who is serious about his or her work. Students from around the world come together to experience MassArt and the environment of a higher education institution in the visual arts. The program is ideal for students who are looking to spend the summer immersed in their creative passion, hoping to develop a portfolio surrounded by creative artists and striving to develop skills and critical thinking.

Contact
(617) 879-7174

Name of College
Manhattan School of Music

Name of Program
MSM Summer

Academic / Career Interest
Music and voice

Website
https://www.msmnyc.edu/programs/msm-summer/

Application Timeline
Contact institution for more information.

Eligibility
Students age 8-17 years.

Tuition Fees
Estimated fees: $3,000

- Residential Participants (ages 12-17):
    - Musical Theater & Classical Voice Majors: $6,100
    - Instrumental & Jazz Voice Majors: $4,755
- Day Participants (ages 8-17):
    - Musical Theater & Classical Voice Majors: $3,500
    - Instrumental and Jazz Voice Majors: $2,770

Information about the program:
MSM Summer provides instruction and performance experience in instrumental music and voice for students ages 8-17. Students will develop their musical skills and join a community of young musicians through a wide variety of musical and social activities. Former participants have hailed from across the United States and from around the world.

Contact
(212) 749-2802

Name of College
University of Michigan, Ann Arbor

Name of Program
MPulse Summer Performing Arts Institutes

Academic / Career Interest
Music

Website
http://smtd.umich.edu/programs-degrees/youth-adult-programs/youth-programs/mpulse/

Application Timeline
Application open for rolling admissions

Eligibility
MPulse Summer Performing Arts Institutes are open to high school students completing grades 9-12 before start of summer program. Exceptions: The Theatre & Drama Academy is open to students completing grades 10-11. The Musical Theatre Workshop is open to high school juniors, although applications from current tenth graders of exceptional ability and experience will be considered. Center Stage Strings accepts applications from students ages 13-24. Students under 13 may be considered on a case by case basis depending on level and maturity.

Tuition Fees
Estimated fees are about $1,700

Information about the program:
MPulse Summer Performing Arts Institutes on the Ann Arbor campus inspire students to exciting new levels of excellence in music performance, music technology, musical theatre, theatre, and dance. Sessions are designed for students who are considering studying these areas in college. Participants work with distinguished University of Michigan faculty and alumni while experiencing campus life in Ann Arbor.

Contact
(866) 936-2660

Name of College
Minneapolis College of Art and Design

Name of Program
Pre-College

Academic / Career Interest
Art

Website
https://mcad.edu/academic-programs/pre-college-summer-session

Application Timeline
Contact institution for more information.

Eligibility
Open to high school students who have completed their high school sophomore, junior, or senior year.

Tuition Fees
Estimated fees: $2,300

Information about the program:
Through a combination of personal investigation and group collaboration, this program encourages students to explore new concepts, share ideas, and develop their studio practice. Students will learn what an art college education is like, including:

- Choosing a major
- Exploring their creative abilities
- Improving their critical thinking skills
- Trying new techniques with help from professional artists
- Sharpening their aesthetic senses through critiques
- Developing time-management and classroom participation skills

Contact
(612) 874-3700
info@mcad.edu

Name of College
State University of New York, Purchase College

Name of Program
Summer Precollege Programs in the Arts: Filmmaking Institute

Academic / Career Interest
Filmmaking

Website
https://www.purchase.edu/academics/youth-and-precollege-programs/summer-precollege-programs-in-the-arts/

Application Timeline
Early Registration Discount Deadline: approx. May

Eligibility
Open to student grades 9–12.

Tuition Fees
Estimated fees: $2,100

Information about the program:
This four-week precollege program is for high school students interested in writing, directing, editing, and acting in original movies, while learning the art of visual storytelling. Begin with shooting exercises that strengthen framing and composition skills. Learn how to tell a dramatic and visually interesting story by writing short scenes and then more complicated scripts. Develop and write scripts using professional scriptwriting software. Learn the art of storyboarding and previsualization, gaining comfort with lighting equipment and directing actors. Gain practice working on a set, creating collaboratively, and learn how to "crew." Editing and advanced editing techniques are taught using a professional digital editing system.

Contact
(914) 251-6500
youth.pre.college@purchase.edu

Name of College
University of North Carolina, School of the Arts

Name of Program
Summer Programs

Academic / Career Interest
Art

Website
https://www.uncsa.edu/summer/index.aspx

Application Timeline
Check during late Fall for the next summer's intensive program

Eligibility
Open to high school students.

Tuition Fees
Estimated fees range from $2,000 - $4,000

Information about the program:
Welcome to the University of North Carolina School of the Arts (UNCSA), where summer is intense, exhilarating and all about the students. Whether students have a passion for dance, drama, film-making, music or visual arts, they'll find all the hands-on experience, all the performance opportunities, and all the individual attention from professional artists they've dared to dream of. Current or former college students, can check out summer online academic classes. Summer liberal arts classes at UNCSA offer current college students a jump-start on required classes, and enable former students to complete outstanding graduation requirements in one five-week session that is 100 percent online. Programs in: Dance, drama, filmmaking, music, and visual arts.

Contact
(336) 734-2848
fogartys@uncsa.edu

Name of College
New England Conservatory of Music

Name of Program
Jazz Lab

Academic / Career Interest
Jazz

Website
http://necmusic.edu/jazz-lab

Application Timeline
Contact institution for more information.

Eligibility
Students ages 14 to 18 at all proficiency levels are welcome.

Tuition Fees
Estimated fees: $1,115 (includes lunch and dinner daily)

Information about the program:
Jazz Lab sets out to educate young jazz musicians by promoting art-istry, practical training, and creative music making. NEC's Jazz Lab is a one-week jazz intensive, where students aged 14-18 work with premier jazz faculty and participate in a schedule full of improvisa-tion, small group training, jam sessions, entrepreneurial workshops and creative music making. The program features daily classes in jazz theory and ear training, improvisation, small ensemble rehears-als, masterclasses, and concerts. Renowned guest artists (like Ken Schaphorst, Luis Bonilla, and Joe Morris) have an impact on partici-pants through their innovative teaching, but also with their spectac-ular performances throughout the week.

Contact
jazzlab@necmusic.edu

Name of College
New York University

Name of Program
Tisch Summer High School Production and Design Workshop

Academic / Career Interest
Performing arts

Website
https://tisch.nyu.edu/special-programs/high-school-programs/drama--production-and-design-workshop

Application Timeline
Tisch Summer High School Application Deadline: approx. January

Eligibility
The summer program is open to high school sophomores and juniors from around the world.

Tuition Fees
Estimated fees: $11,551

Information about the program:
The Production and Design Workshop offered through the Department of Undergraduate Drama is for the student who wants to pursue a career in the design, technical, management and other production areas of the performing arts. Each week students will have 28 hours of conservatory style coursework in areas such as management, scenery, costumes, lighting, sound, drafting, drawing, and painting. Students will also take a weekly Introduction to New York Theatre seminar with professional actors, directors, designers, stage managers, and faculty as guests.

Contact
(212) 998-1500
tisch.special.info@nyu.edu

Name of College
New York University

Name of Program
Tisch Summer High School Photography and Imaging Program

Academic / Career Interest
Photography

Website
https://tisch.nyu.edu/special-programs/high-school-programs/
photography-and-imaging

Application Timeline
Tisch Summer High School Application Deadline: approx. January

Eligibility
The summer program is open to high school sophomores and juniors from around the world.

Tuition Fees
Contact institution for more information.

Information about the program:
Through the Summer High School Program in Photography and Imaging, students will focus on using photo-based image-making for communication, creative expression, and personal exploration. Students will gain the visual and verbal vocabulary to further articulate their interests in relation to creating and discussing imagery. Designed for beginning and advanced students, this program is a rigorous combination of cultural, technical, and historical lectures; darkroom work; critiques of student work; and critical discussions and written responses to lectures, readings, and gallery visits. Students will be introduced to 35 mm manual cameras, proper black-and-white film exposure, and darkroom printing, as well as color slide film, scanning, basic Photoshop, and digital color printing

Contact
(212) 998-1500
tisch.special.info@nyu.edu

Name of College
University of North Texas

Name of Program
University of North Texas (UNT) Summer String Institute

Academic / Career Interest
Music

Website
https://ssi.music.unt.edu/home

Application Timeline
All fees must be paid by approx. June

Eligibility
Open to all high school students.

Tuition Fees
Estimated fees:

- Tuition is $470
- Room & Board (for one session)
    - For minors (under 18 years old) double occupancy (7 nights): $180
    - For adults (18 years and older) single occupancy (7 nights): $250

Information about the program:
UNT Summer String Institute students can choose only one session or attend both. Private lessons, chamber music, string orchestra, clinics, masterclasses, and concerts will be the focus of an intense workshop for violinists, violists, cellists, double bassists, and pianists. The internationally acclaimed UNT string faculty, principal players of the Dallas Symphony, and esteemed guest artists will share their ample knowledge and expertise with students. All this in the rich and wonderful environment of the UNT College of Music with its great facilities in the heart of North Texas and the Dallas Fort Worth Metroplex.

Contact
(940) 565-2791
untssi@unt.edu

Name of College
New Hampshire Institute of Art

Name of Program
Pre College Summer Program: VISUAL ARTS SUMMER INTENSIVE

Academic / Career Interest
Art

Website
http://www.nhia.edu/community-programs/youth-programs/
pre-college-summer-program

Application Timeline
Rolling Admissions Deadline is approx. July

Eligibility
Contact institution for more information.

Tuition Fees
Contact institution for more information.

Information about the program:
New Hampshire Institute of Art Pre-College Summer Intensive
offers distinct programs of study in Visual Arts or Writing. Each program is designed with an immersive and intense daily studio focus
to further students' skills and creative voice within their field of art
or writing. There are a variety of workshops, presentations, and
social activities that offer interaction and collaboration between the
programs. The program offers fun and engaging college experience
as students build their portfolio. Students choose from a variety of
studio courses including Portfolio Drawing, Image and Text, Visual
Storytelling, Painting Abstraction, Graphic Novels, Ceramic Design,
Photography, and Printmaking. Each studio course offers the opportunity to learn new techniques, advance and refine skills, and build a
professional portfolio.

Contact
(603) 836-2561
PreCollege@nhia.edu

Name of College
Northwestern University

Name of Program
Theatre Arts Division

Academic / Career Interest
Theater Arts

Website
https://nhsi.northwestern.edu/theatre-arts-division/

Application Timeline
Early Admission Application Deadline: approx. January
Regular Admission Application Deadline: approx. March

Eligibility
Students must be current high school juniors who will be rising into their senior year of high school following their summer at Northwestern.

Tuition Fees
Estimated fees:

- Theatre Arts and Design/Tech: $5,650
- Musical Theatre Extension: $7,650

Information about the program:
Northwestern University Theatre Arts Division is an immersive, hands-on exploration into stage performance and production. A rigorous combination of classes and rehearsals provide students with a challenging and inspiring learning environment every day for 5 weeks. Working with professional theatre practitioners from around the country, students receive extraordinary training in a collaborative and supportive environment.

Contact
(847) 491-3026
nhsi@northwestern.edu

Name of College
Otis College of Art and Design

Name of Program
Summer of Art

Academic / Career Interest
Art

Website
https://www.otis.edu/summer-art

Application Timeline
Full payment or deposit before approx. April is required to reserve Summer of Art enrollment,

Eligibility
Program is for individuals 15 and older.

Tuition Fees
Estimated fees:

- 5-Day Weekly: $3500 ($4371 before discount)
- 3-Day Weekly: $2959
- 2-Day Weekly: $1547

Information about the program:
Small classes ensure personalized, in-depth learning. Rigorous course work includes hands-on studio courses and labs in chosen Specialization Course (three days per week) and/or Drawing Studio Course (two days per week). Indie Game Design meets five days per week (Some outside work is required). Two units of college credit for Specialization Courses and one unit of college credit for Drawing Studio Courses are awarded to eligible students upon successful completion of the program.

Contact
(310) 665-6800

Name of College
Oberlin College and Conservatory

Name of Program
Summer Dance Program

Academic / Career Interest
Dance

Website
https://www.oberlin.edu/arts-and-sciences/departments/dance/
summer-dance-program

Application Timeline
Final deadline: approx. June

Eligibility
Open to dancers ages 13-18.

Tuition Fees
Estimated fees range from $500 - $1,000

Information about the program:
Oberlin Dance Department cosponsors a summer dance intensive
each July, a series of summer workshops led by current students
and dance faculty. Sessions takes place in the college's Dance Studios. The dance intensive welcomes adults and dancers ages 13-18,
who can take introductory, intermediate, and advanced courses offered in a wide range of dance styles: ballet, Contact Improvisation,
hip-hop, and more.

Contact
(440) 775-8411

Name of College
Oklahoma City University

Name of Program
Broadway-Bound Summer Dance Camps

Academic / Career Interest
Dance

Website
https://www.okcu.edu/dance/workshops/summerdance

Application Timeline
June Camp Registration Deadline: approx. May
July Camp Registration Deadline: approx. June

Eligibility
Dance camp is for high school students entering their sophomore, junior, or senior year (high schoolers entering their freshmen year of college are also welcome to attend).

Tuition Fees
Estimated fees range from $1,000 - $3,000

Information about the program:
This program is for the dancer who dreams of being on Broadway or becoming a star in the entertainment industry. Students will learn professional preparation for long and successful careers in dance Students will learn how to use style, technique and their acting ability to get and keep the job; silence their audition fears with successful audition strategies; develop their own emotional connection with all dance styles; discover the secrets of learning multiple roles; maintain their greatest asset through injury prevention and dance health; enhance their technique and personal style in a variety of areas (Musical Theater Dance, Jazz, Tap, Contemporary, Hip Hop, Rhythm Tap, Ballet, Triple Threat Classes, Acting, Singing); unleash their inner star in a final showcase performances for family and friends. Classes are taught by Oklahoma City University's nationally recognized faculty.

Contact
Ryan Barrett
(405) 208-5644

Name of College
Parsons School of Design

Name of Program
NYC Summer Program

Academic / Career Interest
Art

Website
https://www.newschool.edu/parsons/summer-ny/

Application Timeline
Summer Intensive Studies New York Session I deadline: approx.
April
Summer Intensive Studies New York Session II deadline: approx.
May

Eligibility
Students must be 16 years of age by the start of the Summer Intensive Studies New York program.

Tuition Fees
Estimated fees: $3,064 + fees

Information about the program:
Parsons Summer Intensive Studies: New York is an exceptional academic art and design program enriched by the vast resources of New York City. This intensive three-week, three-credit program is open to anyone wishing to deepen their knowledge of art and design in an academically rigorous and artistically stimulating environment. Students spend five days a week in studio classes and receive demanding homework assignments. Courses are supplemented by special events, including portfolio reviews, Parsons alumni career panels, and industry guest lecturers, all designed to prepare students for admission to design school or direct them toward relevant career paths.

Contact
summer@newschool.edu

Name of College
Pennsylvania Academy of the Fine Arts

Name of Program
Summer Academy

Academic / Career Interest
Dance

Website
https://www.pafa.org/community-education/high-school/summer-academy

Application Timeline
The Commuter Program has a rolling application deadline, with applications accepted on a space-available basis.   The Residential Program has a deadline of approx. June to ensure housing availability.

Eligibility
Open to students who will have completed 9th, 10th, 11th or 12th grades by the time of the program.

Tuition Fees
Estimated fees range $3,000 - $7,000

Information about the program:
Summer Academy is the definitive program for talented and motivated high school students: A five-week, college-level art making experience in the nation's first and premier school of art. The program offers rigorous courses in drawing, painting, sculpture, printmaking and illustration taught by PAFA's exceptional faculty of practicing artists. Commuter and Residential program options are offered. Students will participate in field trips to museums and galleries of Philadelphia, New York and Washington D.C. and a culminating exhibition in PAFA's museum, including a reception and awards ceremony.

Contact
Emily Owens, Director of High School Programs
(215) 972-2040
eowens@pafa.edu

Name of College
Pratt Institute

Name of Program
Summer Program

Academic / Career Interest
Dance

Website
https://www.pratt.edu/academics/continuing-education-and-pro-
fessional/precollege/summer-programs/

Application Timeline
Applications and supporting documents are due approx. March

Eligibility
High school students who are at least sixteen years old and have
completed their sophomore year, as well as graduating seniors. Minimum age: 16 years by start of program; maximum age: 18 years. No
exceptions.

Tuition Fees
Estimated fees: $3,839 (four classes, four elective college credits)

Information about the program:
Pratt Institute Summer Program students will:

- Explore the possibility of studying art, design, architecture,
  creative writing, cultural studies or other creative fields.

Students choose a concentration of study modeled after Pratt's undergraduate offerings. Reflecting Pratt's academic culture, Pre-College students are immersed in their studio practice and actively
participating in a rigorous full schedule of classes Monday to Friday.
Classes are led by Pratt's renowned faculty of working artists and
professional designers who are committed to sharing their expertise
in the field.

Contact
(718) 636-3453
preco@pratt.edu

Name of College
Pace University

Name of Program
Summer Scholars

Academic / Career Interest
Theatre

Website
https://www.pace.edu/summer-scholars/courses/theater

Application Timeline
Contact institution for more information.

Eligibility
Open to high school junior and senior students.

Tuition Fees
Contact institution for more information.

Information about the program:
Home to Bravo's Inside the Actors Studio, Pace's performing arts department is one of the best in the country. Consistently the most popular track in the Summer Scholars Institute, these theatre courses will allow students to learn from the best and see if they have what it takes to make it in the thespian world. The Acting Program is a rigorous two-week intensive in which students learn to fully unleash their potential, truth, imagination, and creative energy. Students study acting with current Pace School of Performing Arts faculty all of whom are active artists in the field in New York City, the theater capital of the world, and are offered unique professional opportunities and guidance. Students will learn how to approach a role, develop character, analyze a text, uncover the playwright's intention, and discover the truthful life of the scene.

Contact
(212) 346-1915
summerscholar@pace.edu

Name of College
Virginia Commonwealth University

Name of Program
Fashion Design + Merchandising

Academic / Career Interest
Fashion Design

Website
https://arts.vcu.edu/summerintensive/the-program/majors/fashion-design-merchandising/

Application Timeline
Applications must be received by approx. March to receive priority processing.

Eligibility
Contact institution for more information.

Tuition Fees
Estimated fees: $3,300

Information about the program:
Fashion is the vehicle people use to express who they are and who they would like to be. Today, the ever-changing world of fashion is one of the greatest economic forces in the world and the fashion industry provides careers for millions of individuals in design, manufacturing, retailing, marketing, advertising, publishing and many auxiliary services. It is both creative and scientific, with careers at every point in between. During this exciting three-week course student will try on many roles including fashion designer, stylist, product development specialist, buyer, and fashion show director. One half of the course work focuses on the business side of fashion and the other half focuses on design. Participants also learn how to publicize the fashion show and to create the program.

Contact
(804) 827-1353
summerarts@vcu.edu

Name of College
Rochester University

Name of Program
Summer @ Eastman

Academic / Career Interest
Art

Website
https://summer.esm.rochester.edu/courses/age/high-school/

Application Timeline
Contact institution for more information.

Eligibility
Open to all high school students.

Tuition Fees
Estimated fees: $6,020

Information about the program:
The Eastman School of Music Summer at Eastman program offers students and the community an individualized and world-class music education experience. Students choose between residential music programs and camps for middle and high school students, week-long institutes devoted to various instruments or specialties, half-day music workshops for youths, and collegiate classes in Music Education, Music History, and Music Theory.

Contact
(585) 274-1974
summer@esm.rochester.edu

Name of College
Rhode Island Institute of Design

Name of Program
Pre-College

Academic / Career Interest
Art

Website
http://precollege.risd.edu/program/about-pre-college/

Application Timeline
Contact institution for more information.

Eligibility
Open to high school juniors and seniors.

Tuition Fees
Contact institution for more information.

Information about the program:
Founded in 1877, Rhode Island School of Design (or "RIZ-dee" for the acronym RISD) is one of the oldest and best-known colleges of art and design in the U.S. RISD has consistently upheld its mission to educate the public about the vital role of art and design in society. RISD Pre-College offers high school juniors and seniors the opportunity to access life as a RISD student and experience college culture. For six weeks, students will live like a college student and follow a college-level studio curriculum. Not only will students build confidence as an artist and as an individual, but they'll get to master a range of tools, materials and techniques, study with award-winning faculty in RISD art studios, create supplementary pieces for their college admission portfolio, and forge the kind of friendships that last a lifetime. Pre-College students also have access to RISD's well-equipped and internationally renowned studio facilities.

Contact
(401) 454-6200
cemail@risd.edu

Name of College
School of Visual Arts

Name of Program
Pre-College Program

Academic / Career Interest
Art

Website
http://www.sva.edu/special-programs/pre-college-program/summer-program

Application Timeline
Contact institution for more information.

Eligibility
Pre-College is open to all students who are 14-18 years of age and are current high school students when applying.

Tuition Fees
Estimated fees:

- Nonrefundable Program Fee: $500 + Tuition Fee: $2,300 = $2,800
- Housing Fee: $1,725 Meal Plan Fee: $550 (breakfast and dinner only)
- Meal Plan Fee: $550 (breakfast and dinner only)

Information about the program:
Summer Pre-College is an intensive three-week program that provides the experience of attending art school in the heart of New York City. Students are immersed in their chosen field of study through unique studio projects and instruction from SVA's award-winning faculty. The program is further enhanced by a robust offering of evening and weekend chaperoned activities and events that take full advantage of the social and cultural life of New York City.

Contact
(212) 592-2101
precollege@sva.edu

Name of College
University of Southern California

Name of Program
Acting Intensive

Academic / Career Interest
Acting

Website
https://summerprograms.usc.edu/programs/4-week/acting/

Application Timeline
Domestic Student Application due approx. April

Eligibility
Students must have completed at least the 9th grade by start of program

Tuition Fees
Estimated fees:

- Residential: $8,534
- Commuter: $6,059

Information about the program:
University of Southern California School of Dramatic Arts offers an opportunity for students to work with theatre professionals and explore a creative experience in the dramatic arts. This conservatory-style training course will challenge students and offer a strong foundation in the craft of acting. The program, taught by the school's world-class faculty, emphasizes process and includes scene study, movement, voice, as well as Shakespeare technique workshops & a monologue audition master class. The four-week class culminates in a public workshop performance for family and friends.

Contact
(213) 740-5679
summer@usc.edu

Name of College
University of Southern California

Name of Program
USC Cinematic Arts

Academic / Career Interest
Art

Website
https://cinema.usc.edu/summer/index.cfm

Application Timeline
The program has a rolling admission.

Eligibility
Anyone ages 16 and above are welcomed to apply.

Tuition Fees
Estimated fees: $1,800 per unit

Information about the program:
Summer Program classes are taught by leading industry professionals during two separate six-week sessions. Students spend time
on the state of-the-art campus taking classes focused on feature
filmmaking, editing, animation, writing, computer graphics, interactive game design, and the business of the industry, among many
others. Besides having access to the school's unparalleled facilities
and equipment, Summer Program students will have many unique
opportunities. Several classes take place on major studio lots such
as Warner Bros. and Walt Disney Studios.

Contact
(213) 740-8358
admissions@cinema.usc.edu

Name of College
Syracuse University

Name of Program
Acting & Musical Theatre

Academic / Career Interest
Acting & Musical Theatre

Website
http://summercollege.syr.edu/program/acting-musical-theater/

Application Timeline
Contact institution for more information.

Eligibility
Students must be a minimum of 15 years of age by the orientation and move-in date.

Tuition Fees
Estimated fees range from $3,500 - $5,000

Information about the program:
This creative summer program was created for talented students who have been inspired by the energy and sophistication of theater and musical theater. The program develops the abilities of experienced performers who are serious about the field and eager to work hard. The program's goal is to help students grow creatively through full-time, college-level theater training under the direction of acclaimed professional performers and teachers. The three-week program develops students' performance skills and provides a behind-the-scenes view of theater that combines music, drama, and dance. Students complete the program with improved audition skills with experience in college level work in the field.

Contact
(315) 443-5000
sumcoll@syr.edu

Name of College
San Francisco Art Institute

Name of Program
Pre-College

Academic / Career Interest
Art

Website
https://www.sfai.edu/public-youth-education/precollege

Application Timeline
Approx. May

Eligibility
For students who have completed the tenth grade, but haven't yet started college

Tuition Fees
Contact institution for more information.

Information about the program:
San Francisco Art Institute Pre-College program gives students a jumpstart on the college experience with an intensive and transformative program in the arts. This four-week, four college credit program combines in-depth study and practice with SFAI's renowned faculty to help students build foundational skills, develop a portfolio, experiment with new media, and collaborate with like-minded peers who are driven to create. Visits to local museums and exhibition opportunities complement this immersive experience. Pre-College takes place on SFAI's legendary campus at 800 Chestnut Street in the heart of San Francisco's historic Russian Hill neighborhood. Inspiring views of the Bay, a monumental Diego Rivera fresco, and a constant stream of visiting artists and visionaries are part of daily life at SFAI.

Contact
(415) 749-4554
precollege@sfai.edu

Name of College
Vassar College

Name of Program
Powerhouse Theater Training Program

Academic / Career Interest
Theater

Website
https://powerhouse.vassar.edu/apprentices/

Application Timeline
Applications are accepted between approx. January 1 and April 1.

Eligibility
Contact institution for more information.

Tuition Fees
Estimated fees: $5,200 (including Room/Board and access to professional offerings)

Information about the program:
Participants in the Powerhouse program choose a discipline (acting, directing, or writing) and then work alongside some of the country's leading and emerging theater practitioners for five weeks, observing and participating in the process through which new works are brought to life. A Powerhouse day includes morning and early afternoon classes. The core classes for all disciplines are acting, movement, and Sound painting. Powerhouse afternoons and evenings feature rehearsals, performances, crew calls to assist in the shops, and more. Master Classes for all disciplines are scheduled based upon the availability of visiting artists and professionals who are on campus working on various productions.

Contact
(845) 437-5907
powerhouse@vassar.edu

Name of College
Watkins College of Art

Name of Program
Pre-College Program

Academic / Career Interest
Art

Website
https://www.watkins.edu/admissions/pre-college-program/

Application Timeline
May 1

Eligibility
Open to rising sophomore, junior, or senior year in high school

Tuition Fees
Estimated fees: $3,850

Information about the program:
What students will do:

- Spend two intensive weeks immersed in the life and culture of a world-class art college studying and creating with like-minded students and professors.
- Learn from Watkins faculty while creating a college portfolio and earning college credit.
- Meet practicing artists, filmmakers, and design professionals.
- Explore new techniques and media.
- Discover contemporary trends and potential career tracks.
- Challenge themselves grow artistically and personally.
- Earn a college scholarship to Watkins.

Contact
(866) 887-6395
info@watkins.edu

Name of College
Wagner College

Name of Program
Summer Musical Theater Institute

Academic / Career Interest
Musical Theater

Website
http://wagner.edu/theatre/smti/

Application Timeline
Approx. March

Eligibility
Open to high school students 16-19 years old from around the country

Tuition Fees
Estimated fees:

- Standard: $3,500
- Early bird (by approx. February): $3,400.00

Information about the program:
Summer Musical Theatre Institute (SMTI) at Wagner College gives high school students from around the country the opportunity to learn about all aspects of musical theatre performance from theatre professionals in the Wagner College and New York City community. In a two-week, on-campus intensive, students receive rigorous, college caliber training in acting, singing, improvisation, and dancing--taught in a supportive, professional environment. Students gain insights into the professional world of New York City theatre through visits from industry experts and trips to Broadway productions. Students are encouraged to apply early as there are a limited number of spots available. We only accept 12 students each year.

Contact
Susan Fenley, Director
smti@wagner.edu

Name of College
Yale University

Name of Program
Summer Drama Program

Academic / Career Interest
Drama

Website
https://summer.yale.edu/academics/summer-drama-program

Application Timeline
Contact institution for more information.

Eligibility
Open to rising juniors and seniors.

Tuition Fees
Contact institution for more information.

Information about the program:
The Yale Summer Conservatory for Actors is an intensive introduction to the basic techniques of acting. Based on the principles of Stanislavski, this five-week program focuses on building a foundation that is applicable to all further study in theatre.

Sections concentrate on the following:

- Text Analysis: to comprehend the material being acted.
- Acting Technique: a laboratory to explore the basic concepts of acting introduced at the -Summer Conservatory
- Voice and Speech: to improve vocal production, articulation, and interpretive skills.
- Games: to develop imagination and spontaneous self-expression

Contact
(203) 432-2430

Name of College
The Cooper Union

Name of Program
Summer Art Intensive

Academic / Career Interest
Drawing / art

Website
http://cooper.edu/academics/outreach-and-pre-college/summer-art-intensive

Application Timeline
Approx. April

Eligibility
The Cooper Union Summer Art Intensive accepts resident and non-resident students, ages 15-18, who will be living in New York City or surrounding areas during the course of the summer program. Preference is given to rising Juniors and Seniors.

Tuition Fees
Estimated fees: $2,700

Information about the program:
The Cooper Union Summer Art Intensive helps high school students prepare a portfolio for college applications, worthy of top undergraduate programs. Participants choose a two-day studio concentration, devoting the rest of the week to intensive drawing instruction and the study of contemporary art issues. A faculty of professional working artists teach all portfolio preparation classes. A mix of local, out-of-town and international students will engage with the vast cultural resources of New York City through visits to major museums and gallery districts. Guest Artists in Residence offer a close-up view of professional practice in action. The program culminates with a student exhibition, a publication of art and writings, and a public animation screening with a reception in Cooper's Great Hall.

Contact
(212) 353-4202

Business / Economics Collegiate Programs

Name of College
American University

Name of Program
Precollege: Discover the World of Communication

Academic / Career Interest
Communications

Website
https://www.american.edu/summer/high-school.cfm

Application Timeline
Approx. May

Eligibility
Open to all high school students

Tuition Fees
Estimated Fees: $1,587

Information about the program:
Discover the World of Communication is open to all high school students grades 9 through 12, including students entering 9th grade in the fall. Classes are taught by American University School of Communication faculty and communication professionals. Topics include Scriptwriting and Video Production, Professional Newswriting, Backpack Journalism, International Communication, Entertainment Communication, Investigative Journalism, Video Game Design, 16 mm film and many more. Activities, guest speakers, events, and field trips occur regularly throughout the summer. Past trips include a Washington Post editorial meeting, a Nationals baseball game, a behind-the-scenes visit to NBC, interviews at National Public Radio, a visit to the Newseum and press box seats with the opportunity to blog for a WNBA game.

Contact
(202) 885-1000

Name of College
University of Arizona

Name of Program
Eller College of Management, Business Careers Awareness Program

Academic / Career Interest
Accounting

Website
https://accounting.eller.arizona.edu/bcap

Application Timeline
Approx. March

Eligibility
Current high school juniors are eligible to apply.

Tuition Fees
Estimated Fees: Free, covered by EY Scholarship. The week long BCAP program will include on-campus housing, transportation, and all meals.

Information about the program:
EY, an international public accounting firm, has teamed up with University of Arizona's Eller College of Management Accounting Department and the McGuire Center for Entrepreneurship to create the Business Careers Awareness Program (BCAP). BCAP provides students who are under-represented in college business classes an opportunity to explore the business world and experience college life through a one-week residential program. Students will stay in on-campus housing, take business courses, compete in a business case study competition, and visit the EY Phoenix office and a Tucson business.

Contact
(520) 621-2620

Name of College
Babson College

Name of Program
Introduction to the Entrepreneurial Experience

Academic / Career Interest
Entrepreneurial thought and action

Website
http://www.babson.edu/admission/visiting-students/high-school/
Pages/entrepreneurial-development-experience.aspx

Application Timeline
Contact institution for more information.

Eligibility
All applicants must be age 16 or older by the start of the program
and complete their sophomore or junior year before the start of the
summer study program.

Tuition Fees
Estimated Fees: $8,500 (includes room and board, tuition for 4 col-
lege credits, activities, and Blue Cross Blue Shield health insurance
plan)

Information about the program:
This four-week, on-campus course gives students a unique opportunity to focus on their growth as an entrepreneur. Students will be
immersed in Entrepreneurial Thought & Action (ET&A™)—Babson's
renowned methodology that encourages combining reflection, experimentation, and analysis with action—all while building leadership, communication, presentation and critical thinking skills in a
hands-on, team-based environment.

Contact
(781) 235-1200

Name of College
Bauer College

Name of Program
EXPLORE Entrepreneurship Summer Institute

Academic / Career Interest
Entrepreneurship

Website
https://www.bauer.uh.edu/undergraduate/prospective-students/high-school/summer-camps.php

Application Timeline
Approx. May

Eligibility
Open to current 10th and 11th graders in the United States.

Tuition Fees
Estimated Fees: free, residential

Information about the program:
Hosted by the Bauer College Wolff Center for Entrepreneurship (WCE), one of the top undergraduate entrepreneurship programs in the nation, students will get a CEO's perspective on starting a business from the ground up and hands-on experiences - from elevator pitches to implementation of their business ideas!

Contact
exploresummercamp@bauer.uh.edu

Name of College
Bauer College

Name of Program
EXPLORE Business Summer Institute

Academic / Career Interest
Business concepts

Website
https://www.bauer.uh.edu/undergraduate/prospective-students/
high-school/summer-camps.php

Application Timeline
Approx. May

Eligibility
Open to current 10th and 11th graders in the United States.

Tuition Fees
Estimated Fees: free, residential

Information about the program:
Students are introduced to basic business concepts through presentations by faculty and industry professionals. This is an opportunity to develop leadership skills. Students will have the opportunity to work in teams to develop solutions to real-life business solutions, perfect their presentation skills, have fun and most of all, explore their interest in business

Contact
exploresummercamp@bauer.uh.edu

Name of College
Bentley College

Name of Program
Wall Street 101

Academic / Career Interest
Financial industry / Business

Website
https://www.bentley.edu/centers/trading-room/wall-street-101

Application Timeline
Contact institution for more information.

Eligibility
Admission is open to high school students who complete their high school sophomore or junior year by June of the program year.

Tuition Fees
Estimated Fees: $1,200

Information about the program:
This 5-day non-residential program provides a fun and interactive opportunity for high school students to learn about the financial industry and other business fields, from NASDAQ to IPO to Dow Jones. Through classroom participation and hands-on exercises, students will explore the stock market and discover the process of investment. They will also experience the excitement and challenges of working in a real trading room environment. Students will work in small teams to utilize the financial technology of the Bentley Trading Room to construct a diversified portfolio of equity securities. Students will develop a formal presentation that explains the reasons for investment selections, including a detailed financial analysis of at least one company.

Contact
awhittaker@bentley.edu

Name of College
Boston College

Name of Program
Business & Leadership Institute

Academic / Career Interest
Business Leadership

Website
https://www.bc.edu/bc-web/sites/bc-experience/programs/
non-credit-programs/business---leadership-institute.html

Application Timeline
Approx. Application Deadlines:
February
March
April
May

Eligibility
Students entering grades 10, 11 & 12.

Tuition Fees
Estimated Fees: resident: $4500; commuter: $2500

Information about the program:
Interdisciplinary in approach, in the Business & Leadership Institute, students will be exposed to the foundations of business and
will have the opportunity to develop their personal leadership capabilities. This three-week program is focused on providing a solid
foundation in core business areas like management, marketing and
finance & economics but will also include engagement in areas such
as civics, social justice and the role of government to frame business
in a larger global and ethical context.

Contact
(617) 552-3800
bce@bc.edu

Name of College
University of California, Los Angeles

Name of Program
Managing Enterprise in Media, Entertainment, and Sports (MEMES) Summer Institute

Academic / Career Interest
Management

Website
https://summer.ucla.edu/institutes/MEMES

Application Timeline
Approx. May

Eligibility
High school students age 14 years or older by the start of the program may participate in Pre-college Summer Institutes.

Tuition Fees
Estimated Fees: $4,621

Information about the program:
Students will spend the summer learning the legal, management, marketing, and financial aspects of managing a global entertainment and media enterprise by undertaking a high-profile, team-based capstone project for a major entertainment enterprise.

Field experience days allow students to further develop and influence their experience, as they will visit companies, speak to executives and learn, first-hand, about these businesses.

Students will experience from the following concentrations:

- Managing the Entertainment and Media Enterprise
- Sports Marketing and Management
- Film & Television Marketing and Management
- Integrated Marketing: A New World of Advertising

Contact
(310) 825-4101
info@summer.ucla.edu

Name of College
University of Chicago

Name of Program
Pathway Program in Economics

Academic / Career Interest
Economics

Website
https://summer.uchicago.edu/course/pathway-program-economics

Application Timeline
Approx. May

Eligibility
This course is open to high school students. This session is for students who have not yet completed Calculus.

Tuition Fees
Estimated Fees: $5,700 (includes tuition, housing, dining, and fees)

Information about the program:
This program introduces students to the approaches to economic research and experimentation that make UChicago a world leader in the field. Full-time lecturers in the Kenneth C. Griffin Department of Economics teach classes on topics in macroeconomics, microeconomics, game theory, and field experiments, which are supplemented by guest lectures delivered by preeminent UChicago faculty in economics and other departments whose research applies the tools and insights of the field in new and exciting ways. Participants can apply what they learn in lectures during small group discussion sections facilitated by a team of outstanding current UChicago students, as well as in labs and site visits to locations such as the Federal Reserve Bank of Chicago.

Contact
(773) 702-2149
summersession@uchicago.edu

Name of College
University of Chicago

Name of Program
Pathway Program in Economics C

Academic / Career Interest
Economics

Website
https://summer.uchicago.edu/course/pathway-program-economics-c

Application Timeline
Approx. May

Eligibility
This course is open to high school students. Students must complete high school calculus before starting this program.

Tuition Fees
Estimated Fees: $5,700 (includes tuition, housing, dining, and fees)

Information about the program:
This program introduces students to the approaches to economic research and experimentation that make UChicago a world leader in the field. Full-time lecturers in the Kenneth C. Griffin Department of Economics teach classes on topics in macroeconomics, microeconomics, game theory, and field experiments, which are supplemented by guest lectures delivered by preeminent UChicago faculty in economics and other departments whose research applies the tools and insights of the field in new and exciting ways. Participants can apply what they learn in lectures during small group discussion sections facilitated by a team of outstanding current UChicago students, as well as in labs and site visits to locations such as the Federal Reserve Bank of Chicago.

Contact
(773) 702-2149
summersession@uchicago.edu

Name of College
Cornell University

Name of Program
Fundamentals of Modern Marketing

Academic / Career Interest
Marketing

Website
https://www.sce.cornell.edu/sc/programs/index.php?v=206

Application Timeline
Approx. May

Eligibility
Students entering their high school sophomore, junior or senior year by the time of the program. Must be younger than 18 years old by the start of the June programs.

Tuition Fees
Estimated Fees: $6,310

Information about the program:
From buying sneakers to choosing political candidates, consumer decisions are shaped at least in part by professional marketers who create and use strategies to influence consumer behavior. Whether students hope to use such strategies in their own career or just want to be an informed consumer, this course will help students under-stand the forces at work in the buying and selling of goods, services, and ideas.

In this rigorous and comprehensive three-week program, students will:

- become familiar with the principles and fundamentals of modern marketing
- learn to analyze complex business situations
- improve teamwork skills, a critical component of academic and career success

Contact
(607) 255-6203
summer_college@cornell.edu

Name of College
Cornell University

Name of Program
Macroeconomics and Current Economic Issues

Academic / Career Interest
Macroeconomics

Website
https://www.sce.cornell.edu/sc/programs/index.php?v=208

Application Timeline
Approx. May

Eligibility
Students entering their high school sophomore, junior or senior year at the start of the program are eligible. Must be younger than 18 years old by the start of the June programs.

Tuition Fees
Estimated Fees: $6,310

Information about the program:
National economies are the result of a complex interplay of relation-ships, and many of those relationships are shifting dramatically in the U.S. What does that mean for us and why should we care? In this program students will learn basic principles of macroeconomics in order to develop a framework for understanding these forces, the U.S. economy, the complex variables that affect it, and the state of many current issues in our national economy.

Students will identify the basic structure of the U.S. Economy, explain a simple macroeconomic model of how the economy works to generate growth and employment, llustrate how macroeconomic aggregates such as GDP, inflation and employment are measured

Contact
(607) 255-6203
summer_college@cornell.edu

Name of College
Cornell University

Name of Program
Secrets of Business Success

Academic / Career Interest
Entrepreneurship

Website
https://www.sce.cornell.edu/sc/programs/index.php?v=204

Application Timeline
Approx. May

Eligibility
Students entering their high school sophomore, junior or senior year at the start of the program are eligible. Must be younger than 18 years old by the start of the June programs.

Tuition Fees
Estimated Fees: $6,310

Information about the program:
Entrepreneurship is global; it is not limited by borders or time zones but fueled by connecting multiple perspectives to create value by seizing opportunity. Every student embodies talents necessary to innovate, create, and contribute to the global entrepreneurial landscape. Whether students have a big idea, are intrigued by the startup culture, or dream of one day running an international company, putting their talents to use is key to business success. This course will expose students to perspectives from successful business leaders, giving them the opportunity to learn from their lessons on culture, industry, and resources while also providing the opportunity to grow their network.

Contact
(607) 255-6203
summer_college@cornell.edu

Name of College
Cornell University

Name of Program
Hospitality Operations Management: Entrepreneurship in the Food and Beverage Industry

Academic / Career Interest
Hospitality Management

Website
https://www.sce.cornell.edu/sc/programs/index.php?v=203

Application Timeline
Approx. May

Eligibility
Students entering their high school sophomore, junior or senior year at the start of the program are eligible. Must be younger than 18 years old by the start of the June programs.

Tuition Fees
Estimated Fees: $6,310

Information about the program:
This intensive and engaging program is taught in the world-renowned School of Hotel Administration (SHA), currently ranked number one in the world for hospitality management, in Cornell's SC Johnson College of Business. Students will:

- deepen their understanding of the food and beverage industry, from market segmentation to menu planning, food safety, supply chain, and service issues
- learn what it means, and takes, to be an entrepreneur in the food and beverage industry
- identify the considerations required to develop a viable and sustainable food and beverage concept
- strengthen their business, marketing, and management knowledge
- develop their oral and written business communication skills and write a concise, well-organized business report

Contact
(607) 255-6203
summer_college@cornell.edu

Name of College
Cornell University

Name of Program
Introduction to Negotiations and Conflict Resolution

Academic / Career Interest
Negotiation and conflict resolution

Website
https://www.sce.cornell.edu/sc/programs/index.php?v=205

Application Timeline
Approx. May

Eligibility
Students entering their high school sophomore, junior or senior year at the start of the program are eligible. Must be younger than 18 years old by the start of the June programs.

Tuition Fees
Estimated Fees: $6,310

Information about the program:
Whether it's with parents, friends, enemies, political adversaries, or other countries, conflicts large and small are inevitable throughout life. How does one navigate them so that all parties get enough of what they want to be satisfied? How does one move forward when the outcome one desires is very different from the outcome desired by an opponent? And in what context does one enlist the help of a third party? Led by Rocco Scanza, director of the Scheinman Institute on Conflict Resolution at Cornell University, this three-week program combines classroom discussion and analysis of dispute resolution techniques, including negotiation, arbitration, and mediation, with opportunities to participate in realistic exercises and group discussions.

Contact
(607) 255-6203
summer_college@cornell.edu

Name of College
Cornell University

Name of Program
The Business World

Academic / Career Interest
Business management

Website
https://www.sce.cornell.edu/sc/programs/index.php?v=166

Application Timeline
Approx. May

Eligibility
Students entering their high school sophomore, junior or senior year at the start of the program are eligible. Must be younger than 18 years old by the start of the June programs.

Tuition Fees
Estimated Fees: $6,310

Information about the program:
Learning about business management can be a great investment in a student's future. It can help students better manage their life, career, and own business (if they ever want to own one). It also could help students begin to solve some of the world's most pressing issues.

Leading the program is David Taylor, director of external relations for the SC Johnson College of Business. With his guidance, students will learn about the basics of business management in today's fast-paced and fascinating business world. From a strategic, managerial decision-making perspective, students will become familiar with the functional areas of business.

Contact
(607) 255-6203
summer_college@cornell.edu

Name of College
Davidson College

Name of Program
The Business World

Academic / Career Interest
Game theory

Website
https://www.davidson.edu/offices/july-experience/courses

Application Timeline
Available approx. December

Eligibility
Program is for students entering their high school junior or senior year at the start of the program.

Tuition Fees
Estimated Fees: $4,000. Tuition covers the following areas: Room and board (all meals and self-service laundry), textbooks for use during the duration of the program, scheduled activity costs/fees.

Information about the program:
Game theory is the study of strategic situations in which the payoff for one person depends directly on the actions of other people. For example, how should one wager in Final Jeopardy? The answer is obvious if one expects to answer correctly. However, it becomes more complicated by the fact that one might not have extensive knowledge of the topic and also isn't sure about an opponents' wagers or how much an opponent knows about the topic. Students will learn about the concept of Nash equilibrium and use it to solve mathematical models of strategic situations. Students will play games in class! Then they will compare their class's data to what theory predicts and discuss how their mathematical models might be improved to better predict the results.

Contact
(704) 894-2508
julyexp@davidson.edu

Name of College
Drexel University

Name of Program
Camp Business

Academic / Career Interest
Business

Website
https://www.lebow.drexel.edu/admissions/undergraduate/pre-college-programs/camp-business

Application Timeline
Approx. May

Eligibility
Exceptional high school students, currently in their sophomore or junior year, are encouraged to apply.

Tuition Fees
Estimated Fees:

- Residential Program: $1500
- Commuter Program: $750

Information about the program:
Camp Business, sponsored by Drexel University's LeBow College of Business, is an enriching summer program designed to give rising high school juniors and seniors an intensive introduction to both collegiate and corporate business education — and it shows them that business can be both fun and exciting. Students work closely with outstanding LeBow faculty and instructors from the corporate world. Students will examine the disciplines of accounting, marketing, finance and management, and learn the core concepts of business including leadership, professional image, etiquette, team building, and strategy.

Contact
(215) 571-3767

Name of College
George Washington University

Name of Program
College Intensive: ECON 1011: Principles of Economics I: Microeconomics

Academic / Career Interest
Economics

Website
https://summer.gwu.edu/business

Application Timeline
Approx. May

Eligibility
The program is open to students entering their high school junior or senior year at time of program (ages 15-18).

Tuition Fees
Estimated Fees: ranges from $3,000 - $6,500

Information about the program:
The College Intensive program offers rising juniors and seniors (ages 15-18) the opportunity to earn college credit by engaging in challenging undergraduate level courses.

Students in this program will earn official GW credit that may be transferable to other institutions, depending on the individual institution policies.

In addition to instruction through lectures, students in the College Intensive program spend time outside of the classroom working on projects, research assignments, readings, papers and other assignments. Major economic principles, institutions and problems in contemporary life. The class focuses on microeconomics: supply and demand, the price system and how it works and competitive and monopolistic markets.

Contact
(202) 994-6360
gwsummer@gwu.edu

Name of College
George Washington University

Name of Program
College Intensive: ECON 1012: Principles of Economics II: Macro-economics

Academic / Career Interest
Economics

Website
https://summer.gwu.edu/business

Application Timeline
Approx. May

Eligibility
The program is open to high school students entering their junior or senior year at start of program (ages 15-18).

Tuition Fees
Estimated Fees: ranges from $3,000 - $6,500

Information about the program:
The College Intensive program offers rising juniors and seniors (ages 15-18) the opportunity to earn college credit by engaging in challenging undergraduate level courses. Students in this program will earn official GW credit that may be transferable to other institutions, depending on the individual institution policies.

In addition to instruction through lectures, students in the College Intensive program spend time outside of the classroom working on projects, research assignments, readings, papers and other assignments. Students also participate in co-curricular site visits, college preparation workshops, personal development and cultural enrichment programs each week, designed to enhance their understanding of and preparation for undergraduate study.

Contact
(202) 994-6360
gwsummer@gwu.ed

Name of College
George Washington University

Name of Program
Summer Immersion: Principles of Real-World Economics

Academic / Career Interest
Economics

Website
https://summer.gwu.edu/business

Application Timeline
Approx. May

Eligibility
The program is open to high school students entering their sophomore, junior or senior year by start of program (ages 14-18).

Tuition Fees
Estimated Fees: ranges from $3,000 - $6,500

Information about the program:
Summer Immersion is a full-day, rigorous, noncredit program for rising sophomores, juniors and seniors (ages 14-18). Participants enroll in 1 or 2-week programs that integrate lectures with guest speakers, experiential and applied activities. Students expand and deepen their knowledge of a topic through collaborative learning and an exploration of the diverse intellectual and cultural resources of Washington, D.C. As the world economy continues to become more globally integrated, understanding the keys to economic efficiency and growth is more important than ever. Students in this course will investigate how economic principles translate into real world processes that affect goods and services, market prices, output, unemployment, inflation and the distribution of resources.

Contact
(202) 994-6360
gwsummer@gwu.edu

Name of College
Georgetown University

Name of Program
Economics Policy Immersion

Academic / Career Interest
Economics

Website
https://summer.georgetown.edu/programs/SHS08/economics-pol-icy-immersion/how-to-apply

Application Timeline
Priority application deadline: approx. April
Last day to submit application: two weeks prior to the start of student's preferred program

Eligibility
The program is open to high school students entering their sophomore, junior or senior year by start of program (ages 14-18).

Tuition Fees
Estimated Fees: $6,199 (includes tuition, housing, and 19 meals per week)

Information about the program:
Georgetown's Economics Policy Immersion provides an interdisciplinary exploration of the complex role played by states and other governing entities in relation to markets, through the lens of both economics and political science. Students will study theoretical concepts from both fields and practice applying them to real-world problems—both in the U.S. and abroad—to assess the situations and evaluate policy solutions. By the end of the program, students will have a deeper understanding of key philosophical and theoretical concepts behind economic policy which affect all facets of life, such as price interventions and regulations as well as he main issues the U.S. economy faces today.

Contact
(202) 687-7087
highschool@georgetown.edu

Name of College
Georgetown University

Name of Program
Entrepreneurship Institute

Academic / Career Interest
Entrepreneurship

Website
https://summer.georgetown.edu/programs/SHS10/entrepreneurship-institute

Application Timeline
Priority application deadline: approx. April
Last day to submit application: Two weeks prior to the start of student's preferred program

Eligibility
The program is open to high school students entering their sophomore, junior or senior year by start of program (ages 14-18).

Tuition Fees
Estimated Fees: $2,895

Information about the program:
Students explore the advantages and challenges of managing their own enterprise in the Entrepreneurship Institute. The one-week program takes an in-depth look at ethical entrepreneurship, social responsibility, risk management, and the business operations of both the private and nonprofit sectors. Over the course of the week, students will have opportunities to hear from faculty members of Georgetown's prestigious McDonough School of Business as well as local entrepreneurs. With an emphasis on personal development, the program incorporates practical, hands-on experience to help students build and improve their public speaking and communications skills, networking strategies, and team-building techniques.

Contact
(202) 687-7087
highschool@georgetown.edu

Name of College
Georgetown University

Name of Program
Business & Leadership Immersion

Academic / Career Interest
Business and leadership

Website
https://summer.georgetown.edu/programs/SHS03/business-leadership-immersion

Application Timeline
Priority application deadline: approx. April
Last day to submit application: Two weeks prior to the start of student's preferred program

Eligibility
The program is open to high school students entering their sophomore, junior or senior year by start of program (ages 14-18).

Tuition Fees
Estimated Fees: $6,199 (includes tuition, housing, and 19 meals per week)

Information about the program:
Georgetown's Business & Leadership Immersion introduces students to the ins and outs of the business world. Combining investment challenges and group presentations with dynamic faculty lectures and case studies, the program prepares students with the practical skills and critical thinking abilities that will benefit them in their future academic and professional endeavors. Students will gain valuable exposure to important business topics and methods of analysis while learning from Georgetown professors and leading experts in the field. Throughout the program, students will also participate in business simulations that take them through the process of becoming an entrepreneur and starting a company.

Contact
(202) 687-7087
highschool@georgetown.edu

Name of College
University of Georgia

Name of Program
Accounting Residency Program

Academic / Career Interest
Accounting

Website
http://www.terry.uga.edu/academics/certificates/accounting-residency-program

Application Timeline
Approx. March

Eligibility
Open to current high school sophomores, juniors, and seniors planning to attend the University of Georgia.

Tuition Fees
Estimated Fees: $95(non-residential)

Information about the program:
As accounting is the language of business, this program is designed to provide exceptional high school students an overview of the many career opportunities in the accounting profession and a brief introduction of business.
ARP students will attend instructional sessions during the day, with fun activities scheduled in the evenings. The daytime sessions will provide insights into career opportunities in accounting and related fields through panel discussions with national and regional accounting firms and representatives from industry groups and government agencies.
Other sessions will introduce important job skills, including:

- Workplace ethics
- Business etiquette
- Financial literacy
- Leadership development

Contact
(706) 542-1379
rgroomes@uga.edu

Name of College
University of Georgia

Name of Program
Terry Business Academy

Academic / Career Interest
Business

Website
http://www.terry.uga.edu/academics/certificates/terry-business-academy

Application Timeline
Approx. March

Eligibility
Open to current high school sophomores, juniors, and seniors planning to attend the University of Georgia.

Tuition Fees
Estimated Fees: $495(non-residential)

Information about the program:
The Terry Business Academy is a highly selective, pre-collegiate program at the University of Georgia's Terry College of Business. This intensive one-week program will expose approximately 30 high school rising juniors and senior to the various fields of business. Each student will gain practical experience developing and presenting a business plan. Participants will learn about different business majors and career paths and will visit corporate headquarters to meet executives and professionals in various industries.

Contact
(706) 542-1379
rgroomes@uga.edu

Name of College
University of Hartford

Name of Program
Summer Business Institute

Academic / Career Interest
Business

Website
http://www.hartford.edu/barney/career-ready/summer_business_institute/

Application Timeline
Contact institution for more information.

Eligibility
Students entering high school junior or senior year at start of program and incoming Barney School freshmen are eligible to apply

Tuition Fees
Estimated Fees: $2,590

Information about the program:
Pe-college students (rising high school juniors, seniors, and incoming Barney School freshmen) enrolled in this course will be introduced to the economic, marketing, financial accounting, ethical and societal dimensions of business. Problem-solving and critical-thinking skills are developed through participation in an interactive team-based simulation. The specific modules of the simulation will be preceded and/or followed by analysis and discussion facilitated by student's own professional faculty who bring their deep professional expertise to help students understand the intricacies of business success.

Summer Business Institute students will also gain general exposure to the academic, residential and social support systems available at the Barney School and the University of Hartford.

Contact
(860) 768-4362
lofink@hartford.edu

Name of College
Ithaca College

Name of Program
Sport Media and Marketing

Academic / Career Interest
Sports media

Website
https://www.ithaca.edu/summercollege/mini/coursedescriptions/?item=5667

Application Timeline
Approx. May

Eligibility
Current high school freshmen, sophomores, and juniors who will be between 15 years and 18 years of age at the start of the summer college program are encouraged to apply.

Tuition Fees
Estimated Fees: One-Week Session $1,680.

Information about the program:
Interested in pursuing a career in sports media? In this workshop students get hands-on experience writing their own material while learning about a professional career in sports media. Students work in a computer lab, shoot video in a television studio, and also visit a professional sports organization to observe media members in action.

Throughout the week, this workshop will cover:

- Sport media relations
- Sport public relations
- Sport radio broadcasting (Park studio)
- Sport television broadcasting day (Park TV studio)
- Sport writing for print/web publications

Contact
(607) 274-5774
kwoody@ithaca.edu

Name of College
Lehigh University

Name of Program
Leadership Education and Development Summer Business Institute

Academic / Career Interest
Business

Website
https://cbe.lehigh.edu/academics/undergraduate/pre-college-pro-grams

Application Timeline
Contact institution for more information.

Eligibility
Open to current high school juniors.

Tuition Fees
Contact institution for more information

Information about the program:
The Summer Business Institute (SBI) program is the longest running Leadership Education and Development (LEAD) summer program and is considered the "flagship" program. The SBI program exposes scholars to business principles and the skill sets needed for successful business careers. The program challenges them through applied learning experiences often facilitated by college professors, links scholars to corporate executives in business fields and peers with similar aspirations and abilities.

During LEAD SBIs, scholars reside and attend classes on-campus at a select number of the nation's top business schools for two or three weeks. SBIs provide diverse, high-achieving rising high school seniors the opportunity to explore finance, entrepreneurship, accounting and marketing, among other business sectors.

Contact
Twana L. Walker
(610) 758-3400

Name of College
Loyola Marymount University

Name of Program
Intro to Entrepreneurship

Academic / Career Interest
Entrepreneurship

Website
https://summer.lmu.edu/pre-collegeacademics/2019non-credit-programs/introtoentrepreneurship/

Application Timeline
Contact institution for more information.

Eligibility
This course is open to high school students entering their sophomore, junior or senior year at time of program.

Tuition Fees
Estimated Fees: 2019 Program Cost: Tuition for next year's program will be announced in September

Information about the program:
This pre-college program is perfect for entrepreneurial minded students who love to dream big, want to make a difference in the world, and believe that anything is possible with a small spark of passion and a lot of hard work.
Considered to be among the top Entrepreneurship programs in the country by U.S. News & World Report and The Princeton Review, LMU is located in the heart of Silicon Beach - one of the most vibrant startup communities in the world - and offers a truly unique environment for enhancing one's entrepreneurial capacity.

Under the guidance of LMU College of Business Administration (CBA) faculty, participants will receive an introduction into the exciting world of building a business from the ground up.

Contact
(310) 338-2700

Name of College
Miami University of Ohio

Name of Program
The Entrepreneurial Experience: Building Your Dreams and Passions into Fun and Profitable Ventures

Academic / Career Interest
Entrepreneurship

Website
https://miamioh.edu/admission/high-school/summer-scholars/session-one/index.html#entrepreneurship

Application Timeline
Approx. May

Eligibility
To be eligible for the Summer Scholars Program, students must:

- Complete their sophomore or junior year of high school by end of June, and not graduate before January the following year.
- Demonstrate strong academic ability in a challenging curriculum. Students typically have a high school grade point average of 3.5 on a 4.0 scale.

Tuition Fees
Estimated Fees: $1,450

Information about the program:
The secret to success in life and business can be found in the entrepreneurial mindset. The entrepreneurship track of the Summer Scholars Program exposes students to the fun and excitement of bringing ideas to life. Students will participate in interactive, hands-on projects where they will be exposed to what it takes to build companies, teams, and insight. Whatever their interests – building a small start-up company, creating a major corporation, driving meaningful social change, or working in creative fields – they will build ideas, form teams, and create the structure that builds success.

Contact
(513) 529-1440
friedmj2@miamioh.edu

Name of College
Miami University of Ohio

Name of Program
Taking Care of Business

Academic / Career Interest
Business

Website
https://miamioh.edu/admission/high-school/summer-scholars/
session-one/index.html#business

Application Timeline
Approx. May

Eligibility
To be eligible for the Summer Scholars Program, students must:

- Complete their high school sophomore or junior year by end of June, and not graduate before January of the following year.
- Demonstrate strong academic ability in a challenging curriculum. Students typically have a high school grade point average of 3.5 on a 4.0 scale.

Tuition Fees
Estimated Fees: $1,450

Information about the program:
What do people "do" in business? What makes a business successful? What does it take to be a business professional? The "Basics of Business" track of the Summer Scholars Program will allow students to investigate all of the functional areas of business, better understand business processes, and develop basic competency in the language of business. Students will work in competitive teams to solve a real-world business problem while thinking creatively and working collaboratively. Students will also have an opportunity to practice how to present in a professional environment.

Contact
(513) 529-1440
friedmj2@miamioh.edu

Name of College
University of Michigan, Ann Arbor

Name of Program
Michigan Business & Entrepreneurship Academy

Academic / Career Interest
Business and entrepreneurship

Website
https://www.summerdiscovery.com/u-michigan/academic-options#michigan-business-and-entrepreneurship-academy

Application Timeline
Contact institution for more information.

Eligibility
For students completing grades 9, 10, 11, 12 (ages 14-18).

Tuition Fees
Estimated Fees:

- 2-Weeks: $4,499
- 3-Weeks: $6,399

Information about the program:
The Michigan Business and Entrepreneurship Academy provides an engaging and hands-on opportunity where students investigate all aspects of a real-life entrepreneurial venture, including opportunity recognition, marketing and sales, negotiation, financials, and legal structures; through the lens of their own business ideas. However, the majority of students are not receiving the education and practical experience in their schools to help fulfill their entrepreneurial goals and aspirations. The program lays the foundation for meaningful participation in looking at, and interacting with, examples from the business world. pricing to guarantee a profitable business.

Contact
(516) 621-3939
info@summerdiscovery.com

Name of College
University of Michigan, Ann Arbor

Name of Program
BBYO Business & Entrepreneurship Academy

Academic / Career Interest
Business and entrepreneurship

Website
https://www.summerdiscovery.com/u-michigan/academic-options#michigan-business-and-entrepreneurship-academy

Application Timeline
Contact institution for more information.

Eligibility
For students completing grades 9, 10, 11, 12 (ages 14-18).

Tuition Fees
Estimated Fees: range from $4,500 - $6,000
Information about the program:
The BBYO Michigan Business and Entrepreneurship Academy highlights Jewish business leadership and engages teens to learn through classroom activities and field trips. On campus at the University of Michigan, participants will learn about competitive advantage, marketing, finance and product development. The two-week program, powered by the Network for Teaching Entrepreneurship, concludes with a competition where students present their original business plans to a panel of judges from the local business community and the winners are awarded prizes for their business plan. In addition, BBYO will offer exciting and meaningful content from a Jewish perspective, including Shabbat programming, opportunities to learn about entrepreneurship in Israel and more. BBYO Michigan Business and Entrepreneurship Academy also features additional afternoon and evening activities including Detroit Tigers baseball games, The Rock 'n Roll Hall of Fame in Cleveland, Cedar Point Amusement Park, plus sports and recreation.

Contact
(516) 621-3939
info@summerdiscovery.com

Name of College
University of Michigan, Ann Arbor

Name of Program
Courses: Business

Academic / Career Interest
Business

Website
https://www.summerdiscovery.com/u-michigan/courses#business

Application Timeline
Contact institution for more information.

Eligibility
For students completing grades 9, 10, 11, 12 (ages 14-18)

Tuition Fees
Estimated Fees:

- 2-Weeks: $4,499
- 3-Weeks: $6,399

Information about the program:
Game Changers: Business Disruptors, this course explores the ways in which innovative companies have revolutionized the way we do business. Students will explore how the business models of modern disruptors such as Amazon, WeWork, Netflix, Uber, Airbnb, and Tesla have changed the world and altered the way we think, behave, and act about a certain idea, item, product, or service. This course provides the framework to understand the nature of disruption that is happening to industry after industry in order for students to apply these same techniques as part of a final project where they will work in groups to create their own (perhaps, disruptive) business.

Contact
(516) 621-3939
info@summerdiscovery.com

Name of College
The College of New Jersey

Name of Program
Pre-College: The Summer Academy for Business and Entrepreneur-ship

Academic / Career Interest
Business and entrepreneurship

Website
https://precollege.tcnj.edu/academy-series/createyourbusiness/

Application Timeline
Approx. May

Eligibility
The Bonner Summer Pre-College Program is geared towards high school students entering their junior or senior year at time of program.

Tuition Fees
Estimated Fees: $1,100.00

Information about the program:
All businesses – small, large, corporate, family – are created, operate and grow following core principles. Complex and diverse, today's global business environment demands leaders with the forethought to anticipate and pivot toward changing opportunity. Leaders are required to analyze and imagine, to find solutions that create value for a company and its community. From business innovation to socially responsible citizenship, success is more than the bottom line. Our program provides students with hands-on learning experience to test-drive business majors. During the week, students will attend class for three hours a day and participate in a business simulation and team-building events.

Contact
Graduate and Advancing Education
Pre-College Programs, Green Hall, Room 111
The College of New Jersey
PO Box 7718, 2000 Pennington Rd, Ewing, NJ 08628

Name of College
New York University

Name of Program
Summer @ Stern

Academic / Career Interest
Business

Website
http://www.stern.nyu.edu/programs-admissions/undergraduate/
high-school-summer-program

Application Timeline
Approx. March

Eligibility
Open to high school students entering their junior or senior year at
time of program.

Tuition Fees
Estimated Fees: $12,494

Information about the program:
All students who are admitted to NYU Precollege and then admitted
to Summer @ Stern will be automatically enrolled in the two Summer @ Stern courses. Both courses are mandatory. Summer @ Stern
through NYU Precollege offers rising high school juniors and seniors
the opportunity to learn fundamental concepts of business—including accounting, finance, economics, marketing, and psychology—
from NYU Stern's world-renowned faculty. If students are thinking
about pursuing business in college or are just interested in knowing
a little more about the basics and want to spend an unforgettable
summer in New York City, then Summer @ Stern through NYU Pre-
college is for them. Summer @ Stern is a two-course program that
will give high school students an introduction to business, college
life, and the cultural vibrancy of New York City.

Contact
(212) 998-0100

Name of College
Northeastern University

Name of Program
Experiential Entrepreneurship

Academic / Career Interest
Entrepreneurship

Website
https://www.northeastern.edu/precollegeprograms/programs/
experiential-entrepreneurship/

Application Timeline
Contact institution for more information.

Eligibility
Contact institution for more information.

Tuition Fees
Estimated Fees:

- Residential: $5,995
- Commuter: $3,995

Information about the program:
Experiential Entrepreneurship (E2) is a summer program designed for future entrepreneurs who want to change the world with their ideas. In this program, students learn to be an entrepreneur by being an entrepreneur. They will form teams and build a startup from an idea to a pitch in front of a panel of entrepreneurs. Along the way, they will have access to industry professionals who will provide guidance in topics, such as finding and growing an audience, business planning, product development, negotiation, pitch presentations, and more. Students will also visit start-up businesses and have other field trips to bring what they are learning to life. This opportunity to go from an idea to a pitch for high school students is a one of a kind experience.

Contact
(617) 373-2200
precollegeprograms@northeastern.edu

Name of College
Notre Dame University

Name of Program
The Language of Business: Accounting in a Global Society

Academic / Career Interest
Accounting

Website
https://precollege.nd.edu/courses/the-language-of-business/

Application Timeline
Summer application will be available approx. October

Eligibility
Current sophomores and juniors.

Tuition Fees
Estimated Fees: $3,500

Information about the program:
From Wall Street to Main Street, accounting shapes and informs all aspects of life. The Summer Scholars Accounting course introduces students to fundamental accounting concepts and processes in addition to the important roles that CPAs (certified public accountants) play with every type of organization, from the local flower shop to the multi-national pharmaceutical company. The framework for this innovative course consists of an overview of accounting concepts and techniques, financial statements, and case studies based on current events, such as proposed changes to U.S. tax law and European Union fines on Apple Computer. The course enables students to see how CPAs protect investors, influence public policy, analyze businesses, and advise companies, ranging from start-ups to Fortune 500 companies.

Contact
(574) 631-0990
precoll@nd.edu

Name of College
University of Pennsylvania

Name of Program
Leadership in the Business World

Academic / Career Interest
Leadership

Website
https://www.wharton.upenn.edu/leadership-business-world/

Application Timeline
Application open from approx. November – February

Eligibility
Students entering their high school senior year at time of program.

Tuition Fees
Estimated Fees: $7,725

Information about the program:
LBW offers opportunities to learn about leadership in 21st century organizations through a dynamic and rigorous mix of classes with Wharton professors and business leaders, company site visits, and team-building activities. Students will attend lectures and presentations from outstanding Wharton faculty and guest speakers, and engage in classroom discussions about core business subjects, entrepreneurship, and leadership.

Contact
(610) 265-9401
LBW-inquiries@wharton.upenn.edu

Name of College
University of Pennsylvania

Name of Program
Wharton Moneyball Academy

Academic / Career Interest
Statistics

Website
https://www.jkcp.com/program/wharton-moneyball-academy.php

Application Timeline
Contact institution for more information

Eligibility
Ages: 16-18. Grades: high school students entering 11th and 12th grade at time of program.

Tuition Fees
Estimated Fees: $6,500

Information about the program:
The hit movie Moneyball opened audiences' eyes to the world of sports statistics. The Wharton Moneyball Academy lets students delve deeper into this fascinating realm, showing them how to turn simple data into deep discoveries that defy conventional wisdom. Hosted by the Wharton School of the University of Pennsylvania and the Wharton Sports Business Initiative (WSBI), the Moneyball Academy welcomes talented high school juniors and seniors intrigued by statistics.

Moneyball is taught by Wharton faculty and graduate students. The program covers much of Wharton's Statistics 101 course as well as many of its advanced level statistical courses. As students learn to read and write code in R (the powerful statistical programming language) and develop key data analysis skills, they will be primed to be a leader in an increasingly data-driven economy.

Contact
(610) 265-9401
Imagine@JKCP.com

Name of College
University of Pennsylvania

Name of Program
Knowledge@Wharton High School Global Young Leaders Academy

Academic / Career Interest
Entrepreneurship

Website
http://www.wharton.braingainmag.com/

Application Timeline
Contact institution for more information.

Eligibility
Students must be at least 15 years of age (upon start date of the program) and in high school.

Tuition Fees
Estimated Fees: $5,110 plus a refundable security deposit of US $500.

Information about the program:
Organized by Knowledge@Wharton High School (KWHS), the Global Young Leaders Academy (GYLA) is an intensive two-week summer program for a select group of domestic (USA) and international high school students. Students must be at least 15 years of age (upon start date of the program) and in high school. The program introduces students to entrepreneurship and other business concepts and provides cultural immersion. It features Wharton faculty presentations, in-depth learning from high school teachers in the KWHS network, residential activities, field trips, community service and relationship building with other teens. GYLA draws its content from hundreds of engaging KWHS lesson plans and online business journal articles.

Contact
wharton@braingainmag.com

Name of College
University of Pennsylvania

Name of Program
Management and Technology Summer Institute

Academic / Career Interest
Management

Website
https://fisher.wharton.upenn.edu/summer-mt

Application Timeline
Approx. February

Eligibility
Program is open to students entering their high school senior year at time of program and a select few students entering their junior year.

Tuition Fees
Estimated Fees: $7,000 (including tuition, housing, meals, and weekend excursions)

Information about the program:
The Management & Technology Summer Institute (M&TSI) is a rigorous and rewarding for-credit summer program for students who will be entering their high school senior year at start of program and a select few students who will be entering their high school junior year, interested in exploring the integration of technological concepts and management principles. Sponsored by the Jerome Fisher Program in Management & Technology, Penn Engineering, and the Wharton School, M&TSI features classes taught by leading faculty and successful entrepreneurs, field trips to companies and R&D facilities, intensive team projects, as well as other activities designed to give students the opportunity to learn about the principles and practice of technological innovation. M&TSI 2018 will run July 8th-July 28th, 2018.

Contact
mtsi@jkcp.com

Name of College
Rowan University

Name of Program
Think Like an Entrepreneur Summer Academy

Academic / Career Interest
Entrepreneurship

Website
https://fisher.wharton.upenn.edu/summer-mt

Application Timeline
Approx. June

Eligibility
Program is for high school juniors and seniors.

Tuition Fees
Estimated Fees: Participation in the academy is free of charge

Information about the program:
Students will:

- Learn how to conceive, develop, prototype, and sell their ideas!
- Work alongside Rowan University faculty and student leaders to learn the basics of how to transform an idea into a feasible and viable business.
- Gain exposure to student life on a college campus and the excitement of working with a team toward a common goal.

The program focuses on the development of soft skills - including fostering of an entrepreneurial mindset – and on the development of specific entrepreneurial knowledge and expertise. Regardless of intended major, all future business students, and the organizations that will eventually employ them, benefit from the type of creative mindset, hard work, and initiative that power startups.

Contact
Jessica Wolk
wolk@rowan.edu

Name of College
Saint Louis University

Name of Program
Allsup Entrepreneurship Academy

Academic / Career Interest
Entrepreneurship

Website
https://www.slu.edu/summer/k-12-camps.php#/camp-details/
Allsup-Entrepreneurship-Academy

Application Timeline
Contact institution for more information.

Eligibility
Students grades 9-12 and College freshmen are eligible to apply
Age Level: 14-18

Tuition Fees
Estimated Fees: $695 (non-residential)

Information about the program:
This program shows high school students what it takes to start and operate a business, be their own bosses and have fun while doing so. The week is full of hands on learning, innovation challenges, field trips to local business incubators, and meeting some of the coolest entrepreneurs in Saint Louis. Camp is led by the students and faculty members of Saint Louis University's entrepreneurship program which was ranked 9th in the nation by U.S. News & World Report in 2017.

Contact
Laura Gardner
(314) 977-3282
laura.gardner@slu.edu

Name of College
University of South Carolina

Name of Program
Adventures in Business - Entrepreneurship

Academic / Career Interest
Entrepreneurship

Website
https://www.sc.edu/about/offices_and_divisions/continuing_ed-ucation/youth_and_teen_pre-university_programs/carolina_mas-ter_scholars_adventure_series/summer_2018_camps/business_en-trepreneurship/index.php

Application Timeline
Contact institution for more information.

Eligibility
Students entering 9 -12 grade at the start of the program are eligible.

Tuition Fees
Estimated Fees range from $600 - $900.

Information about the program:
This program is for any student who's dreamed about creating and launching a project and pitching it like on the popular TV show "Shark Tank." Students will enhance their entrepreneurial skills in this dynamic business-oriented adventure through University of South Carolina's Darla Moore School of Business Proving Ground which began as a competition in 2010 to give University of South Carolina students a chance to get their projects funded. Students will learn how to:

- find a product or service that solves a problem
- identify a clearly defined market
- uncover a clear advantage
- learn what it takes to create a capacity to bring a product or service to the market
- discover how their project will be profitable
- learn how to pitch their product in front of investors

Contact
(803) 777-944

Name of College
University of Southern California

Name of Program
Exploring Entrepreneurship

Academic / Career Interest
Entrepreneurship

Website
https://summerprograms.usc.edu/programs/4-week/entrepreneurship/

Application Timeline
Approx. April

Eligibility
Must have completed at least 10th grade by June.

Tuition Fees
Estimated Fees:

- Residential $8,534
- Commuter $6,059

Information about the program:
This program is for any student with an entrepreneurial mind who's ever thought about starting a business. In this course, students will be immersed in the real world of establishing and building a company. The course blends business theory and the practice of being an entrepreneur. Exploring Entrepreneurship students will:

- Hear from guest entrepreneurs and other speakers
- Participate in off-campus field trips to experience the Los Angeles business and entrepreneurial environment
- Previous trips have included Santa Monica's Silicon Beach to meet with startups and venture firms, leading retailers in the active sports business, manufacturing facilities in Downtown LA and some leading food concepts by Los Angeles top entrepreneurs

Contact
(213) 740-5679
summer@usc.edu

Name of College
University of Southern California

Name of Program
Ethical Business Strategies

Academic / Career Interest
Ethics, business and economics

Website
https://summerprograms.usc.edu/programs/4-week/ethics/

Application Timeline
Approx. April

Eligibility
High school students who have completed at least the 9th grade by the start of the program

Tuition Fees
Estimated Fees: Residential $8,534 Commuter $6,059

Information about the program:
In the course, students will explore the somewhat uneasy relation-ship between ethics, business, and economics, including the ethical issues people confront as individual employees, and as managers of people and projects. How should a person who wants to act ethically conduct business? Is there a place for ethics in business? How do business people evaluate the risks associated with different business plans? What are the duties and responsibilities to various stakeholders, including employees, customers, investors, and the general public? In this course students will explore and apply deci-sion-making frameworks to ethical dilemmas that arise in business management and the workplace as a whole to equip the business leaders of tomorrow with the skills that they will need.

Contact
(213) 740-5679
summer@usc.edu

Name of College
University of Southern California

Name of Program
Introduction to Business

Academic / Career Interest
Business

Website
https://summerprograms.usc.edu/programs/4-week/introduction-to-business/

Application Timeline
Approx. April

Eligibility
High school students who have completed at least the 9th grade by the start of the program.

Tuition Fees
Estimated Fees:

- Residential $8,534
- Commuter $6,059

Information about the program:
This course provides students with an insight as to how a business is managed and run. There are many factors that determine a company's success including marketing, operations, finance and leadership. This course will give students the basics for understanding how these different departments work independently yet are reliant on each other for a company to prosper. To accomplish this goal, the course is divided into different themes:

- Organization
- Ethics & Social Responsibility
- Marketing
- Accounting
- Operations
- Finances
- Management & Leadership

Contact
(213) 740-5679 / summer@usc.edu

Name of College
Syracuse University

Name of Program
Economic Ideas & Issues

Academic / Career Interest
Economics

Website
http://summercollege.syr.edu/program/economic-ideas-issues/

Application Timeline
Scholarship applications deadline: approx. April
Completed applications deadline: approx. June

Eligibility
Students applying to Summer College are expected to be in good academic standing with a minimum cumulative GPA of 3.0. Students must be a minimum of 15 years of age by the orientation and move-in day of their selected program. Students who will be entering their junior or senior year at the start of the program are welcome to apply to any Summer College program. Students who will be entering their sophomore year are only eligible for non-credit courses.

Tuition Fees
Estimated Fees:

- Residential: $4,666
- Commuter: $3,767

$60 non-refundable application fee.

Information about the program:
This course introduces students to the principles of economics and how these principles can be applied to current issues facing individuals and society today.

This is a regularized undergraduate course delivered through classroom-based instruction and homework. The class may consist of both Summer College and undergraduate students.

Contact
(315) 443-5000
sumcoll@syr.edu

Name of College
Syracuse University

Name of Program
Launching a Business: Strategic Leadership & Innovation

Academic / Career Interest
Entrepreneurship

Website
http://summercollege.syr.edu/program/business/

Application Timeline
Scholarship applications deadline: approx. April
Completed applications deadline: approx. June

Eligibility
Students applying to Summer College are expected to be in good
academic standing with a minimum cumulative GPA of 3.0.

Tuition Fees
Estimated Fees:

- Residential: $4,666
- Commuter: $3,767

$60 non-refundable application fee.

Information about the program:
High school students will learn the art and science of planning and
starting a business in this two-week intensive Summer College
program. The primary objective of the program is to help students
develop the skills, knowledge, mindset, and global perspective
they need to succeed as an entrepreneur or corporate innovator.
Taught through a combination of small group discussions, guest
lectures, online and hands-on learning tools, this program provides
actionable content specifically designed to help students succeed in
business. Flipping the classroom allows students to spend valuable
class time working with peers and instructors to craft the perfect
business plan.

Contact
(315) 443-5000
sumcoll@syr.edu

Name of College
Washington University in Saint Louis

Name of Program
Olin Fleischer Scholars Program

Academic / Career Interest
Business and entrepreneurship

Website
http://apps.olin.wustl.edu/conf/ofsp/Home/Default.aspx

Application Timeline
Approx. April

Eligibility
Olin Fleischer Scholar Program is open to students entering their high school sophomore, junior or senior year in beginning fall who are from underrepresented and low-income backgrounds, and/or potential first-generation college students.

Tuition Fees
Estimated Fees: free

Information about the program:
The Olin Fleischer Scholars Program for high school students is a FREE week-long residential program geared toward underrepresented and first-generation college student populations. The program is designed to expose students to the importance of a college education, leadership, and careers in business and entrepreneurship. The students will be exposed to the Olin Business School's faculty, students, and alumni as well as leaders within the St. Louis community.

Contact
Paige LaRose, Coordinator of Fleischer Scholars Program
(314) 935-6315
OLIN-FSO@email.wustl.edu

Name of College
University of Wisconsin Madison

Name of Program
Business Emerging Leaders Program

Academic / Career Interest
Business

Website
https://wsb.wisc.edu/programs-degrees/undergrad-
uate-bba/leadership-personal-development/bel-pro-
gram?_ga=2.162730558.34570880.1534457096-
1920770542.1532741380

Application Timeline
Approx. March

Eligibility
High School Students (Grades 9-12) are eligible.

Tuition Fees
Estimated Fees: there is no cost for students to participate in the Business Emerging Leaders Program once they arrive on campus.

Information about the program:
The Business Emerging Leaders Program is designed for promising students who come from diverse backgrounds and have strong academic records and demonstrated leadership skills. Program participation gives students a distinct competitive advantage when adjusting to college life, learning in classes, applying for internship opportunities and preparing them for successful careers in business.

Contact
(608) 262-1550

Name of College
University of California, Berkeley

Name of Program
Berkeley Business Academy for Youth

Academic / Career Interest
Business

Website
http://haas.berkeley.edu/businessacademy/high-school/

Application Timeline
Approx. April 30

Eligibility
We look for academically motivated, mature students who are interested in attending a rigorous college prep summer business academy. B-BAY is for youth who want to develop their knowledge of business or have a passion for business. The application and accompanying materials should convey and communicate your level of maturity and motivation.

Tuition Fees
Estimated fees: $5,500

Information about the program:
Every year, 50 high-school students from around the globe spend two weeks at B-BAY on the Berkeley Haas campus, where:

- They immerse themselves in the culture, academics, and life at Berkeley.
- Berkeley Haas professors and corporate guest speakers share their insights and real-world experience
- Classroom instruction is supplemented with independent research and computer lab assignments and team projects.
- Teams work together to create a comprehensive business plan.
- Teams present their business plans at the end of the session.

Contact
(510) 643-0923

Name of College
Cornell University

Name of Program
Fundamentals of Modern Marketing

Academic / Career Interest
Marketing

Website
https://www.sce.cornell.edu/sc/programs/index.php?v=206

Application Timeline
Approx. May 4

Eligibility
Current sophomores, juniors, and seniors.

Tuition Fees
Estimated fees: $6,310

Information about the program:
In this rigorous and comprehensive three-week program, you'll become familiar with the principles and fundamentals of modern marketing, learn to analyze complex business situations, and improve your teamwork skills, a critical component of academic and career success. Led by Sherif Nasser, a visiting assistant professor in Cornell's top-ranked Dyson School of Applied Economics and Management, you'll learn how organizations plan, price, promote, and distribute their goods and services in today's global economy. You'll discuss the issues marketing managers face and delve into the techniques they use in choosing and evaluating their marketing strategies.

Contact
(607) 255-6203
summer_college@cornell.edu

Name of College
University of Pennsylvania

Name of Program
Leadership in the Business World

Academic / Career Interest
Leadership

Website
https://www.wharton.upenn.edu/leadership-business-world/

Application Timeline
Approx. February 2

Eligibility
Students with demonstrated leadership ability who will enter 12th grade in Fall.

Tuition Fees
Estimated fees: $7,725

Information about the program:
LBW offers opportunities to learn about leadership in 21st century organizations through a dynamic and rigorous mix of classes with Wharton professors and business leaders, company site visits, and team-building activities. Work in teams to design and present an original business plan, evaluated by a panel of venture capitalists and business professionals. Contact Institution for more information.

Contact
(610) 265-9401
LBW-inquiries@wharton.upenn.edu

Name of College
Cornell University

Name of Program
Macroeconomics and Current Economic Issues

Academic / Career Interest
Macroeconomics

Website
https://www.sce.cornell.edu/sc/programs/index.php?v=208

Application Timeline
Approx. May 4

Eligibility
Current juniors and seniors.

Tuition Fees
Estimated fees: $6,310

Information about the program:
National economies are the result of a complex interplay of relation-ships, and many of those relationships are shifting dramatically in the U.S. What does that mean for you, and why should you care?

In this program, taught by Arnab Basu and Steven Kyle from Cor-nell's acclaimed Charles H. Dyson School of Applied Economics and Management, you'll learn basic principles of macroeconomics in or-der to develop a framework for understanding these forces, the U.S. economy, the complex variables that affect it, and the state of many current issues in our national economy.

Contact
(607) 255-6203

Name of College
Cornell University

Name of Program
The Business World

Academic / Career Interest
Business management

Website
https://www.sce.cornell.edu/sc/programs/index.php?v=166

Application Timeline
Approx. May 4

Eligibility
Current sophomores, juniors, and seniors.

Tuition Fees
Estimated fees: $6,310

Information about the program:
Learning about business management can be a great investment in your future. It can help you better manage your life, your career, and your own business (if you ever want to own one). It also could help you begin to solve some of the world's most pressing issues.

Leading the program is David Taylor, director of external relations for the SC Johnson College of Business. With his guidance, you'll learn about the basics of business management in today's fast-paced and fascinating business world. From a strategic, managerial decision-making perspective, you'll become familiar with the functional areas of business such as:

- Human resources management
- Marketing management
- Operations management
- Finance and accounting
- Information and technology management

Contact
(607) 255-6203

Name of College
Yale University

Name of Program
EXPLO Sports Management

Academic / Career Interest
Sports management

Website
https://www.explo.org/focus/sports-management/

Application Timeline
Contact Institution for more information

Eligibility
Entering grades 10-12.

Tuition Fees
Estimated fees: $5,215

Information about the program:
Get insider access to the fields that make sports a multi-billion-dollar industry. You'll learn from the best — from agents and news producers to directors of sabermetrics, media reps, and marketing VPs. You'll bring the vision, the innovation, and the awareness of what the sports industry looks like now — and what you want it to look like once you're the one calling the shots.

Contact
(781) 762-7400

Gaming / Animation Collegiate Programs

(Please see Art Programs for additional related content)

Name of College
University of California, Los Angeles

Name of Program
Game Lab Summer Institute

Academic / Career Interest
Game-making

Website
https://www.summer.ucla.edu/institutes/GameLab

Application Timeline
Contact institution for more information.

Eligibility
To participate for the Game Lab Summer Institute, students must meet the following qualifications:

- 14 years of age or older prior to June
- Enrolled in grades 9th – 12th

Tuition Fees
Estimated fees: $2,286

Information about the program:
The University of California, Los Angeles (UCLA) Game Lab Summer Institute introduces high school students to game-making as a form of artistic practice, teaching them the techniques and tools that will help them develop analog and digital games that reflect their own creative voice and vision. No previous game-making skills are required, but students with an interest in games and in the visual arts in particular will find the curriculum especially stimulating and rewarding. Students in the program develop a solid aesthetic and technical foundation in various aspects of game design--but just as importantly, they begin learning how to express their own, personal ideas through game-making and game art.

Contact
https://www.summer.ucla.edu/contactus

Name of College
University of California, Los Angeles

Name of Program
Design Media Arts Summer Institute

Academic / Career Interest
Design and media arts

Website
https://www.summer.ucla.edu/institutes/DesignMediaArts

Application Timeline
Summer Scholars Support for California High School Students Application Period: approx. February - April
Full Payment via MYUCLA due for Precollege Summer Institutes: approx. May
Refund Deadline for Precollege Summer Institutes: approx. June

Eligibility

- Enrolled in grades 9th – 12th during Spring
- 14 years of age or older prior to June

Tuition Fees
Estimated fees: $3,310

Information about the program:
The Department of Design Media Arts (DMA) at University of California, Los Angeles is one of the nation's top design departments offering a comprehensive, multidisciplinary education in media creation, which fosters individual exploration and innovative thinking. Geared specifically for high school students, the department offers the DMA Summer Institute, a two-week program with morning and afternoon classes in graphic design, web design, audio/video, and gaming. Taught by professionally trained and well-experienced instructors using the most current software and technology, the program culminates in the creation of an online portfolio students can use for college applications.

Contact
helen.tran@arts.ucla.edu

Name of College
Carnegie Mellon University

Name of Program
National High School Game Academy

Academic / Career Interest
Video game development

Website
https://admission.enrollment.cmu.edu/pages/access-nhsga

Application Timeline
Approx. March

Eligibility
Contact institution for more information.

Tuition Fees
There are limited fee waivers available for students applying for National High School Game Academy. Fee waivers cover the cost of tuition, housing and dining. All students are responsible for the costs of materials/supplies, transportation and recreational expenses, with an average cost of $300. Students who are awarded fee waivers will be notified in their decision letter.

Information about the program:
The National High School Game Academy (NHSGA) allows dedicated high school students to experience the modern video game development process and, in so doing, learn skills used in those processes. NHSGA provides an opportunity for students in all disciplines (art, music, design and programming) to experience the rigorous demands of college-level instruction. Students are encouraged to expand their own creative possibilities in a unique blend of left- and right-brain college-level work. Students' rigor and discipline and prepare them for the college experience

Contact
(412) 268-2082

Name of College
University of Pennsylvania

Name of Program
Art: Summer at Penn

Academic / Career Interest
Art

Website
https://www.jkcp.com/program/art-summer-at-penn.php

Application Timeline
Rolling admission

Eligibility
Students must be in grades 9-12

Tuition Fees
Estimated fees: $6,250

Information about the program:
The University of Pennsylvania's School of design presents an unparalleled four-week intensive studio art program. Students can unleash their creative genius and add new pieces to their portfolio.

Diverse teaching styles are combined with open studio hours and field trips to various art institutions. Students choose their own schedule by pairing a major studio with one supplemental elective course, allowing them to experience different genres and styles. Classes are small to encourage ample interaction between students and Penn design instructors.

Faculty-led portfolio workshops help students strengthen their art portfolio for college admissions and boost their college acceptance odds with professional images and world-renowned experience that will "wow" admissions offices.

Contact
(610) 265-9401
imagine@JKCP.com

Name of College
University of North Carolina, School of the Arts

Name of Program
Animation Summer Intensive

Academic / Career Interest
Animation

Website
https://www.uncsa.edu/summer/film-summer-intensives/anima-tion/index.aspx

Application Timeline
Approx. April

Eligibility
All students in high school are accepted.

Tuition Fees
Estimated fees: $1,869

Information about the program:
This program, open to rising high school freshmen through incoming college freshmen, will introduce first-time students to the fundamentals of animation and returning students to more advanced studies in the field. Within the conservatory approach to learning, students will experience all the elements of animation first–hand: visual storytelling, screenwriting, storyboarding, cinematography, directing, animation production, and editing. Students will also gain hands-on knowledge of various forms of animation such as hand-drawn animation, stop motion animation and 3D computer animation, all with state-of-the-art animation facilities, individual instruction from highly-experienced professional animators and the collaborative efforts of fellow student animators.

Contact
Community & Summer Programs
University of North Carolina School of the Arts
1533 S. Main St.
Winston-Salem, NC 27127
(336) 734-2848

Name of College
Syracuse University

Name of Program
Computer Animation & Game Design

Academic / Career Interest
Computer animation and game development

Website
http://summercollege.syr.edu/program/animation-game-design/

Application Timeline
Approx. April

Eligibility
Students applying to Summer College are expected to be in good academic standing with a minimum cumulative GPA of 3.0. Students must be a minimum of 15 years of age by the orientation and move-in day of their selected program. Rising Juniors and Seniors are welcome to apply to any Summer College program. Rising Sophomores are encouraged to contact the Summer College office to discuss their potential eligibility, as admission of rising Sophomores is considered on a case-by-case basis and in select Summer College programs.

Tuition Fees
Estimated fees: $4,670

Information about the program:
Students will be registered for CPS 185, Introduction to Computer Animation and Game Development. This summer program for high school students offers a highly visual, non-mathematical introduction to computing and computer programming. The vehicle is the Alice development environment, which allows students without prior experience to rapidly create 3D virtual worlds like those seen in video games. Students become the master of domains of their own creation!

Contact
(315) 443-5000
sumcoll@syr.edu

Name of College
University of Southern California

Name of Program
Intro to Video Game Design

Academic / Career Interest
Video game design

Website
https://summerprograms.usc.edu/programs/4-week/game-design/

Application Timeline
Contact institution for more information.

Eligibility
Contact institution for more information.

Tuition Fees
Contact institution for more information.

Information about the program:
This program is perfect for students who love video games and want to create their own. This course will provide students with an overview of the video game production process. Students will gain hands-on experience by developing video games and utilizing various software applications. Upon completion of the course, students will be able to conceptualize, design, develop, implement and integrate current and emerging video game features and technologies.

Contact
(213) 740-5679
summer@usc.edu

History Collegiate Programs

Name of College
Boston College

Name of Program
Boston College Experience (BCE): Introductory Sociology

Academic / Career Interest
Sociology

Website
https://www.bc.edu/bc-web/sites/bc-experience/programs/undergraduate-courses.html

Application Timeline
BCE summer program application review occurs during approx. February – May.

Eligibility
Students entering grades 11 & 12 are eligible to apply.

Tuition Fees
Estimated fees:

- Resident: $8,500
- Commuter: $5,500

Information about the program:
This course conveys a sense of the history of sociology and introduces students to the most essential concepts, ideas, theories, and methods of the discipline. Special topics may include interaction in everyday life, sociology of the family, gender roles, race and ethnic relations, and the sociology of work, among others. Students will deal with fundamental questions about what it means to be a human being living in a society at a given moment in history.

Contact
(617) 552-3800
bce@bc.edu

Name of College
Brown University

Name of Program
Summer@Brown: Black Panthers, Brown Berets: Radical Social Movements of the Late-20th Century

Academic / Career Interest
History

Website
https://precollege.brown.edu/catalog/course.php?course_code=C-EAC0919

Application Timeline
Rolling admission, applications available approx. December

Eligibility
Students completing grades 9-12, ages 15-18 by June, are eligible to apply.

Tuition Fees
Estimated fees range from $2,000 - $6,000

Information about the program:
This course examines the histories of radical social movement organizations and individuals from the Black, Latinx, Asian, and Native American communities. Students will explore their greatest achievements along with their deepest pitfalls and ponder the teachings these experiences can provide for us today. Students will heavily utilize primary sources--film, theater, paintings, and autobiography--to learn about this history from the perspective of those who took part in the movements.

Between 1950 and 1980, the United States witnessed a mobilization of radical social movements led by Black, Latinx, Asian, and Native American communities. The legacy of this activism lives on in popular memory, as names like Malcolm X and the Black Panthers have become iconic--even controversial--in the American mainstream.

Contact
(401) 863-7900
precollege@brown.edu

Name of College
Brown University

Name of Program
Summer@Brown: Girl Power Through the Ages: An Introduction to Feminist Theory and Practice

Academic / Career Interest
History

Website
https://precollege.brown.edu/catalog/course.php?course_code=CEAN0929

Application Timeline
Rolling admission, applications available approx. December

Eligibility
Students completing grades 9-12, ages 15-18 by June are eligible to apply.

Tuition Fees
Estimated fees range from $2,000 - $6,000

Information about the program:
This course is any students who's wondered what it means to be a feminist? This course is a basic introduction to feminist theories and practices both historically and contemporarily. Reading and discussing seminal texts, engaging with depictions of feminists (both in popular culture and other forms), and exploring feminist activism will introduce students to the intersection of theory, representation, and practice.

By engaging this process of exploration and reflection through a conscientious, nuanced, and purposeful feminist framework, students will also open themselves to understanding the impact of gender construction and variant articulations of feminism as issues that concern us all equally.

Contact
(401) 863-7900
precollege@brown.edu

Name of College
University of California, Los Angeles

Name of Program
Introductory Sociology

Academic / Career Interest
Sociology

Website
https://summer.ucla.edu/academiccourses/hscourselist

Application Timeline
Approx. February – April: Summer Scholars Support for California High School Students Application Period

Eligibility
Students must be at least 15 years of age by the first day of summer to enroll in academic courses.

Tuition Fees
Estimated fees:

- Registration Fee: $150
- Service Fee: $200
- Course Fee: $351 per unit
- IEI Fee: $61 per summer (students without a bachelor's degree)
- Document Fee: $50 assessed only for the first summer term at UCLA

Information about the program:
Survey of characteristics of social life, processes of social interaction, and tools of sociological investigation.

Contact
(310) 825-4101
info@summer.ucla.edu

Name of College
University of California, Santa Cruz

Name of Program
United States History, 1877 to 1977

Academic / Career Interest
History

Website
https://summer.ucsc.edu/courses/his.html

Application Timeline
Contact institution for more information.

Eligibility
As part of Summer Session, high school students from all over the world who completed their sophomore or junior year with a GPA of 3.0+ can live and learn at University of California, Santa Cruz.

Tuition Fees
Estimated fees:

- Total one course tuition plus living on campus = $2,464.50 - $2,892.50
- Total one course tuition living off campus = $985.50

Information about the program:
Surveys the political, social, and cultural history of the United States from 1877 to 1977. Focuses on national politics with emphasis on how class, race, ethnicity, and gender changed the nation's agenda.

Contact
(831) 459-5373

Name of College
University of California, Santa Cruz

Name of Program
Early Modern East Asia

Academic / Career Interest
History

Website
https://summer.ucsc.edu/courses/his.html

Application Timeline
Contact institution for more information.

Eligibility
As part of Summer Session, high school students from all over the world who completed their sophomore or junior year with a GPA of 3.0+ can live and learn at University of California, Santa Cruz.

Tuition Fees
Estimated fees:

- Total one course tuition plus living on campus = $2,464.50 - $2,892.50
- Total one course tuition living off campus = $985.50

Information about the program:
Surveys the history of East Asia from 1500 to 1894. Covers political, social, economic, and cultural histories of China, Japan, and Korea with the goal of perceiving a regional history that encompassed each society.

Contact
(831) 459-5373

Name of College
University of California, Santa Cruz

Name of Program
Colonial Mexico

Academic / Career Interest
History

Website
https://summer.ucsc.edu/courses/his.html

Application Timeline
Contact institution for more information.

Eligibility
As part of Summer Session, high school students from all over the world who completed their sophomore or junior year with a GPA of 3.0+ can live and learn at University of California, Santa Cruz.

Tuition Fees
Estimated fees:

- Total one course tuition plus living on campus = $2,464.50 - $2,892.50
- Total one course tuition living off campus = $985.50

Information about the program:
Covers the social, cultural, economic, and political history of colonial Mexico (New Spain). Special attention paid to colonial identity formation, religion, and labor systems. Begins by examining indigenous societies prior to the arrival of Europeans and concludes with Mexico's independence movement in the early 19th century.

Contact
(831) 459-5373

Name of College
University of California, Santa Cruz

Name of Program
Issues and Problems in American Society

Academic / Career Interest
History

Website
https://summer.ucsc.edu/courses/socy.html

Application Timeline
Contact institution for more information.

Eligibility
As part of Summer Session, high school students from all over the world who completed their sophomore or junior year with a GPA of 3.0+ can live and learn at University of California, Santa Cruz.

Tuition Fees
Estimated fees:

- Total one course tuition plus living on campus = $2,464.50 - $2,892.50
- Total one course tuition living off campus = $985.50

Information about the program:
Exploration of nature, structure, and functioning of American society. Explores the following: social institutions and economic structure; the successes, failures, and intractability of institutions; general and distinctive features of American society; specific problems such as race, sex, and other inequalities; urban-rural differences.

Contact
(831) 459-5373

Name of College
University of California, Santa Cruz

Name of Program
Race and Law

Academic / Career Interest
History

Website
https://summer.ucsc.edu/courses/socy.html

Application Timeline
Contact institution for more information.

Eligibility
As part of Summer Session, high school students from all over the world who completed their sophomore or junior year with a GPA of 3.0+ can live and learn at University of California, Santa Cruz.

Tuition Fees
Estimated fees:

- Total one course tuition plus living on campus = $2,464.50 - $2,892.50
- Total one course tuition living off campus = $985.50

Information about the program:
An introduction to comparative and historical analyses of the relation between race and law in the U.S. Emphasis on examinations of continuous colonial policies and structural mechanisms that help maintain and perpetuate racial inequality in law, criminal justice, and jury trials.

Contact
(831) 459-5373

Name of College
Calvin College

Name of Program
History of the West & World II

Academic / Career Interest
History

Website
https://calvin.edu/

Application Timeline
Contact institution for more information.

Eligibility
Open to high school students.

Tuition Fees
Estimated fees: $413 per credit hour

Information about the program:
A survey of world history from the onset of European overseas
expansion (c. 1500 CE) to the present, highlighting developments
and problems in social, political and cultural history that have
continuing relevance in today's world, such as cultural change and
exchange, imperialism and colonization, industrialization, political
reform and revolution, the interplay between religion and society,
class and gender relations, and the causes and forms of human
conflict. Attention will be paid to both "western" and "non-western"
cultures and to the dynamic and often violent relations between
cultures.

Contact
(616) 526-6000
info@calvin.edu

Name of College
Calvin College

Name of Program
Environmental History

Academic / Career Interest
History

Website
https://calvin.edu/

Application Timeline
Contact institution for more information.

Eligibility
Open to high school students.

Tuition Fees
Estimated fees: $413 per credit hour

Information about the program:
An introduction to environmental history, the course gives particular attention to the North America and in each unit makes global comparisons or examines transnational trends. Key topics include the methods of environmental history, pre-human natural history, the relationship between hunter-gathers and the environment, the development of agriculture, the impact of European colonization globally, the consequences of the industrial revolution and urbanization, the emergence of environmental movements, changing cultural patterns in conceptualizing nature and humanity's place in it, and the relationship between religious traditions, particularly Christianity, and environmental issues.

Contact
(616) 526-6000
info@calvin.edu

Name of College
University of Chicago

Name of Program
Summer Immersion: Stones and Bones

Academic / Career Interest
Paleontology

Website
https://summer.uchicago.edu/programs/stones-and-bones

Application Timeline
Approx. May

Eligibility
Open to high school students.

Tuition Fees
Estimated fees: $11,400.

Information about the program:
Join the Field Museum's Distinguished Service Curator Lance Grande for a four-week intensive practicum in paleontology in Chicago and Wyoming. Go into the field and behind the scenes at The Field Museum to learn how fossils are collected, analyzed, and conserved. Students work alongside museum scientists in the lab and in the field.

In Chicago, Dr. Grande and other Field Museum scientists will take students into the labs and galleries where they work and study as they introduce students to important concepts in geology, paleontological methods, stratigraphy, and earth history. Students will also learn about basic techniques for the study of evolutionary biology including comparative skeletal anatomy of fishes and other freshwater animals. Students will examine methodological concepts such as fossil preparation, illustration, and description. In this way, students will acquire the fundamental scientific background needed to discover and understand the significance of fossils in the field.

Contact
(773) 702-2149
summersession@uchicago.edu

Name of College
Colorado College

Name of Program
Pre-College: American History, American Film

Academic / Career Interest
History

Website
https://www.coloradocollege.edu/offices/summersession/course-descriptions/2018-course-descriptions/2018-block-a-courses/hy-200-american-history-american-film.html

Application Timeline
Contact institution for more information.

Eligibility
Open to rising juniors and seniors.

Tuition Fees
Estimated fees: $4,600

Information about the program:
This course addresses the challenge of representing history in the Hollywood film. This class will focus upon the Vietnam War and 9/11 in particular, as they are historical subjects deeply connected to American Exceptionalism, an idea closely connected to the American national identity and US foreign policy. Students will watch an array of movies connected to these subjects such as "Apocalypse Now," "Platoon," "United 93," "World Trade Center" among others. Finally, this course will examine the ways 9/11 has affected the Hollywood movie landscape, especially with the superhero genre such as those films in the Christopher Nolan "Batman" trilogy and the Marvel Cinematic Universe.

Contact
(719) 389-6000

Name of College
Columbia University

Name of Program
Summer Immersion: The United States Presidency in Historical And Global Perspective

Academic / Career Interest
History

Website
https://sps.columbia.edu/highschool/summer-immersion/new-york-city-3-week/courses/the-united-states-presidency-in-historical-and-global

Application Timeline
The application will go live in approx. November.

Eligibility
Open to students entering grades 11 or 12 or freshman year of college in the fall.

Tuition Fees
Estimated fees from $5,000 - $11,000

Information about the program:
This course considers the successes and failures of presidents from George Washington to Donald Trump. Lectures and class discussions based on assigned readings are supplemented by hands-on projects in which students take on the roles of press secretary, strategist, and president. Participants work individually and in teams to complete assignments that hone writing and public speaking skills. They draft State-of-the-Union addresses and op-eds in support of Supreme Court nominees. In a mock town hall, they field questions from constituents about their legislative agendas. From the Situation Room, they manage simulated global crises based on real-world events. The course also features field trips to locations such as the United Nations Headquarters and Federal Hall, the first capitol of the United States.

Contact
(212) 854-9889
hsp@columbia.edu

Name of College
Columbia University

Name of Program
Understanding the Arts: Art History and Architecture

Academic / Career Interest
Art History

Website
https://sps.columbia.edu/highschool/summer-immersion/
new-york-city-3-week/courses/understanding-the-arts-art-histo-
ry-and-architecture

Application Timeline
The application will go live in approx. November.

Eligibility
Open to students entering grades 9 or 10 in the fall.

Tuition Fees
Estimated fees:

- Residential: $11,064 per session
  Commuter: $5,600 per session

Information about the program:
A two-course curricular option for students wishing to develop their appreciation of art and architecture. Both courses meet daily, one in the morning, the other in the afternoon. Both courses incorporate numerous field trips so as to take full advantage of Columbia University's location in New York City.

What is Art History? This course introduces students to selected monuments of painting, sculpture, and architecture and to basic trends and concepts in the history of art. Students are introduced to aspects of visual analysis, historical context, and problems of interpretation. Participants engage in discussions centered around slide presentations, videos, and, most importantly, field trips.

Contact
(212) 854-9889
hsp@columbia.edu

Name of College
Connecticut University

Name of Program
Pre-College Summer @ UConn: Sociology: Social Justice

Academic / Career Interest
Sociology

Website
https://precollege-summer.uconn.edu/academic-areas/sociology-social-justice/

Application Timeline
Applications close one week prior to each session start date.

Eligibility
PCS participants must be rising juniors or seniors in high school and at least 15 years of age to apply.

Tuition Fees
Estimated fees: $1,950

Information about the program:
Using a variety of films and field trips to the Mashantucket Pequot Museum, this 1-week course introduces students to sociological and human rights understandings of social justice and their relationship to historical and present-day inequalities.

The course will focus on cases related to race, class, and gender. By investigating social justice primarily in a North American context, students will explore the social structures and organizations that frame the choices people make and possibilities for social justice. Through short readings and films, engaged discussion, interactive group activities, and engagement with different types of primary sources, students will examine how social justice and human rights can work together to promote social change.

Contact
(860) 486-0149
PreCollegeSummer@UConn.edu

Name of College
Cornell University

Name of Program
Summer College: Introduction to Western Civilization

Academic / Career Interest
History

Website
https://www.sce.cornell.edu/sc/programs/courses.php?v=688

Application Timeline
Approx. May

Eligibility
Open to rising sophomores, juniors, and seniors. Must be younger than 18 years old by the start of the June programs.

Tuition Fees
Estimated fees: $12,825

Information about the program:
The West and its relations with the rest of the world are central topics today, but just what is the West and what is its history? This course surveys the history of the West from remote antiquity to the 16th century. Students will consider developments in technology, economy, politics, religious institutions and faiths, cultural media and social ideals. Together, these themes add up to civilization in the west. Students will acquaint themselves with these dimensions of the past while seeking to acquire the basic skills professional historians use to learn about this past.

Contact
(607) 255-6203
summer_college@cornell.edu

Name of College
Cornell University

Name of Program
Summer College: A Global Approach to Modern Chinese History

Academic / Career Interest
History

Website
https://www.sce.cornell.edu/sc/programs/courses.php?v=3075

Application Timeline
Approx. May

Eligibility
Open to rising sophomores, juniors, and seniors. Must be younger than 18 years old by the start of the June programs.

Tuition Fees
Estimated fees: $12,825

Information about the program:
This course surveys modern Chinese history from a global perspective starting from the 19th century to the dawn of the 21st century. It is a lecture and discussion course that aims to help the students develop a better understanding of the major events that have, for better or worse, shaped China and made it what it is today. The key themes of the course include: Chinese response to the demands of Western powers, foreign images of China, the Opium Wars, the rise of a new order, the fragmentation and reform of the Qing Empire, the rise and fall of the nationalist government, the rise of communism and the People's Republic, the challenge of Deng's reforms and China's impact on the world.

Contact
(607) 255-6203
summer_college@cornell.edu

Name of College
Cornell University

Name of Program
Summer College: Introduction to U.S. Labor History

Academic / Career Interest
History

Website
https://www.sce.cornell.edu/sc/programs/courses.php?v=2701

Application Timeline
Deadline is approx. Mid-May

Eligibility
Open to rising sophomores, juniors, and seniors. Must be younger than 18 years old by the start of the June programs.

Tuition Fees
Estimated fees: $12,825

Information about the program:
Introductory survey covering the major changes in the nature of work, the workforce, and the institutions involved in industrial relations from the late 19th century to the present. Outcome 1: Students will develop a firm understanding of some of the major historical themes and general discourses shaping U.S. labor relations throughout the nineteenth and twentieth centuries. Outcome 2: Students will learn to examine the sources and consequences of change in labor relations over time within the context of the broader patterns and issues of American political, social and economic history. Outcome 3: Students will learn to think about work, class, and the economy as fluid concepts that are shaped by diverse perspectives and interests, and influenced by race, gender, and national identity. Outcome 4: Students will learn to evaluate the evolving actions of workers, labor unions, employers, and the American public to establish government policies for regulating labor relations.

Contact
(607) 255-6203
summer_college@cornell.edu

Name of College
Cornell University

Name of Program
Summer College: History and Politics of the Modern Middle East

Academic / Career Interest
History

Website
https://www.sce.cornell.edu/sc/programs/index.
php?v=197&s=Overview

Application Timeline
Deadline is approx. Mid-May

Eligibility
Open to rising sophomores, juniors, and seniors. Must be younger than 18 years old by the start of the June programs.

Tuition Fees
Estimated fees: $6,310

Information about the program:
From the exodus of millions of Syrians from their homeland, to ISIS, the Israeli-Palestinian conflict, the Cold War competition in the Middle East between the U.S. and the Soviet Union, and the consequences of the fall of the Ottoman Empire in the early twentieth century, the modern Middle East has been a place of political upheaval, shifting alliances, sectarian violence, and competing economic interests.

In this timely course, taught by Ross Brann, the acclaimed M. R. Konvitz Professor of Judeo-Islamic Studies at Cornell, student will examine the modern history and politics of this volatile region, beginning with European colonization following World War I and concluding with Russia's involvement in the Syrian civil war.

Contact
(607) 255-6203
summer_college@cornell.edu

Name of College
Davidson College

Name of Program
July Experience: Developing Your Lens: Introduction to Cultural Anthropology (Anthropology)

Academic / Career Interest
Journalism

Website
https://www.davidson.edu/offices/july-experience/courses

Application Timeline
Rolling admissions until approx. early May

Eligibility
Open to rising high school juniors and seniors.

Tuition Fees
Estimated fees: $4,000

Information about the program:
In the multicultural and digital world in which we inhabit, the acquisition of cultural competency has been deemed an important element of higher education. This course will introduce students to the concepts, methods and theories used in the study of cultures, regardless of where they are geographically situated. Most importantly, the comparative study of the social patterns and practices, institutions, beliefs, and values found in human communities will help students recognize that cultures are concurrently unique and distinct. Students will study an array of cultural institutions and social phenomena: class, kinship, gender, political economy, religion, and sexuality. Two major objectives of this course include: to provide students the tools for comprehending and negotiating diverse cultures, and to develop a less ethnocentric lens through which to view the world.

Contact
(704) 894-2000

Name of College
Davidson College

Name of Program
July Experience: Defining Us: Drawing the Boundaries of the Nation in Nationalistic Times (Sociology)

Academic / Career Interest
Journalism

Website
https://www.davidson.edu/offices/july-experience/courses

Application Timeline
Rolling admissions until approx. early May

Eligibility
Open to rising high school juniors and seniors.

Tuition Fees
Estimated fees: $4,000

Information about the program:
Make America Great Again. Unless this is the slogan of an environmentalist movement, then it seems unlikely this refers to a physical space. Rather, it refers to a people. Recognizing there can be no in-group without an out-group, students are challenged to explore the myriad ways in which some US communities are constructed as separate from "America". Drawing on theories of citizenship, race, and gender, seminar members will come to appreciate the degree to which the boundaries of not only belonging, but even of morality, are drawn to legitimize the existence of the nation and its people. Students will anchor their inquiry into nationalism with contemporary cases of marginalization in the United States–including communities of poor African Americans and undocumented immigrants–before moving to current examples that transcend the US. The course will make use of the instructor's research materials – including original, proprietary data and resultant publications.

Contact
(704) 894-2000

Name of College
Davidson College

Name of Program
July Experience: Finding Nemo, Finding Culture (Sociology)

Academic / Career Interest
Sociology

Website
https://www.davidson.edu/offices/july-experience/courses

Application Timeline
Contact institution for more information.

Eligibility
Open to rising high school juniors and seniors.

Tuition Fees
Estimated fees: is $4,000.

Information about the program:
The program goal is to interrogate how sociologists use culture to understand social problems. The class will be organized around five different definitions of culture put forth by David Harding, Michele Lamont and Mario Smalls. They include culture as values, frames, repertoires, capital, and boundaries. Students will consider theoretical foundation and an empirical application for each way of defining culture. Students will also watch films and television shows that illustrate each of these approaches to culture.

Contact
(704) 894-2000

Name of College
Davidson College

Name of Program
July Experience: Hitler and Nazi Germany (History)

Academic / Career Interest
History

Website
https://www.davidson.edu/offices/july-experience/courses

Application Timeline
Contact institution for more information.

Eligibility
Open to rising high school juniors and seniors.

Tuition Fees
Estimated fees: $4,000

Information about the program:
This course provides an overview of Hitler and National Socialism.
Students will study the rise and fall of Nazism, learn about its ideol-
ogy, look at the organization of the Nazi state, and examine the kind
of culture it promoted (and that which it sought to oppress). The
scope of the course is thus interdisciplinary, ranging from political,
social, and economic aspects of Nazi Germany to various forms of
cultural production: literature, film, sports, architecture, music, and
the visual arts. Students will conclude with a study of the Holocaust
and consider issues of remembrance, representation, and human
rights today.

Contact
(704) 894-2000

Name of College
Davidson College

Name of Program
July Experience: Race, Religion and Donald J. Trump (Sociology)

Academic / Career Interest
Sociology

Website
https://www.davidson.edu/offices/july-experience/courses

Application Timeline
Contact institution for more information.

Eligibility
Open to rising high school juniors and seniors.

Tuition Fees
Estimated fees: $4,000

Information about the program:
The purpose of this course is to gain appreciation for sociological analysis at the intersection of race-ethnicity and religion through the phenomenon of Donald J. Trump's election as the 45th president of the United States. Let me be clear: the course is not an opportunity for the professor and students to air their opinions, and students will not be focused on Trump's personality. Instead, the class constitutes a careful exploration centering on racial and religious dynamics as they touch on the historical context of the Trump presidency. The class will discuss distinctively sociological issues at a macro-level of analysis that includes dynamics of continuing relevance: the perpetuation of systemic/institutionalized racism over the past 200+ years, various racially and religiously motivated political movements, debates over macroeconomic theory, business and corporate strategies regarding profitability, patterns of financial inequality and concentrations of elite wealth, and processes of globalization, immigration, and transnationalism.

Contact
(704) 894-2000

Name of College
Davidson College

Name of Program
July Experience: Skulls, Bones, and Clandestine Graves (Anthropology)

Academic / Career Interest
Sociology

Website
https://www.davidson.edu/offices/july-experience/courses

Application Timeline
Contact institution for more information.

Eligibility
Open to rising high school juniors and seniors.

Tuition Fees
Estimated fees: $4,000

Information about the program:
Locating graves, excavating human remains, and analyzing the remains at any stage of the decomposition process are within the scope of forensic anthropology. Forensic anthropology is the application of the methods and theories used in biological anthropology to the law. Students will learn various methodologies for identifying human skeletal remains, including estimation of age-at-death, sex, stature, and ancestry. The course is designed for students interested in forensic sciences and they will discuss other relevant disciplines such as forensic entomology, mass disasters, facial reconstruction, etc. The format of the course is mainly lectures with hands-on modules.

Contact
(704) 894-2000

Name of College
George Washington University

Name of Program
College Intensive: Introduction to Peace Studies & Conflict Resolution

Academic / Career Interest
Journalism

Website
https://summer.gwu.edu/humanities

Application Timeline
Deadline is approx. mid-May

Eligibility
Open to rising juniors and seniors (ages 15-18).

Tuition Fees
Estimated fees:

- Residential: $7,385 (tuition, program fee, room and board)
- Commuter: $6,003 (tuition, program fee, lunch)

Information about the program:
Major thinkers and themes in the field of peace studies and conflict resolution. Focus on philosophical and religious foundations of peace and justice movements in the twentieth century. Examination of peace and conflict through an interdisciplinary lens and on personal, local and international levels.

Contact
(202) 994-6360
gwsummer@gwu.edu

Name of College
George Washington University

Name of Program
College Intensive: European Civilization in Its World Context

Academic / Career Interest
History

Website
https://summer.gwu.edu/humanities

Application Timeline
Deadline is approx. mid-May

Eligibility
Open to rising juniors and seniors (ages 15-18).

Tuition Fees
Estimated fees:

- Residential (tuition, program fee, room & board)
    - 1 course (3 credits): $7,579.75
    - 2 courses (6 credits): $11,348.50
- Commuter (3 credits): $5,326.75

Information about the program:
Introduction to the history of Europe, emphasizing primary sources and their interpretation. From the beginning of written culture through 1715.

Contact
(202) 994-6360
gwsummer@gwu.edu

Name of College
George Washington University

Name of Program
College Intensive: World History, 1500-Present

Academic / Career Interest
History

Website
https://summer.gwu.edu/humanities

Application Timeline
Deadline is approx. mid-May

Eligibility
Open to rising juniors and seniors (ages 15-18).

Tuition Fees
Estimated fees:

- Residential (tuition, program fee, room & board)
    o 1 course (3 credits): $7,579.75
    o 2 courses (6 credits): $11,348.50
- Commuter (3 credits): $5,326.75

Information about the program:
An introduction to world history over the past half millennium, stressing themes of exchange and integration, tracing the ways various peoples of the world became bound together in a common system.

Contact
(202) 994-6360
gwsummer@gwu.edu

Name of College
Gettysburg College

Name of Program
High School Student Scholarship Program, Civil War Institute Summer Conference

Academic / Career Interest
History

Website
http://www.gettysburg.edu/cwi/conference/registration/

Application Timeline
Contact institution for more information.

Eligibility
Current high school sophomores, juniors, and seniors are eligible to apply.

Tuition Fees
Estimated fees:

- Tuition, Meal Plan, & On-Campus Lodging (Single Bedroom, Shared Suite): $1,025
- Tuition, Meal Plan, & On-Campus Lodging (Shared Bedroom, Suite-Style Residence Hall): $922

Information about the program:
The High School Student Scholarship Program component of Gettysburg College's annual Civil War Institute summer conference provides high school students an opportunity to explore the history of the Civil War era on the site of the war's most decisive battle. Participants will join conference sessions, interact with noted historians, and participate in special tours and programming geared toward high school students, including a historical simulation activity revolving around the 1863 New York City Draft Riots.

Contact
(717) 337-6590
civilwar@gettysburg.edu

Name of College
Harvard University

Name of Program
Pre-College: American History through Musicals

Academic / Career Interest
History

Website
https://www.summer.harvard.edu/courses/american-history-through-musicals/34102

Application Timeline
Deadline is approx. early May

Eligibility
The Pre-College Program admissions committee is looking for mature, academically motivated students who will be entering Sophomore or junior year.

Tuition Fees
Estimated fees: $4,500

Information about the program:
In this course, students explore the American past through musicals such as Hamilton, 1776, Miss Saigon, and Ragtime, among others. While watching and listening, students will ask themselves: what kinds of stories about the American past are being told? Whose voices are being heard, and who is left out? What do the plot, characters, and musical styles of each show say about the time period when it was produced, and what do their reactions say about their own moment in time? When comparing the narrative of these musicals with narratives told by historians, students learn that the kinds of stories we tell about the past are constantly changing and continually intertwined with the events of the present.

Contact
(617) 495-4024
precollege@summer.harvard.edu

Name of College
Harvard University

Name of Program
Pre-College: Social Reform and Revolution: Theory and Practice

Academic / Career Interest
History

Website
https://www.summer.harvard.edu/courses/social-reform-revolu-tion-theory-practice/34123

Application Timeline
Deadline is approx. early May

Eligibility
The Pre-College Program admissions committee is looking for mature, academically motivated students who will be entering Sophomore or Junior year.

Tuition Fees
Estimated fees: $4,500

Information about the program:
This course is designed to introduce students to the study and practice of social change. Interdisciplinary in nature, it combines case studies, theory, field trips, museum visits, and classroom exercises to push students to consider the question: how does long-term social change happen? Students explore the role elements of culture as diverse as art, economics, religion, and technological shifts have played in significant social changes such as political revolutions, the abolition of chattel slavery, and the advent of feminism. Throughout the course, students take advantage of the rich resources of Harvard and Boston so that students encounter objects and physical spaces central to social change.

Contact
(617) 495-4024
precollege@summer.harvard.edu

Name of College
Harvard University

Name of Program
Pre-College: More Than Just a Meal: American Food, a Global History

Academic / Career Interest
History

Website
https://www.summer.harvard.edu/courses/more-just-meal-american-food-global-history/34121

Application Timeline
Deadline is approx. early May

Eligibility
The Pre-College Program admissions committee is looking for mature, academically motivated students who will be entering Sophomore or Junior year.

Tuition Fees
Estimated fees: $4,500

Information about the program:
This course provides an introduction to early American history through food. While we often think a lot about lunch, we rarely give much thought to the history of what we have for lunch. Food is a connection to the past, although sometimes in ways we don't expect. The food we eat is more than just a meal. The content of the course starts around 1200 C.E. and stops just after the Civil War. While the course material often intersects with major political events, the material read discusses historical actors other than elite white men. Students reconstruct how working-class people, slaves, Native Americans, women, and others not only contributed to the food ways of the United States, but also to the formation of the country. Students spend time learning how to read difficult texts like journal articles and chapters from academic books, but also look at objects.

Contact
(617) 495-4024
precollege@summer.harvard.edu

Name of College
University of Pennsylvania

Name of Program
Penn Summer: Introduction to Human Evolution

Academic / Career Interest
Human Evolution

Website
https://www.sas.upenn.edu/summer/courses/term/2018B/subject/ANTH/course/ANTH003920

Application Timeline
Deadline is approx. early May

Eligibility
10th to 11th grade students from the Philadelphia area are eligible to apply.

Tuition Fees
Estimated fees: $4,224

Information about the program:
How did humans evolve? When did humans start to walk on two legs? How are humans related to non-human primates? This course focuses on the scientific study of human evolution describing the emergence, development, and diversification of our species, Homo sapiens. First, students cover the fundamental principles of evolutionary theory and some of the basics of genetics and heredity as they relate to human morphological, physiological, and genetic variation. They then examine what studies of nonhuman primates (monkeys and apes) can reveal about our own evolutionary past, reviewing the behavioral and ecological diversity seen among living primates. Students conclude the course examining the "hard" evidence of human evolution - the fossil and material culture record of human history from our earliest primate ancestors to the emergence of modern Homo sapiens.

Contact
(215) 898-7326
summer@sas.upenn.edu

Name of College
University of Pennsylvania

Name of Program
Penn Summer: World Film History to 1945

Academic / Career Interest
World Film History

Website
https://www.sas.upenn.edu/summer/courses/term/2018B/subject/ARTH/course/ARTH108910

Application Timeline
Deadline is approx. early May

Eligibility
10th to 11th grade students from the Philadelphia area are eligible to apply.

Tuition Fees
Estimated fees: $4,224

Information about the program:
This course surveys the history of world film from cinema s precursors to 1945. Students will develop methods for analyzing film while examining the growth of film as an art, an industry, a technology, and a political instrument. Topics include the emergence of film technology and early film audiences, the rise of narrative film and birth of Hollywood, national film industries and movements, African-American independent film, the emergence of the genre film (the western, film noir, and romantic comedies), ethnographic and documentary film, animated films, censorship, the MPPDA and Hays Code, and the introduction of sound. Students will conclude with the transformation of several film industries into propaganda tools during World War II (including the Nazi, Soviet, and US film industries).

Contact
(215) 898-7326
summer@sas.upenn.edu

Name of College
Smith College

Name of Program
Hidden Lives: Discovering Women's History

Academic / Career Interest
Women's History

Website
https://www.smith.edu/academics/precollege-programs/womens-history

Application Timeline
Approx. June: Last day applications will be accepted for domestic students.

Eligibility
Summer Precollege Programs at Smith are open to academically talented young women who will enter grade 9, 10, 11 and 12 in Fall.

Tuition Fees
Estimated fees: $3,000

Information about the program:
Smith College and the surrounding area are home to unparalleled collections and cultural heritage institutions that offer an immersive experience in women's history. During their time at Smith, students will explore women's lives through archival research, visits to local museums and tours of historic sites. With a focus on women and social change, students will be introduced to women who have altered the course of American history through reform, mobilization, cultural interventions and outright rebellion.

Contact
(413) 584-2700

Name of College
Stanford University

Name of Program
Topics in Sociology

Academic / Career Interest
Sociology

Website
https://summerinstitutes.spcs.stanford.edu/courses/2018/top-ics-sociology

Application Timeline
Application Rounds – approx. Due Dates

- Early Deadline: January
- Early Notification: February
- Regular Deadline: February
- Regular Notification: April
- Extended Deadline: March
- Extended Notification: April

Eligibility
Open to students in grades 9-11 at the time of application.

Tuition Fees
Estimated fees: $6,850

Information about the program:
Why do some people have better ideas than others? Why are some more likely to be bullied in school, get a job, or catch a disease? Why do some innovations, apps, rumors, or revolutions spread like a wildfire, while others never get off the ground?

In this class, students will learn to see the world as a web of relations: not only are people, ideas/concepts and things all increasingly connected to each other; the pattern of these relations can tell us a great deal about many phenomena in our social world that defy traditional explanations.

Contact
precollegiate@stanford.edu

Name of College
Tufts University

Name of Program
Pre-College: Famous Trials in U.S. History

Academic / Career Interest
U.S. History

Website
https://summer.tufts.edu/study-pre-college-courses.asp

Application Timeline
Deadline is approx. early May

Eligibility
Students entering grades 11-12 are eligible. Must be at least 15 by program start.

Tuition Fees
Estimated fees: $10,000

Information about the program:
The course premise is that trials act as a mirror held up to society, in which is reflected the social mores and cultural trends of the time. We can learn much about society, about the tacit assumptions and underlying realities that shaped and were reflected in the trials. This concept, often referred to as the "law as mirror" school of thought, was best summarized by Oliver Wendell Holmes: "this abstraction called the Law is a magic mirror, where we see reflected not only our own lives, but the lives of all men that have been." Trials provide us with invaluable unconscious testimony: we can glean what issues are in contention; what things are tacitly agreed upon and therefore not verbalized; what aspects of culture are in flux. Famous trials in particular are useful for the purposes of analyzing an array of historical forces: legal, literary, sociological, psychological, cultural, economic, political, and an almost-infinite number of other potential connections and dependencies.

Contact
(617) 981-7008
summer@tufts.edu

Name of College
Tufts University

Name of Program
Pre-College: Origins of Electronic Music, 1890-1980

Academic / Career Interest
History of Electronic Music

Website
https://summer.tufts.edu/study-pre-college-courses.asp

Application Timeline
Deadline is approx. early May

Eligibility
Students entering grades 11-12 are eligible. Must be at least 15 by program start.

Tuition Fees
Estimated fees: $10,000

Information about the program:
The history and technology of electronic music starting from its beginnings in the age of Edison and Bell, to the dawn of the digital era. Topics include composers' search for new sounds; technological developments enabling the electronic creation and manipulation of sounds; inventors of new instruments and compositional techniques; and development of schools of electronic music in various cultures in North America, Europe, and Asia. Emphasis on listening to and analyzing important works, viewing and reading interviews with composers and inventors, and hands-on sound manipulation using modern simulations of historical electronic-music tools.

Contact
(617) 981-7008
summer@tufts.edu

Name of College
American University

Name of Program
Community of Scholars

Academic / Career Interest
Global affairs

Website
https://www.american.edu/sis/CommunityofScholars/index.cfm

Application Timeline
Contact institution for more information.

Eligibility
The program is designed for students who will be rising junior and senior high school students by the summer. This means that current sophomore and juniors are eligible to apply.

Tuition Fees
Estimated fees: $3,110

Information about the program:
Community of Scholars will introduce students to the advancing field of global affairs through college-level coursework. Whether online or in class at American University instructors will provide dynamic lectures and engage students in discussions as well as simulations, such as a mock National Security Council debate. By the end of the program, students might find themselves developing a national security strategy or conducting a conflict assessment of an ongoing insurgency. Students will visit government agencies and non-profit organizations to see how leading policy-makers put ideas into action. Students will experience the excitement of Washington at work and see first-hand what others only read about.

Contact
School of International Service
(202) 885-2442
communityofscholars@american.edu

Journalism Collegiate Programs

Name of College
Agnes Scott College

Name of Program
High School Creative Writing Summer Intensive

Academic / Career Interest
Creative writing

Website
https://www.agnesscott.edu/agnesengage/summeratagnes/programs/high-school-creative-writing-program.html

Application Timeline
Contact institution for more information.

Eligibility
Highly motivated high school student writers are welcome to apply.

Tuition Fees
Estimated fees: $800

Information about the program:
The course begins survey-style, with the young writers studying various genres of fiction and nonfiction storytelling before constructing individual projects reflective of their writing interests. Writers may complete the workshop with the opening chapter(s) of a novel, a one-act stage or screenplay, a short story, or a collection of poems. Each project is undertaken with the support of two course instructors, and writers receive peer feedback as they work. To help them pen truly vivid work that captures their readers, the young writers engage in creative writing activities through which they study the classic fundamentals of storytelling as well as practice its more diverse tributaries, such as spoken word poetry.

Contact
Leslie Quigless
lquigless@gmail.com

Name of College
University of Alabama Tuscaloosa

Name of Program
The Long Weekend - Summer Multimedia Journalism Camp

Academic / Career Interest
Journalism

Website
https://k12summer.ua.edu

Application Timeline
Approx. May. Applications will be reviewed on a rolling basis but must be submitted by approximately July 6.

Eligibility
Middle school and high school students are eligible to apply.

Tuition Fees
Estimated fees: $150

Information about the program:
The camp is designed to teach creative and efficient ways to communicate through scholastic newspapers, newsmagazines, yearbooks, literary magazines, broadcast programs and digital media. It allows students to enjoy a taste of college life and invigorate their interest in scholastic media.

The Long Weekend will feature day and evening classes to help participants gain the tools to produce prize-winning results next school year. When festivities and classes wrap up with a showcase by campers, students will have a great start on the upcoming year and will leave with a solid plan for their school newspaper, yearbook, broadcast program, website or literary magazine. If they attend the camp without a staff, they will leave with skills they need to do great journalism in any medium.

Contact
(205) 348-2772
aspa@ua.edu

Name of College
Allegheny College

Name of Program
Summer Academy: Stories and Knowledge

Academic / Career Interest
Communication

Website
https://sites.allegheny.edu/admissions/summer-academy/

Application Timeline
Applications will be reviewed on a rolling basis but must be submitted by July 6

Eligibility
Motivated high school students are welcome to apply.

Tuition Fees
Estimated fees: $1,600

Information about the program:
An investigation into the ways that narrative shapes life and the ways writers can use it to communicate. Stories supply us with the building blocks of knowledge and help us make sense of the world. Students examine how to create and understand stories through creative, intellectual, and intuitive approaches. Students use theatre-based techniques to explore effective communication.

Contact
(800) 521-5293
summeracademy@allegheny.edu

Name of College
Amherst College

Name of Program
Pre-College: Journalism

Academic / Career Interest
Journalism

Website
http://goputney.com/programs/pre-college-program-in-am-herst-massachusetts/

Application Timeline
Contact institution for more information.

Eligibility
Students completing grades 9 – 12 are eligible.

Tuition Fees
Estimated fees: $5,590

Information about the program:
Join an international community of high school students at Amherst College, one of the most prestigious liberal arts colleges in the country. Students choose two exciting seminars to study throughout the program time on campus.

The rise of the Information Age, plummeting newspaper circulations, the proliferation of the soundbite, and the immediacy of social media, blogs and digital video mean that being well-informed is a more complex proposition than ever before. In this timely seminar, students read and analyze contemporary media, then hit the streets to research and prepare their own stories. Use interviews, observation, and opinion to explore issues of contemporary life, culture, science, and politics. Emphasis is placed on basic news writing, as well as features, opinion pieces, and sports writing.

Contact
(802) 387-5000

Name of College
Arizona State University

Name of Program
Cronkite Sports Broadcast Boot Camp

Academic / Career Interest
Journalism

Website
https://cronkite.asu.edu/outreach/cronkite-high-school-programs/broadcast-boot-camp

Application Timeline
Early bird application deadline: approx. April
Final application deadline: approx. May

Eligibility
All high school students are eligible to apply.

Tuition Fees
Estimated fees:

- Regular deadline: $3,250
- Early bird discount rate: $2,950

Information about the program:
This on-campus journalism summer camp puts participants in the middle of the action covering professional sports teams such as the Arizona Diamondbacks and Phoenix Mercury.

At this broadcasting camp, participants learn under the direction of veteran sports journalists. They are exposed to play by play and sideline reporting, hosting, studio production and more. Participants also produce segments and full sports programs inside Cronkite's state-of-the-art studios and discover how to use digital television field reporting equipment and Adobe Premiere Pro editing software. Participants stay in the heart of downtown Phoenix at ASU's Taylor Place residence hall.

Contact
anita.luera@asu.edu

Name of College
University of Arizona

Name of Program
Journalism Diversity Workshop for Arizona High School Students

Academic / Career Interest
Journalism

Website
https://journalism.arizona.edu/journalism-diversity-workshop-arizona-hs-students

Application Timeline
Approx. April

Eligibility
Rising juniors and seniors are eligible to apply.

Tuition Fees
Estimated fees: free

Information about the program:
A tradition for 36 years, the Donald W. Carson Journalism Diversity Workshop for Arizona High School Students in early June teaches teens about reporting basics, media ethics, broadcast and multimedia journalism, design and editing, and different storytelling techniques.

Students will live on the University of Arizona campus for a week and will produce a newspaper, website, and multimedia projects as part of the Journalism Diversity Workshop for Arizona High School Students.

Students will learn how to produce a news site and multimedia using equipment in our publication and photojournalism labs. They will gain experience in news writing, reporting, editing, digital design and photojournalism techniques. They'll also learn about ethics and media law

Contact
(520) 621-7556

Name of College
University of the Arts

Name of Program
Summer Institute: Creative Writing

Academic / Career Interest
Creative Writing

Website
https://www.uarts.edu/academics/pre-college-programs/summer-institute-creative-writing

Application Timeline
Priority application deadline: approx. March
Scholarship application deadline: approx. March

Eligibility
Rising juniors and seniors or international students of equivalent grade level (residential or commuter).
Rising sophomores (commuter only).

Tuition Fees
Estimated fees $3,700 - $5,000

Information about the program:
Students develop their voice in a constructive workshop setting that focuses on creative nonfiction, fiction, poetry, and scriptwriting across four weeks. They'll gain access to published authors and professional editors as they sharpen their skills and expand their imagination. Students will focus on one writing area per week and choose one Art, Media + Design elective that lets them explore an area of interest or discover new media.

Writing prompts and observational exercises throughout Philadelphia drive discussion and critique. Cross-disciplinary electives and collaborations allow students to explore an area of strength or branch out into something new, equipping them to tell their unique story.

Contact
(215) 717-6430
precollege@uarts.edu

Name of College
University of the Arts

Name of Program
One-Week Commuter Intensives: Screenwriting

Academic / Career Interest
Screenwriting

Website
https://www.uarts.edu/academics/pre-college-programs/sum-mer-institute-one-week-intensives

Application Timeline
Space permitting, registrations for One-Week Commuter Intensives will be accepted on an on-going basis.

Eligibility
Rising 9th - 12th graders are welcome to apply.

Tuition Fees
Estimated fees: $560 per class

Information about the program:
All great films began with a brilliant script. An engaging screenplay is essential to a compelling movie. Effectively-written screenplays help directors cast the right actors and turn a story into a captivating visual narrative. Learn industry terminology, character development, scene building, story structure, and the importance of conflict. Through screenings, class discussions, and exercises, students will learn how to conceive of a story for the screen, write a detailed outline, and create a draft of a short screenplay. Students will workshop ideas with their classmates and turn their movie premise into a screenplay reality.

Contact
(215) 717-6430
precollege@uarts.edu

Name of College
Ball State University

Name of Program
Ball State Journalism Workshop

Academic / Career Interest
Journalism

Website
http://bsujournalismworkshops.com/index.php/summer-media-academy/

Application Timeline
Scholarship application deadline is in approx. May. Registration and payment must be submitted online before approx. May.

Eligibility
Middle school and high school students are eligible to apply.

Tuition Fees
Estimated fees:

- $400 for students
- $300 for students living within 20 miles of Ball State's campus

Information about the program:
Ball State Journalism Workshop experience includes:

- 5-day format
- Team-taught, staff-focused and leadership-driven curriculum
- Award-winning faculty
- Innovative daily schedule
- Special Adviser course
- Cutting-edge facilities

Contact
bsuworkshops@bsu.edu

Name of College
Bard College

Name of Program
Young Writers Workshop

Academic / Career Interest
Writing

Website
https://simons-rock.edu/academics/beyond-the-classroom/
young-writers-workshop/index.php?utm_source=summer&utm_
medium=301&utm_campaign=Redirects

Application Timeline
Rolling admissions begin in approx. January and continue until the
program is full, usually sometime in approx. May.

Eligibility
The program is for students currently completing grades 9,10, and
11.

Tuition Fees
Estimated fees: $2,975

Information about the program:
Each year 84 academically motivated students are chosen to participate in the workshop at Simon's Rock. Former participants have
gone on to such colleges as Amherst, Bard, Harvard, Haverford,
Kenyon, Princeton, Simon's Rock, Smith, Williams, and Yale.

Unlike more traditional workshops in creative writing, the Young
Writers Workshop focuses on using informal, playful, and expressive
writing as a way to strengthen skills of language and thinking. Out of
these informal writing activities, using techniques of peer response,
students develop more polished pieces, ranging from personal narratives to short stories, poems, brief dramatic works, and experiments in creative nonfiction.

Contact
(413) 528-7231
jamieh@simons-rock.edu

Name of College
Brown University

Name of Program
Summer @ Brown: Introducing The Craft of Journalism

Academic / Career Interest
Journalism

Website
https://precollege.brown.edu/catalog/course.php?course_code=-CEEL0913

Application Timeline
Contact institution for more information.

Eligibility
For students completing grades 9-12, ages 15-18 by June

Tuition Fees
Estimated fees range from $2,000 - $7,000

Information about the program:
This course is designed to introduce students who are already strong writers to the craft of Journalism. They will learn to report stories, how to conduct interviews, and to become close observers of everyday life. In the process, they will become even stronger writers, learning how to rid their writing of clutter, focus on the essentials, and learn what it takes to become a good reporter.

The course teaches news writing as a thought process as well as a set of skills, and as a vital function in a democracy. Students will learn how to think as a journalist, weighing news values and making decisions on the importance of facts and how to use them to tell a compelling story.

Contact
(401) 863-7900
precollege@brown.edu

Name of College
Boston University

Name of Program
Pre-College Summer Journalism Institute

Academic / Career Interest
Journalism

Website
http://studentprograms.necir.org/pre-college-summer-institute/

Application Timeline
Rolling admission.

Eligibility
Students age 15 to 18 entering grades 9 through 12 in fall, plus graduating seniors are eligible to apply.

Tuition Fees
Estimated fees range from $1,000 - $2,500

Information about the program:
Each two-week session expands student skills through hands-on, real-life learning. Uniquely, the program makes the entire city of Boston the reporting beat. Guided by award-winning working journalists, students report and write on what's happening in real time: government, business, sports, crime, courts, the arts and more. The program exposes students to techniques for hard core investigations, too.

The Institute also serves as an exploration of campus life. Students not commuting from home live in Boston University residence halls and eat at the student dining hall. Instructors use the same textbook from Boston University's journalism fundamentals course and give students the freedom to pursue their own stories.

Contact
studentprograms@necir.org

Name of College
Carleton College

Name of Program
Summer Writing Program

Academic / Career Interest
Writing

Website
https://apps.carleton.edu/summer/writing/

Application Timeline
Approx. March

Eligibility
Students who are currently in 10th and 11th grade (rising junior and senior while the program is in session) are eligible to apply.

Tuition Fees
Estimated fees: $3,250.

Information about the program:
The Summer Writing Program (SWP) emphasizes a writing process approach, teaching students how to compose academic papers similar to those they will write in college.

SWP is a full residential college experience. Students can experience what it means to be completely absorbed in the learning process at a nationally ranked liberal arts college. SWP classes feature hands-on experiences and group work to broaden learning experiences. Students will live with a roommate in a Carleton residence hall, attend class, and study like a college student while learning to balance their academic responsibilities with a variety of social and co-curricular activities.

Contact
(866) 767-2275
summer@carleton.edu

Name of College
University of Chicago

Name of Program
University of Chicago Immersion: Collegiate Writing: Awakening into Consciousness

Academic / Career Interest
Writing

Website
https://summer.uchicago.edu/course/collegiate-writing-awakening-consciousness

Application Timeline
Approx. May

Eligibility
Open to all high school students.

Tuition Fees
Estimated fees: $6,500

Information about the program:
How might we, as individuals and societies, sometimes remain unaware or ignorant? How can our lives – psychological, social, political, and spiritual – be reshaped by awakening from this lack of awareness? What does it mean to achieve true consciousness? This intensive course in analytical writing at the collegiate level will offer a chance to think through these questions and to craft rhetorically-effective essays that explore the enduring struggle to understand what it means for us to awaken into consciousness. This exploration will take students on a journey through many fields – from religion and mythology to politics, philosophy, literature, and the arts.

Contact
(773) 702-2149
summersession@uchicago.edu

Name of College
Colorado College

Name of Program
Cross Genre Writing Workshop

Academic / Career Interest
Writing

Website
https://www.coloradocollege.edu/offices/summersession/
course-descriptions/2017-course-descriptions/pre-college/en-
104-cross-genre-writing-workshop.html

Application Timeline
Contact institution for more information.

Eligibility
Open to high school juniors and seniors.

Tuition Fees
Estimated fees:

- Tuition: $3,450
- Program Fee: $75

Information about the program:
This high energy workshop allows creative writers to try their hands at a range of styles. From prose to spoken word to plays, students will explore across genre, building a tool box for literary adventure. This two-and-a-half-week course will culminate in a public reading, where students will have the opportunity to put their talents on display.

Contact
(719) 389-6000

Name of College
Columbia College Chicago

Name of Program
Summer at Columbia: Investigative Reporting and Podcasting

Academic / Career Interest
Journalism

Website
https://learn.colum.edu/summer/

Application Timeline
Open enrollment program, student is accepted by registering.

Eligibility
Program is open to high school students.

Tuition Fees
Estimated fees:

- Residential: $4,400
- Commuter: $3,300

Information about the program:
In this program, students will learn reporting, research, production and writing skills through hands-on, real-world training in the heart of the nation's third-largest city.

Pulitzer Prize-winning Chicago Tribune reporter Sam Roe will teach the basics of investigative reporting, helping students learn how to expose injustice and wrongdoing. Veteran newspaper editor Suzanne McBride will show participants how to produce impactful journalism on deadline by conducting interviews, using social media and covering events alongside professional journalists. WCRX radio station manager Matt Cunningham will share the aesthetics of audio and give students a chance to make their own original podcast.

Contact
(312) 369-3100

Name of College
Columbia University

Name of Program
Summer Immersion: Expository Writing Intensive: How to Write
Great Papers(1-Week)

Academic / Career Interest
Journalism

Website
https://sps.columbia.edu/highschool/summer-immersion/
new-york-city-1-week/courses/expository-writing-inten-
sive-how-write-great-papers

Application Timeline
Priority Application Deadline: approx. May
Application Deadline: approx. July

Eligibility
Open to students entering grades 9 through 12 or freshman year of
college in the fall.

Tuition Fees
Estimated fees range from $1,000 - $2,500

Information about the program:
Participants learn how to read challenging texts and write about
them clearly and coherently, assess and think critically about their
own writing, and improve writing skills through in-class exercises,
homework, and revisions. Readings for the course are taken from
several disciplines, including literature, history, journalism, and
social sciences.

This course enables students to identify their strengths and weaknesses in writing and to improve their skills through individual and
group work. Students read and analyze short essays that exemplify
good writing, and they learn how to define a thesis, organize an
essay, and incorporate appropriate vocabulary

Contact
(212) 854-9889
hsp@columbia.edu

Name of College
Columbia University

Name of Program
Summer Immersion: Writing Young Adult Fiction (1-Week)

Academic / Career Interest
Journalism

Website
https://sps.columbia.edu/highschool/1-week/courses/writing-young-adult-fiction/highschool/summer-immersion/new-york-city-1-week/courses/writing-young-adult-fiction

Application Timeline
Priority Application Deadline: approx. May
Application Deadline: approx. July

Eligibility
Open to students entering grades 9 through 12 or freshman year of college in the fall.

Tuition Fees
Estimated fees range from $1,000 - $2,500

Information about the program:
Young Adult Literature is one of the fastest growing and most marketable genres. The success of books like The Fault in Our Stars, Twilight, and The Hunger Games have brought YA into the spotlight in recent years, creating a boom in publishing and changing the way we view coming-of-age stories. This course will explore past and current YA trends, from contemporary love stories to science fiction series. Students will learn how to write in the style of authors like John Green or Cassandra Clare as students dive into how to craft a successful YA story. Whether they're working on short fiction or a full-length novel, this course will help students develop a deeper understanding of how to write, read, and appreciate YA.

Contact
(212) 854-9889
hsp@columbia.edu

Name of College
Columbia University

Name of Program
Summer Immersion: Creative Writing: Advanced Workshop
(3-Weeks)

Academic / Career Interest
Creative Writing

Website
https://sps.columbia.edu/highschool/summer-immersion/new-york-city-3-week/courses/the-creative-writer-work-advanced-workshop

Application Timeline
Priority Application Deadline: approx. January

Eligibility
Open to students entering grades 11 or 12 or freshman year of college in the fall.

Tuition Fees
Estimated fees range from $5,000 - $6,500

Information about the program:
This workshop is geared toward students who have considerable experience in creative writing or who demonstrate unusual talent. Students read and write free verse poetry, short prose, drama, fiction, and creative nonfiction with the goal of developing a final portfolio of revised work.

Two daily workshops expose students to many aspects of the writing process, including generating ideas, writing and revising drafts, and editing. Participants practice their literary craft with an attentive group of their peers, under the guidance of an experienced instructor.

Contact
(212) 854-9889
hsp@columbia.edu

Name of College
Drake University

Name of Program
Media Now Drake Journalism Camp

Academic / Career Interest
Journalism

Website
https://medianow.press/drake/

Application Timeline
Registration Deadlines:

- Early Bird: approx. through early April
- Regular Open Registration: approx. April – June
- Late Fee: approx. June

Eligibility
Program is open to high school students.

Tuition Fees
Estimated fees range $300

Information about the program:
Join Drake University in Des Moines, where students and advisers choose a single-track to immerse themselves in for the four days in the program. Students participate in hands-on projects and show-case them in a campus-wide awards ceremony to cap off their time together. It's an awesome opportunity for students to deep dive into that area of interest and hone their skills. No matter what level students arrive with, the program will push them, encourage and train them to move to the next.
Classes include: Editorial Leadership, Beginning Writing, Advanced Writing, Photography, Video, Design, Yearbook, Political Communication, Sports Journalism, Advising Publications and School Newspapers Online (SNO) will be there to help staffs with their online news sites.

Contact
(314) 252-8816
kate@medianow.press

Name of College
Duquesne University

Name of Program
Summer Creative Writing Camp

Academic / Career Interest
Creative Writing

Website
https://www.duq.edu/academics/schools/liberal-arts/sum-mer-creative-writing-camp

Application Timeline
Registration begins approx. January

Eligibility
Program is open to high school students.

Tuition Fees
Estimated fees is $475

Information about the program:
This one-week intensive creative writing camp offers high-school writers the opportunity to hone their understanding of the crafts of fiction and/or poetry. Classes are limited to 12 writers each. Established authors (who are also seasoned teachers) guide the writers through exercises, discussions, and workshops, and provide personal feedback on individual work. At the end of the week, the writers will work together to produce a small journal of the week's work and participate in a public reading for friends and family.

Contact
(412) 396-6222

Name of College
Emerson College

Name of Program
Pre-College Journalism 3-Week Institute

Academic / Career Interest
Journalism

Website
https://www.emerson.edu/academics/pre-college/journalism

Application Timeline
Approx. May

Eligibility
Open to rising sophomores, juniors, and seniors.

Tuition Fees
Estimated fees:

- Tuition: $3,225
- Room and Board Fee: $1,785
- Non-refundable program application fee: $60

Information about the program:
The Summer Journalism Institute helps rising sophomores, juniors and seniors explore digital journalism techniques in a variety of multimedia formats. Students move beyond the traditional methods of communicating news and explore using Twitter and other social media through their mobile devices to find and interview sources, take and format pictures, and shoot and edit video. These elements get scripted to create packages online and on the air. The program takes advantage of Emerson College's state-of-the-art journalism labs giving students access to the ultimate multimedia learning environment.

Contact
(617) 824-8500

Name of College
Emory College

Name of Program
Dramatic Writing Studio

Academic / Career Interest
Creative Writing

Website
http://precollege.emory.edu/program/courses/non-credit.html

Application Timeline
Rolling admission - applications evaluated upon completion.

Eligibility
Applicants must be 15 years of age by the date of attendance and must have completed the 10th or 11th grade in high school.

Tuition Fees
Tuition:

- Commuter $2,861
- Residential $4,100

Information about the program:
This intensive college-level foundation course teaches the basic principles of dramatic writing craft through in-class writing exercises, workshops, text analysis and the completion of a full first draft of a dramatic text. The course is designed to deliver as much value to the dedicated dramatic writer as it does to the pre-collegiate student interested in improving his/her narrative writing skills. By the end of this course, students will be able to identify and employ basic elements of effective dramatic writing and will have experience presenting and responding to creative work in a rigorous workshop setting.

Contact
precollege@emory.edu

Name of College
University of Georgia

Name of Program
Media & Leadership Academy: Journalism

Academic / Career Interest
Journalism

Website
http://grady.uga.edu/apply/high-school-discovery/

Application Timeline
Rolling admission until approx. May.

Eligibility
Open to rising sophomores, juniors, and seniors.

Tuition Fees
Estimated fees: $550

Information about the program:
Rising high school sophomores, juniors and seniors interested in the mass communication field will choose from one of the three offered tracks: journalism, advertising and public relations or entertainment (video production).
The journalism field is evolving to encompass multiple platforms. In this track, students will acquire some of the tools to needed become a multi-skilled journalist in this digital age. In the first part of the week, students will review and learn the essentials of writing for print, online and broadcast. They will practice the art of interviewing and reporting. Furthermore, they will learn the basics of producing a broadcast and the fundamentals of photojournalism. During the second half of the week, students will experience teamwork and collaboration firsthand in a newsroom. They will be divided into two groups and each will produce a project. One group will produce a news website, while the other group will produce a broadcast show.

Contact
(706) 542-1704

Name of College
Hollins University

Name of Program
Hollins Summer: Summer Writing Camp

Academic / Career Interest
Writing

Website
https://www.hollins.edu/academics/hollinsummer/a-summer-writing-camp-for-teens/

Application Timeline
Subject to change. Campers who register and pay the nonrefundable $200 deposit by approx. March receive a 10% discount on the total camp cost. All payments are due in full by approx. June, or registration will be canceled, and deposit will not be refunded.

Eligibility
For rising 9th-12th-grade girls.

Tuition Fees
Estimated fees:

- Residential: $950
- Commuter: $400

Information about the program:
This one-week summer writing retreat provides students with individualized attention and a choice of activities to develop skills in fiction, poetry, and personal narrative. Lectures, workshops, and special events with Hollins faculty and visiting authors encourage participants to hone their writing skills. Each day includes unstructured time for students to practice writing and get to know the other students.

Contact
Meghan Richardson
(540) 362-6212
(800) 456-9595

Name of College
University of Illinois Urbana Champaign

Name of Program
Young Writers Camps: Secondary Summer Camp

Academic / Career Interest
Writing

Website
https://engage.illinois.edu/entry/33882

Application Timeline
Contact institution for more information.

Eligibility
Middle school and high school students are eligible to apply.

Tuition Fees
Estimated fees range from $300 - $500

Information about the program:
Students will work with technology and learn how to write in a variety of genres including:

- Poetry
- Short stories
- Flash fiction
- Novels
- Personal Essays

Students come to the camp to experience being in a community of writers. The camp teachers guide that community and teach students skills to expand their writing abilities. The students work in small groups, as well as getting some focused attention from teachers.

Students will be free to create unique original pieces of writing in this communal environment. Students will make friends, learn

Contact
Check website for contact inquiry.

Name of College
Indiana University Bloomington

Name of Program
High School Journalism Institute: Reporting and Writing

Academic / Career Interest
Journalism

Website
http://mediaschool.indiana.edu/hsji/students/student-work-shops/reporting-and-writing/

Application Timeline
Approx. June

Eligibility
The institute is designed for high school students who have accepted a position in high school media or for those interested in learning about journalism prior to their senior year.

Tuition Fees
Estimated fees: $425

Information about the program:
Students will examine the role of the media, develop both a sense of news and news judgment, and practice their own writing, decision-making and editing skills. Participants will learn to edit the work of others, explore basic principles of design and discuss staff motivation.

Other topics covered include organizing effective news beats, generating story ideas, developing good staff relationships and organization and learning legal and ethical issues.

Contact
Director Teresa White
(812) 855-9822
terwhite@indiana.edu

Name of College
Indiana University Bloomington

Name of Program
High School Journalism Institute: Yearbook Workshops

Academic / Career Interest
Journalism

Website
http://mediaschool.indiana.edu/hsji/students/student-work-shops/yearbook-workshops/

Application Timeline
Approx. June

Eligibility
The institute is designed for high school students who have accepted a position in high school media or for those interested in learning about journalism prior to their senior year.

Tuition Fees
Estimated fees: $425

Information about the program:
Editors and staffers who enroll in one of the yearbook workshops will study theme development, copy preparation, editing, design and photography. Armed with specific plans for the upcoming yearbook, they prepare for their leadership roles.

Students will immerse themselves in working with printers, developing advertising and business practices, and understanding legal and ethical issues as applied to successful yearbooking. Sessions are personal, challenging and demanding. Much instruction is one-to-one.

Contact
Director Teresa White
(812) 855-9822
terwhite@indiana.edu

Name of College
University of Iowa

Name of Program
Summer Journalism Workshops: Investigative Reporting

Academic / Career Interest
Journalism

Website
http://www.iowajournalism.com/workshops/investigative-report-ing/

Application Timeline
Open enrollment.

Eligibility
The course is not recommended for students who have never taken a high school journalism class OR participated in their school's publication.

Tuition Fees
Estimated fees:

- Early Registration (before June): $470
- Full Registration (after June): $570

Information about the program:
The exclusive workshop gives students a transformational week working with a professional award-winning investigative journalist. By the end of this hands-on week, students will be ready to produce their own investigative work. This program will help students find the perfect intersection of data, human interest, and public impact.

Contact
(319) 335-4141
conferences@uiowa.edu

Name of College
University of Iowa

Name of Program
Summer Journalism Workshops: Publication Leadership Academy

Academic / Career Interest
Journalism

Website
http://www.iowajournalism.com/workshops/publication-leadership-academy/

Application Timeline
Open enrollment.

Eligibility
Contact institution for more information.

Tuition Fees
Estimated fees:

- Early Registration (before June): $470
- Full Registration (after June): $570

Information about the program:
Whether it's online news, a newspaper or yearbook, editorial leadership starts with the writer. As the cliché goes, writers will get too much credit for their paper's success, and too much blame for its struggles.

In addition to media training, participants in this workshop will meet with captains of industry beyond journalism to better understand what it means to lead, accept responsibility, and thrive in real-world environments.

Contact
(319) 335-4141
conferences@uiowa.edu

Name of College
University of Iowa

Name of Program
Iowa Young Writers' Studio

Academic / Career Interest
Journalism

Website
https://iyws.clas.uiowa.edu

Application Timeline
Approx. February

Eligibility
Students must have completed at least their sophomore year in high school by June.

Tuition Fees
Estimated fees: $2,350

Information about the program:
The Iowa Young Writers' Studio is a creative writing program for high school students at the University of Iowa, housed in The Frank N. Magid Center for Undergraduate Writing. The Iowa Young Writers' Studio offers a summer residential program as well as online courses. The Studio gives promising high school-age creative writers the opportunity to share their writing with teachers and peers, receive constructive critique, participate in writing exercises and activities, and attend (actually or virtually) readings and literary events.

Contact
Stephen Lovely, Director
(319) 335-4209
iyws@uiowa.edu

Name of College
Johns Hopkins University

Name of Program
Mini Term: College Writing Workshop

Academic / Career Interest
Writing

Website
https://summerprograms.jhu.edu/program/pre-college-students-summer-mini-term/

Application Timeline
Applications are reviewed on a rolling basis through the application deadline or until programs have reached full capacity.

Eligibility
Open to high school students. Students must have achieved at least a 3.0 grade point average (on a 4.0 scale).

Tuition Fees
Estimated fees:

- Residential: $3,600
- Commuter: $1,020

Information about the program:
Residential students must enroll in two courses during each Mini-Term session to be eligible for housing.
Commuter students are also encouraged to apply and are only required to take up to 1 course during each Mini-Term.

In College Writing, students will ask well-informed questions and attempt to answer those questions with the support of evidence. In the process, students will treat good writing not only as a product of good thinking, but also as a tool for effective communication. To that end, students will plan, draft, and revise original essays in several genres in order to create finished pieces of writing.

Contact
(410) 516-4548
summer@jhu.edu

Name of College
Kansas State University

Name of Program
Young Writers' Workshop

Academic / Career Interest
Writing

Website
http://www.k-state.edu/english/summer/youngwritersworkshop.html

Application Timeline
Approx. May

Eligibility
Applicants must be entering 8th, 9th, or 10th grades.

Tuition Fees
Estimated fees: FREE

Information about the program:
For one week on the campus of Kansas State University, students will work with experienced teachers, dig into their imagination, and command the language to create original, inventive works of writing.

Students will meet with published writers -- slam poets, graphic novelists, oral historians, and playwrights -- who will share advice on where to get ideas, how to get going, and why they write.

Join us for a week of creative immersion!

Contact
english@ksu.edu

Name of College
Lewis & Clark College

Name of Program
Fir Acres Workshop

Academic / Career Interest
Writing

Website
https://college.lclark.edu/programs/fir_acres/

Application Timeline
Contact institution for more information.

Eligibility
Application open to students who have recently completed from 8th through 12th grades.

Tuition Fees
Contact institution for more information.

Information about the program:
During the two-week session, participants assemble two portfolios containing informal writing, works in progress, and finished pieces. After students compile each portfolio, students will have a one-on-one student-teacher conference with their Workshop faculty leader, to receive comments and suggestions on their work.

Participants also present their thoughtful work at two community-wide readings (Saturday of the first week and Friday of the second week) and in a final anthology.

Students' portfolios, readings, and anthology provide opportunities to share what they have discovered about writing during the Workshop.

Contact
(503) 768-7200
firacres@lclark.edu

Name of College
University of Maryland

Name of Program
Terp Young Scholars: Creative Writing—Cross Cultural Perspectives in Poetry and Fiction

Academic / Career Interest
Writing

Website
https://oes.umd.edu/middle-high-school-students/terp-young-scholars/terp-young-scholars-courses/terp-young-scholars-creative-writing

Application Timeline
Approx. July

Eligibility
To apply and participate, a student must:

- Be a rising high school freshmen, sophomore, junior, senior, or graduating senior
- Have an academic average of 3.25 or better (unweighted)

Tuition Fees
Estimated fees range from $2,500 - $3,500

Information about the program:
Students immerse themselves in the writing of fiction and poetry that encourages creativity while expanding knowledge. Students will hone their writing craft in a nurturing, interactive environment while developing skills that help uncover their own distinctive voice. Students will read great poems and stories from across cultures and engage in related writing exercises. They'll also refine their skill through close reading, radical revision, and the delivery of constructive criticism on peer work. Morning sessions emphasize assigned readings, writing, analysis, and discussions of craft.

Contact
(301) 405-7762

Name of College
University of Miami

Name of Program
Peace Sullivan/James Ansin High School Workshop in Journalism and New Media

Academic / Career Interest
Journalism

Website
http://com.miami.edu/high-school-journalism-workshop

Application Timeline
Approx. April

Eligibility
To be eligible, students cannot have attended this or any other Dow Jones-funded workshop in the past.

Tuition Fees
Estimated fees: FREE

Information about the program:
The James Ansin / Peace Sullivan High School Journalism and New Media Workshop at the University of Miami is a fully-funded, incredible summer educational opportunity for up to 20 high school students interested in journalism and new media.

Accepted students live in the University of Miami residence halls, work with experienced faculty and professionals. They produce both a printed newspaper and a website on a topic of interest to South Florida. In past years, the publication (Montage) has been a national award winner and the program has been a transformative experience for the students.

Contact
Sam Terilli
Program Director
(305) 284-8451
sterilli@miami.edu

Name of College
Michigan State University

Name of Program
Michigan Interscholastic Press Association (MIPA) Summer Journalism Workshop

Academic / Career Interest
Journalism

Website
https://mipamsu.org/events/mipa2018/

Application Timeline
Open enrollment.

Eligibility
Middle school and high school students are eligible to apply.

Tuition Fees
Estimated fees is $450

Information about the program:
Journalists may not be able to leap a tall building in a single bound, but they certainly have the power to make the world a better place.

Students explore their journalism superpowers at the MIPA Summer Journalism Workshop. Students will spend five days on Michigan State University's campus working with some of the best instructors in the nation. Then take what they learn back to their school newspaper, yearbook, video production or news website.

Don't work on a student media staff? MIPA journalism-focused curriculum provides skills and techniques that students can apply in a variety of areas — from class to life. Students become a better writer, explore print or digital media creation and find their voice.

Contact
(517) 353-6761
mipa@msu.edu

Name of College
University of Mississippi

Name of Program
Pre-College: Creative Writing - Poetry

Academic / Career Interest
Creative Writing

Website
http://www.outreach.olemiss.edu/pre_college/creativewriting_poetry/

Application Timeline
Approx. May

Eligibility
Rising 9th through 12th grade students are eligible to apply.

Tuition Fees
Estimated fees:

- Residential: $700
- Commuters: $400

Information about the program:
In the program students use language and image to express themselves creatively. Everyone has a unique voice and important stories to tell. In a safe and encouraging workshop environment, students will read dynamic work by contemporary poets, write and revise new poems, share work with their peers, offer each other helpful feedback, and hone their voice in an effort to help them improve as a poet and increase confidence in their writing.

Contact
(662) 915-7621
precollege@olemiss.edu

Name of College
University of Missouri

Name of Program
Missouri Investigative Journalism Workshop

Academic / Career Interest
Journalism

Website
https://journalism.missouri.edu/admissions/summer-workshops/

Application Timeline
Approx. May

Eligibility
High school students are eligible to apply.

Tuition Fees
Estimated fees: $700

Information about the program:
Students learn how investigative journalists find information, track people down, conduct better interviews, analyze data and find great stories. Students will leave with skills they need to do their own investigations. The workshop is taught by investigative reporters who have worked at top news organizations such as The New York Times and by experienced University of Missouri faculty.

Highlights include:

- How to use the web and social media to find information and background people.
- How to conduct better interviews that get people talking.
- How to analyze data to pull meaning from numbers and lists.
- How to tell better stories.
- How to find better story ideas.

Contact
horvitm@missouri.edu

Name of College
University of Missouri

Name of Program
Missouri Urban Journalism Workshop

Academic / Career Interest
Journalism

Website
https://journalism.missouri.edu/admissions/summer-workshops/

Application Timeline
Approx. May

Eligibility
High school students are eligible to apply.

Tuition Fees
Estimated fees: $675

Information about the program:
Discover the fast-paced world of professional journalism! Learn how to cover issues, news and current events. Instruction will be guided by faculty experts at the Missouri School of Journalism and industry professionals.
Skills students will work on include:

- Mobile Technologies: Learn how to interview sources, shoot video, take photos – do everything they need for the story – while on location. In today's world, journalists can work from anywhere.
- Social Media: Use Twitter, Snapchat, Facebook and other social platforms to engage with the public, gather information and more for all stages of reporting.

Contact
horvitm@missouri.edu

Name of College
New York University

Name of Program
Urban Journalism Workshop

Academic / Career Interest
Journalism

Website
https://journalism.nyu.edu/about-us/institute-projects/urban-journalism-workshop/

Application Timeline
Approx. April

Eligibility
Students must be at least 16 years of age and live in the New York City metropolitan area to be eligible.

Tuition Fees
Estimated fees: FREE

Information about the program:
During the workshop students will receive hands-on instruction from New York University (NYU) faculty and visiting professionals and get the opportunity to report and produce their own multimedia stories.

Below is a list of what to expect at the Urban Journalism Workshop:

- Experience life away from home, living in the East Village in one of the NYU dorms.
- Produce stories to be published on the program's website: The Spectrum.
- Visit some of New York's most prestigious newsrooms and meet with top journalists.
- Gain valuable insight into the college admissions process from NYU admissions counselors.

Contact
jms36@nyu.edu

Name of College
University of North Carolina, Chapel Hill

Name of Program
North Carolina Scholastic Media Institute

Academic / Career Interest
Journalism

Website
http://ncsma.unc.edu/institute-information/

Application Timeline
Approx. June

Eligibility
Students who are rising ninth-graders through 12th-graders are eligible to apply.

Tuition Fees
Estimated fees:

- Residential: $250 ($200 before May)
- Commuter: $150

Information about the program:
Students are invited to attend the annual Summer Institute, which offers a variety of events and opportunities, such as:

- Courses in design, literary magazine, news, online news, photojournalism, broadcast news and yearbook.
- Networking opportunities with student media across the state.
- Immersive classes in UNC-Chapel Hill's School of Media and Journalism.
- An awards brunch celebrating the best in N.C. student journalism.

Contact
(919) 962-4639
ncsma@unc.edu

Name of College
Northwestern University

Name of Program
Medill-Northwestern Journalism Institute

Academic / Career Interest
Journalism

Website
http://cherubs.medill.northwestern.edu/2017/about/

Application Timeline
Approx. March

Eligibility
Rising seniors are eligible to apply.

Tuition Fees
Estimated fees: $5,700

Information about the program:
The Institute, also known as "Medill cherubs," is a five-week journalism program for about 80 rising high school seniors at Northwestern University in Evanston, Illinois. It is sponsored by Northwestern's Medill School of Journalism, Media, Integrated Marketing Communications. Students learn from accomplished journalists and university professors while gaining practical experience in the field. By the end of the summer, students create a body of work, build connections and meet aspiring journalists from around the world. In the summer of 2017, students came from 23 states and the District of Columbia in the United States as well as from China (5), South Korea (3) and Sweden.

Contact
Prof. Roger Boye
rboye@northwestern.edu

Name of College
New England Center for Investigative Reporting

Name of Program
Pre-College Summer Journalism Institute

Academic / Career Interest
Journalism

Website
https://www.necir.org/training/precollege-summer-journalism-institute/

Application Timeline
Contact institution for more information.

Eligibility
Open to students ages 14-18.

Tuition Fees
Contact institution for more information.

Information about the program:
The New England Center for Investigative Reporting presents a once-in-a-lifetime experience for high school students interested in journalism, communications or writing.

Celebrating its 10th Anniversary, the Pre-College Summer Journalism Institute gives students ages 14 to 18 the opportunity to expand their skills, experience college life and explore Boston.

Each instructor is also a working journalist, so what's taught is grounded in real-life experience. Each lesson is tied to its practical application, by giving students reporting assignments on campus and in the city. Each day is an opportunity to taste what's it like to work in the news field, live on a campus, and make new friends from all over the country.

Contact
(617) 531-1685
info@necir.org

Name of College
Ohio University

Name of Program
High School Journalism Workshop

Academic / Career Interest
Journalism

Website
http://scrippsjschool.org/hsjw/

Application Timeline
Approx. June

Eligibility
Rising juniors and seniors are eligible to apply.

Tuition Fees
Estimated fees: $300

Information about the program:
Ohio University's High School Journalism Workshop will include:

- Opportunities to experience the latest journalism techniques
- Diversity scholarships that cover up to 100 percent of the cost of the workshop for students
- An opportunity to spend time on Ohio University's historic Athens campus
- And the chance to earn college credit!

Contact
(740) 593-2590
info@scrippsjschool.org

Name of College
University of Oregon

Name of Program
Next Generation Storytelling camp

Academic / Career Interest
Journalism

Website
http://journalism.uoregon.edu/news/high-school-journal-ists-get-hands-learning-next-generation-storytelling-camp/

Application Timeline
Approx. April

Eligibility
Applications will be accepted from high school students entering 10th, 11th and 12th grade.

Tuition Fees
Estimated fees: $850

Information about the program:
This summer the University of Oregon School of Journalism and Communication will offer a camp for high schoolers interested in pursuing journalism or communications at the college level. Students at the camp will learn through experience and from working professionals in the journalism and media field. Students who complete the camp can earn one general elective college credit from the University of Oregon.

Contact
(503) 412-3662

Name of College
Pennsylvania State University

Name of Program
Broadcast Journalism Camp

Academic / Career Interest
Journalism

Website
https://bellisario.psu.edu/departments/summer-camps

Application Timeline
Rolling admission through approx. June.

Eligibility
High-school-age students are eligible to apply.

Tuition Fees
Estimated fees: $895

Information about the program:
Penn State's state-of-the-art television studio provides a home for campers who choose this option. Students will work in the same newsroom and studio used by award-winning Penn State students as they learn about TV news and sports productions. It's an opportunity to explore essential broadcast journalism skills, newsgathering techniques, storytelling and more.

They'll also gain insight into other areas of TV news/sports from experienced professionals who have worked in the TV industry for years. Along with faculty, students in the broadcast journalism major at Penn State will serve as counselors, providing an additional resource for those interested in the field. This camp is a good option for those students considering a career in either on-air or off-air television news and sports (including reporting, anchoring, producing and videography).

Contact
(814) 867-2495
epc10@psu.edu

Name of College
Princeton University

Name of Program
The Princeton University Summer Journalism Program

Academic / Career Interest
Journalism

Website
https://www.princeton.edu/sjp/

Application Timeline
Contact institution for more information.

Eligibility
This program is intended for low-income students with excellent academic records who are committed to pursuing a career in journalism. Must be a junior in high school at the time of application.

Tuition Fees
Estimated fees: FREE

Information about the program:
Classes at the program are taught by reporters and editors from The New York Times, The Washington Post, The New Yorker, New York Magazine, The Daily Beast, Politico, Sports Illustrated and CNN, among other media outlets. Students tour The New York Times, New York Magazine, The Daily Beast and Bloomberg; cover a professional sports event; cover news events in the Princeton area; film and produce a TV segment; conduct an investigative project; author a group blog; and report, write, edit and design their own newspaper, The Princeton Summer Journal, which is published on the program's last day. The program is also designed to give students a taste of what life is like at one of the best colleges in the country—students live on campus and eat in one of the university's cafeterias—and to prepare them to apply to top schools.

Contact
sjp@princeton.edu

Name of College
Sarah Lawrence College

Name of Program
Writer's Week: A Creative Writing Workshop

Academic / Career Interest
Creative Writing

Website
https://www.sarahlawrence.edu/summer/pre-college/writ-ers-week.html

Application Timeline
Contact institution for more information.

Eligibility
Students entering the 9th, 10th, 11th, or 12th grades the following fall. Students must be age 14 or older at the start of the program.

Tuition Fees
Estimated fees is $250

Information about the program:
Each day, participants attend writing and theatre workshops led by prose writers, poets, and performance artists.
The day's work begins with a creative writing workshop, giving students the chance to investigate what defines a poem, a story, and the best way to communicate ideas through writing. This course is a place for students to write, to read one another's work, to learn to observe what is familiar and what is not, and to transform what the writer sees into words. Members work as professional writers do: generating material, collaborating, and talking, revising, and rewriting. This course, the creative process is explored in an intuitive and spontaneous fashion through improvisation, group projects, and games. Faculty and students participate together to give form and shape to both individual and collective expression. No prior theatre experience is necessary.

Contact
(914) 395-2205
summer@sarahlawrence.edu

Name of College
San Jose State University

Name of Program
Mosaic Journalism Workshop

Academic / Career Interest
Journalism

Website
http://mosaicjournalism.blogspot.com/p/program.html

Application Timeline
Approx. April

Eligibility
Applicants must be a current sophomore, junior or senior in high school.

Tuition Fees
Estimated fees: FREE

Information about the program:
The program strives to inspire future journalists who grew up in disadvantaged communities as well as those from more privileged backgrounds to widen their world views and smash stereotypes. Mosaic students cover real stories and subject matter that is of interest to youth and bring a new prospective to the media. All of our staff have hands-on experience in the real world of journalism and emphasize ethics across the curriculum.

The students learn reporting, writing, visual media techniques, then hit the streets to gather real-life news stories about people who make the news and those whose lives are affected by the news. Professional guest speakers share their stories and advice about the wonderful world of journalism and the media industry. On the final day, Mosaic students visit a real newsroom and see their Mosaic newspaper run off the presses at the Mercury News.

Contact
Joe Rodriguez
(408) 920-5767
Jrodgriguez@mercurynews.com

Name of College
University of Southern California

Name of Program
News Reporting in the Digital Age

Academic / Career Interest
Journalism

Website
https://summerprograms.usc.edu/programs/4-week/news-reporting/

Application Timeline
Domestic Student Application: approx. April
International Student Application: approx. March

Eligibility
Students must have completed at least the 9th grade by mid-June.

Tuition Fees
Estimated fees:

- Residential: $8,534
- Commuter: $6,059

Information about the program:
Students spend four weeks in our state-of-the-art media center. In this course, students will report and write stories about real people and issues in Los Angeles. Students will explore online reporting and writing, blogging and multimedia news technology. Students will gain an understanding of the challenges and opportunities for journalists in the digital world. Students will be encouraged to experiment and bring to class their own technical skills and life perspective. Their thinking and analytical skills will expand.

Contact
(213) 740-5679
summer@usc.edu

Name of College
University of Southern California

Name of Program
Sports Journalism: Multi-Platform Storytelling

Academic / Career Interest
Journalism

Website
https://summerprograms.usc.edu/programs/4-week/sportsjournalism/

Application Timeline
Domestic Student Application: approx. April
International Student Application: approx. March

Eligibility
Students must have completed at least the 9th grade by mid-June.

Tuition Fees
Estimated fees range from $6,000 - $8,000

Information about the program:
Learn multi-platform sports journalism at University of Southern California Annenberg in Los Angeles–the epicenter of sports media and entertainment, and home to an unparalleled combination of both professional and big-time college sports, including the Dodgers, Lakers, Clippers, Rams, Chargers, Kings, Sparks, Galaxy and expansion LAFC of MLS, and, yes, the USC Trojans! No city or region in America offers a stronger mix of sports at all levels, even high school–where the No. 1-ranked football team in the country, Mater Dei High from nearby Orange County, recently completed an undefeated championship season.

Contact
(213) 740-5679
summer@usc.edu

Name of College
University of South Carolina

Name of Program
Carolina Journalism Institute

Academic / Career Interest
Journalism

Website
https://www.sc.edu/study/colleges_schools/cic/journalism_and_
mass_communications/scholastic_organizations/sipa/cji/index.php

Application Timeline
Approx. May

Eligibility
High-school-age students are eligible to apply.

Tuition Fees
Estimated fees is $300

Information about the program:
After Carolina Journalism Institute (CJI) students will be able to take
their projects back with them to their media production class, no
matter what type of publication or production they work on. Literary magazine, yearbook, newsprint, broadcast and online media
students alike can benefit and learn from sessions, and the project
teaches all students how to work in a group and to use programs
and resources they can use in their journalism classrooms.

At CJI, students will be placed in a group with three or four other
students, and their group will be assigned a beat to cover for a final
project. Each group member should take a different angle or approach to covering the assigned beat. By the end of the week, each
person should have one written, one visual and one social media
element.

Contact
(803) 777-6146

Name of College
St. Johns College

Name of Program
Summer Academy: Poets & Perception

Academic / Career Interest
Journalism

Website
https://www.sjc.edu/summer-academy/sessions/poets-and-perception

Application Timeline
Applications are accepted on a rolling basis.

Eligibility
Open to high school students ages 15 to 18.

Tuition Fees
Estimated fees:

- $1,100 per week-long session if deposit paid before June
- $1,250 per week-long session if deposit paid during or after June

Information about the program:
Playful fairies spin love stories out of magic and illusion in A Midsummer Night's Dream, inviting us to contemplate the deception of perception. What is really true if we cannot trust our own senses? Alongside Shakespeare, students will read Plato's Theaetetus, where Socrates attempts to define what it means to know, and Dickinson and Wordsworth, two poets whose beautiful words challenge our notion of sight and speech. In laboratory, students use works by Aristotle and Boethius to examine the senses, their objects, and our access to them.

Contact
(410) 263-2371

Name of College
Washington University in Saint Louis

Name of Program
Introduction to Reading and Writing About Literature

Academic / Career Interest
Journalism

Website
General: http://summerexperiences.wustl.edu/scholars/course-listings
Course Listing: http://summerexperiences.wustl.edu/files/summerexperiences/imce/2018_session_a_course_listings_9.pdf

Application Timeline
Approx. May

Eligibility
To be eligible for the High School Summer Scholars Program students should be a current sophomore or junior in high school.

Tuition Fees
Estimated fees:

- Session A or B (five weeks): $8,085
- Session C (eight weeks): $10,585
- $35 application fee. This fee is waived if students apply before mid-February

Information about the program:
Intro to Reading and Writing about Literature is a discussion based, writing-intensive course. It focuses on analytical reading skills and on the principles of effective writing. Through weekly writing assignments and revision, students learn the importance of critical thinking and questioning that are required for the development of ideas and good, clear writing.

Contact
(314) 935-4807
summerexperiences@wustl.edu

Name of College
Washington University in Saint Louis

Name of Program
Topics in English and American Literature: Banned Books: From The Giver to The Lord of the Flies

Academic / Career Interest
Journalism

Website
General: http://summerexperiences.wustl.edu/scholars/course-listings

Course Listing: http://summerexperiences.wustl.edu/files/summerexperiences/imce/2018_session_a_course_listings_9.pdf

Application Timeline
Approx. May

Eligibility
To be eligible for the High School Summer Scholars Program students should be a current sophomore or junior in high school.

Tuition Fees
Estimated fees range from $8,000 - $10,000

Information about the program:
In this course students will read a number of Young Adult novels that have been banned and examine what leads to the banning of a book. The novels students will cover, by Toni Morrison, Stephen Chbosky, William Golding, and Lois Lowry, among others, have been banned in the United States on political, religious, sexual, or social grounds. Students will gain insight into the controversies these novels started and also consider the themes and questions raised by the texts and their moral implications. Students will be asked to engage critically with the texts they encounter and to hone their close reading skills while also considering historical and cultural contexts of the novels.

Contact
(314) 935-4807
summerexperiences@wustl.edu

Name of College
Washington University in Saint Louis

Name of Program
Critical Reading and Writing

Academic / Career Interest
Journalism

Website
General: http://summerexperiences.wustl.edu/scholars/
course-listings

Application Timeline
Approx. May

Eligibility
To be eligible for the High School Summer Scholars Program students should be a current sophomore or junior in high school.

Tuition Fees
Estimated fees:

- Session A or B (five weeks): $8,085
- Session C (eight weeks): $10,585
- $35 application fee. This fee is waived if students apply before mid-February

Information about the program:
This course teaches students to engage critically with scholarship, construct convincing arguments, and write persuasive research papers. Students will study how other writers achieve these goals, then use a proven model of researched writing to write an argument and paper about a text of their own choosing that includes accurate use of primary and secondary sources. Concentrating on a single research project throughout the session, attention will be given to revision and organization, library research strategies, academic citation conventions, and electronic search engines and sources.

Contact
(314) 935-4807
summerexperiences@wustl.edu

Name of College
Western Kentucky University

Name of Program
Xposure Journalism Workshop

Academic / Career Interest
Journalism

Website
https://www.wku.edu/journalism/summer_workshops/xposure/
xposure.php

Application Timeline
Approx. April

Eligibility
All high school students are welcome to apply, especially rising
juniors and seniors.

Tuition Fees
Contact institution for more information.

Information about the program:
The program seeks students with interests in news writing, editing, photography and journalism as a career. During the workshop,
students gain important skills through classes, seminars, educational field trips and work with WKU journalism professors and other
professional journalists in a learn-by-doing environment. Students
report, write, edit and shoot photos for stories published in a newspaper and posted on the workshop's website.
The Xposure High School Journalism Workshop will continue that
tradition. The alumni of these workshops fill media outlets throughout the country, helping to ensure that the news gatherers at media
outlets mirror the diverse communities they serve.

Contact
Chuck Clark, Workshop Director
(270) 745-4206
chuck.clark@wku.edu

Name of College
Yale University

Name of Program
Summer Journalism Program

Academic / Career Interest
Journalism

Website
https://yaledailynews.com/about-us/sjp/

Application Timeline
Approx. May

Eligibility
The program is limited to Connecticut residents and is geared toward those with writing or journalism experience, but any Connecticut high school student with an interest in journalism, writing or photography is encouraged to apply.

Tuition Fees
Estimated fees: free

Information about the program:
Summer Journalism Program (SJP) is an intensive, one-week program in journalism for high school students. The program is completely free and is run entirely by Yale undergraduates, who are also staff members of the Yale Daily News. SJP is based at the Yale Daily News building on the campus of Yale.

Students participate in workshops introducing them to the fundamentals of journalism, attend lectures by guest speakers from major news outlets such as the New York Times, the Huffington Post and ABC News, and receive mentorship from staff of the Yale Daily News. Throughout the week, they gain hands-on experience by pitching, writing their own stories and taking photographs. At the end of the week, they produce an issue of the Yale Daily News.

Contact
sjp@yaledailynews.com

COLLEGE
CONSULTING
EXPERTS

Law Collegiate Programs

Name of College
Brigham Young University

Name of Program
BYU Law Camp

Academic / Career Interest
Law

Website
https://lawcamp.ce.byu.edu

Application Timeline
Approx. June

Eligibility
All high school students interested in leadership, law, and/or government are encouraged to apply, especially those who will be sophomores, juniors or seniors.

Tuition Fees
Estimated fees: $575

Cost includes on-campus housing accommodations (Monday-Friday), meals (Monday lunch through Saturday breakfast), counselor supervision, all program classes, activities, and fieldtrips. Participants will also receive some awesome swag from the BYU Law School!

Information about the program:
BYU's Law Camp is a hands-on, interactive learning experience. Throughout the course of the week, you will:

- Work personally with judges, professors, and practicing attorneys
- Be personally mentored by current law students
- Engage in realistic and interactive trials, appeals, and jury deliberations.
- Visit a Federal Courthouse
- Build friendships through fun social activities including a movie night, dance and more!

Contact
(801) 442-7871
admissionscamp@law.byu

Name of College
University of British Columbia

Name of Program
Law and Society: Fundamental Concepts Future Global Leaders

Academic / Career Interest
Law

Website
https://extendedlearning.ubc.ca/courses/law-society-fundamental-concepts/sa012

Application Timeline
Contact institution for more information

Eligibility
Must be 15- to 18-years-old on or before the course start date.

Tuition Fees
Estimated fees range from $1,600 - $3,000

Information about the program:
This academic course is part of the UBC Future Global Leaders pre-university program for high school students ages 15-18.

Why do we have laws in our society? How is law made and implemented in Canada and other jurisdictions? Explore fundamental legal concepts and questions. Find out what role law plays when it confronts questions of justice, ethics and morality. Study the workings of a trial, and how a legal question is presented and adjudicated. This is an ideal course for an aspiring lawyer, or students interested in politics and democracy. This 2-week course is part of the UBC Future Global Leaders pre-university program at the University of British Columbia in Vancouver, Canada, which has the option to stay in a UBC student residence during the program.

Contact
(604) 822-144

Name of College
Brown University

Name of Program
Summer@Brown: Political Theory and the Law

Academic / Career Interest
Theory and Law

Website
https://precollege.brown.edu/catalog/course.php?course_code=-CEPS0919

Application Timeline
Contact institution for more information

Eligibility
Students completing grades 9-12, ages 15-18 by June are eligible to apply.

Tuition Fees
Estimated fees ranges from $2,500 - $6,000

Information about the program:
How should we evaluate the laws that govern and bind society? This course will examine the moral and political value of American law through the lens of political theory. As such, students will be able to evaluate for themselves whether laws are legitimate.

During the course, we will read contemporary and classic political theory in light of the history of American jurisprudence. In doing so, we will use cases to illuminate and theories to help solve the following kinds of puzzles: This course will serve as an introduction to three areas: American constitutional law, the study of contemporary and historical political theory, and the practice of normative political theory.

Contact
(401) 863-7900
precollege@brown.edu

Name of College
Brown University

Name of Program
Summer@Brown: The U.S. In World Politics

Academic / Career Interest
Politics

Website
https://precollege.brown.edu/catalog/course.php?course_code=-CEPS0902

Application Timeline
Contact institution for more information

Eligibility
Students completing grades 9-12, ages 15-18 by June are eligible to apply.

Tuition Fees
Estimated fees range from $2,500 - $6,000

Information about the program:
Globalization is transforming the relationship between world events and U.S. politics. This course analyzes some of the main challenges, threats, and questions facing the United States in the first decades of the twenty-first century. In addition to introducing students to core theoretical perspectives, concepts, and debates in the study of International Relations and American foreign policy, the course focuses on a number of substantive issues, ranging from the spread of nuclear weapons, transnational terrorism, the role of human rights in American foreign policy, and the appropriate grand strategy for the United States in the twenty-first century.

Contact
(401) 863-7900
precollege@brown.edu

Name of College
Brown University

Name of Program
Summer@Brown: The Power of Political Ideas

Academic / Career Interest
Politics

Website
https://precollege.brown.edu/catalog/course.php?course_code=-CEPS0926

Application Timeline
Contact institution for more information

Eligibility
Students completing grades 9-12, ages 15-18 by June are eligible to apply.

Tuition Fees
Estimated fees range from $2,500 - $6,000

Information about the program:
This course gives students a chance to undertake a fascinating and highly challenging process of political and intellectual exploration. In addition to well-established far right- and left-wing ideas, you will be exposed to and asked to evaluate such ideologies as Nihilism, Radical Feminism, Radical Environmentalism, and Radical Islam.

This will be an intense, deeply personal and highly intellectual experience, as you engage the passionate arguments of leading political thinkers and explore your own feelings about them. Here in America the two predominant ideological orientations are Liberalism and Conservatism, so it behooves us to understand both of them thoroughly.

Contact
(401) 863-7900
precollege@brown.edu

Name of College
Brown University

Name of Program
Summer@Brown: Introduction to U.S. Law and The Way Lawyers Think

Academic / Career Interest
Law

Website
https://precollege.brown.edu/catalog/course.php?course_code=-CEPS0960

Application Timeline
Contact institution for more information

Eligibility
Students completing grades 9-12, ages 15-18 by June are eligible to apply.

Tuition Fees
Estimated fees range from $2,500 - $6,000

Information about the program:
The law touches nearly all aspects of our lives, and a certain amount of basic legal knowledge is necessary to identify important legal issues that arise in daily life and in various industries. Learn at an introductory level about: the legal system in the U.S., what lawyers really do, and how to analyze issues like an attorney, all through real examples and interactive hypotheticals and exercises.

Contact
(401) 863-7900
precollege@brown.edu

Name of College
Brown University

Name of Program
Summer@Brown: How the Judicial System Works: Trials and the Law

Academic / Career Interest
Law

Website
https://precollege.brown.edu/catalog/course.php?course_code=-CEPS0970

Application Timeline
Contact institution for more information

Eligibility
Students completing grades 9-12, ages 15-18 by June are eligible to apply.

Tuition Fees
Estimated fees range from $2,500 - $6,000

Information about the program:
Taught by the Honorable Dennis J Curran, Justice of the Massachusetts Superior Court (Ret.), this course is intended for those who wish to have a "behind the scenes" look at how the judicial system works - at the legal mechanics behind the dramas and the way the law functions in practice when human lives and living is at issue.

Contact
(401) 863-7900
precollege@brown.edu

Name of College
Brown University

Name of Program
Summer@Brown: Creating Change Through Public Policy

Academic / Career Interest
Public policy

Website
https://precollege.brown.edu/catalog/course.php?course_code=-CEPS0958

Application Timeline
Contact institution for more information

Eligibility
Students completing grades 9-12, ages 15-18 by June are eligible to apply.

Tuition Fees
Estimated fees range from $2,500 - $6,000

Information about the program:
How do major, transformative changes in public policy take place? Major public policy changes often begin in the orderly world of analysis - but end in the messy world of partisan politics. To succeed, a new initiative has to coincide with a political climate and a leadership capacity that allows the proponents to overcome the natural resistance to change.

Public policy is the set of laws, rules, and regulations enacted and enforced by government. Policy is made in response to a societal issue or problem that requires attention and is made on behalf of the public. Policy affects virtually every aspect of our daily lives yet the average citizen has limited understanding of how public policy is made or how to impact public policy.

Contact
(401) 863-7900
precollege@brown.edu

Name of College
University of California, Irvine

Name of Program
High School Summer Institute in Law

Academic / Career Interest
Law

Website
https://ce.uci.edu/areas/legal/hslaw/

Application Timeline
Contact institution for more information

Eligibility
Students are encouraged to attend upon completion of their sophomore year of high school.

Tuition Fees
Estimated fees: $1,110

Information about the program:
This week-long experience led by distinguished UC Irvine School of Law faculty in a law school setting is designed to equip students with knowledge, understanding, and skills that will benefit them as they continue their education and chart their future—to perform better in high school, prepare for college, and explore a possible career as a lawyer.

Renowned faculty will lead engaging morning lectures of current relevance, introducing participants to the legal system and to major areas of law important to students, such as First Amendment rights and crime and punishment. In the afternoon, students will have an opportunity to participate in mock debates, hearings, and workshop-style sessions. This specialized program advances college readiness on a UC campus in actual law school classrooms.

Contact
Gina Cho
(949) 824-4598
LegalPrograms@ce.uci.edu

Name of College
University of California, Los Angeles

Name of Program
Mock Trial Summer Institute

Academic / Career Interest
Law

Website
https://summer.ucla.edu/institutes/MockTrial

Application Timeline
Approx. April

Eligibility
To participate for the Mock Trial Summer Institute, you must meet the following qualifications:

- 14 years of age or older prior to June 25
- Enrolled in grades 8th – 12th during Spring

Tuition Fees
Estimated fees range from $1,000 - $1800

Information about the program:
This week-long program is a great way to broaden a student's knowledge base, explore college and career options, boost self-confidence and powers of persuasion - all while making new friends and having fun! Come to Los Angeles to train with the National Champion UCLA Mock Trial Team Coach and Team Members! Learn effective trial advocacy techniques and improve public speaking skills. UCLA has won the Collegiate National Championship four times in the last decade (most recently 2014) and students will have the chance to work with current students and coaches.

Due to the rigorous and intense nature of the program, the residential plan, which includes housing, a meal plan, a schedule of activities, and supervision, is mandatory for all students.

Contact
(310) 825-4101
info@summer.ucla.edu

Name of College
University of Chicago

Name of Program
Summer Immersion: American Law and Litigation

Academic / Career Interest
Law

Website
https://summer.uchicago.edu/course/american-law-and-litigation

Application Timeline
Approx. May

Eligibility
Open to high school students

Tuition Fees
Estimated fees: $6,500 + $50 application fee

Information about the program:
Students will explore how the American legal system operates, and hone critical thinking skills through extensive reading and analysis, while learning to think like a litigator. After an overview of how the American common law system developed into the court structure that exists today, students will read the full text of actual U.S. landmark Constitutional cases, while learning how to decipher legal terminology and to conduct legal analysis. Through critical examination, students will gain insight into the ways in which law is continually interpreted and reinterpreted, and how courts attempt to dispense justice while balancing competing social interests.

Contact
(773) 702-2149
summersession@uchicago.edu

Name of College
Claremont McKenna College

Name of Program
High School Debate (HSPDP)

Academic / Career Interest
Debate

Website
https://claremontsummer.org/portfolio/high-school-debate-hspd-pchssa/

Application Timeline
Contact institution for more information

Eligibility
Students entering 9th-12th grades in the fall are eligible to participate in high school sessions

Tuition Fees
Estimated fees:

- Residential student: $1,450
- Commuting student: $900

Information about the program:
This summer, students will have the opportunity to learn competitive and professional skills in an innovative college bridge program offering the following:

- 16 small group instructional sessions, including 6 student-selected elective sessions
- 12 full debates, critiqued by certified judges
- experienced debaters will work on advanced debate theory and sophisticated refutation in supplemental seminars led by John Meany
- 10 hours of open forum sessions – students have the opportunity to discuss and practice any element of debate and argumentation theory, as well as arrange for additional speech and debate practice.

Contact
(909) 607-9246
john.meany@cmc.edu

Name of College
Columbia University

Name of Program
Summer Immersion: Introduction To Global Economics And Public Policy

Academic / Career Interest
Global Economics and Public Policy

Website
https://sps.columbia.edu/highschool/3-week/courses/introduction-to-global-economics-and-public-policy

Application Timeline
Contact institution for more information

Eligibility
Open to students entering grade 9 or 10 in the fall

Tuition Fees
Estimated fees: $11,064

Information about the program:
Is inequality an unavoidable consequence of the global economic system? How do current policies on foreign investment, offshoring labor, and immigration impact globalization and economic development? Is debt relief by international organizations to federal governments a helpful policy in the long-run? Was the 2008 financial crisis predictable? Does economic development necessarily entail a negative impact on the natural environment?
This course provides students with an understanding of current macroeconomic debates and the reasoning behind significant global policy decisions.

Contact
(212) 854-9889
hsp@columbia.edu

Name of College
Columbia University

Name of Program
Summer Immersion: Constitutional Law

Academic / Career Interest
Law

Website
https://sps.columbia.edu/highschool/3-week/courses/introduction-to-global-economics-and-public-policy

Application Timeline
Contact institution for more information

Eligibility
Open to students entering grade 9 or 10 in the fall

Tuition Fees
Estimated fees: $11,064

Information about the program:
This is a course designed for students interested in law, government, and politics. It examines a wide range of contemporary issues subject to constitutional interpretation, introducing students to the constitution, the fundamental concepts of constitutional law, the role of the courts, and the legal limitations on governmental policy making.

Students discuss and analyze topics including separation of powers, federalism, freedom of speech, affirmative action, the death penalty, gun control, civil rights, and abortion. They are exposed to current constitutional challenges and are given the opportunity to explore the relationship between law and society.

Contact
(212) 854-9889
hsp@columbia.edu

Name of College
Columbia University

Name of Program
Summer Immersion: We the People? Understanding Democracy

Academic / Career Interest
Understanding Democracy

Website
https://sps.columbia.edu/highschool/summer-immersion/new-york-city-3-week/courses/we-the-people-understanding-democracy

Application Timeline
Contact institution for more information

Eligibility
Open to students entering grade 9 or 10 in the fall

Tuition Fees
Estimated fees: $11,064

Information about the program:
Is democracy the rule of the people, by the people, and for the people? Or is it a form of government in which selected elites rule, leaving individuals to pursue their private interests? What is the role of a constitution in preserving individual rights and enabling the will of the majority? To answer these questions we analyze both ancient Athenian democracy and our current form of representative democracy, identifying the core features of democratic politics and the kinds of liberty they foster.

To review the origins of democracy and identify its basic principles and institutions, students engage with the works of Herodotus, Thucydides, Plato, and Aristotle.

Contact
(212) 854-9889
hsp@columbia.edu

Name of College
Connecticut College

Name of Program
Pre-College Summer @ UConn: Pre-Law

Academic / Career Interest
Law

Website
https://precollege-summer.uconn.edu/academic-areas/pre-law/

Application Timeline
Contact institution for more information

Eligibility
Application is open to juniors and seniors

Tuition Fees
Estimated fees:

- 1 Session: $1,950
- Additional Course Fee: $35

Information about the program:
Oliver Wendell Holmes famously stated that "the life of the law has not been logic; it has been experience." In accordance with this observation, this one-week course is designed to provide participants with both academic and practical understandings of the law, legal education, and the operations of the American judicial system.

Participants are expected to reflect upon each one of these experiences daily as well as prepare for the Moot Court simulation at the end of the week. This course may be of particular interest to aspiring legal professionals as well as to those who have a curious interest in current legal issues.

Contact
(860) 486-0149
PreCollegeSummer@UConn.edu

Name of College
Cornell University

Name of Program
Introduction to American Government and Politics

Academic / Career Interest
American Government and Politics

Website
https://www.sce.cornell.edu/sc/programs/courses.php?v=3081

Application Timeline
Approx. May

Eligibility
Open to sophomores, juniors, and seniors. Must be younger than 18 years old by the start of the June programs.

Tuition Fees
Estimated fees: $12,825

Information about the program:
A policy-centered approach to the study of government in the American experience. Considers the American Founding and how it influenced the structure of government; how national institutions operate in shaping law and public policy; who has a voice in American politics and why some are more influential than others; and how existing public policies themselves influence social, economic, and political power. Students will gain an introductory knowledge of the founding principles and structure of American government, political institutions, political processes, political behavior, and public policy.

Contact
(607) 255-6203
summer_college@cornell.edu

Name of College
Davidson College

Name of Program
July Experience: The Supreme Court in American Politics

Academic / Career Interest
Politics

Website
https://www.davidson.edu/offices/july-experience/courses

Application Timeline
Contact institution for more information

Eligibility
Open to high school juniors and seniors

Tuition Fees
Estimated fees: $4,000.

Information about the program:
This course will provide an overview of the Supreme Court as an institution that exists at the intersection of law and politics in the United States. We will discuss the operations of the Court and its role in the federal government, both historical and current. We will also discuss the politics of judicial appointments and Supreme Court decision-making. Finally, we will discuss several landmark Court opinions as well as cases and issues currently on the Court's docket.

Contact
(800) 768-0380

Name of College
Davidson College

Name of Program
July Experience: Equality and Inequality

Academic / Career Interest
Equality

Website
https://www.davidson.edu/offices/july-experience/courses

Application Timeline
Contact institution for more information

Eligibility
Open to high school juniors and seniors

Tuition Fees
Estimated fees: $4,000

Information about the program:
Although liberals and conservatives embrace the ideal of equality, they often understand this ideal in very different ways and recommend very different policies to attain it. Liberals characteristically denounce economic and social inequality, and recommend energetic government policies to remedy it, from raising taxes on the wealthy and regulating corporations to providing universal welfare benefits (like Bernie Sanders' call for "Medicare for All"). Conservatives, on the other hand, view precisely these kinds of proposals as threats to civil equality and political liberty. In their view, inequality arises more from individual choices than from unjust social structures or political policies – and that government actions to combat it are ineffective and even counterproductive. To help us explore these debates, we will read liberal and conservative responses to the plight of the poor Americans movingly depicted in J. D. Vance's Hillbilly Elegy. We will also examine the ways which these contrasting views might help explain Donald Trump's surprising presidential victory.

Contact
(800) 768-0380

Name of College
Emerson College

Name of Program
Pre-College Politics, Activism, & Leadership

Academic / Career Interest
Politics

Website
https://www.emerson.edu/academics/pre-college/political-com-munication

Application Timeline
Approx. May

Eligibility
Students entering grades 10, 11 and 12 are eligible to apply

Tuition Fees
Estimated fees:

- Politics, Activism, & Leadership Institute Tuition: $2,495
- Residential Room and Board Fee: $1,190
- Non-Refundable Application Fee: $60

Information about the program:
The Politics, Activism, and Leadership Institute (PAL) is for high school students who wish to understand how communication is at the heart of politics, activism and leadership in a democratic society. The Institute is focused on a number of important issues, including, community activism, social justice, civic engagement, public service, scandal/crisis management, speechwriting, grassroots organizing, and communicating with the media. Students will be encouraged to "find their voice" through the various activities, seminars, guest speakers, and field trips. Whether interested in what takes place behind the scenes or in front of an audience, the Institute rests upon the belief that young people can be active agents within your communities, and serve as ambassadors and advocates for various causes and issues.

Contact
(617) 824-8280
precollege@emerson.edu

Name of College
Emory College

Name of Program
Pre-College Program: Law and Litigation

Academic / Career Interest
Law

Website
http://precollege.emory.edu/program/courses/non-credit.html

Application Timeline
Contact institution for more information

Eligibility
Application is open to juniors and seniors

Tuition Fees
Estimated fee range from $2,800 - $4,000

Information about the program:
The Emory Pre-College Program offers a diverse selection of two-week non-credit courses in a variety of disciplines. Students will experience college-level academics in a small class setting with some of Emory's leading experts in their respective fields and will receive written feedback on their work at the end of the course. Pre-College students will also receive a grade of Satisfactory/Unsatisfactory and a certificate of completion at the conclusion of the program.
All non-credit courses meet from 9:00-11:30am daily and may have additional requirements (excursions, film viewings, etc.) in the afternoons or evenings. In addition to their coursework, each Pre-College student will participate in College 101 sessions which are held in the afternoons. Taught by Emory Law School faculty, this course introduces students to law as a profession and to some of the most fundamental legal concepts and skills.

Contact
precollege@emory.edu

Name of College
Emory College

Name of Program
Pre-College Program: Civil Rights and Social Justice

Academic / Career Interest
Civil Rights and Social Justice

Website
http://precollege.emory.edu/program/courses/non-credit.html

Application Timeline
Contact institution for more information

Eligibility
Application is open to juniors and seniors.

Tuition Fees
Estimated fees from $2,800 - $4,000

Information about the program:
Civil Rights and Social Justice in the US is a course designed to provide students with the history, theory, and academic tools that are foundational for critical thinking, college success, and making positive political and cultural change. The course introduces students to a brief history of civil rights and social justice in the United States through college-level critical reading and writing practices. Students will learn about civil rights—the legal mandates that guarantee equal treatment and freedom from discrimination—and social justice—the manifestation of civil rights in individuals' everyday lives. More specifically, students will practice dissecting arguments, developing sound definitions, and articulating historical narratives, as they learn about Indigenous Rights, Civil Rights and Black Lives Matter, Women's Rights, and LGBTQ Rights.

Contact
precollege@emory.edu

Name of College
George Washington University

Name of Program
College Intensive: International Organizations & Global Governance

Academic / Career Interest
International Organizations and Global Governance

Website
https://summer.gwu.edu/law-politics

Application Timeline
Approx. May

Eligibility
Open to juniors and seniors (ages 15-18)

Tuition Fees
Estimated fees ranges from $4,000 - $6,000

Information about the program:
This course provides an overview of major international organizations and investigates how they effect change in global governance. Students will learn about the political cooperation needed to successfully negotiate responses to global financial crises and promote multilateral trade agreements, as well as confront challenges to international security and environmental concerns. Importantly, by understanding how international organizations, such as the United Nations, International Monetary Fund, World Bank Group and the World Trade Organization influence global peace and security, as well as economic and human development, students will be better positioned to assess the role played by emerging economies and newly formed international organizations, such as the Asian Infrastructure and Investment Bank.

Contact
(202) 994-6360
gwsummer@gwu.edu

Name of College
George Washington University

Name of Program
Summer Immersion: Principles of International Law

Academic / Career Interest
International Law

Website
https://summer.gwu.edu/law-politics

Application Timeline
Approx. May

Eligibility
Open to sophomores, juniors and seniors (ages 14-18)

Tuition Fees
Estimated fees:

- Residential Students:
    o One-Week Session: $1,800
    o Two-Week Session: $3,600
    o Multiple Course Discount:
        - 2 two-week sessions: $6,336
        - 3 two-week sessions: $9,533
- Commuter Students (Two-Week Session Only): $2,700

Information about the program:
What do killer robots, lethal drones, and acts of global terrorism have in common with disappearing polar regions, space exploration and nuclear war? These issues--and many others of increasing importance--are all governed by, and thus must adhere to, multinational agreements that form the foundation of international law. In this course, students will employ an interactive, hands-on methodology to think critically about the various topics, raise questions about how the different structures work and make individual contributions within a cooperative framework.

Contact
(202) 994-6360
gwsummer@gwu.edu

Name of College
George Washington University

Name of Program
Summer Immersion: U.S. Foreign Policy: Multilateralism

Academic / Career Interest
Foreign policy

Website
https://summer.gwu.edu/law-politics

Application Timeline
Approx. May

Eligibility
Open to sophomores, juniors and seniors (ages 14-18)

Tuition Fees
Estimated fees:

- Residential Students:
    o One-Week Session: $1,800
    o Two-Week Session: $3,600
    o Multiple Course Discount:
        ▪ 2 two-week sessions: $6,336
        ▪ 3 two-week sessions: $9,533
- Commuter Students (Two-Week Session Only): $2,700

Information about the program:
The globalization of economic, political, social and cultural activity has increased society's need for international understanding and cooperation. This course will expose students to viewpoints and perspectives of foreign policymakers and explore multilateral approaches to international issue. Students will gain a basic understanding of how to analyze and articulate foreign policy.

Contact
(202) 994-6360
gwsummer@gwu.edu

Name of College
George Washington University

Name of Program
Summer Immersion: Public Policy on Capitol Hill

Academic / Career Interest
Public policy

Website
https://summer.gwu.edu/law-politics

Application Timeline
Approx. May

Eligibility
Open to sophomores, juniors and seniors (ages 14-18)

Tuition Fees
Estimated fees:

- Residential Students:
    - One-Week Session: $1,800
    - Two-Week Session: $3,600
    - Multiple Course Discount:
        - 2 two-week sessions: $6,336
        - 3 two-week sessions: $9,533
- Commuter Students (Two-Week Session Only): $2,700

Information about the program:
Public policy is the way in which public issues are addressed through modifying existing laws and regulations or creating new ones altogether. In this course, students will think strategically, creatively and critically about current issues shaping the public debate, and learn to analyze and evaluate policies and programs in pursuit of public interest.

Contact
(202) 994-6360
gwsummer@gwu.edu

Name of College
George Washington University

Name of Program
Summer Immersion: Pre-Law: Trial & Advocacy

Academic / Career Interest
Pre-Law Trial

Website
https://summer.gwu.edu/law-politics

Application Timeline
Approx. May

Eligibility
Open to sophomores, juniors and seniors (ages 14-18)

Tuition Fees
Estimated fees:

- Residential Students:
    - One-Week Session: $1,800
    - Two-Week Session: $3,600
    - Multiple Course Discount:
        - 2 two-week sessions: $6,336
        - 3 two-week sessions: $9,533
- Commuter Students (Two-Week Session Only): $2,700

Information about the program:
In this course, students will learn what it takes to prepare cases: interview clients; negotiate out of court settlements; act as an advocate at trial and argue cases on appeal. Given the university's location in Washington, D.C., students will benefit from a vibrant and engaging legal community and learn about different settings in which lawyers practice. Students will also have an opportunity to explore legal ethics and the role lawyers play in helping to ensure fairness in the justice system.

Contact
(202) 994-6360
gwsummer@gwu.edu

Name of College
George Washington University

Name of Program
Summer Immersion: American Politics

Academic / Career Interest
American Politics

Website
https://summer.gwu.edu/law-politics

Application Timeline
Approx. May

Eligibility
Open to sophomores, juniors and seniors (ages 14-18)

Tuition Fees
Estimated fees:

- Residential Students:
    o One-Week Session: $1,800
    o Two-Week Session: $3,600
    o Multiple Course Discount:
        - 2 two-week sessions: $6,336
        - 3 two-week sessions: $9,533
- Commuter Students (Two-Week Session Only): $2,700

Information about the program:
This course is ideal for students without prior background in political studies and who are interested in a survey of American political systems and processes, including topics such as the U.S. Constitution, media and politics, policy studies, international relations and survey research, among others.

Contact
(202) 994-6360
gwsummer@gwu.edu

Name of College
George Washington University

Name of Program
Summer Immersion: Introduction to Comparative Politics

Academic / Career Interest
Politics

Website
https://summer.gwu.edu/law-politics

Application Timeline
Approx. May

Eligibility
Open to sophomores, juniors and seniors (ages 14-18)

Tuition Fees
Estimated fees:

- Residential Students:
    - One-Week Session: $1,800
    - Two-Week Session: $3,600
    - Multiple Course Discount:
        - 2 two-week sessions: $6,336
        - 3 two-week sessions: $9,533
- Commuter Students (Two-Week Session Only): $2,700

Information about the program:
Concepts and principles of comparative analysis, with an examination of politics and government in selected countries.

Contact
(202) 994-6360
gwsummer@gwu.edu

Name of College
Georgetown University

Name of Program
Law Institute

Academic / Career Interest
Law

Website
https://summer.georgetown.edu/programs/SHS16/law-institute

Application Timeline
Contact institution for more information

Eligibility
To apply to the Summer Programs for High School Students, students must meet the following criteria:

- Be a current high school freshman, sophomore, or junior during the upcoming academic year
- Show evidence of good academic standing, with at least a 2.0 GPA
- Have no history of suspension from high school

Tuition Fees
Estimated fees: $2,895

Information about the program:
From corporate attorneys and prosecutors to politicians and a sitting Supreme Court justice, many of the nation's lawmakers, administrators, and interpreters received their education at Georgetown. Through lectures, field trips, guest speakers, and discussion sections, our program offers not only an introduction to jurisprudence, but also a firsthand look at how laws are adjudicated and administered. Students examine the most vexing issues of our day and explore how America's legal institutions change as popular values, standards, and perspectives evolve. At the end of the program, students will have the opportunity to put their skills to practice and take part in a complete mock trial.

Contact
(202) 687-7087
highschool@georgetown.edu

Name of College
Georgetown University

Name of Program
American Politics Institute

Academic / Career Interest
American Politics

Website
https://summer.georgetown.edu/programs/SHS01/american-politics-institute

Application Timeline
Contact institution for more information

Eligibility
To apply to the Summer Programs for High School Students, students must meet the following criteria:

- Be a current high school freshman, sophomore, or junior during the upcoming academic year
- Show evidence of good academic standing, with at least a 2.0 GPA
- Have no history of suspension from high school

Tuition Fees
Estimated fees: $2,895

Information about the program:
In the American Politics Institute, students take an in-depth look at the three branches of government through a blend of classroom lectures and hands-on debate and simulation exercises. Students will learn about the important role that political parties, public opinion, and special interest groups can have on shaping political behavior and decisions while exploring how America's changing culture impacts political movements, and ultimately, federal, state, and local policies.

Contact
(202) 687-7087
highschool@georgetown.edu

Name of College
Georgetown University

Name of Program
Social Justice & Public Policy Institute

Academic / Career Interest
Social Justice and Public Policy

Website
https://summer.georgetown.edu/programs/SHS21/social-jus-tice-public-policy-immersion

Application Timeline
Contact institution for more information

Eligibility
To apply to the Summer Programs for High School Students, students must be a current Sophomore or Junior.

Tuition Fees
Estimated fees: $6,199

Information about the program:
The Social Justice & Public Policy Immersion introduces students to the complex role of public policy through the lens of social justice. Students explore models and methods of public policy to gain an interdisciplinary understanding to analyze real-world problems. Students will reflect on the meaning of democracy, freedom, justice and equality; investigate how advocacy leads to change in public policy; develop capacity for leadership; and become part of a community committed to personal growth.
Taking advantage of our location in the heart of the nation's capital, students have the opportunity to engage with policy think tanks and organizations that defend and work in areas of civil, economic, labor, and human rights.
Focusing on one of four issues—Women & Gender Issues, LGBT Issues, Racial Justice, and Economic Justice—students will work in groups to explore and implement advocacy strategies to promote public awareness-building and policy reform.

Contact
(202) 687-7087
highschool@georgetown.edu

Name of College
Harvard University

Name of Program
Pre-College Program: Introduction to American Law

Academic / Career Interest
Law

Website
https://www.summer.harvard.edu/courses/introduction-american-law/33407

Application Timeline
Contact institution for more information

Eligibility
Students must meet the following requirements:

- Will graduate in 2019 or 2020
- Are at least 15 years old by December 1, and will not turn 19 years old before July 31,

Tuition Fees
Estimated fees:

- Application fee (nonrefundable): $50
- Full program fee: $4,500
- Health insurance fee: $100

Information about the program:
This course introduces students to the US legal system by considering several central or important procedural and substantive aspects of American law. Included among the topics covered are the basic structure and function of US legal institutions; basics of subject matter and personal jurisdiction of American courts; the interaction of state and federal law in the American system of federalism; selected doctrines of constitutional law; selected topics pertaining to the American criminal and civil justice systems; and trial by jury.

Contact
(617) 495-4024
precollege@summer.harvard.edu

Name of College
Harvard University

Name of Program
Pre-College Program: On the Witness Stand: Scientific Evidence in the American Judicial System

Academic / Career Interest
Law

Website
https://www.summer.harvard.edu/courses/witness-stand-scientific-evidence-american-judicial-system/33641

Application Timeline
Contact institution for more information

Eligibility
Students must meet the following requirements:

- Are at least 15 years old by December 1, and will not turn 19 years old before July 31

Tuition Fees
Estimated fees:

- Application fee (nonrefundable): $50
- Full program fee: $4,500
- Health insurance fee: $100

Information about the program:
Scientific evidence can serve as a powerful witness in the courts. In this course, we evaluate the legal response to novel scientific evidence (x-rays, fingerprints, polygraphs) and consider recent challenges to ballistics, arson science, interrogation, and identification techniques—exploring science and law as they negotiate the complex relationship between justice and truth.

Contact
(617) 495-4024
precollege@summer.harvard.edu

Name of College
Harvard University

Name of Program
Pre-College Program: Constitutional Law, Civil Rights, and Civil Liberties

Academic / Career Interest
Law

Website
https://www.summer.harvard.edu/courses/constitutional-law-civil-rights-civil-liberties/33814

Application Timeline
Contact institution for more information

Eligibility
Students must meet the following requirements:

- Are at least 15 years old by December 1, and will not turn 19 years old before July 31

Tuition Fees
Estimated fees:

- Application fee (nonrefundable): $50
- Full program fee: $4,500
- Health insurance fee: $100

Information about the program:
This course provides a broad introduction to American constitutional law and to contemporary debates about civil rights and civil liberties in the United States. Students learn about fundamental principles of constitutional interpretation, the basic legal limitations on governmental power, the relationship between law and society, and arguments around controversial topics such as affirmative action, free speech, freedom of religion, abortion, and government surveillance. In the process, students also deepen their understanding of US politics and see how the judiciary often functions as a key player in our political system.

Contact
(617) 495-4024
precollege@summer.harvard.edu

Name of College
Harvard University

Name of Program
Pre-College Program: Intellectual Property Law for the Start-up and Entrepreneur

Academic / Career Interest
Law

Website
https://www.summer.harvard.edu/courses/intellectual-property-law-start-entrepreneur/33839

Application Timeline
Contact institution for more information

Eligibility
Students must meet the following requirements at least 15 years old by December 1, and will not turn 19 years old before July 31

Tuition Fees
Estimated fee is $4,500

Information about the program:
This course covers the intersection between start-ups, entrepreneurship, and intellectual property (IP) law. Students gain skills with navigation of major tenets of intellectual property law including patents, trademarks, copyrights, and trade secrets as these concepts relate to start-ups and entrepreneurship. Students also gain experience in presenting "shark tank" and more formal pitches, which incorporate references to the IP holdings of start-ups or small businesses. Further, students receive an introduction to the basics of contract instruments which allow for sharing of IP with entities outside of a start-up while protecting the IP of the start-up. Students are also exposed to the IP litigation landscape which start-ups face using actual litigation matters.

Contact
(617) 495-4024
precollege@summer.harvard.edu

Name of College
Harvard University

Name of Program
Pre-College Program: Introduction to Criminal Law and Criminal Procedure

Academic / Career Interest
Law

Website
https://www.summer.harvard.edu/courses/introduction-criminal-law-criminal-procedure/33961

Application Timeline
Contact institution for more information

Eligibility
Students must meet the following requirements:

- Are at least 15 years old by December 1 and will not turn 19 years old before July 31

Tuition Fees
Estimated fees:

- Application fee (nonrefundable): $50
- Full program fee: $4,500
- Health insurance fee: $100

Information about the program:
This course introduces students to the relevant constitutional, statutory, and common law, and the procedural process of the US criminal legal system. In exploring criminal law and criminal procedure, students gain an understanding of the organization of the US criminal legal system, how to review and analyze constitutional and statutory provisions, the key players (including police officers, prosecuting and criminal defense attorneys, judges, witnesses, and juries), and how criminal cases move through this system from investigation and arrest to conviction and sentencing

Contact
(617) 495-4024
precollege@summer.harvard.edu

Name of College
Harvard University

Name of Program
Pre-College Program: Introduction to Litigation Practice

Academic / Career Interest
Law

Website
https://www.summer.harvard.edu/courses/introduction-litigation-practice/34097

Application Timeline
Contact institution for more information

Eligibility
Students must meet the following requirements:

- Are at least 15 years old by December 1 and will not turn 19 years old before July 31

Tuition Fees
Estimated fees:

- Application fee (nonrefundable): $50
- Full program fee: $4,500
- Health insurance fee: $100

Information about the program:
This course introduces students to the US civil legal system, specifically litigation practice within this system. Students gain legal analysis, research, writing, and advocacy skills through involvement in two mock trial cases. Specifically, students gain experience in drafting common pleadings including a complaint and a motion for summary judgment, and developing and delivering opening and closing statements. Students are also exposed to activities related to litigation which occur outside of the courtroom such as discovery, which includes document requests, interrogatories, and depositions. In addition, students are provided with the ethical framework which governs attorneys in the litigation context.

Contact
(617) 495-4024
precollege@summer.harvard.edu

Name of College
Harvard University

Name of Program
Secondary School Program: Global Law, Global History: A Comparative Perspective

Academic / Career Interest
Law

Website
https://www.summer.harvard.edu/courses/global-law-global-history-comparative-perspective/33649

Application Timeline
Contact institution for more information

Eligibility
Students must meet the following requirements:

- Are at least 15 years old by December 1 and will not turn 19 years old before July 31

Tuition Fees
Estimated fees is $4,500

Information about the program:
In this course, students read and discuss writings on global law and history from the eighteenth century to the present. In the process, they develop insight into the relation between the disciplines of law and history. This course allows students to discuss a variety of perspectives on state-building, nationalism, revolutions, empire, religion, and their relation to the world. This course also questions concepts such as civilization and progress and their impact in the history of global order. By introducing questions, themes, and approaches to the study of global law and history, this course provides a conceptual toolbox that may further students' interest in international relations, political science, international law, or global studies.

Contact
(617) 495-4024
precollege@summer.harvard.edu

Name of College
John Hopkins University

Name of Program
Pre-College: Political Science: The City in American Political Development

Academic / Career Interest
Political science

Website
https://summerprograms.jhu.edu/program/pre-college-students-summer-university/

Application Timeline
Contact institution for more information

Eligibility
Program Requirements:

- Must be at least 16 years old by June 30
- Have achieved at least a 3.0 grade point average (on a 4.0 scale)

Tuition Fees
Estimated fees:

- Residential:$10,070
- Commuter: $5,620

Information about the program:
The city is central to American life yet is underexplored in political science. This class explores urban politics through the lens of American Political Development (APD), which explores the historical progression of institutions both formal (legislature, executive, judiciary) and informal (parties, interest groups). Students will learn key research topics in APD, be able to explain American institutional development from founding to present, and understand American urban politics, including issues of race, class and gender.

Contact
(410) 516-4548
summer@jhu.edu

Name of College
University of Maryland

Name of Program
Terp Young Scholars: Public Policy- Leadership for the Common Good

Academic / Career Interest
Leadership

Website
https://oes.umd.edu/middle-high-school-students/terp-young-scholars/terp-young-scholars-courses/terp-young-scholars-public-policy

Application Timeline
Approx. June

Eligibility
To apply and participate, a student must:

- Be a high school freshmen, sophomore, junior, senior, or graduating senior
- Have an academic average of 3.25 or better (unweighted)

Tuition Fees
Estimated fees:

- $ 3,975: Residential Package Fee
- $ 2,795: Commuter Package Fee

Information about the program:
This course is designed to provide undergraduate students an introduction to leadership theory and a chance to practice a core set of practical skills relevant to transformational and collaborative leadership.

Contact
(301) 405-7762

Name of College
Miami University of Florida

Name of Program
Law - Litigation and the Legal Profession

Academic / Career Interest
Law

Website
https://ssp.dcie.miami.edu/program-information/academic-areas-of-study/index.html#law

Application Timeline
Contact institution for more information

Eligibility
Student Requirements:

- Completed sophomore or junior year of high school
- Grade point average of at least 3.0 (based on a 4.0 scale)

Tuition Fees
Estimated fees ranges from $6,000 - $7,000

Information about the program:
Consists of two courses.

Courtroom 101: Litigation Basics: This course will enhance the student's abilities to participate in mock trials, by incorporating techniques of witness direct and cross examination, exhibits, objections, opening statements and closing arguments. It will incorporate technology in the courtroom, as well as for preparation. The skills acquired will be helpful in almost any persuasion presentation, including lobbying, debate and negotiation.

Contact
(305) 284-4000
ssp@miami.edu

Name of College
University of Minnesota, Twin Cities

Name of Program
Just The Beginning Summer Legal Institute

Academic / Career Interest
Law

Website
https://www.law.umn.edu/events/just-beginning-summer-legal-in-stitute

Application Timeline
Approx. June

Eligibility
Program is open to all high school students

Tuition Fees
Estimated fees: free

Information about the program:
The Twin Cities Summer Legal Institute is a fun, educational, and interactive program hosted by the University of Minnesota Law School. The SLI provides high school students with exposure to legal careers, the opportunity to build legal and professional skills, and connections with judges, lawyers, and other leaders in the legal profession.

Contact
Krystle McNeely, Program Director, Just The Beginning – A Pipeline Organization
(312) 258-5930
kmcneely@jtb.org

Name of College
University of Notre Dame

Name of Program
Summer Scholars: The Law

Academic / Career Interest
Law

Website
http://precollege.nd.edu/courses/the-law/

Application Timeline
Approx. February

Eligibility
High school students who meet the following criteria may apply to Summer Scholars:

- Current sophomores and juniors
- Strong academic standing with solid extracurricular activities
- At least 16 years old by or on August 1

Tuition Fees
Estimated fees is $3,200

Information about the program:
From Capitol Hill to the county courthouse, the workings of law in American society have shaped, and continue to shape, our way of life. The Law course exposes Summer Scholars students to the many facets of the American legal system. The groundwork for this exciting track will be laid in the exploration of the United States Constitution as well as current legal issues.

Students participate in an active investigation of the court system, from both a civil and criminal law perspective.

Contact
(574) 631-0990
precoll@nd.edu

Name of College
Ohio University

Name of Program
Summer Law & Trial Institute

Academic / Career Interest
Law

Website
https://www.ohio.edu/cas/lawcenter/about/summer-institute.cfm

Application Timeline
Contact institution for more information

Eligibility
Preference will be given to high achieving, high school juniors and seniors from Southeast Ohio, though outstanding sophomores and high school students outside Southeast Ohio will be considered if space permits.

Tuition Fees
Estimated fees: free

Information about the program:
The Summer Law & Trial Institute is a 12-day immersive residential program that aims to increase understanding of the law and its possibilities among Ohio high school students from Southeast Ohio. The program also seeks to foster an interest in all aspects of legal education, service, and issues, and to create the next generation of legal, advocacy, and community professionals.

Students will gain exposure, through immersive academic study and experiential learning, to the criminal justice system and to law and justice issues relevant to Southeast Ohio, especially access to justice.

Contact
Larry Hayman, Program Director
(740) 593-0835
hayman@ohio.edu

Name of College
Oxford University

Name of Program
Law Academy

Academic / Career Interest
Law

Website
https://summerinoxford.com/courses/law-academy/

Application Timeline
Contact institution for more information

Eligibility
Students must be proficient in English and between the ages of 14 – 19. Only high school students are allowed to participate or students who just graduated from high school but not yet attending college or university.

Tuition Fees
Estimated fees: $3,980

Information about the program:
Thinking of becoming a lawyer or a judge? Interested in international business law, human rights, or criminal justice? Then join our Law School Academy to learn about the different options you will have when studying law at university. Find out about the different law subjects and learn how to work on actual cases.

Laws, regulations, and our whole legal systems heavily influence our professional lives, education system, health care, and many other aspects of our lives. As part of the Law School Academy students will find out how the law impacts all of us and how important legal contracts are. Additionally, we will analyze study options for law in Oxford, Cambridge, and other outstanding universities worldwide.

Contact
(703) 938-0897

Name of College
Patrick Henry College

Name of Program
Constitutional Law

Academic / Career Interest
Law

Website
https://www.phc.edu/constitutional-law-camp-2018

Application Timeline
Approx. June

Eligibility
Students must be 14-18 at the start of the camp they are attending

Tuition Fees
Estimated fees: $575

Information about the program:
At Constitutional Law Camp, students will explore our nation's founding documents and precedent-setting Supreme Court decisions. Students will get familiar with legal terms and complex judicial and legislative concepts, while learning to reflect critically about the Constitution's original intent. Students will receive cases to decide, as if they were a member of the Supreme Court, and you will get to apply the legal principles that they have learned, to come up with an oral opinion as Supreme Court Justices. Students will leave camp with a thorough understanding of the world's first and longest standing written constitution, the basis for how our country and its freedoms work.

Contact
(540) 441-8105
teencamps@phc.edu

Name of College
University of Pennsylvania

Name of Program
Summer Discovery: Law Academy

Academic / Career Interest
Law

Website
https://www.summerdiscovery.com/upenn-law/academic-options

Application Timeline
Contact institution for more information

Eligibility
For students completing grades 10, 11, 12 (ages 15-18)

Tuition Fees
Estimated fees:

- 3 Weeks: Pre-College $7,999
- 3 Weeks: Pre-College (Commuter) $5,999

Information about the program:
The Penn Law Pre-College Academy is a rigorous academic program that gives high school students the opportunity to experience law school at a world-class university. During this 3 week intensive Academy, learn what it means to be a lawyer while gaining a better understanding of the role of laws in modern society.

Taught and sponsored by the University of Pennsylvania Law School, classes mirror those taken by first year law students. Develop legal reasoning skills, review case briefings, and unravel constitutional, criminal, and contract law. Receive coaching and constructive feedback on writing assignments and oral argument skills.

Contact
(516) 621-3939
info@summerdiscovery.com

Name of College
Pennsylvania State University

Name of Program
Summer Discovery: Learning the Law & Its Impact

Academic / Career Interest
Law

Website
https://www.summerdiscovery.com/penn-state/cours-es#law-and-government

Application Timeline
Contact institution for more information

Eligibility
For students completing grades 9, 10, 11, 12 (ages 14-18)

Tuition Fees
Estimated fees: $4,399

Information about the program:
Penn State University offers over 20 different enrichment classes in a wide range of subjects. Students can take 2 classes or a full-day academy of their choice.

Engage in questions central to the foundation of law. What is law? Where does it come from? Why have law? Class will be structured similarly to a law school class, and will thus require students to use critical thinking and applied analytical skills in reading and discussing case law. Discussions will be fundamental when considering questions such as, how law has a societal impact on current events in America. Class discussion will cover constitutional rights, criminal law/procedures, civil procedure, contracts, torts, and property.

Contact
(516) 621-3939
info@summerdiscovery.com

Name of College
Rutgers University

Name of Program
Summer Scholars Course: American Government

Academic / Career Interest
American Government

Website
https://summerscholars.rutgers.edu/courses/american-government

Application Timeline
Contact institution for more information

Eligibility
High school students who are age 16 or above, with a minimum grade-point average of 3.0, are invited to apply to the Summer Scholars Program. Students under the age of 16 will be considered on a case-by-case basis.

Tuition Fees
Estimated fees:

- NJ Resident per Credit: $374
- Non-resident per credit: $894
- Student Fee: $162

Information about the program:
Comprehensive analysis of American political institutions. Issues and problems faced by federal, state, and local governments under the impact of modern conditions. The leading political, economic, and social influences affecting democratic government.

Contact
(848) 932-7565
wsru@docs.rutgers.edu

Name of College
Rutgers University

Name of Program
Summer Scholars Course: Nature of Politics

Academic / Career Interest
Politics

Website
https://summerscholars.rutgers.edu/courses/nature-politics

Application Timeline
Contact institution for more information

Eligibility
High school students who are age 16 or above, with a minimum grade-point average of 3.0, are invited to apply to the Summer Scholars Program. Students under the age of 16 will be considered on a case-by-case basis.

Tuition Fees
Estimated fees:

- NJ Resident per Credit: $374
- Non-resident per credit: $894
- Student Fee: $162

Information about the program:
Crucial issues in politics: individual and community; political obligation and civil disobedience; stability, revolution, and change; legitimacy and justice; freedom and power.

Contact
(848) 932-7565
wsru@docs.rutgers.edu

Name of College
Sam Houston State University

Name of Program
CJ Summer Camp

Academic / Career Interest
Criminal justice

Website
http://www.shsu.edu/academics/criminal-justice/events/camp.html

Application Timeline
Approx. March

Eligibility
Open to high school students age 15-17

Tuition Fees
Estimated fees: $700

Information about the program:
For students who dream of a career in criminal justice, come get a glimpse of the real deal. Visit with law enforcement agents, professors, and criminal justice students, as well as go on tours of a prison, crime lab, and morgue. Participate in activities that give you hands-on experience, such as investigating a mock crime scene, being arrested, arresting someone else, and the like.

Contact
(936) 294-3170
cjadvising@shsu.edu

Name of College
University of Southern California

Name of Program
Exploring Criminal Justice

Academic / Career Interest
Criminal Justice

Website
https://summerprograms.usc.edu/programs/4-week/explor-ing-criminal-justice/

Application Timeline
Approx. April

Eligibility
High school students who have completed at least the 9th grade by the start of the program are eligible to apply

Tuition Fees
Estimated fees:

- Residential $8,534
- Commuter $6,059

Information about the program:
Should our criminal justice system seek to punish criminals, or to promote rehabilitation? How should we treat individuals who commit crimes in their youth? Is there a better way to spend the $71,000 a year that it costs to house an inmate in California?

In this course, students will critically examine criminal justice from a legal, political, economic, and historical perspective. Through guest speakers, field trips, documentaries, and reports from the front lines, students learn about California's recent efforts to reduce prison populations and increase community investments. Most powerfully, students will have first-hand interactions with the individuals who are most impacted by the criminal justice system.

Contact
(213) 740-5679
summer@usc.edu

Name of College
University of Southern California

Name of Program
Legal Reasoning and Argumentation

Academic / Career Interest
Law

Website
https://summerprograms.usc.edu/programs/4-week/legal-reasoning/

Application Timeline
Approx. April 27

Eligibility
High school students who have completed at least the 9th grade by the start of the program are eligible to apply.

Tuition Fees
Estimated fees:

- Residential $8,534
- Commuter $6,059

Information about the program:
Students learn how lawyers think, and why they think, differently from other people. Learn the skills necessary for successful legal reasoning and how to relate this knowledge to everyday problems.

Attend federal appellate court proceedings and see these skills applied (and mis-applied) in real life. At the end of the course, students will have a portfolio of documents that demonstrate your experience with legal analysis and writing.

Contact
(213) 740-5679
summer@usc.edu

Name of College
Stanford University (Envision Summer Program)

Name of Program
Intensive Law & Trial

Academic / Career Interest
Law

Website
https://www.envisionexperience.com/explore-our-programs/intensive-law-and-trial

Application Timeline
Contact institution for more information

Eligibility
Application open to high school students

Tuition Fees
Estimated fees: $3,995

Information about the program:
Intensive Law & Trial allows students to become immersed in the theory and practice of law and to develop a roadmap for becoming a lawyer. At this 10-day program students will be exposed to the practice of law, legal rhetoric, and ethics from pre-eminent legal professionals, including Stanford Law School professors. Students also develop and practice essential legal skills such as making impactful opening and closing arguments, preparing cases, and readying witnesses for cross-examinations.

In a simulation endorsed by the American Mock Trial Association, students will prepare for a court case, just as any attorney does—they'll practice the art of creating effective oral arguments, directly examine and cross-examine witnesses, gain an understanding of evidence and its integrity, and learn how to manage a courtroom. Powerful skills workshops will help students develop their own personal mission statement to set and attain future academic and career goals.

Contact
(703) 584-9380
envisioninfo@envisionexperience.com

Name of College
Stanford University

Name of Program
Pre-Collegiate Summer Institutes: Topics in Politics and Public Policy: Deliberative Democracy

Academic / Career Interest
Politics and Public Policy

Website
https://summerinstitutes.spcs.stanford.edu/courses/2018/topics-politics-and-public-policy-deliberative-democracy

Application Timeline
Early Deadline: approx. January
Regular Deadline: approx. February
Extended Deadline: approx. March

Eligibility
Students must be in grades 9-11 at the time of application.

Tuition Fees
Estimated fees: $6,850

Information about the program:
This reading and writing intensive course examines the theory and practice of democracy, deliberative democracy and engages in a dialogue with critics. The course will discuss whether a democracy, which emphasizes people thinking and talking together on the basis of good information, can be made practical in the modern age. What kinds of distortions arise when people try to discuss politics or policy together? The course draws on ideas as well as criticisms from the jury literature, from the psychology of group processes and from the most recent normative and empirical literature on deliberative forums.

Contact
precollegiate@stanford.edu

Name of College
Stanford University

Name of Program
Pre-Collegiate Summer Institutes: Political Science

Academic / Career Interest
Political Science

Website
https://summerinstitutes.spcs.stanford.edu/courses/2018/political-science-0

Application Timeline
Early Deadline: approx. January
Regular Deadline: approx. February
Extended Deadline: approx. March

Eligibility
Students must be in grades 9-11 at the time of application.

Tuition Fees
Estimated fees: $6,850

Information about the program:
In the 1990s, political scientists believed that the "end of history" was inevitable: that with the triumph of liberal capitalist democracy world wide, the age of ideological conflict was over. Few predictions have turned out to be so wrong. Today, in Europe, Latin America, the Middle East, East Asia and in the US, we have seen the reemergence of ideological conflict, debates over the nature of populism and fascism, calls for socialism and the critique of capitalism, a re-energized conservatism and the revolutionary reappearance of religious political movements.
The first aim of this course is to help us interpret the ideologies that make up our current political world by exploring the classical political ideologies of the modern political age: liberalism, conservatism, fascism, socialism and capitalism.

Contact
precollegiate@stanford.edu

Name of College
Stanford University

Name of Program
Pre-Collegiate Summer Institutes: Legal Studies

Academic / Career Interest
Legal Studies

Website
https://summerinstitutes.spcs.stanford.edu/courses/2018/legal-studies

Application Timeline
Early Deadline: approx. January
Regular Deadline: approx. February
Extended Deadline: approx. March

Eligibility
Students must be in grades 9-11 at the time of application.

Tuition Fees
Estimated fees: $6,850

Information about the program:
This course provides students with an introduction to the American legal system. Students will begin developing the imaginative, critical, analytical, and technical skills necessary to "think like a lawyer". Students will be exposed to a wide variety of legal topics, discuss and debate legal issues and real life cases, and learn practical methods for dealing with legal problems. Civil, criminal, and constitutional law issues will be included. While this course is of particular value for those who contemplate becoming attorneys, any student interested in developing and refining their communication and public speaking skills will enjoy the lively debates and discussions which are the primary means of instruction. Past activities of this course have included role-playing, mock trials, computer simulations, negotiations, a lecture by a guest speaker, and a field trip.

Contact
precollegiate@stanford.edu

Name of College
State University of New York, Binghamton

Name of Program
Speech and Debate

Academic / Career Interest
Speech and Debate

Website
https://www.binghamton.edu/admissions/summer-college/pro-grams-offered.html

Application Timeline
Contact institution for more information

Eligibility
Contact institution for more information

Tuition Fees
Estimated fees: $985

Information about the program:
In this accelerated one-week program students will learn to form, research and deliver arguments through a variety of different debate styles. The course is designed to be challenging and interesting for all students, whatever their level of prior debate experience. Most days will be spent learning through hands-on activities that emphasize participation. By the end of the one-week class, students will be better able to deliver and write speeches, research and prepare arguments, as well as navigate the information overload that comes with debating in the age of the Internet. Students who participated in the two-week program will serve as student leaders, coaches and judges.

Contact
BSC@binghamton.edu

Name of College
Syracuse University

Name of Program
Criminal and Corporate Law

Academic / Career Interest
Law

Website
http://summercollege.syr.edu/program/criminal-justice/

Application Timeline
Approx. June

Eligibility
Students must be a minimum of 15 years of age by the orientation and move-in date

Tuition Fees
Contact institution for more information

Information about the program:
This program provides an extensive survey of criminal law and procedure and corporate law.
While exploring criminal law, the course will track what happens from apprehension and arrest to due process and sentencing. We will also learn about the policies and various participants in modern criminal law.
In corporate law, we will dedicate our time to hands-on areas such as Business Formation, Wills and Estates, Real Estate, and Contracts.

A field trip to the court each week is the highlight of the summer program.

Contact
(315) 443-5000

Name of College
University of Texas, Austin

Name of Program
Law Academy

Academic / Career Interest
Law

Website
https://www.summerdiscovery.com/u-texas-austin

Application Timeline
Contact institution for more information.

Eligibility
For students completing grades 9, 10, 11, 12 (ages 14-18)

Tuition Fees
Estimated fees $3,000- $5,000

Information about the program:
Law Academy Interested in law? This academy provides high-achieving students an introduction to the core areas of U.S. law (constitutional, contract, and criminal law), covered in all 1st year law schools, and a preview of the type of attorney you might want to become, transactional or litigation law. This academy combines the Intro to Law and Trial Tactics classes.

Intro to Law: Learn about the U.S. law and the legal system, including an overview of the U.S. Constitution and basic procedures of civil and criminal courts, and consider the relationship between laws and justice. Interactive, discussion-based class focused on key Constitutional issues. Learn to read cases, identify key legal issues, and make cogent legal argument. Taught by practicing attorney.

Contact
(516) 621-3939
info@summerdiscovery.com

Name of College
University of Toronto

Name of Program
Trial Advocacy: Represent Your Client in Court and Win Your Case!

Academic / Career Interest
Law

Website
http://ysp.utoronto.ca/law/

Application Timeline
Applications are open until program is full.

Eligibility
Students in grades 10th to 12th are eligible to apply.

Tuition Fees
Estimated fees: $900 + $98 registration fee

Information about the program:
What makes lawyers successful in court? How do they persuade judges and juries to rule in their favour? How do they ensure they represent their clients to the best of their abilities?

During this module, students develop their individual advocacy styles, acquiring a strong understanding of trail processes and courtroom etiquette. Working with leading litigators and justice sector professionals, students develop trial strategies and put their theories of the case to the test in a final mock trial.

Contact
(647) 649-0829
ysp@lawinaction.ca

Name of College
University of Toronto

Name of Program
Criminal Law: Prosecute and Defend Murder!

Academic / Career Interest
Law

Website
http://ysp.utoronto.ca/law/

Application Timeline
Applications are open until program is full.

Eligibility
Students in grades 10th to 12th are eligible to apply.

Tuition Fees
Estimated fees: $900 + $98 registration fee

Information about the program:
In contrast to the popular portrayal of criminal law presented in bestselling novels and Hollywood movies, this module engages students in the realities of criminal legal practice by immersing them in the proceedings of a murder trial. In preparation for their culminating mock trials, students work with leading criminal litigators to develop complex legal strategies, weigh evidence, consider possible defenses, prepare and examine witnesses, and deliver persuasive arguments in a courtroom setting.

Contact
(647) 649-0829
ysp@lawinaction.ca

Name of College
University of Toronto

Name of Program
Corporate Law: Negotiate Big Business Deals!

Academic / Career Interest
Law

Website
http://ysp.utoronto.ca/law/

Application Timeline
Applications are open until program is full.

Eligibility
Students in grades 10th to 12th are eligible to apply.

Tuition Fees
Estimated fees: $900 + $98 registration fee

Information about the program:
What is a corporation? What are its legal responsibilities and obligations?

Relationships between corporations and the law are complex, often surrounded by significant degrees of controversy. During this module, students engage with leading corporate lawyers and experts, and visit top Canadian corporate law firms and in-house legal departments. They immerse themselves in complex legal simulations, exploring corporate mergers and acquisitions, contracts, negotiation and corporate social responsibility.

Contact
(647) 649-0829
ysp@lawinaction.ca

Name of College
University of Toronto

Name of Program
International Law: Protect Human Rights and Examine International Norms!

Academic / Career Interest
Law

Website
http://ysp.utoronto.ca/law/

Application Timeline
Applications are open until program is full.

Eligibility
Students in grades 10th to 12th are eligible to apply.

Tuition Fees
Estimated fees: $900 + $98 registration fee

Information about the program:
When is the international community responsible for interfering in cross-border matters? Should global institutions prosecute individuals or censure rogue states? Is there 'one law that binds us all'? Through dynamic workshops, debates, lectures, field trips and interactive activities, students learn to frame issues in the language of international law, explore the world of global human rights, and examine institutions such as the United Nations and the International Criminal Court.

Contact
(647) 649-0829
ysp@lawinaction.ca

Name of College
University of Toronto

Name of Program
Law and Politics: Debate Policy and Create Law!

Academic / Career Interest
Law

Website
http://ysp.utoronto.ca/law/

Application Timeline
Applications are open until program is full.

Eligibility
Students in grades 10th to 12th are eligible to apply.

Tuition Fees
Estimated fees: $900 + $98 registration fee

Information about the program:
Whose role is it to create law in a democratic society? Who gets to vote or to run for office? How and why does the law change over time? In this module, students examine our political framework through a legal lens, develop oral advocacy skills, weigh society's complex needs and interests, and gain a deep understanding of the importance of respectful debate in a democratic society. Engaging with legal experts and exploring leading Canadian political institutions, this module immerses students in a challenging and rewarding political simulation that culminates in a Parliamentary debate.

Contact
(647) 649-0829
ysp@lawinaction.ca

Name of College
Tufts University

Name of Program
College Experience: Foundations of Law & Ethics

Academic / Career Interest
Law

Website
https://summer.tufts.edu/study-pre-college-courses.asp

Application Timeline
Approx. May

Eligibility
Students entering Grades 11-12 are eligible to apply.

Tuition Fees
Estimated fees: $10,000

Information about the program:
Each student must take 2 courses during the application process.
The Foundations of Law & Ethics program will introduce students
to the fundamental concepts of legal thinking, examined through the
lens of historical and contemporary issues. Students will improve
their ability to write and convey viewpoints more clearly, assess the
validity of arguments, and learn to identify mistakes in reasoning.
Exploring these foundations of legal thought and practice will give
students the opportunity to see themselves in the role of an advocate for others and help to assess their interest in this field.

Contact
(617) 981-7008
summer@tufts.edu

Name of College
Tufts University

Name of Program
College Experience: Western Political Thought II

Academic / Career Interest
Law

Website
https://summer.tufts.edu/study-pre-college-courses.asp

Application Timeline
Approx. May

Eligibility
Students entering Grades 11-12 are eligible to apply.

Tuition Fees
Estimated fees: $10,000

Information about the program:
Each student must take 2 courses during the application process. Central concepts of modern political thought. The views of those writers who challenged the dominance of Christianity: Machiavelli, Descartes, Hobbes, and others. Some of the main transformations of political thinking that characterized the Enlightenment: the possibility of scientific thinking and reasoning as the basis for human freedom. Nietzsche's critique of the Enlightenment, and the ability to find political principles that are genuinely true or liberating.

Contact
(617) 981-7008
summer@tufts.edu

Name of College
Vanderbilt University

Name of Program
The Fourth Branch of Government: Welcome to the Administrative State

Academic / Career Interest
Law

Website
https://s3.amazonaws.com/vu-wp0/wp-content/uploads/sites/18/2018/01/05172015/PTY-Summer-Academy-Catalog-2018_FINAL.pdf

Application Timeline
Contact institution for more information

Eligibility
For students who will be entering 9th or 10th grade in fall.

Tuition Fees
Estimated fees: $2,750

Information about the program:
Students have probably heard about the three branches of government—legislative, executive, and judicial— but did they know there is an unofficial fourth? The administrative state refers to the departments that arguably have the most impact on our everyday lives. The breakfast we eat is regulated by the Department of Agriculture; the things we buy by the Federal Trade Commission; the tests students take by the Department of Education. This course will examine the processes that create the agencies that seem to run so much of our lives and the methods used to carry out their missions. As a class, students should expect to engage in judicial review of agency processes and other limits that restrict administrative power. The administrative state influences every part of our lives, so to be an informed citizen or political influencer, take hold of this unofficial branch and explore.

Contact
(615) 322-3173
vsa.pty@vanderbilt.edu

Name of College
Wake Forest University

Name of Program
Summer Immersion: Law Institute

Academic / Career Interest
Law

Website
https://immersion.summer.wfu.edu/institutes/law-institute/

Application Timeline
Applications are open until program is full.

Eligibility
Rising sophomores, juniors, and seniors in high school and incoming college freshmen are eligible to apply.

Tuition Fees
Estimated fees:

- $1,450 (Non-Residential)
- $2,250 (Residential)

Information about the program:
Find out what it's really like to be a lawyer. This is a chance to learn about civil and criminal litigation as well as analyze and argue a case in a moot court simulation. Students have the opportunity to explore corporate, intellectual property and international law practices. They will learn to make an argument, network with judges and attorneys and dive into the legal industry to discover if this is the career path for them.

Contact
(336) 758-5000

Name of College
The College of William & Mary

Name of Program
Introduction to Law

Academic / Career Interest
Law

Website
https://education.wm.edu/centers/cfge/precollegiate/HSLawSummer/flyer-intro-to-law-hs-students-2018.pdf

Application Timeline
Registration is open until program is full.

Eligibility
Registration is open to all high school students.

Tuition Fees
Estimated fees: $330

Information about the program:
This program will explain United States law, how it is made, and how judges can change the law. This interactive and thought-provoking program will help students understand how the judicial branch interprets, creates, and modifies the legal rules.

- Emphasizes logical thinking and writing
- Traces the sources of our laws
- Introduces the separate function of lawmakers and courts
- Uses primary and secondary sources
- Addresses many Virginia SOL requirements for U.S. Government

Contact
(757) 221-2494
clct@wm.edu

Name of College
The College of William & Mary

Name of Program
Introduction to Artificial Intelligence & the Law

Academic / Career Interest
Law

Website
https://education.wm.edu/centers/cfge/precollegiate/HSLawSummer/flyer-for-intro-to-ai-and-the-law-2.6.2018.pdf

Application Timeline
Registration is open until program is full.

Eligibility
Registration is open to all high school students.

Tuition Fees
Estimated fees: $190

Information about the program:
    Open to high school and college students, this one-of-a-kind program in legal education provides an introduction to selected legal issues that we may face as Artificial Intelligence and other groundbreaking technologies advance.

Participants will:

- Understand the concepts of Artificial Intelligence (AI), machine learning, and deep learning, data analytics, and the Internet of Things by reference to real-life examples
- Identify and discuss selected legal risks associated with the combination of AI, data analytics, the Internet-of-Things and related technologies, including cybersecurity, privacy law, civil and criminal liability, and issues under the law of war

Contact
(757) 221-2494
clct@wm.edu

Name of College
The College of William & Mary

Name of Program
Introduction to Evidence

Academic / Career Interest
Law

Website
https://education.wm.edu/centers/cfge/precollegiate/HSLawSummer/flyer-intro-to-evidence-hs-students-2018-4.25.18.pdf

Application Timeline
Registration is open until program is full.

Eligibility
Registration is open to all high school students.

Tuition Fees
Estimated fees: $190

Information about the program:
Available now to high school-aged students, Prove it! Introduction to Evidence is an interactive study of the rules that govern the types of information that can be used in court. To be admissible in court, information – evidence – must logically prove or disprove a matter in issue and must comply with a wide range of restrictions based on reliability concerns and public policy.

Among other topics, the course includes:

- Hearsay
- Relevance
- Best Evidence
- Authentication
- Procedure

Contact
(757) 221-2494
clct@wm.edu

Name of College
The College of William & Mary

Name of Program
Introduction to Search & Seizure

Academic / Career Interest
Law

Website
https://education.wm.edu/centers/cfge/precollegiate/HSLawSummer/flyer-intro-to-search-and-seizure-hs-students-2018.pdf

Application Timeline
Registration is open until program is full.

Eligibility
Registration is open to all high school students.

Tuition Fees
Estimated fees: $190

Information about the program:
This course will study the law of search and seizure. The course covers key aspects of how the Fourth Amendment governs law enforcement's ability to search and seize. Students also will examine how the United States Supreme Court has interpreted the Fourth Amendment.

Topics include:

- The warrant and probable cause requirements of the Fourth Amendment
- Exceptions including consent, border searches, emergency searches, stop and frisk, and searches incident to a lawful arrest

Contact
(757) 221-2494
clct@wm.edu

Name of College
The College of William & Mary

Name of Program
Introduction to Torts

Academic / Career Interest
Law

Website
https://education.wm.edu/centers/cfge/precollegiate/HSLawSummer/flyer-intro-to-torts-hs-students-2018.pdf

Application Timeline
Registration is open until program is full.

Eligibility
Registration is open to all high school students.

Tuition Fees
Estimated fees: $190

Information about the program:
This program will explore the basic foundation of the American tort law system. Through interactive class sessions and thought-provoking discussions, this course will help students understand the basic concepts of negligence and liability in the modern world.

- Emphasizes logical thinking and writing
- Introduces the fundamental elements of negligence, including duty, breach, causation, and damages
- Provides the opportunity for students to read, analyze, and apply case law to real-life
  situations

Contact
(757) 221-2494
clct@wm.edu

Name of College
The College of William & Mary

Name of Program
Introduction to Contract Law

Academic / Career Interest
Law

Website
https://education.wm.edu/centers/cfge/precollegiate/HSLawSummer/flyer-for-intro-to-contract-law-2018.pdf

Application Timeline
Registration is open until program is full.

Eligibility
Registration is open to all high school students.

Tuition Fees
Estimated fees: $210

Information about the program:
This course is aimed at high school and college students who are interested in understanding the basic element of commercial life: contracts. Through interactive and hands-on class sessions, participants will be guided through an introduction to American contract law.

With a mixture of critical thinking and analytical writing, participants will be encouraged to:

- Understand the basic components of a binding contract
- Analyze clauses taken from real-life contracts and discuss their effect
- Explore what happens to a contract when "things go wrong": this will cover areas such as misrepresentation, implied terms, breach of contract and damages
- During the last class, participants will be required to draft their own first contract

Contact
(757) 221-2494
clct@wm.edu

Psychology Collegiate Programs

Name of College
Boston College

Name of Program
Introduction to Psychology Seminar

Academic / Career Interest
Psychology

Website
https://www.bc.edu/bc-web/sites/bc-experience/programs/
non-credit-programs/intro-to-psychology.html

Application Timeline
Rolling Admission Every Two Weeks
Final Deadline: approx. May

Eligibility
Students entering grades 10, 11 & 12 are eligible to apply

Tuition Fees
Estimated cost:
Resident: $4500
Commuter: $2500

Information about the program:
This course covers four units: history of psychology, clinical skills, psychopathology, and research methods (with special topic in neuropsychology). Through a multi-modal class design incorporating lectures, readings, film, field-trips to outstanding Boston institutions, and hands-on class participation in clinical diagnosis, therapy, and case presentation, students gain experience as real-life professionals in the mental health field.

Contact
(617) 552-3800
bce@bc.edu

Name of College
University of California, Riverside

Name of Program
Summer Academy: Introductory Psychology

Academic / Career Interest
Psychology

Website
http://summeracademy.ucr.edu

Application Timeline
Contact institution for more information

Eligibility
Students must be a current (spring) high school freshman, sophomore or junior with a minimum GPA of 3.5

Tuition Fees
$691

Information about the program:
An introduction to psychology as an experimental science. Emphasizes topics in cognitive (including learning, memory, sensation, perception), comparative, and physiological psychology.

Contact
(951) 827-7739
SummerAcademy@ucr.edu

Name of College
University of California, Santa Cruz

Name of Program
Psychology Summer Courses

Academic / Career Interest
Psychology

Website
https://summer.ucsc.edu/courses/psyc.html

Application Timeline
Register approx. April

Eligibility
Students who completed their sophomore or junior year with a GPA of 3.0+ can live and learn at UCSC!

Tuition Fees
Total one course tuition plus living on campus = $2464.50 - $2892.50

Information about the program:
In the Summer University, students will:
-Gain academic credit that transfer to a future college or university (or back to high school)
-Have access to libraries, labs, fitness center and everything Santa Cruz has to offer
-Enjoy a welcome reception on Sunday - parents welcome! (details will be sent to registered students)
-Understand research university culture and academic expectations

Contact
(831) 459-5373
summer@usc.edu

Name of College
University of Chicago

Name of Program
UChicago Immersion: The Psychology of Learning

Academic / Career Interest
Psychology of learning

Website
https://summer.uchicago.edu/course/psychology-learning

Application Timeline
Approx. May

Eligibility
This course is open to high school students

Tuition Fees
$6,500

Information about the program:
Humans' ability to learn from and teach others is a feature that sets our species apart. Students will investigate learning across the lifespan. What hinders learning and what enhances it? We will learn about engagement, memory, analogical reasoning, executive function, social-emotional components of learning, mindset, "grit", insight, stereotype threat and more. Students will observe learning in formal (e.g., classrooms) and informal settings (e.g., museums) and then conduct their own study of learning with human subjects.

Contact
UChicago Summer Session
5845 South Ellis Avenue
Gates-Blake 509 S. Ellis Avenue
Chicago, IL 60637

Name of College
University of Chicago

Name of Program
UChicago Immersion: Developmental Psychology: Theories and Techniques

Academic / Career Interest
Psychology

Website
https://summer.uchicago.edu/course/developmental-psychology-theories-and-techniques

Application Timeline
Approx. May 1

Eligibility
This course is open to high school students

Tuition Fees
$6,500

Information about the program:
In just a few short years, infants go from helpless beings who cannot even hold their heads up to walking, talking, thinking people who are able to understand complex games, infer intentions in others, and even engage in reflexive thought (i.e., thinking about thinking). In this class, we will explore this transition by studying major theories of developmental psychology, examining how the mind (and correspondingly, the brain) changes from infancy through adolescence. We will focus on primary empirical sources investigating the development and integration of perceptual, cognitive, and social skills. Lecture and discussion will emphasize the complex interplay between biological, psychological, and sociocultural elements throughout the life span in domains such as language, emotions, morality, and intelligence.

Contact
Contact the program website

Name of College
Colorado College

Name of Program
Pre-College: Introduction to Psychology

Academic / Career Interest
Psychology

Website
https://www.coloradocollege.edu/offices/summersession/CC-students/2016-courses/2016-on-campus-descriptions/py-100-introduction-to-psychology-bases-of-behavior.html

Application Timeline
Contact institution for more information

Eligibility
Open to rising juniors and seniors

Tuition Fees
$4,600

Information about the program:
Examination of psychological phenomena from bio behavioral and socio behavioral perspectives. Contemporary issues in psychology, such as intelligence, development, perception, learning, abnormal behavior, language, and social behavior are explored. Scientific methodology and its application to psychological phenomena are stressed.

Contact
(719) 389-6000

Name of College
Columbia University

Name of Program
Summer Immersion: The Science of Psychology

Academic / Career Interest
Psychology

Website
http://sps.columbia.edu/highschool/summer-immersion/new-york-city-3-week/courses/the-science-of-psychology

Application Timeline
Approx. March

Eligibility
Admission to the Programs for High School Students is selective. The admissions committee looks for academically exceptional, highly motivated students interested in the program because of a passion for learning and wish to enrich their knowledge of the particular field for which they are applying.

Tuition Fees
$5,600

Information about the program:
This course is designed for students interested in the fundamental concepts, principles, and theories of psychology, the science of mind and behavior. The course provides an overview of the diverse topics within psychology, including biological bases of behavior, learning and memory, sensation and perception, cognitive development, language acquisition, and personality and social influences on behavior. Special emphasis is placed on current psychology research and topics relevant to both individual experience and real-world events.

Contact
(212) 854-9889
hsp@columbia.edu

Name of College
University of Connecticut

Name of Program
Pre-College Summer @ UConn: Pre-Psych: Psychology and Neuro-science

Academic / Career Interest
Psychology

Website
https://precollege-summer.uconn.edu/academic-areas/pre-psy-chology/

Application Timeline
Applications close one week prior to each session start date.

Eligibility
Must be juniors or seniors in high school and at least 15 years of age to apply

Tuition Fees
$1,950

Information about the program:
Ever get a feeling of Déjà vu? What happens when we confront something new? How do we tell if we've seen something before? In this 1-week (17.5 hour) introduction to the field of Behavioral Neuroscience, students learn that what we think, see, hear, and re-member can have little to do with the physical reality. Students will be guided through fascinating human and animal research includ-ing the responses of individual brain cells to changes in the world around us. Students will be exposed to lively discussion, video clips, in-class activities, and visit a Brain Research laboratory in order to come away with a better understanding of how our brains process information about the world. This program is excellent for students interested in Psychology, Cognitive Sciences, and Medicine (espe-cially Neurology).

Contact
(860) 486-09149
PreCollegeSummer@UConn.edu

Name of College
Cornell University

Name of Program
Summer College: Adolescent Psychology

Academic / Career Interest
Psychology

Website
https://www.sce.cornell.edu/sc/programs/index.php?v=215

Application Timeline
Approx. May

Eligibility
Eligibility: current sophomores, juniors, seniors

Tuition Fees
$6,310

Information about the program:
How does society treat adolescents? Does that vary across cultures, and has it changed over time? How should we deal with problems of youth unemployment, underage drinking, teenage pregnancy, and juvenile crime? What is the best way to prepare for adulthood? Answering these questions requires an understanding of the ways in which individuals change as they move through adolescence. How do their hopes and fears alter? How does the brain develop? How do relationships with others evolve?
Students will learn about the major theoretical perspectives, research methods, and controversies in the study of human development. The program will focus on psychology—but it will also touch on education, neuroscience, sociology, psychiatry, criminology, economics, law, medicine, and public health.

Contact
(607-255-6203)
summer_college@cornell.edu

Name of College
Duke University

Name of Program
Duke Summer College: Introductory Psychology

Academic / Career Interest
Psychology

Website
https://summersession.duke.edu/high-school-students/summer-college-for-high-school-students/daytime-courses

Application Timeline
Approx. December

Eligibility
Current 10th and 11th grade students are eligible to apply.

Tuition Fees
$8,895

Information about the program:
This course will provide a broad overview of the field of psychological science, covering the biological, evolutionary, cognitive, social, personality, and clinical perspectives of behavior, as well as the conceptual issues unifying these sub-disciplines. Not only will the course provide a solid grounding in the knowledge of the field, but it will address the historical roots of psychological inquiry and the methods and techniques through which our understanding is advanced. Students will come away with greater insight into human behavior and an enhanced appreciation of the psychological factors that influence their lives and the functioning of society as a whole.

Contact
(919) 684-6259
summer@duke.edu

Name of College
Duke University

Name of Program
Duke Summer College: Adolescence

Academic / Career Interest
Adolescent development

Website
https://summersession.duke.edu/high-school-students/summer-college-for-high-school-students/daytime-courses

Application Timeline
Approx. December

Eligibility
Current 10th and 11th grade students are eligible to apply.

Tuition Fees
$8,895

Information about the program:
This course will explore adolescent development across domains of physical, cognitive, and social development. Topics will include those related to normal/typical development as well as abnormal development, particularly with regard to issues of health and mental health in this age group. Additionally, students will learn about the broader world in which adolescents live and the contexts within which development occurs – families, peer groups, schools, neighborhoods, and cultures. This course features a service learning component that allows class members to interact with adolescents in our community by means of a variety of activities on the Duke campus. This class is particularly appropriate for students interested in counseling or clinical psychology, teaching, educational policy, or medicine.

Contact
(919) 684-6259
summer@duke.edu

Name of College
Emory University

Name of Program
Pre-College Program

Academic / Career Interest
Neuroscience / Psychology

Website
http://precollege.emory.edu/index.html

Application Timeline
Rolling basis admission

Eligibility
Contact institution for more information

Tuition Fees
Estimated Fees:
2-week: $4,100
4-week: $7,825

Information about the program:
The Emory Pre-College Program (noncredit) offers students an opportunity to preview the best of college life: from compelling non-credit courses taught by renowned faculty to life on a vibrant campus, from becoming an active participant in the university, local, and global communities to developing friendships with other students from around the world. Emory Pre-College students will experience a challenging college-level academic course, but they will also gain exposure to other academic disciplines, co-curricular and extra-curricular activities, and residential college life. Two-week noncredit courses and four-week noncredit courses. To experience both a neuroscience AND a psychology class here, the four-week option is recommended. Introduction to Neuroscience for Session A and Cognitive/Social Psychology for Session B.

Contact
(404) 727-6036
admission@emory.edu

Name of College
Gettysburg College

Name of Program
Camp Psych - Summer Camp in Psychology

Academic / Career Interest
Psychology

Website
http://www.gettysburg.edu/camppsych/

Application Timeline
Applications will be reviewed on a rolling until the camp is full.

Eligibility
Open to sophomores, juniors, and seniors.

Tuition Fees
$1,295

Information about the program:
The goal of Camp Psych is to provide a window into how psychological science works . What are some of the major questions investigated by psychologists? Campers will get hands-on experiences that introduce them to research in psychology in a fun, challenging, and engaging environment. Campers will not simply learn about cutting edge issues and research in psychology; they will engage in research themselves. Perfect for students interested in psychology, this camp gives students an insider view of the field as well as preparation for college studies.

Contact
(717) 337-6171
camppsych@gettysburg.edu

Name of College
Harvard University

Name of Program
Pre-College Courses: Mind, Brain, and Consciousness

Academic / Career Interest
Psychology

Website
https://www.summer.harvard.edu/courses/mind-brain-consciousness/33603

Application Timeline
Approx. May

Eligibility
The Pre-College Program admissions committee is looking for mature, academically motivated students who are at least 15 years old.

Tuition Fees
$4,500

Information about the program:
For centuries, we believed ourselves to be unique among creatures because of our consciousness. Only human beings, we thought, are truly conscious of themselves. No other animal or machine can ever experience something like human consciousness because they don't have a mind. Yet, as science evolved, we have come to see consciousness as something that comes from the brain. Other animals have brains. Does that make them conscious? Neuroscientists have invented a new way of studying consciousness by asking what happens to the mind when the brain is impaired. Meanwhile, psychologists have wondered how to prove that an animal is or isn't conscious. In this course, we review what scientists know about consciousness. their experience.

Contact
inquiry@summer.harvard.edu

Name of College
Harvard University

Name of Program
Pre-College Courses: The Science and Practice of Mindfulness

Academic / Career Interest
Psychology

Website
https://www.summer.harvard.edu/courses/science-practice-mind-fulness/33791

Application Timeline
Approx. May

Eligibility
The Pre-College Program admissions committee is looking for mature, academically motivated students who are at least 15 years old.

Tuition Fees
$4,500

Information about the program:
Mindfulness is a way of attending to the experience of the present moment with full awareness and without judgment or reactivity. Studies show the benefits of mindfulness include stress reduction, emotional balance, greater mental focus, and improved physical health, as well as changes in brain biology more supportive of overall well-being. This course explores the theory and practice of mindfulness and current research in brain and neuroscience associated with mindfulness and its outcomes among youth. We also discuss how mindfulness can be helpful during the life challenges of late adolescence, as well as its general application to clinical contexts.

Contact
inquiry@summer.harvard.edu

Name of College
Harvard University

Name of Program
Pre-College Courses: Implicit Bias in Philosophy and Psychology

Academic / Career Interest
Psychology

Website
https://www.summer.harvard.edu/courses/implicit-bias-philoso-phy-psychology/34109

Application Timeline
Approx. May

Eligibility
The Pre-College Program admissions committee is looking for mature, academically motivated students who are at least 15 years old.

Tuition Fees
$4,500

Information about the program:
During the 2016 presidential debates Hillary Clinton said, "I think implicit bias is a problem for everyone, not just police. I think unfortunately too many of us in our great country jump to conclusions about each other." In recent years, there has been growing interest in the psychological phenomenon of implicit bias and its social ramifications. In this course, we ask various questions regarding this phenomenon, including: What are implicit biases? Are implicit biases inescapable? Are people responsible for having implicit biases? The first part of this course focuses on recent psychological research on implicit bias and how best to define this phenomenon.

Contact
inquiry@summer.harvard.edu

Name of College
Harvard University

Name of Program
Pre-College Courses: Introduction to Neuropsychiatry

Academic / Career Interest
Psychology

Website
https://www.summer.harvard.edu/courses/introduction-neuropsy-chiatry/33849

Application Timeline
Approx. May

Eligibility
The Pre-College Program admissions committee is looking for mature, academically motivated students who are at least 15 years old.

Tuition Fees
$4,500

Information about the program:
Our understanding of the human brain has progressed in the past century like never before in history. At the same time, there has been a growing interest in those cases in which the brain does not function properly, giving rise to mental illness. Neurosciences, cognitive sciences, psychology, neurology, and psychiatry all play a role in this frontier of science. Neuropsychiatry seeks to advance our understanding of the neurological bases of psychiatric disorders. In other words, neuropsychiatry integrates what we know from the neurology of the brain and the psychology of the mind to help understand the link between an illness in the brain and an abnormal behavior. Often, doctors observe a behavior and need to figure out its cause.

Contact
inquiry@summer.harvard.edu

Name of College
Ithaca College

Name of Program
Summer College: General Psychology

Academic / Career Interest
Psychology

Website
https://www.ithaca.edu/summercollege/threeweek/threeweek-courses/?item=5673

Application Timeline
Approx. May

Eligibility
Students who will be between 15 years and 18 years of age at the time of the summer college program are welcome to apply.

Tuition Fees
Three-Week Session $4,980

Information about the program:
An introduction to the study of behavior, this course focuses on the influences of physiological, cognitive, social, and personality factors as they pertain to behavior and includes discussion of the major theories in psychology and related research. Taught by Kathryn Caldwell, Assistant Prof., Department of Psychology
In Professor Caldwell's words....I have taught in the Psychology department of Ithaca College since 2005. Previously, I worked as a Research Associate for Casey Family Programs in Seattle, and as a Research Associate for the National Institute of Child Health and Human Development (NICHD) Study of Early Childcare at the University of Washington.

Contact
(607) 274-3011

Name of College
James Madison University

Name of Program
Summer Honors Institute: The Biopsychology of Deceit

Academic / Career Interest
Psychology

Website
https://www.jmu.edu/outreach/programs/all/honorscamp/index.
shtml

Application Timeline
Approx. May

Eligibility
Open to high school juniors and seniors

Tuition Fees
$1,000

Information about the program:
Do polygraphs really work? What are they testing anyways? In this session you will have the opportunity to witness digital detection of concealed information using modern physiology equipment. We will discuss the meaning of these measurements, the psychology of lying and concealing information, other ways psychologists attempt to detect lies, and ways in which liars attempt to conceal information.

Contact
(540) 568-4226
heatwoml@jmu.edu

Name of College
Loyola University, Chicago

Name of Program
Pre-College Summer Scholars: Psychology

Academic / Career Interest
Psychology

Website
https://www.luc.edu/summerscholars/

Application Timeline
Contact institution for more information

Eligibility
-Be a current freshmen, sophomore or junior
-Have a strong academic standing -- a minimum 3.0 GPA (on a 4.0 scale)

Tuition Fees
Residential: $1,320.00
Commuter: $893.00

Information about the program:
Given the broadly applicable nature of the science of psychology, seminars with this focus give students an excellent opportunity to jump into a diverse discipline. Psychology is a strong entry point if a student's career interest exists in psychiatry, research, or the behavioral and social sciences. Students will learn how to apply psychological principles to solve problems on the individual and social level.

Contact
(773) 408-7381
summerscholars@luc.edu

Name of College
University of Pennsylvania

Name of Program
Neuroscience Research Academy

Academic / Career Interest
Psychology

Website
http://www.sas.upenn.edu/summer/programs/high-school/neuro-science

Application Timeline
Approx. May

Eligibility
Current 9th-11th grade students. A successful applicant should have:

- Minimum 3.3 high school GPA
- Writing that shows both technical skill and intellectual depth
- Strong recommendations
- A variety of extracurricular interests

Tuition Fees
$4,299

Information about the program:
The Neuroscience Research Academy explores the biological foundations of the brain, progressing from the cellular foundations of the neuron to an understanding of the sensory systems, and culminating with higher-order cognitive functions such as memory, emotion and morality. Taught by members of Penn's Biological Basis of Behavior program, the Neuroscience Academy introduces students to this cutting-edge field in both research and medicine, which has provided important insights into understanding the mind in both health and disease.

Contact
(215) 898-7326
summer@sas.upenn.edu

Name of College
Stanford University

Name of Program
High School Summer College

Academic / Career Interest
Psychology

Website
https://summer.stanford.edu/program/high-school-high-school-summer-college

Application Timeline
Approx. February

Eligibility
Be a current sophomore, junior, or senior, or a gap year student at the time of application.

Tuition Fees
$14,426 to $17,054 is the estimated range for a student attending Stanford Summer Session taking eight units and living on campus.

Information about the program:
During Stanford University's Summer Quarter, high school students from the United States and around the globe are invited to spend eight or nine weeks living and learning in the heart of Silicon Valley. Alongside visiting undergraduate and matriculated students, participants will have an exclusive opportunity as a student in Stanford Summer Session's High School Summer College program to earn credit and a Stanford University transcript at one of the most competitive universities in the world. Choose from more than 145 courses offered by 30 departments within the schools of Humanities and Sciences, Earth Sciences, and Engineering. Summer courses feature a smaller class size, accessible instructors, and a diverse student body with students from over 30 different countries.

Contact
precollegiate@stanford.edu

Name of College
Stanford University

Name of Program
Pre-Collegiate Summer Institutes: Topics in Psychology

Academic / Career Interest
Psychology

Website
https://summerinstitutes.spcs.stanford.edu/courses/2018/topics-psychology

Application Timeline
Early Deadline: approx. January
Regular Deadline: approx. February
Extended Deadline: approx. March

Eligibility
Students must be in grades 9-11 at the time of application.

Tuition Fees
$6,850.00

Information about the program:
This course introduces students to methodological and theoretical aspects of the field of psychology through in-depth study of some of psychology's most important topics. Students will learn significant works from the historical development of psychology as well as receive an introduction to areas and methods of current research. Possible topics include: social psychology, social and cognitive development, perception, memory, psychological disorders, psychological approaches to the study of behavior, the theories and contributions of major figures in the field, the methodology of psychology and its limitations, ways to apply psychological findings to everyday life, and others.

Contact
precollegiate@stanford.edu

Name of College
Stonehill College

Name of Program
Summer@Stonehill Pre-College Program: General Psychology

Academic / Career Interest
Psychology

Website
https://www.stonehill.edu/precollege/psychology/

Application Timeline
Approx. May

Eligibility
For junior and senior high school students

Tuition Fees
Resident students: $3,900
Commuter students: $2,400

Information about the program:
Psychology is an incredibly diverse, fascinating field. This course will provide students with a foundation for potential further study in the field of psychology.
We will use a scientific approach in exploring psychology – the thoughts, feelings, and behaviors that make up so much of human life – and its many sub disciplines, including biological psychology, learning, altered states of consciousness, human development, human memory and emotion, personality, social behavior, and psychological disorders & treatment. What unites many psychologists from various, diverse perspectives is the common goal of understanding behavior (broadly defined) and using scientific methods toward this end. Each sub discipline brings its own unique perspective to this challenge.

Contact
(508) 565-1754
dhurley1@stonehill.edu

Name of College
University of Southern California

Name of Program
USC Summer Programs: Psychological Science & Society

Academic / Career Interest
Psychology

Website
https://summerprograms.usc.edu/programs/4-week/psychological-science/

Application Timeline
Approx. April

Eligibility
Students must have completed at least the 9th grade by June

Tuition Fees
Resident: $8,534
Commuter: $6,059

Information about the program:
Why are people the way that they are? Why do they do the things that they do? What can psychological science tell me about the world around me? And how can I use it to make the world a better place? If these questions (especially the last two) keep your student up at night, this course might just be for them. Scientifically tackle these questions and more through lectures, group discussions, lab activities, and field trips.

Contact
(213) 740-5679
summer@usc.edu

Name of College
University of Southern California

Name of Program
USC Summer Programs: My Mind & Me: Introduction to Mental Health

Academic / Career Interest
Psychology

Website
https://summerprograms.usc.edu/programs/4-week/mental-health/

Application Timeline
Approx. April

Eligibility
Students must have completed at least the 9th grade by June

Tuition Fees
Resident: $8,534
Commuter: $6,059

Information about the program:
What are mental health & mental illness? What makes them different? How can I improve my own mental health? What is the science behind self-care? How can I use this information to help those around me? If your student is interested in having a discussion about the answers to these questions, and many more, then this course is a good fit for you. For the next four weeks, students will be immersed in the field of mental health and find themselves looking at the world through a new lens. In this course, we will develop individualized methods for improving mental health, study psychopathology, look at case studies of people living with psychological disorders, and study the relationship between social media and mental health.

Contact
(213) 740-5679
summer@usc.edu

Name of College
University of Southern California

Name of Program
USC Summer Programs: The Brain: Introduction to Neuroscience

Academic / Career Interest
Psychology

Website
https://summerprograms.usc.edu/programs/4-week/the-brain/

Application Timeline
Approx. April

Eligibility
Students must have completed at least the 9th grade by June

Tuition Fees
Resident: $8,534
Commuter: $6,059

Information about the program:
Is your student considering a career in healthcare, psychology, or the behavioral sciences? Are they interested in the scientific study of the human brain? In this introduction to the anatomy and function of the brain, students will discover some common and unusual aspects of the brain in everyday life and under abnormal circumstances. Students will explore normal brain development as well as abnormal occurrences in the brain and their effects on human function and behavior over the lifespan.

Contact
(213) 740-5679
summer@usc.edu

Name of College
University of Texas, Austin

Name of Program
Psychology Academy

Academic / Career Interest
Psychology

Website
https://www.summerdiscovery.com/u-texas-austin/academic-options#psychology-academy

Application Timeline
Contact institution for more information

Eligibility
For students completing grades 9, 10, 11, 12 (ages 14-18)

Tuition Fees
Residential:$5,999
Commuter: $3,199

Information about the program:
Why do we think and feel the way we do? Does your student want to understand what makes other people tick? Dive into psychology with award winning UT Psychology faculty at one of the top rated Psychology programs. Learn how psychology affects our lives, deepen the understanding of self, and apply learning to improve life. As part of this academy students will take the following two courses:

FOUNDATIONS OF PSYCHOLOGY: Learn why relationships work, how the brain influences experiences, and how we learn. Cover problems in abnormal, bio, cognitive, developmental, and social psychology, and discover what can be treated and how. Taught by award-winning UT Psychology faculty.

Contact
(516) 621-3939
info@summerdiscovery.com

Name of College
Washington University in Saint Louis

Name of Program
Philosophy, Neuroscience, and Psychology Institute

Academic / Career Interest
Psychology

Website
https://summerexperiences.wustl.edu/pnp

Application Timeline
Approx. April

Eligibility
To be eligible for a High School Summer Institute students should:
-Be a current freshman, sophomore, or junior in high school.
-Have an academic average of B+ (3.3/4.0) or better.

Tuition Fees
$3,885

Information about the program:
The Philosophy, Neuroscience, and Psychology (PNP) Institute explores the intersection of philosophy, neuroscience, and psychology. Students ask philosophical questions, focusing on "what is the Good?" and evaluate philosophical arguments that seek to answer this question. The institute provides a brief introduction to psychology with particular focus on mental health and the intersection between mental illness and morality. Finally, students explore the burgeoning field of neuroscience, learning the basics of brain functioning and research to ask critical questions about the role of neuroscience in philosophy and psychology.

Contact
Contact the program website for information.

Name of College
Westmont College

Name of Program
Summer Scholars: General Psychology

Academic / Career Interest
Psychology

Website
https://www.westmont.edu/summerscholars/#psych.html

Application Timeline
Approx. May

Eligibility
Juniors and seniors are eligible

Tuition Fees
$2,950

Information about the program:
General Psychology is a survey of major areas of psychology with an emphasis on basic concepts, theories, and facts of human thoughts, feelings, and behavior. Students will learn about personality, social psychology, emotion, memory, biological processes, developmental psychology, cognition, consciousness, and therapy. Students will also learn how scientific methodology is utilized in psychological research and will learn critical thinking skills. They will be able to understand and critique how we gain knowledge about people. They will work together and with the instructor to discover how to understand and predict human behavior.

Contact
(805) 565-6239
wss@westmont.edu

Name of College
Yale University

Name of Program
EXPLO Psychology + Neuroscience

Academic / Career Interest
Psychology

Website
https://www.explo.org/focus/psychology-and-neuroscience/

Application Timeline
Contact institution for more information

Eligibility
Students entering grades 10-12

Tuition Fees
$5,215

Information about the program:
From avatar therapy to building business brands to refining pharmacological treatment of mental health through genetic markers, the applications of psychology and neuroscience far exceed the traditional counseling track. These transdisciplinary fields can be applied to nearly any topic that involves a brain — and they help us to unlock the mysteries of how the mind works so that we can better develop solutions to the complex questions of human behavior and experience.

Contact
(781) 762-7400

COLLEGE
CONSULTING
EXPERTS

Aerospace Collegiate Programs

Name of College
University of Arizona

Name of Program
Advanced Teen Astronomy Camp

Academic / Career Interest
Astronomy

Website
http://www.astronomycamp.org/register.html

Application Timeline
Qualified applicants will be accepted on a first-come, first-served basis until the Camp is full.
Consult Institution for more information

Eligibility
Students should be between the ages of 14 and 18 years. Students are required to have completed satisfactorily either Algebra II or Geometry in school.

Tuition Fees
Estimated fees: $995

Information about the program:
Astronomy Camp is all about discovering the Eureka moment! Under the dark skies of Southern Arizona, students of all ages explore "the heavens" with large telescopes and experience the excitement of scientific inquiry. The unique environments at Mount Lemmon Observatory immediately north of Tucson, Arizona, and Kitt Peak National Observatory just west of Tucson, provide outstanding views of the sky and encourage exploration. Astronomy Camp is an "immersion" experience that merges all four STEM letters: Science, technology, engineering, and numerical thinking.

Contact
Dr. Don McCarthy
dmccarthy@as.arizona.edu

Name of College
Auburn University

Name of Program
Aviation Camp

Academic / Career Interest
Aviation

Website
http://www.auburn.edu/outreach/opce/auburnyouthprograms/
aviation.htm

Application Timeline
Contact institution for more information.

Eligibility
Rising 9th – 12th Grade

Tuition Fees
Estimated fees: $875

Information about the program:
Are you thinking about a career in aviation as a pilot? Engineer? Unmanned aircraft operator? Airport manager? Air traffic controller?
Corporate aviation? If you are a rising 9th-12th grade student and
you would like to learn more about these and other aviation career
opportunities, we invite you to attend the Aviation Camp at Auburn
University.

The air transportation industry connects the world's economies
and the demand for aviation professionals has never been stronger.
Auburn University has been a leader in aviation education since
the early 1940s and is proud to offer this youth program to begin
developing the next generation of global aviation leaders. Working
with faculty and staff from Auburn's Aviation Center and Auburn
University Regional Airport, the Harbert College of Business, and
the Samuel Ginn College of Engineering

Contact
(334) 844-5100
auyouth@auburn.edu

Name of College
Embry-Riddle Aeronautical

Name of Program
Aerospace Career Exploration Camp

Academic / Career Interest
Aerospace

Website
http://summercamps.erau.edu/camps/aerospace-career-exploration-camp.html

Application Timeline
Approx. in January

Eligibility
Students Ages 12-18.

Tuition Fees
Estimated fees: $950. Advanced Registration discount of $50 is applied to all completed application packets that are received by early April.

Information about the program:
Aerospace Career Exploration is an in-depth and exciting way for students, ages 12-18, with an interest in aviation and aerospace to explore the fast-paced world of both industries. This program allows participants to learn about a variety of career in Safety, Meteorology, Aviation Maintenance, Engineering, Space Technology, and Flight in a comprehensive and structured environment.

Contact
(386) 226-7945
summer@erau.edu

Name of College
Embry-Riddle Aeronautical

Name of Program
Aviation Voyage Camp

Academic / Career Interest
Aviation

Website
http://summercamps.erau.edu/camps/aviation-voyage-camp.html

Application Timeline
Approx. in January

Eligibility
Students Ages 12-18

Tuition Fees
Estimated fees: $2,250. Advanced Registration discount of $100 is applied to all completed application packets received by early April.

Information about the program:
This program was developed for students ages 12-18. Students will have an opportunity to apply the lessons learned from Flight Exploration to procedures such as flight planning and pre-flighting the aircraft. Students are required to bring their logbook from Flight Exploration with them to continue recording their flight hours[1]. All Aviation Voyage students must obtain an FAA Medical prior to submitting an application.

Contact
(386) 266-7945
summer@erau.edu

Name of College
Embry-Riddle Aeronautical

Name of Program
Drone Flight Exploration

Academic / Career Interest
Drone Flight Exploration

Website
http://summercamps.erau.edu/camps/drone-flight-exploration-uas.html

Application Timeline
Approx. in December

Eligibility
High School Students ages 15-18 who are interested in UAS.

Tuition Fees
Contact institution for more information.

Information about the program:
The Drone Flight Exploration summer program will introduce students to the evolving world of unmanned aircraft operations. Come and learn how Drones are being used in today's world. Students will be introduced to Drone operations through class room instruction, flight simulators, and actual flight operations. Classes will include Ground School, ATC airspace, Unmanned Aircraft Systems Lab (UAS), UAS Sims and Weather. Students will gain an understanding of UAS fixed wing and rotary, and have hands on experience with the aircraft.

Contact
(928) 777-3956
prsummer@erau.edu

Name of College
Embry-Riddle Aeronautical

Name of Program
Flight Exploration Camp

Academic / Career Interest
Flight Exploration

Website
http://summercamps.erau.edu/camps/flight-exploration-camp-daytona-beach-fl.html

Application Timeline
Approx. in January

Eligibility
Students Ages 12-18

Tuition Fees
Estimated fees: $2,050. Advanced Registration discount of $100 is applied to all completed application packets received by early April.

Information about the program:
Developed for students, ages 12-18, Flight Exploration is an introduction to flying and flight training. Students practice flight maneuvers and experience firsthand how the plane responds to the flight controls. This hands-on practical experience will allow students to record flight time while exploring their potential career paths. All Flight Exploration students must obtain an FAA Medical prior to submitting an application. Any student in our Flight Exploration Camp is required to provide TSA approved documentation. This means a valid passport, or driver's license AND original birth certificate.

Contact
(386) 226-7945
summer@erau.edu

Name of College
Embry-Riddle Aeronautical

Name of Program
Flight Exploration Camp

Academic / Career Interest
Flight Exploration

Website
http://summercamps.erau.edu/camps/flight-explora-tion-prescott-az.html

Application Timeline
Approx. in December

Eligibility
High School Students ages 14-18 who are interested in flight

Tuition Fees
Contact institution for more information.

Information about the program:
Future pilots, ready to fly?

ERAU's pre-college Flight Exploration is one of our most popular programs and offers a wide range of opportunities for students wishing to pursue a career in aviation. Flight instructors and professors from our School of Aviation work alongside students to perfect the skills a pilot needs to operate successfully in the national airspace system. Students will learn how to plan and conduct a cross country flight, identify weather sources used for flight planning, and what to expect from air traffic controllers during flight. The program will also focus on a "capstone" cross-country flight. When students earn their "wings" at the end of the program, it will be a result of student efforts during the week, and a model of the skills needed to be a pilot.

Contact
(928) 777-3956
prsummer@erau.edu

Name of College
Embry-Riddle Aeronautical

Name of Program
Helicopter Camp

Academic / Career Interest
Helicopter training

Website
http://summercamps.erau.edu/camps/helicopter.html

Application Timeline
Approx. in December

Eligibility
High School Students ages 15-18 who are interested in flight and helicopters

Tuition Fees
Contact institution for more information.

Information about the program:
Ready to pilot a helicopter?

ERAU's pre-college Helicopter Exploration program is a unique opportunity for students to get in the pilot seat and take control of a Robinson R22 helicopter. The flight instructors are some of the best in the aviation industry and will give students firsthand training on pre-flight, helicopter care, ground school, ATC airspace, aviation weather, safety science, careers in helicopter, and Unmanned Air-craft Systems Lab (UAS).

Throughout 3 hours of flight training, students will take control and experience the adrenaline rush of breaking contact with the ground to soar over the northern Arizona landscape.

Contact
(928) 777-3956
prsummer@erau.edu

Name of College
Embry-Riddle Aeronautical

Name of Program
Next Level Flight

Academic / Career Interest
Aviation

Website
http://summercamps.erau.edu/camps/next-level-flight-prescott-az.html

Application Timeline
Approx. in December

Eligibility
High School Students ages 15-18 who have attended the Flight Exploration Program.

Tuition Fees
Contact institution for more information.

Information about the program:
Are you interested in aviation, but have already attended one of our Flight Exploration programs?
Then Next Level Flight is for you!

This pre-college program explores the more advanced world of aviation and flight training at Embry-Riddle. The culmination of this week-long program includes ground lessons, simulator flights, a refresher flight in our Cessna 172 aircraft, trainings in our DA42 Simulator, and a flight in our multi-engine Diamond DA 42 aircraft over the Grand Canyon.

Students' academic classes will build upon the knowledge they gained in Flight Exploration, with a focus in the Garmin G1000 and the DA42 aircraft systems. Students are required to wear closed toed shoes and long pants during their flight times.

Contact
(928) 777-3956
prsummer@erau.edu

Name of College
Embry-Riddle Aeronautical

Name of Program
SunFlight Custom Flight Training Camp

Academic / Career Interest
Flight training

Website
http://summercamps.erau.edu/camps/sunflight-custom-flight-training-camp.html

Application Timeline
Approx. in January

Eligibility
High School Juniors or Seniors

Tuition Fees
Contact institution for more information.

Information about the program:
The SunFlight Custom Flight Training program is designed for qualified private pilots to continue with their flight training by working toward an instrument rating, multi-engine land rating or upset training. If these have been attained and the student wants to continue with the next rating, we can customize that training as well. Students learn in the same program as our University flight students.

Students must possess an FAA Private Pilot Certificate and FAA Medical prior to the start of this course in order to enroll in one of the customized training programs.

Contact
(386) 226-7945
summer@erau.edu

Name of College
Embry-Riddle Aeronautical

Name of Program
SunFlight Private Pilot Camp

Academic / Career Interest
Private pilot program

Website
http://summercamps.erau.edu/camps/sunflight-private-pilot-camp.html

Application Timeline
Approx. in January

Eligibility
Students aged 17-18 (High School Juniors and Seniors)

Tuition Fees
Estimated fees: $22,500. Advanced Registration discount of $500 is applied to all completed application packets received by early April.

Information about the program:
This structured program allows aspiring pilots to potentially earn their Private Pilot Certificate in the same environment as our University flight students. Regardless of the student's flight experience, this program is designed to provide the knowledge necessary for qualified students to successfully pass the FAA Private Pilot knowledge, flight, and oral exams. However, if the student has previously attended the SunFlight Solo program, they typically finish this course in a more efficient manner.

Contact
(386) 226-7945
summer@erau.edu

Name of College
Embry-Riddle Aeronautical

Name of Program
SunFlight Solo Camp

Academic / Career Interest
Solo flight training

Website
http://summercamps.erau.edu/camps/sunflight-solo-camp.html

Application Timeline
Approx. in January

Eligibility
High School Juniors and Seniors

Students must be 16 years old prior to the end of the program. All participants must obtain an FAA Medical/Student Pilot Certificate prior to submitting an application[2].

Tuition Fees
Estimated fees: $8,500. Advanced Registration discount of $500 is applied to all completed application packets received by early April.

Information about the program:
The goal of SunFlight Solo program is for all qualified students to fly solo under the 14 CFR Part 61 Flight Training Curriculum by the end of the program. Areas of study include air traffic control, meteorology, navigation, and Federal Aviation Regulations. The fundamentals learned in this program give students an advantage when they enroll into the SunFlight Private Pilot program.

Contact
(386) 226-7945
summer@erau.edu

Name of College
Florida Institute of Technology

Name of Program
Advanced Aviation Academy

Academic / Career Interest
Aviation

Website
http://camps.fit.edu/aviation-advanced-academy/

Application Timeline
Approx. June 1

Eligibility
Grades 7-12

Tuition Fees
Estimated fees: $675

Information about the program:
The flight camps give students a unique opportunity to explore the vast and exciting world of aviation. Participants learn about the dynamics of airplanes and the principles of flight during an immerse experience that showcases the broad spectrum of careers in the aviation industry. Participants are also introduced to the Florida Tech community with activities and buffet lunch in Panther Dining Hall on campus.

Contact
FIT Aviation
801 Harry Goode Way
Melbourne, FL 32901

Name of College
Florida Institute of Technology

Name of Program
Aviation/Aerospace Experience

Academic / Career Interest
Aviation

Website
http://camps.fit.edu/aviation-experience/

Application Timeline
Approx. June 1

Eligibility
Grades 7-12

Tuition Fees
Estimated fees: $750

Information about the program:
The flight camps give students a unique opportunity to explore the vast and exciting world of aviation. Participants learn about the dynamics of airplanes and the principles of flight during an immerse experience that showcases the broad spectrum of careers in the aviation industry. Participants are also introduced to the Florida Tech community with activities and buffet lunch in Panther Dining Hall on campus.

Contact
FIT Aviation
801 Harry Goode Way
Melbourne, FL 32901

Name of College
Harvard University

Name of Program
From Stars to Planets: Are We Alone in the Universe?

Academic / Career Interest
Study of the universe

Website
https://www.summer.harvard.edu/courses/stars-planets-are-we-alone-universe/33620

Application Timeline
Approx. May

Eligibility
The Pre-College Program admissions committee is looking for mature, academically motivated students who meet both of the following criteria:

- Will graduate in 2019 or 2020
- Are at least 15 years old by December, and will not turn 19 years old before July.

Tuition Fees
Estimated fees: $4,500

Information about the program:
This course is an introduction to stars, planets, and life in the universe. Topics include the main properties of stars, their formation and evolution, including supernova explosions and black holes; the detection, characterization, and formation of planets and their potential to host life, both outside and in our solar system; and the search for extra-terrestrial intelligence. It conveys some of the main physical concepts such as gravity, electromagnetic radiation, and energy, which are relevant for the study of the universe and that are also used in everyday life.

Contact
(617) 495-4024

Name of College
Harvard University

Name of Program
Life in the Universe

Academic / Career Interest
Study of the universe

Website
https://www.summer.harvard.edu/courses/life-universe/33827

Application Timeline
Approx. May

Eligibility
The Pre-College Program admissions committee is looking for mature, academically motivated students who meet both of the following criteria:

- Will graduate within the upcoming or following year
- Are at least 15 years old by December and will not turn 19 years old before July

Tuition Fees
Estimated fees: $4,500

Information about the program:
This course involves an interdisciplinary study of life in the universe, beginning with the astrophysics of star and planet formation, before moving into the new and exciting field of exoplanet detection and characteristics. It covers planetary processes, with considerations of various bodies in the solar system in the context of potential habitability, introduces the biology and chemistry of life, and explores the origins and future potential of life on Earth. Students evaluate the possibility of life in the universe based on the state of current studies and expected discoveries. their choosing.

Contact
(617) 495-4024

Name of College
University of Illinois, Urbana Champaign

Name of Program
Girls' Astronomy Summer Camp

Academic / Career Interest
Astronomy

Website
http://publish.illinois.edu/astroillini/

Application Timeline
Approx. Mid-July or until maximum capacity reached

Eligibility
For rising 10-11 grade girls

Tuition Fees
Contact institution for more information

Information about the program:
This summer camp for high school girls will be focused on hands-on astronomy projects and learning about real-life research experience as women in science.

Camp highlights include build your own telescope, watch 3D science movies in the NCSA visualization lab, tours to the South Pole Telescope Lab and astrobiology lab, work with scientist on real data in campus computer labs, observation sessions at the University of Illinois observatory (a historical landmark), talk to women astrophysicists about their research.

Contact
https://publish.illinois.edu/astroillini/contact-us/

Name of College
Kent State University

Name of Program
Nikki Kukwa Memorial Aeronautics Camp

Academic / Career Interest
Aeronautics

Website
https://www.kent.edu/NikkiKukwaCamp

Application Timeline
Approx. Mid-June

Eligibility
You must be a female, high school student with an interest in aviation

Tuition Fees
Contact institution for more information

Information about the program:
Fifteen female, high school students will receive a free, three-day camp experience in the July/mid-summer timeframe through the Nikki Kukwa Memorial Aviation Fund and Kent State University's College of Aeronautics and Engineering. Students will explore careers in aviation while staying in dorms on Kent State University Main Campus. The camp includes a tour of the Cleveland Hopkins International Airport, experience at KSU's Air Traffic Control Lab, a tour of Parker Hannifin's Flight Department and a flight out of the KSU Airport. University personnel provide information regarding academic programs, financial aid and campus life.

Contact
(330) 672-2892
cae@kent.edu

Name of College
Liberty University

Name of Program
New Horizons High School Program: Overnight Aviation Camp

Academic / Career Interest
Aviation

Website
http://www.liberty.edu/academics/aeronautics/index.
cfm?PID=31189

Application Timeline
Early Enrollment: Approx. January through end of March
Final Enrollment Dates: Approx. April through end of May

Eligibility
Rising 9th-12th graders

Tuition Fees
Estimated fees:

- Early Enrollment: $650
- Final Enrollment Dates: $750

Information about the program:
The New Horizons High School Camp gives high school students from all over the U.S. the opportunity to explore the exciting career opportunities (and hobbies) that the field of aviation has to offer. Through basic ground school classes and fun hands-on activities, students will be able to get an idea if a career in aviation is something they might be interested in.

At camp, you will be immersed in the world of aviation through ground school classes taught by professionally certified flight instructors as well as a number of fun educational activities.

Contact
kwagner27@liberty.edu

Name of College
Michigan Institute of Technology

Name of Program
The Summer Science Program

Academic / Career Interest
Science

Website
https://summerscience.org/the-ssp-experience/what-is-ssp/

Application Timeline
Applications open Approx. mid December

Eligibility
Current sophomores and juniors are eligible to apply:

- Junior (11th grade): must have taken courses in calculus or physics
- Sophomore (10th grade): must have taken courses in calculus and physics

Tuition Fees
Estimated fees: $6,950. Thanks to donors, fees of all participants can be subsidized to a greater or lesser degree.

Information about the program:
Today's most promising high school students will be tomorrow's scientists and engineers, doctors and entrepreneurs – the people who invent the future – but only if they realize their potential. Gifted teens have unique needs not often met in their schools: for role models, intellectual challenge, true peers, and the confidence to dream bigger dreams.

SSP is an immersion into experimental science, designed to challenge and inspire talented rising seniors from around the world. Working in teams of three, participants complete a research project from beginning to end: either in Astrophysics – near-earth asteroid imaging and orbit determination.

Contact
info2@ssp.org
(866) 728-0999

Name of College
University of North Dakota

Name of Program
International Aerospace Camp

Academic / Career Interest
Aerospace

Website
http://aviation.und.edu/prospective-students/aerocamp.aspx

Application Timeline
Contact institution for more information

Eligibility
Motivated students entering the 11th or 12th grade who have an interest or curiosity about aviation careers and collegiate aviation

Tuition Fees
Estimated fees: $1,450

Information about the program:
The University of North Dakota's International Aerospace Camp is a full week of aviation adventure. This "college seminar" is similar to attending a week of actual college. Additionally, what makes this seminar unique is the amount of flight training each student receives which simulates the collegiate aviation experience.

The counselors, flight instructors and professors are leaders in aerospace education. You'll start with the basics of flying, experience new and exciting technology and explore career opportunities in flight, air traffic control, aviation management, and unmanned aircraft systems (UAS).

Contact
aerospacecamps@aero.und.edu

Name of College
Saint Louis University

Name of Program
Aviation Summer Academy

Academic / Career Interest
Aviation

Website
https://www.slu.edu/parks/about/pre-college-programs/aviation-summer-academy.php

Application Timeline
Approx. Mid-April

Eligibility
Rising high school juniors and seniors who currently have a 2.5 or higher GPA are eligible to participate.

Tuition Fees
Estimated fees: $800

Information about the program:
The Saint Louis University Aviation Summer Academy is a six-day, five-night residential camp that invites students entering grades 11 and 12 to learn more about different areas of study and career paths in aviation.

During the academy, Parks College of Engineering, Aviation and Technology faculty, certified flight instructors and student mentors guide participants through hands-on activities in subjects that include flight science, aviation management, aerial navigation, aircraft design, unmanned aerial vehicles and air traffic control.

Contact
SLU Parks College
Attn: Aviation Summer Academy
3450 Lindell Blvd.
St. Louis, MO 63103

Name of College
Stanford University

Name of Program
Pre-Collegiate Institutes: Astrochemistry: Origins of Life in Space

Academic / Career Interest
Astrochemistry

Website
https://summerinstitutes.spcs.stanford.edu/courses/2018/astro-chemistry-origins-life-space

Application Timeline
Early Deadline: Approx. End of January
Regular Deadline: Approx. End of February
Extended Deadline: Approx. End of March

Eligibility
Students must be in grades 10-11 at the time of application. Must be 15-17 years old on the first day of session. Prerequisites: Completion of high school courses in physics and chemistry.

Tuition Fees
Estimated fees: $6,850

Information about the program:
New experimental techniques, remarkable advancements in quantum chemistry, the development of observational telescopes, and powerful computer algorithms are making the observation of interstellar molecules possible for the first time in human history. Through this cutting-edge science, we are able to better understand the origins of the organic and molecular elements of life first produced by nucleosynthesis at the core of stars, subsequently ejected out into the interstellar medium, physically and chemically processed by the conditions in space over millions of years, and deposited on to the surfaces of primordial planets, ultimately to become the building blocks of life as we know it.

Contact
https://summerinstitutes.spcs.stanford.edu/contact-us

Name of College
Southeastern Oklahoma State University

Name of Program
Take Flight Aviation Camp

Academic / Career Interest
Aviation

Website
https://www.se.edu/news/take-flight-aviation-camp-held-at-south-eastern/

Application Timeline
Contact institution for more information

Eligibility
Students must be enrolled in 8th, 9th, or 10th grade for the current academic year

Tuition Fees
Estimated fees: $250

Information about the program:
Among the week-long activities were:

- Presentation on STEM (Science-Technology-Engineering-Mathematics) related aviation careers
- Basic rocket building and launching
- Airplane — Aerodynamics, design and performance, navigation, weather/atmospheric conditions
- One hour of flight time in Southeastern Cessna C-172
- One hour of flight time in flight simulator
- Tour of Flight Safety International in Dallas

Contact
(580) 745-2000

Name of College
Southern Illinois University

Name of Program
Summer Wings

Academic / Career Interest
Collegiate flight training

Website
https://aviation.siu.edu/management/community/summer-wings.php

Application Timeline
Contact institution for more information

Eligibility
Open to high school students

Tuition Fees
Contact institution for more information

Information about the program:
Welcome to Summer Wings, a week-long camp for high school students interested in learning more about collegiate flight training!

The camp opens on Sunday afternoon with a tour of the SIU Carbondale campus, a pizza party and activities at the Recreation Center. On Monday morning, class is in session. Our week is spent in aircraft and simulators, in ground school classes and with guest speakers. You'll be introduced to a broad range of topics on a very basic level, including:

- Aerodynamics
- weight and balance computations
- aircraft performance
- radio communications
- decoding weather reports and charts
- aircraft systems
- and more!

Contact
Sarah Vanvooren in Conference and Scheduling Services
(618) 536-775

Name of College
South Dakota State University

Name of Program
ACE Camp

Academic / Career Interest
Aviation

Website
https://www.sdstate.edu/consumer-sciences/ace-camp

Application Timeline
Contact institution for more information

Eligibility
Open to high school-aged students

Tuition Fees
Estimated fees: $350

Information about the program:
Hosted at South Dakota State University (SDSU) every summer (mostly July), this four-day camp provides high school-aged students the opportunity to get an early start on aviation careers. At the camp, students will learn about the fundamentals of flight, get behind the controls of an aircraft, build and launch model rockets, look into the workings of a jet engine, explore an F-16 fighter jet, and visit with aviation professionals. This particular ACE Camp focuses more on aviation, but does touch on aerospace activities.

ACE Camp enables students to make informed decisions as they consider college and career options. Having completed the program, students are more knowledgeable about the importance and diversity of aviation careers, how aviation and aerospace industries have developed and grown to what they are today, and are aware of future career opportunities and developments.

Contact
Cody Christensen
acecamp@sdstate.edu
(605) 688-4983

Name of College
Utah Valley University

Name of Program
Up Up and Away

Academic / Career Interest
Aviation

Website
https://www.uvu.edu/aviation/

Application Timeline
Contact institution for more information.

Eligibility
Ages 14-18

Tuition Fees
Estimated fees: $179

Information about the program:
Learn to fly at UVU's state-of-the-art flight facilities. Includes: safety briefing, ground school, flight prep, simulator, tour of the facility and FAA tower, paper airplane flying contest Graduation certificate and T-shirt included. Students will fly for about 45 minutes during their time.

Contact
(801) 863-888

Name of College
Western Michigan University

Name of Program
Aviation Summer Camp

Academic / Career Interest
Aviation

Website
https://wmich.edu/aviation/future/aviationsummercamp

Application Timeline
Contact institution for more information

Eligibility
Open to high school students (entering 9th grade) ages 13-17

Tuition Fees
Estimated fees:

- Aviation Summer Camp cost is $1,450
- Advanced Flight Aviation Summer Camp cost is $2,300 (to participate in advanced flight camp a student must have previously attended an organized aviation summer camp or completed the initial solo of their private pilot training)
- Aviation Maintenance Camp cost is $1,500.

Information about the program:
Aviation Summer Camps are an awesome opportunity for high school students (entering 9th grade) ages 13-17 to experience many aspects of aviation. Two options are available: those who are generally interested in aviation and want to get some experience will find the Aviation Summer Camp to be their best bet. For those with more experience in aviation or who have already experienced an Aviation Summer Camp, the Advanced Aviation Summer Camp will enhance the knowledge already gained and truly prepare participants for a more in-depth career oriented/experienced environment.

Contact
https://wmich.edu/contact

Name of College
Yale University

Name of Program
The Yale Summer Program in Astrophysics

Academic / Career Interest
Astrophysics

Website
https://yspa.yale.edu

Application Timeline
Approx. Early March

Eligibility
Students must be rising juniors or seniors in order to attend, and you must apply when you are a high school sophomore or junior

Tuition Fees
Estimated fees: $5,250

Information about the program:
YSPA is not a camp, it's not a summer course, and it's not a research internship, but it has elements that are like all of those things. You can expect to be challenged academically and personally and to be pushed to explore the boundaries of your comfort zone. You can expect to meet peers who are as smart (or smarter) than you and who are as passionate about science as you are. Some say it's like going on a month-long scientific mission on a research submarine with a group of similarly obsessed and brilliant scientists, because you are all working intensely on a specific problem in close quarters in a somewhat isolated environment. You might forget about the rest of the world for the four weeks of YSPA, and when the submarine resurfaces, you might find that you've changed. You may find that completing the program is one of the hardest and most rewarding things you've ever done.

Contact
https://yspa.yale.edu/contact-us

Name of College
University of Illinois

Name of Program
Computer Engineering and Computer Science (CE & CS)

Academic / Career Interest
Computer Science

Website
http://publish.illinois.edu/astroillini/

Application Timeline
Approx. Early July

Eligibility
Girls in grades 10 to 11. Requirements: online application

Tuition Fees
Estimated fees: Free

Information about the program
This summer camp for high school girls (entering grades 10 to 11) will be focused on hands-on astronomy projects and learning about real-life research experience as women in science.

Camp highlights include build your own telescope, watch 3D science movies in the NCSA visualization lab, tours to the South Pole Telescope Lab and astrobiology lab, work with scientist on real data in campus computer labs, observation sessions at the University of Illinois observatory (a historical landmark), and talk to women astrophysicists about their research.

Contact
(217) 244-3517
wie@illinois.edu

Math Collegiate Programs

Name of College
Stanford University

Name of Program
Stanford University Mathematics Camp (SUMaC)

Academic / Career Interest
Math

Website
http://sumac.stanford.edu/

Application Timeline
Approx. March

Eligibility
Students currently in grades 10 or 11 are eligible. SUMaC is for students who are sophomores and juniors at the time of application, and who have an exceptional interest and ability in mathematics.

Tuition Fees
Estimated fees: $6,500. Financial aid is available in the form of partial and full scholarships. Aid is granted based upon need, as well as other factors including merit. Members of underrepresented groups are encouraged to apply.

Information about the program
SUMaC welcomes an elite group of talented current 10th- and 11th-grade students from around the world for five-weeks of intensive study in advanced mathematics on Stanford campus.
SUMaC leads participants on a journey in advanced mathematics through lectures, guided research, and group problem solving. In a social environment centered on mathematics, participants explore current lines of mathematical research, the historical development of important areas of mathematics, and applications across scientific disciplines.

Contact
precollegiate@stanford.edu

Name of College
Illinois Institute of Technology

Name of Program
Computational Science Course

Academic / Career Interest
Science / Math / Computation

Website
https://admissions.iit.edu/summer/computational-science-course

Application Timeline
Contact institution for more information

Eligibility
One year of science and completion of Algebra II plus strong math and science grades. No coding experience required.

Tuition Fees
Estimated Fees: $1,000

Information about the program:
Are you a college or advanced high school student interested in science, math, and computation? Learn about these topics in exciting and unconventional ways by enrolling in Illinois Tech's Computational Science course in summer 2018. The course will integrate math and science with computation as a unifying concept.

Using real-world tools such as Mathematica, students will learn how to take an idea or question and find ways to formulate it for a computer. The course consists of hands-on activities and minimal lecturing. At the end of the program, students will acquire better computational thinking, a skill that is critical in an increasingly technological world.

Contact
(312) 567-3025
summer@iit.edu

Name of College
Stanford University

Name of Program
High School Summer College

Academic / Career Interest
Humanities and Sciences, Earth Sciences, Engineering

Website
https://summer.stanford.edu/program/high-school-high-school-summer-college

Application Timeline
Approx. February

Eligibility
Be a current sophomore, junior, or senior, or a gap year student at the time of application.

Tuition Fees
Estimated Fees: $14,426 to $17,054, estimated range for a student attending Stanford Summer Session taking eight units and living on campus.

Information about the program:
During Stanford University's Summer Quarter, high school students from the United States and around the globe are invited to spend eight or nine weeks living and learning in the heart of Silicon Valley. Alongside visiting undergraduate and matriculated students, participants will have an exclusive opportunity as a student in Stanford Summer Session's High School Summer College program to earn credit and a Stanford University transcript at one of the most competitive universities in the world

Contact
precollegiate@stanford.edu

Name of College
Ohio State University

Name of Program
Ross Mathematics Program

Academic / Career Interest
Math

Website
http://u.osu.edu/rossmath/

Application Timeline
Approx. April

Eligibility
Ambitious pre-college students with interests in mathematics and science are invited to apply. First-year students range in age from 15 to 18 years old.

Tuition Fees
Estimated fees: $4,500

Information about the program:
The Ross Program at the Ohio State University is an intensive summer experience designed to encourage motivated pre-college students to explore mathematics. During those six weeks, students are immersed in a world of mathematical discovery.

The central goal of the Ross Program has always been to instruct bright young students in the art of mathematical thinking and to inspire them to discover for themselves that abstract ideas are valuable and important.

Contact
ross@math.osu.edu

Name of College
Boston University

Name of Program
Program in Mathematics for Young Scientists (PROMYS)

Academic / Career Interest
Math

Website
http://www.promys.org/

Application Timeline
Approx. March

Eligibility
PROMYS is a program for pre-college students who will be at least 15 years old by the first day of the program (unfortunately, there is no flexibility on this age requirement). Students from throughout the United States participate as well as many international students.

Tuition Fees
Estimated fees: $4,600

Information about the program:
PROMYS is a six-week summer program at Boston University designed to encourage strongly motivated high school students to explore in depth the creative world of mathematics in a supportive community of peers, counselors, research mathematicians, and visiting scientists. Professor Glenn Stevens, the Director of PROMYS, founded the program in 1989 together with other members of the current faculty.

Contact
(617) 353-2563
promys@bu.edu

Name of College
University of Michigan

Name of Program
Michigan Math and Science Scholars

Academic / Career Interest
Mathematics and science

Website
http://www.math.lsa.umich.edu/mmss/

Application Timeline
Contact institution for more information

Eligibility
Applicant must be a rising sophomore, junior or senior in high school.

Tuition Fees
Estimated fees: $100 application fee and $2,150 for one session

Information about the program:
A program designed to introduce high school students to current developments and research in the sciences and to encourage the next generation of researchers to develop and retain a love of mathematics and science.

Contact
(734) 647-4466
mmss@umich.edu

Name of College
Hampshire College

Name of Program
Summer Studies in Mathematics

Academic / Career Interest
Math

Website
http://hcssim.org/

Application Timeline
Rolling admission

Eligibility
Most students come to the program after their sophomore or junior years in high schools.

Tuition Fees
Estimated fees: $4,913

Information about the program:
Hampshire College Summer Studies in Mathematics (HCSSiM) is an intensive six-week encounter with college-level mathematics for talented and highly motivated high school students. It is demanding and expanding. Participants spend a major portion of each day actively engaged in doing mathematics (not simply learning the results of mathematics). HCSSiM students live in the dorms at Hampshire College in Massachusetts for six summer weeks, and study and play in its fields, woods, and academic buildings (not typically in that order).

Contact
Check website for Contact Us google form for questions

Name of College
Carnegie Mellon University

Name of Program
Summer Academy for Mathematics and Science

Academic / Career Interest
Math and Science

Website
https://admission.enrollment.cmu.edu/pages/access-sams

Application Timeline
Approx. March

Eligibility
The Summer Opportunities for Access & Inclusion Programs invite students with strong academic records, who are U.S. citizens/permanent residents, to apply.

Tuition Fees
Because of Carnegie Mellon's commitment to expanding and diversifying the national STEM pipeline, students admitted to the Summer Academy of Math and Science will not be charged tuition, housing or dining fees.

Information about the program:
Summer Academy for Math and Science provides high school seniors with a strong interest in computer science, engineering and/or the natural sciences, with the opportunity to achieve essential skills necessary to pursue and complete majors in STEM fields. The Summer Academy curriculum includes seminars and highly collaborative hands-on projects, designed and taught by Carnegie Mellon faculty, outstanding teachers and graduate students, carefully chosen due to their commitment to teaching.

Contact
(412) 268-2082
admission@andrew.cmu.edu

Name of College
Bryn Mawr College

Name of Program
Mathematics Infused with Levity (MathILy)

Academic / Career Interest
Math

Website
http://www.mathily.org/

Application Timeline
Approx. April

Eligibility
Students who are not in high school are welcome to apply, but preference will be given to high-school students. Additionally, students who are outside the 14-17 age range may be asked to supply more information as part of the admissions process.

Tuition Fees
Estimated Fees: $4,600

Information about the program:
MathILy is an intensive residential summer program for mathematically excellent secondary students.
Want to explore and create mathematics? Then read on, for that's what MathILy is all about! In MathILy classes, instructors provide the framework and students get to make (and prove!) the conjectures. Students will encounter new ideas, improve their problem-solving skills, learn lots and lots of advanced mathematics, and hone their overall thinking skills. Students will meet others like them (Yes, really. It's a promise.) Most of all, students will find serious mathematics infused with levity.

Contact
info-AT-mathily.org

Name of College
Emory University & Louisiana State University

Name of Program
Math Circle Nonprofit

Academic / Career Interest
Logic and math

Website
https://www.mathcircle.us/

Application Timeline
Approx. February

Eligibility
The program accepts rising 9th through 12th graders; that is, students who will be entering 9th through 12th grade in the fall after the program.

Tuition Fees
Estimated fees: $3,200

Information about the program:
At Math Circle, students will participate in hands-on lessons, activities, and games centered around logic and math. Students will test their probability skills at the Math Circle casino - face off against the house and see if they can hit the jackpot. Students will crack codes and unveil a campus-wide mystery in the Cryptography Scavenger Hunt, and more.

Students will take two courses - Combinatorics and Number Theory - taught by graduate students and postdoctoral students in mathematics.

Contact
(225) 892-1981
contact@mathcircle.us

Name of College
University of Pennsylvania

Name of Program
Mathematics Academy

Academic / Career Interest
Math

Website
http://www.sas.upenn.edu/summer/programs/high-school/mathematics

Application Timeline
Approx. May

Eligibility
Current 9th-11th grade students.

Tuition Fees
Estimated fees: $4,299

Information about the program:
The Mathematics Academy is a unique opportunity for students interested in examining mathematical concepts rarely offered at the high school level. This rigorous, proof-oriented program will fuse lectures, problem sessions, demonstrations, and exploratory research to engage students.

Contact
(215) 898-7326
summer@sas.upenn.edu

Name of College
University of Pennsylvania

Name of Program
Wharton Moneyball Academy

Academic / Career Interest
Math

Website
https://www.jkcp.com/program/wharton-moneyball-academy.php

Application Timeline
Contact institution for more information.

Eligibility
Must be in High School.

Tuition Fees
Estimated fees: $75 application fee + $6,500 for program

Information about the program
Moneyball covers much of Wharton's Statistics 101 course as well as many of its advanced level statistics courses. This program also teaches students how to apply the statistical techniques they learn in AP Statistics. By the end of the course, they will be able to understand how to read and write code in R and do many of the analyses one typically sees in a FiveThirtyEight, Fangraphs, or Hardball Times article.

Contact
(610) 265-9401
Imagine@JKCP.com

Name of College
California Institute of Technology

Name of Program
DaVinci Camp

Academic / Career Interest
Math

Website
https://davinci-camp.com/summer-institute/

Application Timeline
Approx. May

Eligibility
6th - 12th grades but certain programs are only high school. Requirements: online application, supplemental student questionnaire (requires applicants to make a short video as well as a short essay). Deposit is required with the application submission

Tuition Fees
Estimated fees: $3,000

Information about the program
The camp activities blend mathematics, engineering, science, and art instruction in the spirit of Leonardo da Vinci's concept of a Renaissance scholar. Hands-on workshops and a mix of other activities reinforce instruction while balancing the students' day. Students engage their entire analytical and creative potentials in a fast-paced academic environment while meeting others who share their interests and abilities. By having the camp at world-renowned academic institutions, the camp provides students with the opportunity to experience life on college campuses while getting to know Alumni from Berkeley, Stanford, MIT, and Caltech who lead the program and expose students to the world of possibilities and opportunities that await them.

Contact
(415) 275-0246
ContactUs@davincicamp.com

Name of College
University of Michigan

Name of Program
MIDAS data science camp

Academic / Career Interest
Math

Website
http://midas.umich.edu/camp/

Application Timeline
Approx. April

Eligibility
Interested high school students. Experience with trigonometry recommended and interest in math + art. Must be local - day camp non-residential. Requirements: online application.

Tuition Fees
Estimated fees: $495

Information about the program
Students will learn the mathematics behind data science and re-al-life applications.

Contact
(734) 615-8945
midas-contact@umich.edu

Name of College
New York University

Name of Program
Summer Math Program for Young Scholars

Academic / Career Interest
Math

Website
https://cims.nyu.edu/cmt/summer.html

Application Timeline
Approx. May

Eligibility
Grades 9, 10 and 11 who are interested in learning advanced mathematical ideas. Algebra I is the only prerequisite course. Requirements: submitted online application, an official school transcript and a teacher recommendation.

Tuition Fees
Estimated fees: $1,000

Information about the program
CMT's Summer Math Program for Young Scholars Program is an intensive 3-week long summer program for mathematically talented high school students. It provides a mathematically rich environment to high school students interested in mathematics and is designed to encourage them to consider careers in the mathematical sciences. In this program, selected high school students in grades 9 through 11 are introduced to undergraduate level math topics while building problem solving skills. In past years, topics included, but are not limited to number theory, group theory, graph theory, combinatorics, as well as logic and methods of mathematical proof.

Contact
cmt@cims.nyu.edu

Name of College
Boston College

Name of Program
Math Experience

Academic / Career Interest
Math

Website
https://www.bc.edu/bc-web/sites/bc-experience/programs/cred-it-programs/math-experience.html

Application Timeline
Approx. Feb 15th

Eligibility
Must be 11th or 12th grade high school student. Requirements: transcript, application, two letters of recommendation, and personal essay.

Tuition Fees
Estimated fees range from $5,000 - $8,000

Information about the program
This engaging and creative program is designed to challenge high school students with a strong interest in and talent for mathematics. Students in this program will participate in math courses that are focused on topics outside of what is typically covered in a high school setting but does not require a background in Calculus. Under the guidance and instruction of faculty from the Mathematics Department and supported by graduate students in the field, students will have the opportunity to learn and explore a variety of problem-solving skills. Their classroom experience will be supplemented with a Math workshop with an emphasis on collaborative problem solving. Students will also have access to supported evening study sessions.

Contact
(617) 552-3800
bce@bc.edu

Name of College
University of Wisconsin Madison

Name of Program
College Access Program (CAP)

Academic / Career Interest
Math

Website
https://www.education.wisc.edu/soe/about/resource-service-units/student-diversity-programs/college-access-program/overview-(english)

Application Timeline
Approx. April

Eligibility
Rising sophomores or juniors, low income/economically disadvantaged backgrounds or first gen, must have a minimum 2.75 GPA. Requirements: a completed program application, 300-word personal statement, a letter of recommendation, a high school transcript, and scholarship application (optional).

Tuition Fees
Estimated fees: $500

Information about the program
The College Access Program (CAP) is a three-week summer enrichment residential program for first-generation college students or students from economically disadvantaged backgrounds. The program is open to 9th and 10th graders who have completed their high school academic year. Students must be completing their freshman or sophomore year in high school when applying. Students must have a minimum 2.75 GPA and course work which will prepare them for college. This program has various math workshops aimed to assist and strengthen students' math backgrounds to college level proficiency.

Contact
(608) 262-8427

Name of College
University of Illinois Urbana Champaign

Name of Program
Summer Illinois Mathematics Camp - Omega Camp

Academic / Career Interest
Math

Website
https://math.illinois.edu/research/illinois-geometry-lab/summer-illinois-mathematics-camp

Application Timeline
Approx. April 15th

Eligibility
Grades 10-12. Must have taken at least one year of algebra. Commuter camp (should be local). Requirements: application + essay responses (within the application).

Tuition Fees
Estimated fees: FREE

Information about the program
Summer Illinois Math (SIM) Camp is a free, week-long math day camp for middle and high school students hosted by the University of Illinois at Urbana-Champaign Department of Mathematics. Campers will see the creative, discovery driven side of mathematics. By showing them some of the ways a mathematician approaches a problem, SIM Camp hopes to encourage students to continue studying math beyond the high school level.

Contact
(217) 333-3350
math@illinois.edu

Name of College
The Ohio State University

Name of Program
Ross Mathematics Program

Academic / Career Interest
Math

Website
http://u.osu.edu/rossmath/

Application Timeline
Approx. April

Eligibility
Rising sophomores and older. Requirements: application, school transcripts; teacher recommendations; essays concerning the applicant's interests and goals; and the applicant's work on some challenging math problems (optional).

Tuition Fees
Estimated fees: $4,500.

Information about the program
The Ross Program at the Ohio State University is an intensive summer experience designed to encourage motivated pre-college students to explore mathematics. During those six weeks, students are immersed in a world of mathematical discovery.

Contact
ross@math.osu.edu

Name of College
Illinois Institute of Technology

Name of Program
Computational Science Course

Academic / Career Interest
Math

Website
https://admissions.iit.edu/summer/computational-science-course

Application Timeline
Approx. April

Eligibility
One year of science and completion of Algebra II plus strong math and science grades. No coding experience required.

Tuition Fees
Estimated fees: $1,000

Information about the program
Are you a college or advanced high school student interested in science, math, and computation? Students learn about these topics in exciting and unconventional ways by enrolling in Illinois Tech's Computational Science course in summer 2018. The course will integrate math and science with computation as a unifying concept.

Using real-world tools such as Mathematica, students will learn how to take an idea or question and find ways to formulate it for a computer. The course consists of hands-on activities and minimal lecturing. At the end of the program, students will acquire better computational thinking, a skill that is critical in an increasingly technological world.

Contact
summer@iit.edu

Name of College
Hampshire College

Name of Program
Summer Studies in Mathematics

Academic / Career Interest
Math

Website
http://hcssim.org/

Application Timeline
Rolling admission

Eligibility
Most students come to Hampshire College Summer Studies in Mathematics (HCSSiM) after their sophomore or junior years in high schools. Recent programs have included students who have just completed their 9th grade and have taken more advanced math, open to an occasional even younger student.

Tuition Fees
Estimated fees: $4,913

Information about the program
HCSSiM is an intensive six-week encounter with college-level mathematics for talented and highly motivated high school students. It is demanding and expanding. Participants spend a major portion of each day actively engaged in doing mathematics (not simply learning the results of mathematics). HCSSiM students live in the dorms at Hampshire College in Massachusetts for six summer weeks, and study and play in its fields, woods, and academic buildings (not typically in that order).

Contact
http://hcssim.org/contact/

Name of College
Humboldt State University

Name of Program
Summer Session

Academic / Career Interest
Math

Website
https://extended.humboldt.edu/extended-education/summer-session/overview-summer-session

Application Timeline
Opens approx. April and closes when the course fills.

Eligibility
Any student who has met the course pre-requisite or gained instructor approval and has registered. Requirements: Fill out registration form, secure instructor approval for any pre-requisites, and pay for the courses.

Tuition Fees
Estimated fees: $289 per unit

Information about the program
The Summer Session program allows continuing (matriculated) Humboldt State University (HSU) students and non-HSU students to enroll in HSU degree classes, provided that there is space available and prerequisites are fulfilled. Program includes various courses including Math courses up to calculus.

Contact
(707) 826-3731
extended@humboldt.edu

Name of College
University of California, Santa Cruz

Name of Program
California State Summer School for Mathematics and Science (COSMOS)
Discrete Math and Number Theory Cluster

Academic / Career Interest
Math

Website
https://cosmos.ucsc.edu/

Application Timeline
Approx. Jan to Feb

Eligibility
9th - 12th graders with one year of high school mathematics, two years preferred. Algebra 1 minimum.

Tuition Fees
Estimated fees:

- Tuition CA Resident: $3,745
- Tuition Non-CA Resident: $6,000

Information about the program
In the Number Theory course students will learn how to prove mathematical theorems. Students will also focus on experimenting with numbers, coming up with conjectures, and hopefully proving their conjectures. Discrete Math: This course will serve as an introduction to three topics, highlighting different ways of thinking and doing mathematics. The first topic is infinity, where the notions of sets and functions will be introduced. Infinity, being a difficult concept to fully grasp gives a taste of abstraction in mathematics, and the discussion of sets introduces language that will be used the rest of the course.

Contact
(831) 459-1766
cosmos@ucsc.edu

Name of College
Northwestern University

Name of Program
Equinox Program from Center for Talent Development

Academic / Career Interest
Math

Website
https://www.ctd.northwestern.edu/program/equinox#details

Application Timeline
Approx. June

Eligibility
Must be above average level on SAT/ACT tests or other state level exams, must in 9th-12th grades, must complete prerequisite courses as noted in course descriptions. Requirements: test scores, transcript, one letter of recommendation, and online application.

Tuition Fees
Estimated fees:

- Commuter: $2,185
- Residential: $3,795

Information about the program
Center for Talent Development's (CTD) Equinox program provides rigorous, credit-bearing acceleration opportunities for academically advanced students completing grades 9 through 12. Taking challenging courses at a world-class university, participating in recreational activities and social events with friends, and developing the self-confidence and self-directed learning skills crucial to success in college define the Equinox experience.

Contact
summer@ctd.northwestern.edu

Name of College
Notre Dame University

Name of Program
Summer Program in Mathematics

Academic / Career Interest
Math

Website
https://www3.nd.edu/~math/ndsummer/

Application Timeline
Approx. March

Eligibility
Must be a sophomore or junior in high school, from the South Bend Indiana School District. Students must provide their own transportation to and from Notre Dame. Requirements: must fill out online form, have a math teacher submit a letter of recommendation.

Tuition Fees
Estimated fees: FREE, students will receive a $400 stipend upon completion of two-week program.

Information about the program
This program allows student to learn interesting mathematics, with a focus on creative problem solving and topics outside the usual high school curriculum. Students will also have panel discussions about things like applying to college, showing students the excitement of a career in math, science, and technology.

Contact
ndsummermath@gmail.com

Name of College
Pomona College

Name of Program
Pomona College Academy for Youth Success (PAYS)

Academic / Career Interest
Math

Website
https://www.pomona.edu/administration/draper-center/pays/pays-experience

Application Timeline
Approx. Feb 2nd

Eligibility
Must be in 9th grade and a high school student in the Los Angeles, Riverside and San Bernardino Counties. Requirements: online form, two completed essays, two recommendation forms, official high school transcript.

Tuition Fees
Estimated fees: FREE

Information about the program
Program participants attend small classes (approximately 15 students) taught by Pomona College faculty. The faculty work with Pomona College students who serve as program teaching assistants.. Each summer, all PAYS scholars participate in two core faculty-taught courses, Math/Problem Solving and Critical Inquiry: Analysis and Writing.

Contact
(909) 607-1810
drapercenter@pomona.edu

Name of College
Texas A&M University

Name of Program
Summer Mathematics Training High School Camp (SMaRT)

Academic / Career Interest
Math

Website
http://www.math.tamu.edu/outreach/SMaRT/

Application Timeline
Contact institution for more information.

Eligibility
High school students (grades 8 through 12 in Spring) of age 14 through 18 are eligible. US citizenship or permanent residency is required. Requirements: application, awaiting email response for the rest.

Tuition Fees
Estimated fees: FREE

Information about the program
SMaRT is a two-week summer program at Texas A&M University. It is intended to facilitate interest in mathematics of advanced high school students. The camp will provide an intensive learning environment in mathematics, where high school students will learn not only useful mathematical facts, but also how to approach mathematical problems, prove mathematical statements, and write the results.

Contact
camp@math.tamu.edu

Name of College
University of Washington

Name of Program
Math Academy

Academic / Career Interest
Math

Website
https://www.engr.washington.edu/admission/k12/mathacademy

Application Timeline
Approx. March

Eligibility
High school Juniors, min 3.0 GPA, must have completed pre-calculus by years end. Must be a resident of Washington state.

Tuition Fees
Estimated fees: FREE

Information about the program
The University of Washington's Math Academy is a four-week program for incoming high school seniors from underserved communities. Math Academy successfully prepares students for rigorous college coursework and inspires them to pursue a degree in STEM and engineering careers. Math Academy provides students with a supportive environment to hone math skills, explore engineering and sample life as a college student. Students who participate in Math Academy are more likely to successfully pursue and graduate with a degree in engineering.

Contact
Priscilla Yoon, Assistant Director, Pre-College Outreach & Recruitment
(206) 616-3280
plyoon@uw.edu

Name of College
University of Washington

Name of Program
Summer Institute for Mathematics

Academic / Career Interest
Math

Website
http://www.simuw.net/

Application Timeline
Approx. Feb

Eligibility
Must be in high school, have taken at least 3 years of math courses - algebra, trigonometry, and geometry, must be a resident of Washington, British Columbia, Oregon, Idaho, or Alaska.

Tuition Fees
Estimated fees: $2,500

Information about the program
Summer Institute for Mathematics University of Washington (SIMUW) provides a carefully selected group of motivated high school students with ample opportunities to acquire a full appreciation of the nature of mathematics: its wide-ranging content, the intrinsic beauty of its ideas, the nature of mathematical argument and rigorous proof, the surprising power of mathematics within the sciences and beyond. Getting a profound understanding of the depth and beauty of mathematics can be a transforming experience for a student whatever interests the student may intend to pursue in the future, and this is the experience SIMUW is designed to provide.

Contact
(305) 707-4689
simuw@math.washington.edu

Name of College
Wellesley College

Name of Program
Pre-College Immersive program

Academic / Career Interest
Math

Website
https://www.wellesley.edu/summer/summerprograms/immersive

Application Timeline
Approx. May

Eligibility
Rising high school juniors and seniors, Requirements: online form, one letter of recommendation (can be from any teacher), transcript, and $100 non-refundable application fee.

Tuition Fees
Estimated fees: $5,400 (Tuition) + $3,150 (Room, Board, and Activities) = $8,550

Information about the program
Students spend the summer experiencing college life first-hand. Wellesley College invites motivated high school junior and senior girls to join us this summer for a unique, immersive college experience—The Wellesley Pre-College Immersive Program. For four weeks, students will have the opportunity to become members of the Wellesley community, taking courses with college students while earning full college credit. Students will also enjoy academic, social, and intellectual opportunities that cannot be found in a high school program.

Contact
summer@wellesley.edu

Name of College
Wellesley College

Name of Program
Precollege exploratory workshops

Academic / Career Interest
Math

Website
http://www.wellesley.edu/summer/summerprograms/exploratory

Application Timeline
Approx. June 15th

Eligibility
Rising high school sophomores, juniors and seniors. Requirements: precollege application form and $50 application fee.

Tuition Fees
Estimated fees:

- One-week workshop - $1,050 (Tuition) + $300 (Room, Board, and Activities) = $1,350
- Two-week workshop - $1,800 (Tuition) + $600 (Room, Board, and Activities) = $2,400

Information about the program
The Calculus of Happiness workshop: The science of happiness is an emerging, multidisciplinary field of research. Much of that research focuses on psychological interventions that have been proven to increase happiness (e.g., meditation). In this course students will focus on interventions suggested by mathematics that hold the potential to improve our lives. Using only pre-calculus level mathematics, students will explore health, wealth, and love from mathematical perspectives and extract concrete steps one can take to improve those core aspects of their daily lives. Neither Pre-Calculus nor Calculus are requirements.

Contact
summer@wellesley.edu

Name of College
University of Alaska, Anchorage

Name of Program
Acceleration Academy (Summer)

Academic / Career Interest
Math

Website
http://www.ansep.net/high-school/acceleration-academy

Application Timeline
Approx. March 2nd

Eligibility
Must be a high school student. Requirements: application, math placement test, Student Records/Transcripts, and two recommendation forms from teachers, 500-word essay explaining student's plan to contribute to the future of Alaska.

Tuition Fees
Estimated fees: FREE

Information about the program
The Acceleration Academy (Summer) is designed to develop students academically and socially for college, while creating excitement around STEM (Science, Technology, Engineering and Mathematics) degree programs and careers. Students develop skills that can be used for the rest of their academic careers. The classes are taught by university faculty for college credit. Students can earn high school credit by applying for credit through their school counselor. Students will learn more about career opportunities in STEM fields while getting a jumpstart in pursuing those degrees. Acceleration Academy students are hyper-prepared for college and beyond.

Contact
Michael Ulroan, Regional Director
(907) 352-0451
mikeu@alaska.edu

Name of College
Arizona State University

Name of Program
Joaquin Bustoz Math-Science Honors Summer Program

Academic / Career Interest
Math

Website
https://jbmshp.asu.edu/summer_program

Application Timeline
Approx. Feb

Eligibility
10th - 12th grades, sophomores may apply, provided they have completed a minimum of three years of high school mathematics by the end of the academic year. Seniors may apply, provided they plan to attend Arizona State University in the fall. Minimum cumulative unweighted GPA of 3.25.

Tuition Fees
Estimated fees: FREE

Information about the program
The Joaquin Bustoz Math-Science Honors Program is intended for mature and motivated students who are interested in academic careers requiring mathematics, science, or engineering-based coursework and who are typically underrepresented in those fields of study. Selected participants include first-generation college bound students and students representing diverse backgrounds from high schools throughout the state of Arizona, including rural communities and the Navajo Nation. Participants live on the Arizona State University (ASU) Tempe campus while enrolled in a university level mathematics course for college credit.

Contact
(480) 965-1690
mshp@asu.edu

Name of College
ProveIt! Math Academy (Non-profit)

Name of Program
Math Summer Academy

Academic / Career Interest
Math

Website
https://proveitmath.org/

Application Timeline
Approx. March

Eligibility
Entering grade 9, 10, 11, or 12, must be at least 14 years old, and currently attending high school in the US or Canada. Requirements: online math assessment and online application.

Tuition Fees
Estimated fees: $3,284

Information about the program
The Purpose of Prove it! Math Academy summer program is to provide an introduction to mathematical proof in a creative, problem-solving context. In a safe, scenic, memorable location, surrounded by like-minded peers and outstanding instructors, students can reach their full potential. The Prove it! Math Academy curriculum is based on experiences teaching mathematical proof at the undergraduate level, NSF-funded research project Lurch (a word processor that checks reasoning), and coaching of proof-oriented mathematics competitions. The program's philosophy is that mathematical proof is best learned by a gradual transition from the rigor of formal proofs to the clarity of traditional mathematical exposition. The curriculum bridges the gap between calculations and proofs.

Contact
(970) 430-6915
info@proveitmath.org

Name of College
Canada/USA Mathcamp

Name of Program
Mathcamp

Academic / Career Interest
Math

Website
https://www.mathcamp.org/prospectiveapplicants/theprocess.php

Application Timeline
Approx. March

Eligibility
Rising 9th grade and above. Expectations: comfortable with high-school algebra, geometry, trig, exponents and logarithms. Students are expected to have completed Precalculus (or the equivalent).

Tuition Fees
Estimated fees: $4,500

Information about the program
Mathcamp is an intensive 5-week-long summer program for math-ematically talented high school students. More than just a summer camp, Mathcamp is a vibrant community, made up of a wide variety of people who share a common love of learning and passion for mathematics. At Mathcamp, students can explore undergraduate and even graduate-level topics while building problem-solving skills that will help them in any field they choose to study.

Contact
https://www.mathcamp.org/contact.php

Name of College
Areteem Institute for Mathematics

Name of Program
Zoom Mathematics Summer Camp

Academic / Career Interest
Math

Website
https://areteem.org/summer-camps/summer-program-overview

Application Timeline
Approx. Feb

Eligibility
Must be in grades 6th-12th. To automatically qualify (meet one of the following): Returning Math Zoom Students, ZIML Winners: Any student who has won a Gold, Silver or Bronze prize in one of the ZIML Monthly Contests Scored in the Top 5% on the AMC 8, Qualified for AIME, Participated in the MathCounts State Competition (Individual or Team), or Top performers in ARML.

Tuition Fees
Estimated fees:

- Georgetown University - $4,775 - $400 = $4,375 (residential)
- UC San Diego - $4,775 - $400 = $4,375 (residential)
- South Bay Area - $1,700 (day camp only)
- Chicago - $1,900 - $200 = $1,700 (day camp only)
- East Bay Area - $1,900 - $200 = $1,700 (day camp only)

Information about the program
Areteem Institute of Mathematics' flagship summer program is the Math Zoom Summer Camp, for gifted and advanced middle school and high school students, that has been running since 2007. Math Zoom Summer Camps are usually hosted on prestigious university campuses.

Contact
(949) 305-1705
info@areteem.org

Name of College
Emory College/Louisiana State University

Name of Program
Math Circle Summer Program

Academic / Career Interest
Math

Website
https://www.mathcircle.us/summer

Application Timeline
Approx. May

Eligibility
Rising 9th through 12th graders, have completed algebra and passion for math, not necessarily ability. Requirements: student application, pay the $50 application fee.

Tuition Fees
Estimated fees:

- Emory - Commuting - $1,650 (early bird), $1,950 (regular), $2,050 (late registration)
- Emory - Residential - $2,900 (early bird), $3,200 (regular), $3,300 (late registration)
- LSU - Commuting - $750 (early bird), $950 (regular), $1,050 (late registration)

Information about the program
Summer programs at Math Circle give talented high school students a unique introduction to the complex world of college mathematics. At Math Circle, students will participate in hands-on lessons, activities, and games centered around logic and math. Test their probability skills at the Math Circle casino - face off against the house and see if they can hit the jackpot! Crack codes and unveil a campus-wide mystery in the Cryptography Scavenger Hunt, and more

Contact
(225) 892-1981
contact@mathcircle.us

Name of College
New York Math Circle (Non-profit)

Name of Program
High School Summer Program

Academic / Career Interest
Math

Website
https://www.nymathcircle.org/summer

Application Timeline
Approx. April

Eligibility
Must be entering grades 9-12. Requirements: completed application and qualifying exam.

Tuition Fees
Estimated fees: FREE

Information about the program
The Summer High School Math Circle is an academically intensive weekday program for students entering grades 9–12 in the fall that runs for three weeks, five hours a day. A typical day consists of a class in the morning, followed by lunch, and a problem-solving session in the afternoon. Instructors and teaching assistants are very friendly and helpful, and the atmosphere is open and collaborative.

Contact
(646) 706-7647
info@nymathcircle.org

Computer Science Collegiate Programs

Name of College
Carleton College

Name of Program
Summer Computer Science Institute

Academic / Career Interest
Computer Science

Website
https://apps.carleton.edu/summer/scsi/

Application Timeline
Approx. February 13

Eligibility
Students who are currently in 10th and 11th grade (rising junior and senior while the program is in session) are eligible to apply. Students who would like to participate in any Summer A

Tuition Fees
Estimated fees: $3,895

Information about the program
Computer Science is about more than computers: it is the systematic study of processes for solving problems. The Summer Computer Science Institute (SCSI) at Carleton focuses on understanding how to think about these processes, how to program computers to implement them, and how to apply computer science ideas to real problems of interest. During a 3-week program, SCSI students, faculty, and Carleton undergraduate research assistants will engage in lab-based and classroom-based computing research related to faculty and student interests. Each participant will self-select into a research group consisting of 12 students. T

Contact
(866)767-2275
summer@carleton.edu

Name of College
Syracuse University

Name of Program
Learn to Code!

Academic / Career Interest
Computer Science

Website
http://summercollege.syr.edu/program/coding/

Application Timeline
Approx. May 1

Eligibility
Students applying to Summer College are expected to be in good academic standing with a minimum cumulative GPA of 3.0. Students must be a minimum of 15 years of age by the orientation and move-in day of their selected program. Rising juniors and seniors are welcome to apply to any Summer College program.

Tuition Fees
Estimated fees: $3,090

Information about the program
In this course students will learn to code in Python: an easy to learn yet powerful computer programming language. Many of the concepts taught for Python transferrable to learning other programming languages. We will take an applied approach to programming, starting with programming essentials, then using this knowledge to solve real world problems with computer applications.

Contact
(315) 443-5000
sumcoll@syr.edu

Name of College
Princeton University

Name of Program
PACT - Theoretical CS program

Academic / Career Interest
Math

Website
https://algorithmicthinking.org/

Application Timeline
Approx. late June
Consult Institution for more information

Eligibility
Statement of Interest, Transcript, 2 Letters of recommendation, Official Transcript: Guidance counselor must email an official transcript to the email address: summertcs@gmail.com.

Tuition Fees
Estimated fees: $1250

Information about the program
In the main group, most students have limited experience with theoretical computer science. Students start the program by studying topics in discrete mathematics such as systematic counting and methods of proof. They then learn proof techniques, such as induction, and basic graph theory to prove various theorems. Additionally, the students are exposed to combinatorics and probability. Though many students have been exposed to probability in school, the program introduces them to more theoretical and fundamental topics, developing sophisticated ideas from basic principles.

Contact
(315) 443-5000
sumcoll@syr.edu

Name of College
Princeton University

Name of Program
i.D. Tech - Coding and Engineering Academy

Academic / Career Interest
Computer Science

Website
https://www.idtech.com/

Application Timeline
Rolling acceptance – Consult Institution for more information

Eligibility
No formal academic requirement - simply pay and sign up.

Tuition Fees
Estimated fees: $4,099 - $4200

- Can add college prep course (SAT/ACT prep) for an additional $198
- For weekend stay, it's an additional $398

Information about the program
Machine Learning Course: If you had to choose between a computer or a doctor to detect and analyze early signs of cancer, which would you choose?

Why not both? Machine learning methods, while formalized in the 1950s, have only recently become powerful enough to make a huge impact. These deep learning methods have performed better at early cancer detection than professional radiologists. From image detection and Snapchat filters to Natural Language Processing and Siri, machine learning is ready to push our technology into the future.

Contact
(888)709-8324

Name of College
Stanford University

Name of Program
AI4ALL

Academic / Career Interest
Computer Science

Website
http://ai4all.stanford.edu/

Application Timeline
Approx. Feb 15th

Eligibility
Women in 9th grade only. Requirements: Application, a copy of any standardized test score reports, transcript (unofficial is ok), teacher recommendations from science and math teachers who can speak on student's aptitude.

Tuition Fees
Estimated fees: Free

Information about the program
Stanford AI4ALL intends to increase diversity in the field of Artificial Intelligence by targeting students from a range of financial and cultural backgrounds. Our mission is to inspire tomorrow's leaders to know, think and use Artificial Intelligence. We aim to educate students through this three-week residential program with a combination of lectures, hands-on research projects, field trips, and mentoring activities.

Contact
precollegiate@stanford.edu

COLLEGE CONSULTING EXPERTS

Name of College
Cornell University

Name of Program
The Digital World Program

Academic / Career Interest
Computer Science

Website
https://www.sce.cornell.edu/sc/programs/index.php?v=113

Application Timeline
Approx. March 4th

Eligibility
Grades 11 and 12. Requirements: Application, transcript, letters of recommendation from science and math teacher

Tuition Fees
Estimated fees: $6,310 for the three-week program

Information about the program
Digital music, web technology, robots, computer games, human-computer interaction, privacy and security in our networked world . . . These are some of the topics you'll explore in this cutting-edge program where the study of computing and information technologies intertwines with the analysis of social, historical, and ethical dimensions.

Contact
(607) 255-6203
summer_college@cornell.edu

Name of College
University of California, Los Angeles

Name of Program
Game Lab Summer Institute

Academic / Career Interest
Computer Science

Website
https://www.summer.ucla.edu/institutes/GameLab

Application Timeline
Approx. April 1st

Eligibility
At least 14 years old, must be in at least 9th grade. Requirement: online application and non-refundable fee ($150)

Tuition Fees
Estimated fees: $2,361 + $150 non-refundable deposit is required

Information about the program
The UCLA Game Lab Summer Institute introduces high school students to game-making as a form of artistic practice, teaching them the techniques and tools that will help them develop analog and digital games that reflect their own creative voice and vision. No previous game-making skills are required, but students with an interest in games and in the visual arts in particular will find the curriculum especially stimulating and rewarding.

Contact
(310) 825-4101
info@summer.ucla.edu

Name of College
University of Michigan

Name of Program
Seth Bonders Summer Camp in Computational and Data Science

Academic / Career Interest
Computer Science

Website
https://cdscamp.engin.umich.edu/

Application Timeline
Approx. April 27th

Eligibility
High school students who can use a web browser and use basic algebra. Must be local (commuter day camp). Requirements: Online application.

Tuition Fees
Estimated fees: $300

Information about the program
The Seth Bonder Summer Camp in Computational and Data Science for Engineering is intended for high school students interested in engineering who have no or minimal background in data science and computer programming. The camp only requires that participants are able to use a browser and have the desire to learn computational and data science through meaningful and exciting applications, in machine learning, optimization, computational social science, and genomics.

Contact
Ted Norris
(734) 764-9269
tnorris@umich.edu

Name of College
University of Michigan

Name of Program
WISE Code Camp

Academic / Career Interest
Computer Science

Website
https://youthhub.umich.edu/marketplace/competitionDe-tails/6d4b9de0-1ab2-4730-9503-f37b507eb0ee

Application Timeline
Approx. April 6th

Eligibility
Will complete 9th,10th, or 11th grade, are a woman, and have an interest in computer science, mathematics, technology, coding or engineering. Must be local - commuter program. Bring own lunch. Requirements: online application + STEM teacher recommendation.

Tuition Fees
Estimated fees: $450. Need-based scholarships are available.

Information about the program
The Girls Code camp introduces students to programming and pro-gramming concepts in a fun and supportive environment. One of the languages our camp will focus on is Python and no previous experi-ence is necessary. The number of campers is limited to 30.

Contact
youth-hub@umich.edu

Name of College
NYU

Name of Program
Computer Science for Cyber Security (CS4CS) Summer Program for High School Women

Academic / Career Interest
Computer Science

Website
http://engineering.nyu.edu/k12stem/cs4cs/

Application Timeline
Approx. April 9th

Eligibility
In grades 9-12 and are a woman. Must be within commuting distance of the NYU engineering school. Requirements: application, unofficial transcript

Tuition Fees
Estimated fees: free

Information about the program
Computer Science for Cyber Security (CS4CS) is a FREE, three-week, full-day summer program providing an introduction for high school women on the fundamentals of cyber security and computer science at the NYU Tandon School of Engineering. No background or experience in cyber security or computer programming is needed in order to apply, only your interest and enthusiasm. The program is led by members of the Department of Computer Science and Engineering and the Offensive Security, Incident Response and Internet Security (OSIRIS) Laboratory.

Contact
k12.stem@nyu.edu

Name of College
Boston University

Name of Program
Codebreakers

Academic / Career Interest
Computer Science

Website
http://www.bu.edu/lernet/cyber/index.html

Application Timeline
Approx. May 1st

Eligibility
Young women entering 10th or 11th grade at a school in greater Boston area in Fall 2018. Must be local (commuter camp). Requirements: online application, 2 letters of recommendation w/ at least 1 STEM recommendation but preferred both be STEM teachers.

Tuition Fees
Estimated fees: $100

Information about the program
Codebreakers is a program for young women who are currently either freshmen or sophomores in high school and who are interested in learning about computer security.

Contact
(774) 606-9367
cyber@bu.edu

Name of College
Brandeis University

Name of Program
App Design Bootcamp

Academic / Career Interest
Computer Science

Website
https://www.brandeis.edu/precollege/app-design/index.html

Application Timeline
Approx. June 4th – rolling application decisions

Eligibility
Student in HS. Requirements: essays, GPA, online application.

Tuition Fees
Estimated fees: $3,300

Information about the program
Developed and taught by Brandeis Computer Science Professor Tim Hickey, App Design Boot Camp combines college-level coursework with field trips and social activities to provide you with an exciting and transformative summer experience. You'll learn what it takes to create your own groundbreaking web application using industry standard technology such as HTML5, CSS and the Meteor Javascript Web Platform!

Contact
(781) 736-8416
precollege@brandeis.edu

Name of College
Georgia Tech

Name of Program
High School App & Game Academy

Academic / Career Interest
Computer Science

Website
https://ceismc.gatech.edu/studentprograms/summer-peaks_programs/highschool/h4

Application Timeline
Contact Institution for more information

Eligibility
Rising grades 10-12. Must be local to metro Atlanta area. Program is non-residential. Requirements: online application

Tuition Fees
Estimated fees: $450 + $10 application fee

Information about the program
High school students can come to this program to explore how to create their own apps and games, and maybe even become the next "app-illionaire!" This fun-filled week for students teaches the basics of app and game creation for a variety of mobile, console, web, and computer platforms using Construct 2. Throughout the week, students will learn the fundamentals of user interface design, touch controls, graphics editing, and app/game design to create their very own app/game projects! On the last day, students will present their projects to be judged by parents. All students finish the week with their own app/game to share with the world!

Contact
(404) 894-0777

COLLEGE CONSULTING EXPERTS

Name of College
Georgia Tech

Name of Program
Java Programming Camp

Academic / Career Interest
Computer Science

Website
http://gtcomputingoutreach.org/summerCamp.html#

Application Timeline
Rolling admission until program fills – Consult Institution for more information

Eligibility
Rising 9th through 12th grades. Must be local (day camp). Requirements: registration form.

Tuition Fees
Estimated fees: $400

Information about the program
This camp is designed to engage in topics of computer science and equip students with the tools of a high level programming language and object-oriented programming. Students will learn programming concepts using the Java language and work to establish skills and facility that can be applied to the AP Computer Science exam. Students will employ iteration, arrays, randomness, and control structures to design programs of increasing complexity. In addition, students will engage in projects designed to connecting programming to relevant real world situations and needs.

Contact
(404) 385-1395
oecoutreachevents@gmail.com

Name of College
Georgia Tech

Name of Program
Programming Games in Unity

Academic / Career Interest
Computer Science

Website
http://gtcomputingoutreach.org/summerCamp.html#

Application Timeline
Rolling admission until program fills – Consult Institution for more information

Eligibility
Rising 9th through 12th grades. Must be local (day camp). Requirements: registration form.

Tuition Fees
Estimated fees: $400

Information about the program
Unity is one of the industry standard development environments for game design in 3D. In this course we will work through the game development pipeline as we design environments, characters, and program game interactions within the Unity development environments. The class will also explore elements of successful and engaging game experiences and study the design and software development process. Students will also work with programming in C# and Javascript.

Contact
(404) 385-1395
oecoutreachevents@gmail.com

Name of College
Google

Name of Program
Google for Education: Computer Science Summer Institute

Academic / Career Interest
Computer Science

Website
https://buildyourfuture.withgoogle.com/programs/computer-science-summer-institute/#!?detail-content-tabby_activeEl=detail-overview-content

Application Timeline
Rolling admission until program fills – Consult Institution for more information

Eligibility
Current high school seniors

Tuition Fees
Estimated fees: Free. Google will provide round-trip transportation within the US and Canada, and housing. Most meals will be provided either at the dorm or at Google. For the day camps, students will be provided with a travel stipend and expected to commute into the respective Google offices for each day of CSSI.

Information about the program
Kick start your university studies in computer science with an unforgettable summer program at Google. Google's Computer Science Summer Institute (CSSI) is a three-week introduction to computer science for graduating high school seniors with a passion for technology — especially students from historically underrepresented groups in the field.

Contact
cssi@google.com

Name of College
University of Florida

Name of Program
Gator Computing Program

Academic / Career Interest
Computer Science

Website
https://www.cpet.ufl.edu/students/rise/

Application Timeline
Approx. March 15th - priority deadline

Eligibility
Grades 10 and 11. Requirements: Online application form, Two 300-500 word essays, One teacher/mentor endorsement from STEM teacher, and A copy of your current report card.

Tuition Fees
Estimated fees: $500

Information about the program
Gator Computing Program is a two-week, non-residential program for students entering 10th and 11th grade. Students enrolled in the Gator Computing Program engage with UF faculty from the engineering, social sciences, medical research, and biotechnology disciplines, and those with expertise in 3-D printing technologies. Each afternoon, students tour various campus laboratories for an up-close view of what scientific work really looks like. One of the tours will be to the UF Data Center, home to HiPerGator, UF's supercomputer. HiPerGator, short for High Performance Gator, is among the top supercomputers owned by a U.S. university. During week one of the program, students will spend the mornings learning how to use computational tools to solve problems. The program is managed by UFIT Research Computing and the Center for Pre-collegiate Education and Training.

Contact
(352) 392-2310

Name of College
Villanova University

Name of Program
Julian Krinsky Coding Academy

Academic / Career Interest
Computer Science

Website
https://www.jkcp.com/program/julian-krinsky-coding-academy.php

Application Timeline
Rolling admissions - program beginApprox. July 8th. Earlier applications have priority
Consult Institution for more information

Eligibility
Grades 9-12. Requirements: online application, deposit, app fee, and cancellation forms, once confirmed, supplemental forms will be sent to your account for completion.

Tuition Fees
Estimated fees: $4,375

Information about the program
Our coding intensive is the summer hub for honing your programming skills. Prepare to be amazed at what you can accomplish in only two weeks! You'll not only take your coding skills to the next level; you'll also get a unique glimpse into the technology industry and potential careers.

Contact
(610) 265-9401
Imagine@JKCP.com

Name of College
Penn State

Name of Program
Computers and Cyber Security Camp

Academic / Career Interest
Computer Science

Website
https://berks.psu.edu/computers-and-cyber-security-camp

Application Timeline
Rolling admission - closes two weeks prior to camp start date
Consult Institution for more information

Eligibility
Grades 9 – 12 HS students who have demonstrated interest in electronics, cybersecurity, and computers. Requirements: online application

Tuition Fees
Estimated fees:

- Residential: $785
- Commuter: $485

Information about the program
The Computers and Cyber Security Camp includes problem-based instruction and hands-on activities with a strong emphasis on exposing students to computer security/information assurance careers, especially in the financial services industry. Students will be involved in many activities designed to protect and defend personal privacy and information systems, and they will learn techniques for information system restoration by incorporating protection, detection, and recovery capabilities.

Contact
Cathleen Phillips
(610) 396-6225
cxp57@psu.edu

Name of College
University of Illinois Urbana Champaign

Name of Program
Computer Engineering and Computer Science (CE & CS)

Academic / Career Interest
Computer Science

Website
https://wie.engineering.illinois.edu/k-12-programs-resources/
gameswyse-camp/camp-tracks/computer-science/

Application Timeline
Approx. April 15th

Eligibility
9th through 12th grades, must be a woman. Requirements: app, email for STEM teacher recommender, transcript, and statement of purpose essay.

Tuition Fees
Estimated fees is $1,000

Information about the program
Computing is all around us, and you can find it almost everywhere. In this camp you'll explore how code intersects with your digital and physical worlds. In this camp you will: Learn fundamental concepts found in any programming language using Scratch, a popular open-source programming language developed at MIT, design and create a mobile app for Android phones or tablets using App Inventor, an open-source app development tool, explore the intersection of art, fashion, and technology through e-textile projects.

Contact
(217) 244-3517
wie@illinois.edu

Name of College
Girls who code

Name of Program
Summer Immersion Program

Academic / Career Interest
Computer Science

Website
https://girlswhocode.com/summer-immersion-programs/

Application Timeline
Approx. March 16th

Eligibility
Must be in HS and a rising Junior or Senior. Requirements: online application.

Tuition Fees
Estimated fees: Free

Information about the program
Students learn computer science through real-world projects in art and storytelling, robotics, video games, web sites, apps and more. This camp also brings its students to local area tech companies where they can meet and speak with female engineers at the company and learn what it's like to be a professional computer scientist as a woman in tech.

Contact
(415) 992-4700
info@naturebridge.org

Engineering Collegiate Programs

Name of College
John Hopkins University

Name of Program
Engineering Innovation

Academic / Career Interest
Engineering

Website
https://ei.jhu.edu/

Application Timeline
Several application deadlines - Approx. (February 15, March 1, March 15, April 1, April 15, May 1, May 15, June 1)

Eligibility
The typical student is a rising junior or senior in high school. Talented 9th graders (rising sophomores) may be considered, however, priority will be given to older students. Graduated seniors are also eligible.

Because the Engineering Innovation course is college level course, for a student to be eligible to apply, the student must meet the following requirements have As and Bs in their high school math and science classes.

Tuition Fees
Estimated fees: $6,700

Information about the program
Engineering Innovation (EI) is an exciting, hands-on summer course for high school students interested in engineering. This program is offered at the JHU Homewood campus in Baltimore, MD and at other sites in Maryland, California, the District of Columbia, Ohio, and Pennsylvania. A residential experience is available at the JHU Homewood campus and Hood College. Through Engineering Innovation, high school students put engineering concepts to the test.

Contact
(410) 516-6224
ei@jhu.edu

Name of College
Washington University St. Louis

Name of Program
Pre-Engineering Institute

Academic / Career Interest
Engineering

Website
http://summerexperiences.wustl.edu/engineering

Application Timeline
Approx. April 1

Eligibility
To be eligible for a High School Summer Institute students should be a current freshman, sophomore, or junior in high school.

Tuition Fees
Estimated fees: $5,585

Information about the program
Engineering is one of the fastest growing career fields in the world. Discover the exciting and diverse fields of engineering and learn how to apply scientific, economic, and social knowledge to solve problems, create new systems, or design a structure. We offer the Pre-Engineering Institute in both June and July.

This institute combines traditional undergraduate class and lab curriculum with organized field trips, guest lectures, and hands-on activities in order for students to gain valuable academic and career experience. The institute is divided into morning and afternoon sessions that include assigned readings, daily assignments, and a final project.

Contact
(314) 935-4807
summerexperiences@wustl.edu

Name of College
Wheaton College

Name of Program
Bioengineering for Girls

Academic / Career Interest
Engineering

Website
https://www.explo.org/focus/bioengineering-for-girls/

Application Timeline
Consult Institution for more information

Eligibility
Grades 9-11

Tuition Fees
Estimated fees: $5,215

Information about the program
Science spans the real world and is applied to our daily lives in more ways than we typically think about. From robotics to genetics to medical technology, STEM scientists are exploring the far limits of the field (and in some cases, redefining them completely). Connect with leading women in STEM and explore the possibilities of careers in biomechanics, prosthetics, environmental science, neuropsychology, tissue engineering, epidemiology, biophotography, pharmacology, and beyond. With this launchpad, you'll feel informed and prepared as you apply to university — and jump right into your major field of study. The most interesting work in bioengineering and medicine transcends a single discipline. At EXPLO, you'll be introduced to these transdisciplinary fields. Work with top researchers and visit leading labs throughout the Boston area to network with future mentors. Hone your foundational science skills in hands-on labs and grapple with real-life cases in medical simulations. Design, build and test a medical device under the guidance of professionals in the field.

Contact
(781) 762-7400

Name of College
MIT

Name of Program
Women's Technology Program

Academic / Career Interest
Engineering

Website
http://wtp.mit.edu/application.html

Application Timeline
Approx. Jan 15th

Eligibility
Eligibility: Must be a female HS Junior. Requirements: Application, 2 letters of recommendations from math and science teachers, Transcript, and test scores from either ACT/SAT/PSAT or AP exams in science & math or SAT II subject tests in math or science

Tuition Fees
Estimated fees: Cost free if household income is under 120K. $3,500 if above that.

Information about the program
The MIT Women's Technology Program (WTP) is a rigorous four-week summer academic and residential experience where female high school students explore engineering through hands-on classes, labs, and team-based projects in the summer after 11th grade

Contact
wtp@mit.edu

Name of College
MIT

Name of Program
LaunchX - entrepreneur summer program

Academic / Career Interest
Engineering

Website
https://launchx.com/summer-program/massachusetts-insti-tute-of-technology.php

Application Timeline
Approx. Priority deadline: Dec 18th. Regular deadline: Feb 20th

Eligibility
Must be in HS. Requirements: transcript, application, test scores, and a video introduction to yourself.

Tuition Fees
Estimated fees: $6,295. There is a $60 application fee. Financial aid is available and scales based on need.

Information about the program
LaunchX gives students the skills and mindset to start real companies. Our programs help students leverage their talents and tenacity to build a viable startup. We'll train you in the skills and innovative thinking that allow founders to create successful businesses, challenging you to take a real startup from idea to execution and impact.

Contact
info@launchx.com

Name of College
MIT

Name of Program
Lincoln Laboratory Radar Introduction for Student Engineers (LL-RISE)

Academic / Career Interest
Engineering

Website
https://www.ll.mit.edu/outreach/LLrise.html

Application Timeline
Approx. Deadline is March 31st

Eligibility
Requirements: application online, copy of test scores, and transcript. Two letters of recommendation from science and math teacher.

- Be a U.S. citizen (foreign citizens who are permanent residents are not eligible)
- Have completed or will complete physics and pre-calculus by end of junior year
- Be passionate about science, math, and engineering
- Be completing your junior year in high school
- Encourages Underrepresented groups and minorities to apply

Tuition Fees
Estimated fees: Free. Students will provide own transport at the beginning and end of the program.

Information about the program
The Lincoln Laboratory Radar Introduction for Student Engineers (LLRISE) program is a summer workshop teaching 18 students how to build small radar systems. This summer STEM program is a FREE two-week residential project-based enrichment program for outstanding students currently in their junior year in high school. This workshop is typically held the end of July.

Contact
LLRISE@LL.mit.edu

Name of College
MIT

Name of Program
National Geographic engineering and robotics @ MIT

Academic / Career Interest
Engineering

Website
http://ngstudentexpeditions.com/technology-and-innovation-workshop-mit/dates-tuition

Application Timeline
Contact Institution for more information

Eligibility
Eligibility: Must be a US HS student. Requirements: online application, applicant statement, two recommendations from teachers, signed applicant agreement form and a $700 application fee + program deposit.

Tuition Fees
Estimated fees: $5,290. There is an additional $200 application fee and $500 deposit. Includes housing and meals and all associated costs except transportation to and from MIT.

Information about the program
Get a first-hand look at new technologies that are being used to address challenges facing the modern world. See a nuclear reactor in action, experiment with 3D printers to create objects of your own design, and visit a garden engineered on the roof of Fenway Park. Robotics Innovation Track: Discover how National Geographic explorers are using emerging technologies to share the stories of our world. Learn about advances in fields ranging from underwater robotics to satellite imagery, and test out devices like an ROV—a high-tech tool that is strengthening our connection with the planet and allowing storytellers to delve deeper into the pressing issues of our time.

Contact
(877) 877-8759

Name of College
Northwestern University

Name of Program
NSLC on Engineering summer program

Academic / Career Interest
Engineering

Website
https://www.nslcleaders.org/youth-leadership-programs/engi-neering-summer-programs/#section-2

Application Timeline
Rolling admissions - Contact Institution for more information

Eligibility
Must be in high school. Requirements: online application, transcript, and contact information for a counselor recommendation and teacher recommendation.

Tuition Fees
Estimated fees: $3,095. This covers all costs except airfare and transportation to and from the program. All meals and housing are included in the cost.

Information about the program
At the NSLC on Engineering summer program for high school students, you'll explore a variety of engineering fields including mechanical, civil, electrical, and biomedical engineering. Professors and professional engineers will tell you about exciting new research endeavors and their latest projects. Then, engineering simulations give you the opportunity to design and build with your teammates.

Contact
(800) 994-6752

Name of College
Cornell University

Name of Program
Robotics and Programming

Academic / Career Interest
Engineering

Website
https://www.sce.cornell.edu/sc/programs/index.php?v=199

Application Timeline
Approx. March 4th

Eligibility
Grades 10-12. Requirements: Application, transcript, letters of recommendation from science and math teacher

Tuition Fees
Estimated fees: $4,250 for housing, tuition, and meals plus an additional $245 for the robotics kit.

Information about the program
In this innovative program, you'll experiment with Arduino microcontrollers to create small robots. You'll then use these robots to explore topics such as programming, control theory, and algorithm design. You'll supplement robotics workshop time with college-level coursework in subjects ranging from engineering to science and technology, and you'll enjoy field trips to Cornell's first-class research facilities, including the synchrotron.

Contact
(607) 255-6203
summer_college@cornell.edu

Name of College
Cornell University

Name of Program
CURIE program

Academic / Career Interest
Engineering

Website
https://sites.coecis.cornell.edu/curieacademy/

Application Timeline
Approx. March 1st

Eligibility
Requirements: application, transcript, HS profile, standardized test scores (PSAT/ACT/SAT/SATII/APs where applicable but if you haven't taken one, it's not required to apply). Have a 3.0/4.0 GPA. Be a high school rising junior or senior, and must be young women interested in learning about engineering.

Tuition Fees
Estimated fees: $1,450 for tuition, room & board, meals, and research supplies. Financial aid is available.

Information about the program
The CURIE Academy is a one-week summer residential program for high school girls who excel in math and science and want to learn more about careers in engineering. Cornell University's world-renowned faculty and graduate students will lead CURIE participants in classes, lab sessions, and project research. Social events, panel discussions, and other out-of-classroom activities will provide participants with opportunities to network informally with Cornell faculty, staff, and students.

Contact
(607) 255-6403
dpeng@cornell.edu

Name of College
Cornell University

Name of Program
CATALYST program

Academic / Career Interest
Engineering

Website
https://sites.coecis.cornell.edu/catalystacademy/academy-over-view/

Application Timeline
Approx. March 1st

Eligibility
A minimum GPA of 3.0/4.0, Be a high school rising junior or senior and be young men and women of diverse racial, socioeconomic, or geographic backgrounds. Requirements: The online application, online teacher recommendation, transcript, high school profile, and financial assistance form (optional), and standardized test scores.

Tuition Fees
Estimated fees: $1450 includes room, board/meals, and research supplies. Financial aid is available.

Information about the program
The CATALYST Academy is a one-week summer residential program for rising high school juniors, and seniors. The mission of the CATALYST Academy is to advance diversity in engineering and its related disciplines. Therefore, applications from students from backgrounds (African American, Latino/a, or Native American) critically under-represented in the fields of science, technology, engineering, and math are especially encouraged. During the CATALYST Academy, Cornell University's world-renowned faculty and graduate students lead participants in classes, lab sessions, and project research.

Contact
(607) 255-6403
dpeng@cornell.edu

Name of College
Rice University

Name of Program
Rice Institute for Dynamic Research

Academic / Career Interest
Engineering

Website
https://www.rstem.rice.edu/ridr

Application Timeline
Approx. Spring 2019

Eligibility
Must be currently in 11th grade. Requirements: Application, Student articulates a clear motivation to attend (essay), completed Participant Agreement Form, resume, statement of purpose, and latest report card/transcript.

Tuition Fees
Estimated fees: Free with funding available to provide small stipends for particularly outstanding students.

Information about the program
The Rice Institute for Dynamics Research (RIDR) is a 6-week program for four current 11th grade students to shadow graduate students and postdocs in their engineering research at Rice University. Dr. Matthew Brake is an Assistant Professor in the Department of Mechanical Engineering at Rice University. Prior to joining the faculty of Rice, Dr. Brake founded and directed the predecessor to this institute, NOMAD, hosted at Sandia National Laboratories and the University of New Mexico. While students will assist with experiments and learn more about mechanical engineering, they will also experience cross-cultural collaboration through their work. This program only occurs every two years.

Contact
(713) 348-8211
selena.zermeno@rice.edu

Name of College
USC

Name of Program
Discover Engineering Summer Program

Academic / Career Interest
Engineering

Website
https://summerprograms.usc.edu/programs/4-week/engineering/

Application Timeline
Approx. April 27th

Eligibility
You must have completed at least the 9th grade by June 17, 2018. You should be pursuing a rigorous high school curriculum to excel in USC Summer Programs.

Tuition Fees
Estimated fees is $5,000

Information about the program
Engineering is a field that impacts every aspect of life, including society, politics and technology. If you have considered the study of engineering at the college level, this course is an excellent way to preview what's ahead. You will explore various disciplines of engineering through academic lectures and classroom discussions. You will gain practical experience through hands-on projects which involve designing, building and testing. You will learn how to conduct research using design thinking and the engineering design process. You will explore Aerospace engineering, Biomedical engineering, Chemical engineering, Civil engineering, Computer science, Electrical engineering, Environmental engineering, Industrial engineering, and Mechanical engineering.

Contact
(213) 740-5679
summer@usc.edu

Name of College
USC

Name of Program
3D Design and Prototyping

Academic / Career Interest
Engineering

Website
https://summerprograms.usc.edu/programs/4-week/3ddesign/

Application Timeline
Approx. April 27th

Eligibility
You must have completed at least the 9th grade by June. You should
be pursuing a rigorous high school curriculum to excel in USC
Summer Programs. You may be either a domestic or international
student. Requirements: online application, including the 300-500
word essay written by you, 60 dollar app fee, letter of recommendation from teacher or guidance counselor (Send the completed
form to the USC Summer Programs Office; email is fine), and official
high school transcript to the USC Summer Programs Office must be
MAILED. Transcripts must be signed and stamped by your school
office. Emailed or faxed transcripts are not accepted.

Tuition Fees
Estimated fees ranges from $5,500 - $8,000

Information about the program
This course explores how significant innovations in the areas of 3D
computer graphics and 3D printing technologies are revolutioniz-
ing how designers, artists, and engineers create products and tools.
You will learn an overview of modern 3D design and modeling
techniques and also explore the range of printing and prototyping
technologies in use today

Contact
(213) 740-5679
summer@usc.edu

Name of College
USC

Name of Program
SHINE program

Academic / Career Interest
Engineering

Website
https://viterbipk12.usc.edu/shine/

Application Timeline
Approx. May 21st

Eligibility
10th through 12th grades, must have 3.4+ GPA unweighted, must be local (non residential program) Requirements: online application, transcript, test scores (PSAT/SAT/ACT - optional but assist in lab placements), Two letters of recommendation from STEM teachers, personal statement, and 35-dollar application fee.

Tuition Fees
Estimated fees: $4,900

Information about the program
Designed specifically for high school students on an ambitious STEM pathway, this is a unique seven-week opportunity to participate in hands-on engineering laboratory research focused on real-world problems at one of the top-ranked engineering schools in the nation. Close mentorship comes from USC Viterbi faculty and staff, graduate student researchers, plus visiting national scholars -- all enveloped within SHINE's cohort activities and network.

Contact
https://viterbipk12.usc.edu/contact/

Name of College
USC

Name of Program
Mission Engineering Program

Academic / Career Interest
Engineering

Website
https://viterbipk12.usc.edu/missionengineering/

Application Timeline
Approx. May 1st

Eligibility
10th through 12th, min 3.0 GPA, must have completed algebra II w/ at least a B avg. Requirements: online application, letter of recommendation from STEM teacher, and complete a school records request form.

Tuition Fees
Estimated fees: $750

Information about the program
Spend two weeks this July exploring various disciplines offered in engineering, including aerospace, biomedical, civil, computer science, and mechanical engineering. Gain engineering skills by designing, building, and testing team-oriented, hands-on projects. Mission Engineering has been a part of USC Viterbi for 11 years.

Contact
Dr. Rochelle Urban
rurban@usc.edu

Name of College
USC

Name of Program
SCIHI

Academic / Career Interest
Engineering

Website
http://viterbiinnovation.usc.edu/scihi/

Application Timeline
Approx. April 15th

Eligibility
10th through 12th grades. minimum 3.5/4.0 GPA. Must be local (non residential program). Requirements: online application, official HS transcripts, 1 letter of recommendation from STEM teacher. Application fee of 35 dollars is required.

Tuition Fees
Estimated fees: $3,500

Information about the program
High school students are invited to participate in a highly experiential course teaching key concepts of engineering entrepreneurship focused on the theme of the "Internet of Things". Students will learn how to think like an entrepreneur, develop a commercialization plan for an invention of your own design, and gain hands-on skills in developing electronic and digital prototypes. Topics covered include entrepreneurial team dynamics, technology and strategic assessments, creativity and business model development, communication to investors and technology managers, and technology plan development.

Contact
Viterbi-innovation@usc.edu

Name of College
Carnegie Mellon

Name of Program
CMU Engineering Workshop

Academic / Career Interest
Engineering

Website
http://www.andrew.cmu.edu/course/24-engineeringworkshop/

Application Timeline
Approx. Jan 1st

Eligibility
Rising 10th and 11th graders only. Must be local (non residential program). Requirements: application, short essay response, teacher recommendation form, and official HS transcript

Tuition Fees
Estimated fees: $900 for tuition and $200 deposit

Information about the program
Do you know what you want to study in college, or what career you want to pursue? Have you considered engineering? How much do you know about it? Come join us for a week to learn more about what engineers do and what it would be like to study engineering in college at one of the nation's top engineering schools! Try out real mechanical engineering practices! Learn how to make your own products with computer-aided design software, and then fabricate them in a CMU makerspace using Laser Cutting, 3D Printing, Resin Casting. Learn about other engineering disciplines (electrical, biomedical, robotics, etc.) through daily presentations and tours of CMU labs.

Contact
(412) 952-5991
engineeringworkshop@cmu.edu

Name of College
University of Michigan

Name of Program
SEE Camp

Academic / Career Interest
Engineering

Website
http://www.swe.engin.umich.edu/seecamp

Application Timeline
Approx. Feb 23rd

Eligibility
High school students in 10th - 12th grades who demonstrate an interest/aptitude for math, science, and engineering. Requirements: application only.

Tuition Fees
Estimated fees: $650

Information about the program
The Summer Engineering Exploration (SEE) Camp is a one week, residential camp for high school students interested in engineering. Hosted by the Society of Women Engineers at the University of Michigan, SEE Camp provides opportunities for the campers to discover the possibilities of engineering. The program costs $650 (current estimate), and there are Financial Aid Scholarships available to all students in need. Please do not let cost keep you from applying. Financial Aid forms will be mailed with letters of acceptance in March.

Contact
swe.seecamp@umich.edu

Name of College
University of Michigan

Name of Program
The Summer College Engineering Exposure Program (SCEEP)

Academic / Career Interest
Engineering

Website
https://cedo.engin.umich.edu/diversity/programs/k12/sea/

Application Timeline
Approx. March 30th

Eligibility
Must be in 11th grade currently. Requirements: A complete application includes biographical and academic information, three recommendations, two essays, and your ACT and/or SAT standardized test scores.

Tuition Fees
Estimated fees: $2,000, however the program is subsidized down to $500 for each participant

Information about the program
The Summer College Engineering Exposure Program (SCEEP) is an 11-day residential program that exposes current U.S. domestic 11th-grade students to the engineering disciplines offered at U-M. The program includes: exposure to life on a college campus while living in Bursley Residential Hall, classes designed to help students develop an understanding of engineering, team-focused project-based learning through engineering design challenges, informal discussions with College of Engineering alumni, faculty, staff, and students, and campus tours and workshops. 40-60 students are excepted every year.

Contact
(734) 647-7120
cedo-admin@umich.edu

Name of College
University of Michigan

Name of Program
Electrify Tech Camp

Academic / Career Interest
Engineering

Website
https://electrify.engin.umich.edu/

Application Timeline
Contact Institution for additional information.

Eligibility
Eligibility: open to any student that has completed at least one year of high school by June. Students entering 9th grade in Fall are not eligible. Must be local - commuter program. Requirements: application - includes self reporting SAT/ACT scores, GPA, Math courses taken, and preference of program.

Tuition Fees
Estimated fees: $500

Information about the program
Electrify Tech Camp consists of three non-residential summer camps for high school students that is sponsored and run by Electrical and Computer Engineering (ECE) at the University of Michigan (U-M). Camp participants will be introduced to college-level topics at an introductory level suitable for high school students.   Sense it: At Sense It you'll learn the fundamentals behind wireless sensors and how they are being used in modern technology. You'll get experience working with remote measuring devices, programming, and connecting circuits. You'll get a closer look at how these devices connect with one another and gather information, and control your own wireless sensors to complete a task of your choice. Power Up: At Power Up you'll learn how systems are powered, the challenges of different sources of energy, and the basics of circuit design.

Contact
https://electrify.engin.umich.edu/contact/

Name of College
University of Michigan

Name of Program
Girls in Music and Technology

Academic / Career Interest
Engineering

Website
https://smtd.umich.edu/programs-degrees/youth-adult-programs/
youth-programs/girls-music-technology/

Application Timeline
Priority Deadline: Approx. March 31st

Eligibility
Students who will complete grades 9-12 before camp begins, experience with music, computer programming, or music software is not required, but will be beneficial, must be a girl, and local (commuter camp). Requirements: online application, 30 dollar application fee, short essay response and a second essay about prior experience in music and computer science.

Tuition Fees
Contact institution for more information.

Information about the program
Girls in Music and Technology (GiMaT) is a summer day camp designed to promote participation by girls in activities at the intersection of music and technology. GiMaT offers the hands-on opportunity to learn creative technologies for making music with computers with faculty from U-M School of Music, Theatre & Dance Department of Performing Arts Technology, one of the world's leading undergraduate programs in music technology.

Contact
(734) 764-5097
smtd.admissions@umich.edu

Name of College
Georgia Tech

Name of Program
H.O.T Day camp - electrical engineering

Academic / Career Interest
Engineering

Website
https://www.ece.gatech.edu/outreach/hot-days

Application Timeline
Approx. April 6th

Eligibility
Sophomore and juniors. Must be local to metro Atlanta (day camp)

Tuition Fees
Estimated fees: $175

Information about the program
The H.O.T. Days @ Georgia Tech camp is a one-week-long summer day camp designed to introduce students attending high schools in Georgia to electrical and computer engineering (ECE) concepts. The goal of the program is to instill an interest in ECE and increase the number of high school graduates majoring in this field.

Contact
Dr. Leyla Conrad, Outreach Director
(404) 385-0439
leyla.conrad@ece.gatech.edu

Name of College
Georgia Tech

Name of Program
Summer Engineering Institute

Academic / Career Interest
Engineering

Website
http://sei.gatech.edu/program-overview

Application Timeline
Approx. April 6th

Eligibility
Rising 11th and 12th graders, must be 16 by program start date,
Have completed a minimum of Algebra II and 2 lab sciences (preferably biology, chemistry or physical science and 3.0/4.0 GPA.
Requirements: online application, 2 STEM teacher letters of recommendation, transcript release form, and emails of your recommenders. Nonrefundable $65 application fee required.

Tuition Fees
Estimated fees: $1500 +$65 application fee

Information about the program
Since 2008 the College of Engineering at Georgia Tech has offered
a 3-week residential Summer Engineering Institute (SEI) which
focuses on underrepresented minority rising 11th and 12th graders
from across the nation. The goal of GT-SEI is to provide students
with a real world engineering experience that prepares them for the
challenges and opportunities of tomorrow.

Contact
GTSEI@coe.gatech.edu

Name of College
Georgia Tech

Name of Program
Tag-Ed summer internship program

Academic / Career Interest
Engineering

Website
https://www.tagedonline.org/programs/tag-ed-summer-intern-ship-program/

Application Timeline
Approx. April 13th

Eligibility
At least 16 years old, rising sophomore, junior, or seniors, able to secure housing and reliable transportation to company work location, and available to work 20-30 hours per week for at least 5-weeks during the summer (June-August).

Tuition Fees
Estimated fees: free

Information about the program
The TAG-Ed Summer Internship Program was created to give students real world STEM experience at companies in metro Atlanta and the state of Georgia. For five weeks or more, you will work with a mentor on a specific project, not only honing your technical skills, but also developing the professional skills you will need to excel through high school and beyond.

Contact
internadmin@tagonline.org

Name of College
Georgia Tech

Name of Program
GTRI summer internship program - robotics

Academic / Career Interest
Engineering

Website
http://gafirst.org/blog/2018/03/18/gtri-georgia-tech-research-in-stitute-summer-internship-for-high-school-students/

Application Timeline
Approx. April 13th

Eligibility
At least 16 local HS students, can demonstrate proficiency in an object oriented programming language, can work full time during the summer, has reliable transportation to Georgia Tech. Requirements: apply online through the application and email resume directly to Stephen.Balakirsky@gtri.gatech.edu.

Tuition Fees
Estimated fees: Free and includes a stipend of $1100.

Information about the program
This is the 4th year that the GTRI (Georgia Tech Research Institute) Robotics and Intelligent Systems Division is hosting a Robotics Summer Internship. This is a 5-week program (starting sometime in June with exact date TBD) that includes an $1100 stipend at the end of the program for your participation. This year's project involves dexterous grasping and manipulation for manufacturing with a robotic arm. What is dexterous grasping and manipulation? It is the ability to have a robot arm pick up objects and use them in simple tasks. For example, grasping a round/square peg and placing it in a hole or connecting a USB plug to a socket. We will be using the project board designed by the National Institute for Standards and Technology (NIST) for this project

Contact
(770) 366-5612

Name of College
Northeastern University

Name of Program
Engineering Innovation and Design

Academic / Career Interest
Engineering

Website
https://www.northeastern.edu/precollegeprograms/programs/engineering-innovation-design/

Application Timeline
Consult Institution for more information

Eligibility
Current 10th and 11th grade HS students. Requirements: application, transcript, resume, and letter of rec.

Tuition Fees
Estimated fees: $5,330

Information about the program
EID is an intensive, experiential, and project-based program for talented high school students who want to deepen their understanding of engineering disciplines and current engineering challenges while building a toolbox of technical skills to set themselves apart from their peers.

Contact
(617) 373-2000

Name of College
Northeastern University

Name of Program
Hacking IoT

Academic / Career Interest
Engineering

Website
https://www.northeastern.edu/precollegeprograms/programs/hackingiot/

Application Timeline
Contact institution for more information.

Eligibility
Current 10th and 11th grade HS students. Requirements: application, transcript, resume, and letter of rec.

Tuition Fees
Estimated fees:

- Residents: $4,595
- Commuter: $2,995

Information about the program
Hacking the Internet of Things is a project-based program for high school students who want to harness the power of technology to change the world. It's designed by Northeastern University's Level using the cutting-edge IoT technology and concepts direct from Silicon Valley, here on our Boston campus.

Contact
(617) 373-2200
precollegeprograms@northeatsern.edu

Name of College
Rensselaer Polytechnic Institute

Name of Program
Aerospace Engineering Summer Camp

Academic / Career Interest
Engineering

Website
http://summer.rpi.edu/programs/aerospace-engineering

Application Timeline
Approx. March 31st

Eligibility
Rising 10th, 11th, and 12th graders. Requirements: application, recommendation letters, transcripts.

Tuition Fees
Estimated fees:

- Commuter: $850
- Residential: $1,835
- Non-refundable deposit: $425

Information about the program
Explore the field of aerospace engineering, tour RPI's top-tier research labs and learn how experimental data is collected by running wind tunnel tests. Participants will apply their new aerodynamic and flight mechanic knowledge by building a balsa glider and an electric radio controlled airplane for test flights.

Contact
(518) 276-6809
soaps@rpi.edu

Name of College
Rensselaer Polytechnic Institute

Name of Program
Engineering Exploration program

Academic / Career Interest
Engineering

Website
http://summer.rpi.edu/programs/engineering-exploration-program

Application Timeline
Approx. March 31st

Eligibility
Open to rising 11th, and 12th graders. Requirements: application, two letters of recommendation, and copy of your transcript.

Tuition Fees
Estimated fees:

- Commuters: $850
- Residential: $1,835

Information about the program
This program is an introduction to engineering concepts with a focus on creativity, teamwork, communication, and working across seven available engineering disciplines. Students will be introduced to various disciplines as well as engineering design processes through a week-long project, providing a design-built-test experience.

Contact
(518) 276-6809
soaps@rpi.edu

Name of College
Rensselaer Polytechnic Institute

Name of Program
Product Innovation: Immerse, Design, and Make

Academic / Career Interest
Engineering

Website
http://summer.rpi.edu/programs/product-innovation

Application Timeline
Approx. March 31st

Eligibility
Rising 10th, 11th, and 12th graders. Requirements: application, recommendation letters, transcripts.

Tuition Fees
Estimated fees:

- Commuter: $850
- Residential: $1,835.
- Non-refundable deposit: $425

Information about the program
Identify real-world problems and design, create, and market new products through mock-ups! Bring your ideas to life! Participants will identify real-world issues and work through an entire design process, starting with the potential new solution, into the creation of the mock-ups and prototypes, and on to marketing new products to a broad audience.

Contact
(518) 276-6809
soaps@rpi.edu

Name of College
Rensselaer Polytechnic Institute

Name of Program
3D Printing and the Chemistry of the Periodic Table

Academic / Career Interest
Engineering

Website
http://summer.rpi.edu/programs/3D-chemistry

Application Timeline
Approx. March 31st

Eligibility
Rising 10th, 11th, and 12th graders, must have completed or be currently enrolled in basic high school chemistry class and have completed one year of high school algebra. Requirements: application, recommendation letters, transcripts.

Tuition Fees
Estimated fees:

- Commuter: $1,300
- Residential: $3,270 for residential
- Non-refundable deposit: $425

Information about the program
This program allows students to learn to use 3D CADD to design and manufacture geometric shapes based on the properties of chemical elements. Students will learn the chemistry of the periodic table of elements and how it is constructed and then discover how to design objects using 3D modelling and printing. In addition, students will research the cultural significance of a variety of elements throughout history and incorporate this into their design work. The program incorporates classroom lectures and hands-on experimentation and learning.

Contact
(518) 276-6809
soaps@rpi.edu

Name of College
Rensselaer Polytechnic Institute

Name of Program
Preface program

Academic / Career Interest
Engineering

Website
https://info.rpi.edu/pre-college-initiatives/preface

Application Timeline
Approx. March 23rd

Eligibility
Must be entering the 11th or 12th grade in the fall. Requirements: application, essay, transcript, letter of recommendation from guidance counselor and one letter of recommendation from STEM teacher.

Tuition Fees
Estimated fees: Free. The only costs to participants are the health center fee, and personal and miscellaneous expenses such as snacks and souvenirs.

Information about the program
This is a two-week residential summer experience for high school sophomores and juniors entering 11th or 12th grade in the fall of the coming year. It is for talented and underrepresented students who have been underserved in the areas of science, engineering, and technological fields who have expressed a strong, early interest in pursuing a career in these areas.

Contact
(518) 276-6000

Name of College
UC Davis

Name of Program
Impact of Design program

Academic / Career Interest
Engineering

Website
https://precollege.ucdavis.edu/programs/design

Application Timeline
Sessions I, II, III – Approx. June 6th, July 3rd, July 18th respectively

Eligibility
Must be Sophomore or Junior in HS. Requirements: HS transcript, personal statement, short essay responses, two letters of recommendation from teachers of your choice, optional materials like test scores, academic writing samples, or other materials with a maximum of 3 uploads allowed.

Tuition Fees
Estimated fees:

- Application fee: $80
- Tuition: $5,400
- Housing/dining fee: $1,600
- International service fee: $250 for international students only

Information about the program
Design is all around you. From the posters hanging on your wall to the chair you're sitting in, almost everything you see, feel and hear has been touched by a designer. Explore the diverse world of design with the only comprehensive academic design department in the entire University of California system.

Contact
(530) 752-1011

Name of College
UC Davis

Name of Program
Innovation & Entrepreneurship

Academic / Career Interest
Engineering

Website
https://precollege.ucdavis.edu/programs/innovation-entrepre-neurship

Application Timeline
Sessions I, II, III – Approx. June 6th, July 3rd, July 18th respectively

Eligibility
Eligibility: Must be Sophomore or Junior in HS. Requirements: HS transcript, personal statement, short essay responses, two letters of recommendation from teachers of your choice, optional materials like test scores, academic writing samples, or other materials with a maximum of 3 uploads allowed.

Tuition Fees
Estimated fees:

- Application fee: $80
- Tuition: $5,400
- Housing/dining fee: $1,600
- International service fee: $250 for international students only

Information about the program
We believe entrepreneurship and innovation fuels human progress. The world needs dreamers who are willing to be doers. And our job is to educate dreamers about what that takes, beyond the idea: vibrant, collaborative networks. Engagement in uncommon partnerships. Restlessness, grit, bravery. All in service of giving great ideas the best possible chance at finding a home and changing people's lives for the better.

Contact
(530) 752-1011

Name of College
UC Davis

Name of Program
Girl+ Code Camp

Academic / Career Interest
Engineering

Website
http://c-stem.ucdavis.edu/students-parents/girls-camp/girl-camp2/

Application Timeline
Contact institution for more information

Eligibility
10th, 11th, or 12th grade and local (commuter camp). Requirements: Application, one letter of recommendation from a teacher, and transcript.

Tuition Fees
Estimated fees: free

Information about the program
Motivating girls in high school through peer mentoring by female college students to learn leadership and STEM concepts through a fun and exciting physical computing with Arduino and robotics curriculum. Providing life-changing experience and inspiration to campers, encouraging them to pursue computing related STEM careers and post-secondary studies. Empowering campers to serve as leaders and inspire other young girls to gain interest in science and technology through creating robotics clubs on their respective school campuses, outreaching to elementary and middle schools, and participating in RoboPlay competition.

Contact
(530) 752-9082

Name of College
University of Wisconsin - Madison

Name of Program
Design & Make (Almost) Anything

Academic / Career Interest
Engineering

Website
https://making.engr.wisc.edu

Application Timeline
Approx. March 1st for submitting ECCP participation form and May 1st for app submission

Eligibility
High school juniors and seniors enrolled in a Wisconsin public HS, 3.0/4.0 min GPA. Requirements: online app, transcript, and a completed UW-Madison Enrollment Plan and Agreement.

Tuition Fees
Estimated fees:

- $50 for the cost of engineering materials
- Residents of Wisconsin: $1,329.45 for 3-unit course
- Non-resident: $4,360.65

Information about the program
Students will work on an interdisciplinary team to prototype a product that addresses a market and/or societal need. The course is extremely hands-on, team-based, interactive and will provide students with a broad set of skills for creating innovative products. There will be a significant field component where students will explore the Madison area to identify needs and test prototypes.

Contact
(608) 571-7023
maker-contact@lists.wisc.edu

Name of College
Penn State

Name of Program
Discovering Engineering

Academic / Career Interest
Engineering

Website
https://berks.psu.edu/engineering-rockets-and-renewable-cars

Application Timeline
Consult Institution for more information - Rolling admissions that close two weeks prior to camp start date

Eligibility
Grades 9-12. No prior experience needed.

Tuition Fees
Estimated fees:

- Residential: $785
- Commuter: $485

Information about the program
This summer camp will introduce the participants to the engineering process via applied projects. The participants will explore basic engineering concepts and they will develop, design, and construct air-powered airplanes, and model rockets throughout the week. Participants will be trained in the use of software including RocSim to analyze the performance of rocket-powered vehicles. All of the projects will be tested, sometimes under competition settings, culminating with a team project.

Contact
(610) 396-6000

Name of College
Penn State

Name of Program
Discovering Engineering

Academic / Career Interest
Engineering

Website
https://berks.psu.edu/engineering-rockets-and-renewable-cars

Application Timeline
Consult Institution for more information - Rolling admissions that close two weeks prior to camp start date

Eligibility
Grades 9-12. No prior experience needed. Requirements: online application.

Tuition Fees
Estimated fees:

- Residential: $785
- Commuter: $485

Information about the program
This summer camp will introduce the participants to the engineering process via applied projects. The participants will explore basic engineering concepts and they will develop, design, and construct air-powered airplanes, and model rockets throughout the week. Participants will be trained in the use of software including RocSim to analyze the performance of rocket-powered vehicles. All of the projects will be tested, sometimes under competition settings, culminating with a team project.

Contact
(610) 396-6000

Name of College
University of Illinois Urbana Champaign

Name of Program
Discover Engineering Summer Program

Academic / Career Interest
Engineering

Website
https://wyse.engineering.illinois.edu/summer-camps/

Application Timeline
Approx. April 15th

Eligibility
Rising freshman and sophomores. Requirements: app, email for teacher recommender, transcript, and statement of purpose essay.

Tuition Fees
Estimated fees: $50 deposit + $1,000 for all housing, tuition, and meal costs

Information about the program
Discover Engineering is a week-long residential camp for rising freshmen and sophomores who are interested in math and science. Students will work on several projects that will incorporate different aspects of engineering. DE is also offering a Bioengineering track; see below for a specific description regarding that camp. The general Discover Engineering camp is meant as a similar version of the Exploring You Options but for rising first year and second year high school students. Campers will get to visit various labs around campus and hear from and talk with many different forms of engineering that take place on campus. They will get to do various different activities in many areas all designed to help educate students on different specialties of engineering.

Contact
(217) 244-3517
wyse@illinois.edu

Name of College
University of Illinois Urbana Champaign

Name of Program
Exploring Mechanical Science and Engineering

Academic / Career Interest
Engineering

Website
https://wyse.engineering.illinois.edu/summer-camps/

Application Timeline
Approx. April 15th

Eligibility
Rising freshman and sophomores. Requirements: app, email for teacher recommender, transcript, and statement of purpose essay.

Tuition Fees
Estimated fees: $50 deposit + $1,000 for all housing, tuition, and meal costs

Information about the program
Exploring Mechanical Science and Engineering is a week-long residential program that introduces high school students whom are rising juniors and seniors to the field of Mechanical Science and Engineering. Mechanical Engineering is all about building things. Mechanical engineers understand how machines work and how to design and construct new ones to solve challenging problems in the world. This camp will explore many of the exciting new topics in Mechanical Engineering.

Contact
(217) 244-3517
wyse@illinois.edu

Name of College
University of Illinois Urbana Champaign

Name of Program
Exploring Your Options Program

Academic / Career Interest
Engineering

Website
https://wyse.engineering.illinois.edu/summer-camps/

Application Timeline
Approx. April 15th

Eligibility
Rising freshman and sophomores. Requirements: app, email for teacher recommender, transcript, and statement of purpose essay.

Tuition Fees
Estimated fees: $50 dollar deposit + $1,000 for all housing, tuition, and meal costs

Information about the program
EYO is a week-long residential program that introduces high school rising juniors and seniors to the field of engineering. EYO is held at the University of Illinois campus in Urbana-Champaign during the normal weeks of camp. Participants will interact with engineering students and faculty members, plan and build a project, and engage in hands-on activities prepared by departments within the College of Engineering. There are two sessions offered: see the camp details below for extra details. In general, the first session is held during the first week of camps and the second is held during the last week. The two sessions are completely identical in how they are run, operated, and activities.

Contact
(217) 244-3517
wyse@illinois.edu

Name of College
University of Illinois Urbana Champaign

Name of Program
GAMES - Chemical Engineering

Academic / Career Interest
Engineering

Website
http://wie.engineering.illinois.edu/k-12-programs-resources/
gameswyse-camp/camp-tracks/chemical-engineering/

Application Timeline
Approx. April 15th

Eligibility
Eligibility: 9th through 12 grades, must be a woman. Requirements:
app, email for STEM teacher recommender, transcript, and statement of purpose essay.

Tuition Fees
Estimated fees: $50 deposit, $1,000 for all housing, tuition, and meal
costs.

Information about the program
The Chemical Engineering program camp explores many of the
exciting new topics within Chemical engineering, such as: Polymers,
Catalysis Reaction, Imaging of Cell Migration, and Bio-transporta-
tion, etc.. Unit Operations: Distillation/Separations, Extruder, and
Bioreactor, Refractometer & Refractive index. These topics are covered through lectures, hands-on activities, and team projects. Some
hands-on activities and projects that campers will be involved in
include: Imaging of Cell Migration Activity, Hydrogel activity, Show-
er gel activity, Utilization of Distillation, Extruder and Bioreactor
equipment.

Contact
(217) 244-3517
wie@illinois.edu

Name of College
University of Illinois Urbana Champaign

Name of Program
Girls Learning Electrical Engineering (GLEE)

Academic / Career Interest
Engineering

Website
http://wie.engineering.illinois.edu/k-12-programs-resources/
gameswyse-camp/camp-tracks/girls-learning-electrical-engineer-
ing-glee/

Application Timeline
Approx. April 15th

Eligibility
9th through 12 grades, must be a woman. Requirements: app, email
for STEM teacher recommender, transcript, and statement of purpose essay.

Tuition Fees
Estimated fees: $50 deposit + $1,000 for all housing, tuition, and
meal costs

Information about the program
Technology and electronics are all around us. At this camp, young
women will have the opportunity to explore current devices
through the eyes of an innovator-engineer by designing and building their own cell phone and light emitting calculator. Campers will
also explore how electrical engineering is used to address socially
relevant issues.

Contact
(217) 244-3517
wie@illinois.edu

Name of College
University of Illinois Urbana Champaign

Name of Program
Aerospace Engineering

Academic / Career Interest
Engineering

Website
http://wie.engineering.illinois.edu/k-12-programs-resources/
gameswyse-camp/camp-tracks/aerospace-engineering/

Application Timeline
Approx. April 15th

Eligibility
9th through 12 grades, must be a woman. Requirements: app, email for STEM teacher recommender, transcript, and statement of purpose essay.

Tuition Fees
Estimated fees: $50 deposit + $1,000 for all housing, tuition, and meal costs

Information about the program
The Aerospace GAMES camp provides young women with the opportunity to explore aerospace engineering through numerous hands-on projects and demonstrations, including a field trip to the local airport where the campers will have the opportunity to take an actual flight in a small aircraft operated by the Institute of Aviation. Utilizing individual and team activities, participants will investigate various aspects of this discipline comprising flight mechanics, aerodynamics, aerospace structures, orbital mechanics, and propulsion systems and apply them to aircraft and spacecraft design.

Contact
(217) 244-3517
wie@illinois.edu

Name of College
University of Illinois Urbana Champaign

Name of Program
Girls Building Awesome Machines (G-BAM) / Mechanical Science & Engineering

Academic / Career Interest
Engineering

Website
http://wie.engineering.illinois.edu/k-12-programs-resources/gameswyse-camp/camp-tracks/girls-building-awesome-machines-g-bammechanical-engineering/

Application Timeline
Approx. April 15th

Eligibility
9th through 12 grades, must be a woman. Requirements: app, email for STEM teacher recommender, transcript, and statement of purpose essay.

Tuition Fees
Estimated fees: $50 deposit + $1,000 for all housing, tuition, and meal costs

Information about the program
Mechanical engineers understand how machines work and how to design and construct new ones to solve challenging problems in the world. This camp will explore many of the exciting new topics in mechanical engineering, such as: constructing 3D printers to make things, building robots to explore and clean up hazardous waste, creating prosthetics to help injured people walk again, and making water treatment systems that run on sunlight for the developing world.

Contact
(217) 244-3517
wie@illinois.edu

Name of College
University of Illinois Urbana Champaign

Name of Program
Illinois Aerospace Institute (IAI) summer camp

Academic / Career Interest
Engineering

Website
http://iai.aerospace.illinois.edu/program/

Application Timeline
Approx. April 15th

Eligibility
9th through 12 grades, must be a woman. Requirements: app, email for STEM teacher recommender, transcript, and statement of purpose essay.

Tuition Fees
Estimated fees: $50 deposit + $1,000 for all housing, tuition, and meal costs.

Information about the program
The Illinois Aerospace Institute (IAI) summer camp is a one-week residential program for students entering grades 9-12 who are interested in learning about the fields of aerospace engineering and aviation. Though most of the students who attend are from the Midwest, students come to us from all over the U.S. and internationally. Many campers have some sort of experience with the aerospace field, through model rockets, remote control airplanes, or having a family member who is a pilot, but no experience is necessary, just an interest in learning about the field of aerospace engineering. The Institute is held on the campus of the University of Illinois at Urbana-Champaign.

Contact
Diane E. Jeffers
(217) 244-8048
il-aero-inst@illinois.edu

Name of College
The Ohio State University

Name of Program
RISEng STARS Summer Camp

Academic / Career Interest
Engineering

Website
https://mep.engineering.osu.edu/future-students/doi-riseng-stars-summer-camp

Application Timeline
Approx. May 1st

Eligibility
Rising juniors and seniors. Requirements: online app, parental consent form, one teacher recommendation, and $175 registration fee.

Tuition Fees
Estimated fees: $175 dollars

Information about the program
This five-day residential camp will include have hands-on engineering activities and lab tours led by engineering faculty and students. Discover Buckeye Engineering that includes in-depth introductions to engineering majors offered at Ohio State. Connect with Ohio State students and staff to learn how to navigate the college admissions and financial aid process. Engage in social and recreational activities designed to introduce you to the undergraduate experience.

Contact
(614) 292-6491

Name of College
University of Arkansas

Name of Program
Engineering Summer Academy

Academic / Career Interest
Engineering

Website
https://engineering-camps.uark.edu/camps/engineering-sum-mer-academy.php

Application Timeline
Contact institution for more information

Eligibility
Must be in 10th through 12th grades. Requirements: online application, personal essay responses.

Tuition Fees
Estimated fees: $675

Information about the program
The Engineering Summer Academy (ESA) is a one-week residential engineering academy for students who have recently completed 9th, 10th, or 11th grade. This intensive summer academy provides students with the opportunity for in-depth exploration into a concept that crosses engineering disciplines. Each course allows students to participate in hands-on activities in our cutting-edge labs, working alongside engineering faculty and current students.

Contact
Amy Warren, Asst. Director, Summer Programs
(479) 575-2562
engrcamp@uark.edu

Name of College
Colorado School of Mines

Name of Program
Engineering Design Summer Camp

Academic / Career Interest
Engineering

Website
https://students.csmspace.com/edsc2018.html?20180411

Application Timeline
Consult Institution for more information - Open until space closes.
Program begins Approx. June 25th

Eligibility
Students entering 9th through 12th grade. Requirement: online registration.

Tuition Fees
Estimated fees: $450 - $465

Information about the program
These camps, designed for those entering 9th through 12th grade, provide exposure to real-world problem solving in a team environment and provide opportunities to learn design skills that are applicable to many fields of engineering. The mission of the camp is to offer high school students an opportunity to participate in a creative challenge as they explore the world of engineering. The goal of the camp is to guide participants through a fun and rewarding hands-on experience of authentic engineering design practices. The expected outcomes of this program is to address the fundamentals of the engineering design process. This camp aims to provide: challenges of designing and marketing a product, early exposure to engineering design processes, opportunities to apply basic mathematics and science concepts, learn importance of team and communications skills, and challenges to step beyond your comfort zone.

Contact
(303) 384-2692
te@mines.edu

Name of College
Colorado Space Business Roundtable

Name of Program
Aerospace Internship

Academic / Career Interest
Engineering

Website
https://www.coloradosbr.org/csbr-summer-internship-program

Application Timeline
Contact institution for more information

Eligibility
Colorado Resident, U.S. Citizen, High School student, Interested in Science, Technology, Engineering, or Mathematics Careers. Requirements: online application.

Tuition Fees
Estimated fees: free. Unpaid internship.

Information about the program
CSBR offers a Colorado Aerospace Internship for rural high school and college students interested in pursuing careers in the aerospace industry. All students pursuing STEM - (Science, Technology, Engineering, and Mathematics) related disciplines are encouraged to apply; however, please note that students from rural locations will be given first priority into the program. If there is still space available, we will accept students from the Front Range. The Colorado Aerospace Internship will run for two weeks during the summer which gives students ample time to experience what it's like to work in various facets of the aerospace industry.

Contact
Christie Lee
(303) 258-6957
Christie.j.lee@lmco.com

Name of College
US Air Force

Name of Program
Society of American Military Engineers (SAME) - US Air Force STEM Camp

Academic / Career Interest
Engineering

Website
https://www.same.org/Portals/0/same.org/inside_pages/
SAME_Camps/documents/USAFA%20Camp%20Flyer.pd-
f?ver=2018-01-24-100320-130

Application Timeline
Approx. April 1st

Eligibility
Must be at least a sophomore in HS, US citizen, demonstrate proof of medical insurance, minimum 3.2 GPA, physically fit, and have not previously attended a SAME week-long summer Camp. Requirements: online application, transcript.

Tuition Fees
Estimated fees: $580

- Students generally pay half the registration fee ($290)
- The sponsoring SAME Post will pay the remainder of the fee and will work with the student on transportation cost

Information about the program
This is a week-long, live-in STEM camp, with full emersion in engineering and STEM activities. The AFA provides world class facilities for this program. Campers work as teams of 12 to complete engineering tasks in a competitive environment. Campers are supervised, mentored, coached, lead and guided by young STEM professionals and college students in a STEM major.

Contact
Scott Prosuch
(719) 337-0346
sprosuch@earthlink.net

Name of College
University of Connecticut

Name of Program
Explore Engineering Program

Academic / Career Interest
Engineering

Website
http://edoc.engr.uconn.edu/explore-engineering/

Application Timeline
Approx. June 1st

Eligibility
Sophomore or Junior in HS. Requirements: Online application, teacher recommendation letter (must be on official school letter-head).

Tuition Fees
Estimated fees: $700

Information about the program
Explore Engineering (E2) is a one-week residential summer program for current high school sophomores and juniors. During this exciting week at the University of Connecticut Storrs Campus, participants explore engineering careers by working in small groups with faculty and college students. They will learn what various engineers do in the workplace and see engineering concepts demonstrated. During the evenings, through the YESS Program, students focus on a single engineering discipline by fabricating a discipline-specific device. The week wraps up with demonstrations of items the students created during the week. Examples include: rudimentary EKG devices, Smart Lego vehicles that can follow a trail, fuel cell and other energy efficient devices, wooden bridges, environmentally friendly processes, and how to resolve differences.
Contact
Velda Alfred-Abney
(860) 486-5536
engr-explore@uconn.edu

Name of College
University of Connecticut

Name of Program
Explore Engineering Program

Academic / Career Interest
Engineering

Website
http://edoc.engr.uconn.edu/explore-engineering/

Application Timeline
Approx. June 1st

Eligibility
Sophomore or Junior in HS. Requirements: Online application, teacher recommendation letter (must be on official school letter-head).

Tuition Fees
Estimated fees: $700

Information about the program
Explore Engineering (E2) is a one-week residential summer program for current high school sophomores and juniors. During this exciting week at the University of Connecticut Storrs Campus participants explore engineering careers by working in small groups with faculty and college students. They will learn what various engineers do in the workplace and see engineering concepts demonstrated. During the evenings, through the YESS Program, students focus on a single engineering discipline by fabricating a discipline-specific device. The week wraps up with demonstrations of items the students created during the week. Examples have included: rudimentary EKG devices, Smart Lego vehicles that can follow a trail, fuel cell and other energy efficient devices, wooden bridges, environmentally friendly processes, and how to resolve differences.

Contact
Velda Alfred-Abney
(860) 486-5536
engr-explore@uconn.edu

Name of College
University of Arizona

Name of Program
Summer Engineering Academy

Academic / Career Interest
Engineering

Website
http://www.engineering.arizona.edu/k12/k12_SEA#experience

Application Timeline
Approx. April 1st

Eligibility
Contact institution for more information

Tuition Fees
Estimated fees:

- Explore Engineering Programs: $675, plus non-refundable service fee
- Themed Programs: $775, plus non-refundable service fee

Information about the program
High school students attending the Summer Engineering Academy (SEA) can expect some exciting new options in their quest to learn about how engineers change people's lives.   SEA will be focus on the Grand Challenges for Engineering. Themes for the weeklong STEM residential camps range from health and security to sustainability and infrastructure. Plus, the first of two Explore Engineering camp sessions – which introduce the range of UA Engineering majors and related careers – features NeuroBytes by NeuroTinker.

Contact
Lori Huggins, SEA director
(520) 621-8103
engr-sea@email.arizona.edu

COLLEGE
CONSULTING
EXPERTS

Science Collegiate Programs

Name of College
University of Chicago

Name of Program
Summer Immersion Program for HS students

Academic / Career Interest
Science

Website
https://summer.uchicago.edu/programs/uchicago-immersion

Application Timeline
Approx. May 1st.

Eligibility
Contact institution for more information

Tuition Fees
Estimated fees: $6500

Information about the program
There are three STEM courses: The Laws of Physics - This course treats our current understanding of the role that the laws of physics play in the development, existence, persistence, and prevalence of life in the universe. Starting with the big bang theory, we will explore how the laws of physics guided the evolution of the universe through the processes most likely to have produced life on earth as it exists today; Mathematical and Computational Research in Biological Sciences - Using computation to model and study biological systems is one of the leading edges of current scientific research. In this hands-on exploration of the latest techniques, students will learn how macromolecules, such as DNA, RNA, and proteins, perform their functions and how to visualize and quantify their behavior.

Contact
(773) 702-2149
summersession@uchicago.edu

Name of College
University of Chicago

Name of Program
Research in the Biological Sciences (RIBS)

Academic / Career Interest
Science

Website
https://summer.uchicago.edu/course/research-biological-scienc-es-ribs

Application Timeline
Approx. March 2nd

Eligibility
Requirements: must have completed 10th grade and have completed HS biology with excellent academic record. Only for Sophomores and Juniors

Tuition Fees
Estimated fees: 11,400

Information about the program
This four-week intensive training program is designed to expose students to a broad range of molecular, microbiological, and cell biological techniques currently used in research laboratories. Students are immersed in the research experience, giving them a taste of "life at the bench". Using a project-based approach, the course progresses from a survey of basic lab techniques to the application of current molecular techniques in developmental biology and microbiology. Most of a typical RIBS day is spent in lab. Lectures will also be presented to provide background and introduce new concepts. Since communication skills are important in science, students will keep lab notebooks and they will make several group presentations.

Contact
(773) 702-2149
summersession@uchicago.edu

Name of College
University of Chicago

Name of Program
Neubauer Family Adelante Summer Scholars

Academic / Career Interest
Science

Website
https://summer.uchicago.edu/programs/neubauer-family-adelan-te-summer-scholars

Application Timeline
Approx. March 2nd

Eligibility
Requirements: Of Hispanic/Latino descent. High School Juniors Only

Tuition Fees
Estimated fees: free

Information about the program
Thanks to the vision and the generosity of the Neubauer family, top students engaged in Hispanic/Latino communities can now partic-ipate in select University of Chicago Summer Session courses free of charge. Students selected will receive a full scholarship to par-ticipate in one of two Summer Session courses: Collegiate Writing: Awakening Into Consciousness and Contagion: Infectious Agents and Emerging Diseases. Even if you don't plan to study English or Bi-ology in college, being a Neubauer Family Adelante Summer Scholar is a great way to get an early look at college-level classes and get a feel for life on campus--and to have a ton of fun in the process. You'll spend the morning gaining hands-on experience from teachers who are experts in their fields and the evening exploring Chicago with your classmates. Biology Related Course for STEM focused appli-cants available.

Contact
(773) 702-2149
summersession@uchicago.edu

Name of College
Yale University

Name of Program
Research Experience for HS Students (REHS)

Academic / Career Interest
Science

Website
https://crisp.yale.edu/education/research-experi-
ence-high-school-students-rehs

Application Timeline
Approx. April 1st

Eligibility
High school juniors and seniors that are currently attending a New
Haven Public School. Minorities, women and persons with disabili-
ties are strongly encouraged to apply. Requirements: The selection
of HS participants is based on a personal statement, academic transcript, resume and one letter of recommendation. Also must enroll
in the Yale Pathways to Science Program.

Tuition Fees
Estimated fees: Free but must provide their own transportation to
Yale. There is a $500 stipend for students

Information about the program
The CRISP High School (HS) Research Fellowship provides participants with the opportunity to conduct team-based interdisciplinary
materials research. Participating students conduct a four-week
research project as members of a research team including university faculty, undergraduate and graduate students. Students will be
exposed to professional development opportunities through weekly
meetings and faculty seminars. The program begins in the late June/
early July timeframe just after the school year ends.

Contact
(203) 392-8959

Name of College
Yale University

Name of Program
Yale Summer Program in Astrophysics

Academic / Career Interest
Science

Website
https://yspa.yale.edu/program-overview

Application Timeline
Approx. March 4th

Eligibility
Must be rising junior or senior. Requirements: complete app, current transcript including fall semester and 2 letters of recommendation from teachers.

Tuition Fees
Estimated fees: $5,250. Financial aid is need based and available but limited and can cover up to 50%.

Information about the program
The Yale Summer Program in Astrophysics (YSPA) is a research and enrichment program that's hosted at the Leitner Family Observatory and Planetarium (LFOP) at Yale for 32 rising high school juniors and seniors (high school students who are juniors or sophomores when they apply) who have shown an aptitude for science and math, an interest in astrophysics, and who are considering going into careers in science or tech. The program consists of a two-week online, directed self-study program followed by a four-week residential program. Students at YSPA live together on campus in one of the dorms, take classes at the Leitner Planetarium, learn to program and analyze data in the computer lab at the Leitner Observatory, and use the telescopes at the Leitner Observatory to collect data for their research project. At the end of the program, students write up their results in the form of a scientific paper and then present those results at our YSPA mini-conference.

Contact
https://yspa.yale.edu/contact-us

Name of College
Rockefeller University

Name of Program
Summer Science Research Program

Academic / Career Interest
Science

Website
https://www.rockefeller.edu/outreach/lab-initiative/summer-science/

Application Timeline
Approx. Jan 8th

Eligibility
Must be 16 years old and in HS. Must commit to the full 7 weeks. No exceptions. Requirements: Online App, 1 essay question response, a 750-word commentary on one of 4-5 articles linked in the application on research being done at Rockefeller, school transcript, a resume, 2 letters of recommendation from math and science teachers and a 3rd optional recommendation from a mentor or advisor.

Tuition Fees
Estimated fees: Free

Information about the program
The Rockefeller University Summer Science Research Program (SSRP) provides high school students with a unique and personalized opportunity to conduct hands-on research under the mentorship of leading scientists at one of the world's premier biomedical research facilities. During this rigorous 7-week program, SSRP students become immersed in scientific culture while gaining an appreciation for the process of biomedical discovery.

Contact
(212) 327-7930
hsresearch@rockefeller.edu

Name of College
MIT

Name of Program
Research Summer Institute

Academic / Career Interest
Science

Website
https://www.cee.org/academic-program

Application Timeline
Approx. Jan 22nd

Eligibility
Eligibility: Must be in HS. Requirements: transcript, all standard-ized test scores included AP, SAT, SATII (if applicable), MAA tests (international Olympiad exams), research publications if applicable. Full application must be completed as well. Link to old application: https://www.cee.org/sites/default/files/RSIapp/RSI_2016_App.pdf

Tuition Fees
Estimated fees: Free

Information about the program
At the core of the RSI academic program is an intensive, six-week introduction to scientific research.
In fields ranging from category theory to cancer research, partici-pants gain first-hand experience with open-ended, scientific inquiry in leading laboratories in the Boston area. Academic, corporate, and government-sponsored research teams invite RSI students to join in their ongoing projects, providing students an opportunity to make an original contribution.

Contact
(212) 327-7930
hsresearch@rockefeller.edu

Name of College
MIT

Name of Program
Summer Science Program (SSP)

Academic / Career Interest
Science

Website
https://summerscience.org/

Application Timeline
Approx. Dec 15 open date - Mar 2nd close date

Eligibility
Eligibility: HS Sophomore or Junior. Must have completed or currently enrolled in physics or calculus for Astrophysics. Must have completed biology and chemistry for biochemistry track. Requirements: Application, official transcript, standardized test scores, recommendation letters from current science and math teachers and a third of your own choice.

Tuition Fees
Estimated fees: $6,950 but no student pays that amount due to financial aid and alumni donations. Full scholarships and partial awards are granted based on need.

Information about the program
SSP is an immersion into experimental science, designed to challenge and inspire talented rising seniors from around the world. Working in teams of three, participants complete a research project from beginning to end: either in Astrophysics – near-earth asteroid imaging and orbit determination – or Biochemistry – fungal enzyme inhibition and drug discovery. Each team acquires its own original data and performs its own analysis. Field trips and guest speakers round out an intense 39-day schedule. The experience changes their lives, and the benefits continue for life.

Contact
(866) 728-0999
info2@ssp.org

Name of College
Stanford University

Name of Program
Stanford Medical Youth Science Program

Academic / Career Interest
Health

Website
http://smysp.stanford.edu/

Application Timeline
Approx. Feb 15th

Eligibility
Are a current sophomore or junior high school student (at the time of your application) who lives and attends high school in one of the 20 Northern or Central California counties from which we recruit. Preference is given to students who are juniors at the time of their application. Are from a low-income family whose members have little or no history of attending college.

Tuition Fees
Estimated fees: Free

Information about the program
Stanford Medical Youth Science Program is a five-week residential enrichment program focused on science and medicine that is open to low-income and underrepresented minority high school sophomores and juniors who live in Northern and Central California.

Contact
youth-science@stanford.edu

Name of College
Stanford University

Name of Program
Genomics Research Internship Program

Academic / Career Interest
Health

Website
http://med.stanford.edu/genecamp.html

Application Timeline
Approx. March 5th

Eligibility
SF Bay Area High School Students who are 16 or older by internship start date. Students must live locally, no housing assistance is provided with this internship.

Tuition Fees
Estimated fees: Free

Information about the program
At the Stanford Center for Genomics and Personalized Medicine (SCGPM), we are applying our expertise on the science and ethics of genomics to build a new collaborative model of science focused on transforming the practice of medicine. As part of our commitment to education, we offer a summer internship program to SF Bay Area High School students. Our Center has unofficially hosted dozens of students every summer since 2000. We formalized the process starting 2015 with the Gene Camp program.

Contact
http://med.stanford.edu/genecamp/contact.html

Name of College
Stanford University

Name of Program
Science, Technology, and Reconstructive Surgery (STaRS) Summer
Internship Program

Academic / Career Interest
Health

Website
https://www.stanfordstars.org/

Application Timeline
Approx. Jan 31st

Eligibility
Candidate must be at least 16 years old by the time the internship
begins. This is an unpaid opportunity.

Tuition Fees
Estimated fees: free

Information about the program
Each year, we host 15-30 talented high school and undergraduate
students in our research laboratories. During their 7-week internship, students master basic lab techniques, present their scientific
discoveries to colleagues in oral and poster presentations, and join
research teams led by experienced (PhD level) mentors who dedicate invaluable time to inspire and guide them on their first steps
towards a successful career in science.

Contact
(650) 736-3640
cpmoreau@stanford.edu

Name of College
University of Pennsylvania

Name of Program
Teen Research and Education in Environmental Science (TREES)

Academic / Career Interest
Science

Website
http://ceet.upenn.edu/training-career-development/summer-programs/teen-research-and-education-in-environmental-science/

Application Timeline
Approx. Mar 1st

Eligibility
Students must have completed grade 9, 10, or 11 by the summer.

Tuition Fees
Estimated fees: Free

Information about the program
The Teen Research and Education in Environmental Science (TREES) program is a unique summer research and mentorship program offering hands-on environmental research opportunities to motivated high school students. Each summer, approximately eight high-school students work one-on-one with mentors on projects that they choose and design.

Contact
(215) 746-3030
Webster@upenn.edu

Name of College
Duke University

Name of Program
STAR program

Academic / Career Interest
Science

Website
https://dcri.org/education/dukes-star-program/

Application Timeline
Contact institution for more information

Eligibility
Must be in High School.

Requirements:

- Completed application
- School transcript
- Two letters of support provided by non-relatives
- Essay (300 to 500-word limit)

Tuition Fees
Estimated fees: Free. Students will receive a stipend of $2,600 dollars

Information about the program
The summer training in academic research takes place over 8 weeks and focuses on pharmaco-epidemiological research methodology and writing skills. Participants are placed in teams and matched with Duke faculty mentors to work on an original, hypothesis-driven project, originating as a one-page précis and progressing through draft figures and tables, an abstract, a PowerPoint presentation, and a written thesis. A goal of the program is to have every trainee qualify for co-authorship on a peer-reviewed manuscript related to their team's project.

Contact
(919) 668-8700

Name of College
Duke University

Name of Program
Duke TIP Summer Studies

Academic / Career Interest
Science

Website
https://tip.duke.edu/programs/summer-studies

Application Timeline
Consult Institution for more information

Eligibility
The Summer Studies Program is TIP's original program, and only students who score at the very top of their grade level on the ACT or SAT are eligible to attend. TIP students must qualify for either our Center or Academy Summer Studies Program to apply.

Tuition Fees
Estimated fees: $4,300-$4,375

Information about the program
Duke TIP's Summer Studies Program is demanding, intense, and rewarding. Students take part in interactive, inquiry-based learning that challenges them to think critically about themselves and their world. Led by content experts, courses are equivalent to a semester-long college course or a year of high school instruction. Our high-energy classrooms encourage students to take academic risks in a supportive environment and to stretch their intellectual abilities. TIP's active residential program is a lot like a structured version of the college experience, providing opportunities for friendship and fun.

Contact
(919) 668-9100

Name of College
Dartmouth

Name of Program
ACS Project SEED Summer Internship

Academic / Career Interest
Science

Website
http://www.dartmouth.edu/~academicoutreach/research_intern.html

Application Timeline
Approx. June 1st

Eligibility
Must be Junior or Senior and must be recognized as economically disadvantaged. Preference will be given to students whose maximum family income does not exceed 200% of the current Federal Poverty Guidelines based on family size (http://aspe.hhs.gov/poverty). An economically disadvantaged student applicant who is physically disabled must be considered on the same basis as any other applicant and may not be discriminated against in any way.

Tuition Fees
Estimated fees: Free

Information about the program
The American Chemical Society Project SEED summer research program opens new doors for economically disadvantaged students to experience what it's like to be a chemist. Students entering their junior or senior year in high school are given a rare chance to work alongside scientist-mentors on research projects in industrial, academic, and federal laboratories, discovering new career paths as they approach critical turning points in their lives.

Contact
(415) 275-0246
ContactUs@davincicamp.com

Name of College
Cornell University

Name of Program
Plant Genome Research Program Internship

Academic / Career Interest
Science

Website
https://btiscience.org/education-outreach/internships/?-card#page=PGRPSummerInternships

Application Timeline
Approx. Feb 2nd

Eligibility
Must be at least 16 years old enrolled in a HS. Requirements: application, recommendation forms (sent via email in the application), transcripts, resume, personal statement.

Tuition Fees
Estimated fees: Free. High School students receive a $2,400 stipend but are responsible for their own housing, meals, and transportation

Information about the program
Undergraduate and high school students participate in the Plant Genome Research Program (PGRP) summer internship program and learn how basic plant research can be applied to protect the environment, enhance human health, and improve agriculture. PGRP interns gain knowledge of plant genomics and scientific research by working closely with scientists, postdoctoral fellows, and graduate students in a laboratory setting. PGRP interns learn the latest molecular biology techniques and bioinformatics tools while working on a supervised, independent research project within the framework of the assigned laboratory's research program.

Contact
(607) 254-1234
contact@btiscience.org

Name of College
Cornell University

Name of Program
Research Apprenticeship in Biological Sciences

Academic / Career Interest
Science

Website
https://www.sce.cornell.edu/sc/programs/index.php?v=170

Application Timeline
Approx. March 4th

Eligibility
Must be sophomore, junior, or senior. Must have completed AP biology and received a 4 or 5 on the exam. Requirements: application, transcript, a letter of recommendation from your research mentor, a copy or sample of the research completed (picture of your poster is fine), If you have taken a didactic research skills course, please include a letter from an instructor who personally knows your work, a recommendation from your AP biology teacher, and another letter of recommendation from another teacher or guidance counselor.

Tuition Fees
Estimated fees: $12,825

Information about the program
The Cornell University Research Apprenticeship in the Biological Sciences (RABS) offers serious, research-oriented students the rare opportunity to join a top-notch laboratory at one of the world's leading research institutions. Students develop your research skills, becoming familiar with the lab procedures, protocols, techniques, and equipment used in cutting-edge facilities. All the while, students work closely with some of Cornell's leading professors, post-doctoral fellows, and graduate and undergraduate researchers.

Contact
(607) 255-6203
summer_college@cornell.edu

Name of College
Rice University

Name of Program
Solar Academy

Academic / Career Interest
Science

Website
https://www.rstem.rice.edu/solar-academy

Application Timeline
Contact institution for more information.

Eligibility
Must be in 10th or 11th grades. Must be from the Houston area (non-residential camp). Requirements: Transcript (official & un-official), letter of recommendation submitted by a STEM teacher, Submit a 1-page statement about why you want to participate in the program, signed Participation Agreement Form and completed application.

Tuition Fees
Estimated fees: free

Information about the program
The Rice Office of STEM Engagement offers two-week summer program for 10th and 11th grade students enrolled in schools in the Greater Houston area. This program is funded by a grant from the National Science Foundation and led by Dr. Stephen Bradshaw, Associate Professor of Physics and Astronomy at Rice University. The goal of Solar Academy is to help students explore our understanding of the center of our solar system, the sun, while also learning about collaboration in science and how to use available resources.

Contact
Selena Zermeno
(713) 348-8211
selena.zermeno@rice.edu

Name of College
Emory University

Name of Program
Institute on Neuroscience (ION) - for High School Students

Academic / Career Interest
Science

Website
http://sites.gsu.edu/ion-teach/application/

Application Timeline
Approx. Feb 4th

Eligibility
Junior or Senior in HS, 3.0/4.0 GPA, must self-arrange housing &
all meals for the duration of the 8-week program. Requirements:
Online Application, Personal Statement, Current Resume, Recommendation by a high school science teacher, Recommendation by
an adult not related to applicant (both emailed to ION@gsu.edu by
the recommender), Official High School Transcripts sent by the High
School (emailed to ION@gsu.edu)

Tuition Fees
Estimated fees: $25 application fee + hourly pay set by the institu-
tion

Information about the program
ION seeks applications from highly motivated high school students
who have taken at least one college-level science course (e.g., AP
Biology, Honors Chemistry, etc.). After participating in an introductory neuroscience course, ION Scholars are matched with mentors
by interest to conduct a seven-week mentored laboratory research
project. Weekly professional development workshops focus on topics such as scientific communication, the ethical conduct of research
and special topics in neuroscience.

Contact
http://sites.gsu.edu/ion-teach/connections/

Name of College
Emory University

Name of Program
Summer College for HS students

Academic / Career Interest
Science

Website
http://precollege.emory.edu/summer-college/index.html

Application Timeline
Session I deadline: Approx. May 7th.
Session II deadline: Approx. June 18th

Eligibility
Must be at minimum a sophomore and able to commute to campus.
Requirements:

Tuition Fees
Estimated fees:

- $75 application fee
- $350 deposit
- $4,698 tuition for a three-credit course
- $6,220 tuition for a four-credit course.

Information about the program
Emory Summer College is a nonresidential program in which exceptional high school students who have completed their sophomore or junior year may enroll in Emory undergraduate courses and earn college credit. Credit students are expected to commute (use their own mode of transportation) to campus daily. Out-of-state students will need to arrange their own accommodations locally. Emory University does not provide any residential options. This program allows students to take various STEM courses in college mathematics, physics + lab, Introductory CS, and various bio/chemistry courses.

Contact
Jennifer Combs
(404) 727-9279
jcombs@emory.edu

Name of College
University of California, Berkeley

Name of Program
Summer Science Intensive: iCLEM

Academic / Career Interest
Science

Website
https://www.jbei.org/education/research-experiences/iclem-program/

Application Timeline
Approx. March 9th

Eligibility
Be 15 years old by the end of December. Be currently enrolled as a sophomore or junior at a high school in Alameda, Contra Costa, or San Francisco county.

Requirements: Application, emails from one science/math teacher and another general teacher email for recommendations.

Tuition Fees
Estimated fees: Free with a $2,000 stipend

Information about the program
The Introductory College Level Experience in Microbiology (iCLEM) is an eight-week paid summer science intensive for economically disadvantaged high school sophomores and juniors. The program seeks to broaden students' understanding of biotechnology, microbiology, and biofuels. In addition to completing a research project, the program also exposes students to career exploration and preparation for the college application process.

Contact
Lauchlin Cruickshanks
lcruickshanks@lbl.gov

Name of College
University of California, Los Angeles

Name of Program
Applications of Nanoscience Institute

Academic / Career Interest
Science

Website
https://www.summer.ucla.edu/institutes/ApplicationsofNanoscience

Application Timeline
Approx. April 1st

Eligibility
Must be in 9th - 12th grades. Requirements: two short essay responses (found on website), online application. Instructors selection solely based on responses and application. Additional documents such as transcripts or recommendations were not listed as requirements or as supplementary application material. Consult Institution for more information.

Tuition Fees
Estimated fees: $3,651 + $150 non-refundable deposit is required

Information about the program
The Applications of Nanoscience course is designed for high school students to learn the basics of pursing a scientific research project. As a model-student, you will explore important applications of nanoscience, learn the basics of reviewing existing scientific literature, and go through the process of proposing a research project in pursuit of new scientific data.

Contact
(310) 825-4101
info@summer.ucla.edu

Name of College
University of California, Los Angeles

Name of Program
Nanoscale Microscopy Lab Summer Institute

Academic / Career Interest
Science

Website
https://www.summer.ucla.edu/institutes/NanoscaleMicroscopyLab

Application Timeline
Approx. April 1st

Eligibility
Eligibility: at least 14 years old, must be in at least 9th grade. Requirement: online application, two essay responses, and non refundable deposit payment ($150).

Tuition Fees
Cost: 1,872.00. Includes registration and document fees, housing, dining, and tuition. 150 dollar non refundable deposit is required. Qualified students attending grades 9th – 11th in the state of California are eligible for Summer Scholars

Information about the program
Nanoscale Microscopy Lab is a one-week, hands-on, science learning opportunity for high school students on scientific imaging, a topic that is typically only accessible in an advance college level course. Specifically, students will be able to explore three key microscopy techniques for nanoscience research: fluorescence microscopy, scanning probe microscopy, and electron microscopy. This one-week summer course offers an exploratory introduction to this important scientific skill for students as early as 10th grade at the high school level.

Contact
(310) 825-4101
info@summer.ucla.edu

Name of College
University of California, Los Angeles

Name of Program
Westwood Hospital Volunteers program

Academic / Career Interest
Health

Website
https://www.uclahealth.org/volunteer/high-school-students

Application Timeline
Approx. April 11th

Eligibility
Minimum age 16 years old. Agreement to volunteer for 100 hours; commitment of four hours per month

Tuition Fees
Estimated fees: free

Information about the program
Patient Transport: Patient Transport assists in the Patient Transport office at the Ronald Reagan UCLA Medical Center. They are responsible for discharging patients, assisting in transfers, and helping the patient transport staff. This is a great opportunity for students to see all areas of the hospital and get clinical exposure. Shifts are available seven days a week.

Contact
(310) 267-8180

Name of College
USC

Name of Program
Introduction to Neuroscience

Academic / Career Interest
Health

Website
https://summerprograms.usc.edu/programs/4-week/the-brain/

Application Timeline
Approx. April 27th

Eligibility
You must have completed at least the 9th grade by June 17, 2018.
You should be pursuing a rigorous high school curriculum to excel in
USC Summer Programs.

Tuition Fees
Estimated fees:

- $8,534 for residential
- $6,059 for commuter
- $500 non-refundable deposit
- $60 application fee

Information about the program
Are you considering a career in healthcare, psychology, or the
behavioral sciences? Are you otherwise interested in the scientific
study of the human brain? In this introduction to the anatomy and
function of the brain, you will discover some common and unusual
aspects of the brain in everyday life and under abnormal circumstances. You will explore normal brain development as well as abnormal occurrences in the brain and their effects on human function
and behavior over the lifespan.

Contact
(213) 740-5679
summer@usc.edu

Name of College
USC

Name of Program
My Mind & Me: Intro to Mental Health

Academic / Career Interest
Health

Website
https://summerprograms.usc.edu/programs/4-week/mental-health/

Application Timeline
Approx. April 27th

Eligibility
You must have completed at least the 9th grade by June. You should be pursuing a rigorous high school curriculum to excel in USC Summer Programs.

Tuition Fees
Estimated fees:

- $8,534 for residential
- $6,059 for commuter
- $500 non-refundable deposit
- $60 application fee

Information about the program
What are mental health & mental illness? What makes them different? How can I improve my own mental health? What is the science behind self-care? How can I use this information to help those around me? If you are interested in having a discussion about the answers to these questions, and many more, then this course is a good fit for you. For the next four weeks, you will immerse yourself in the field of mental health and find yourself looking at the world through a new lens.

Contact
(213) 740-5679
summer@usc.edu

Name of College
University of Michigan

Name of Program
High School Summer Program

Academic / Career Interest
Science

Website
https://cphom.engin.umich.edu/education-and-outreach/high-school-research/

Application Timeline
Approx. March 1st

Eligibility
Must be 16 years old by the start of the program (no exceptions).

Tuition Fees
Estimated fees: free + $2,800 stipend for student researchers

Information about the program
The C-PHOM High School Research Program is a program that allows students to participate in research within the Center for Photonic and Multiscale Nanomaterials (C-PHOM) at the University of Michigan. The program begins in June with orientation, training, and matching of lab groups. The 8-week residential component on the UM campus begins Approx. mid-June. During the Fall, participants will continue research with UM advisors, preparing presentations and papers for science fair competitions. The local, regional, and national science fair competitions are discussed during the program.

Contact
Ted Norris
(734) 764-9269
tnorris@umich.edu

Name of College
University of Michigan

Name of Program
Biotechnology Camp for High School Students (Focus on Nucleotide Hybridization)

Academic / Career Interest
Science

Website
http://www.mircore.org/2018-summer-camps/2018-bt-camp/

Application Timeline
Contact Institution for more information

Eligibility
Academically motivated high school students interested in computers, math, science, and medicine; Must have previously completed the Computational Biology camp. Must be local - commuter program. Must bring own laptop and lunch. Requirements: application including personal essay responses.

Tuition Fees
Estimated fees: $540 (financial aid is available)

Information about the program
This camp combines UNIX usage, wet-lab experiments, and thermodynamics calculation of nucleotide hybridization to teach current nucleotide biotechnology (qRT-PCR, microarray, next-generation sequencing). Wet-lab experiments will include PCR and gel-electrophoresis. As part of the camp, students will be encouraged to make a plan using new technology or improve technology, design it, and pitch the idea. No prior knowledge besides DNA and RNA is necessary except for students' motivation.

Contact
(734) 288-8647
info@mircore.org

Name of College
University of Michigan

Name of Program
R Programming Camp for High School Students

Academic / Career Interest
Science

Website
http://www.mircore.org/2018-summer-camps/2018-r-camp/

Application Timeline
Consult Institution for more information

Eligibility
Academically motivated current high school students interested in computers, math, science, and medicine. Must be local (commuter program). Must bring own laptop and lunch. Requirements: just application form and essay responses w/in app.

Tuition Fees
Estimated fees: $530

Information about the program
This camp provides statistical methods in the context of disease research. It is for current (2017-18) high school and exceptional 8th grade students who want to learn computer programming in relation to future biomedical applications. R is a statistical tool and programming language with excellent graphic options, useful in various application areas such as medicine, public policy, and economics. After R is introduced, the students will assess current biomedical problems and identify useful tools for research. Students will be encouraged to write a program to aid in biological research and to share the program online as authors such as through GitHub.

Contact
(734) 288-8647
info@mircore.org

Name of College
Tufts University

Name of Program
Teachers and High School Students Program (TAHSS)

Academic / Career Interest
Science

Website
http://medicine.tufts.edu/About-Us/Administrative-Offices/Office-of-Multicultural-Affairs/Pipeline-Programs/Teachers-and-High-School-Student-Program_tabs

Application Timeline
Approx. Jan 22nd

Eligibility
Must be at least 16 years old and in grades 10-12. Must be a local resident of the greater Boston area.

Tuition Fees
Estimated fees: Free. Students will receive a stipend.

Information about the program
The Teachers and High School Students (TAHSS) Program was founded in the fall of 1989 with the goals of exposing interested high school students of varied backgrounds to health care and related professions, and providing support in their academic and personal development. Today, TAHSS continues as a key Tufts University School of Medicine (TUSM) community outreach program for high school students in the Greater Boston area. The program is supported by the Dean's Office and aims to stimulate and support interest in careers in the biomedical sciences among high school students.

Contact
Marlene Jreaswec, Program Administrator
(617) 636-0992
marlene.jreaswec@tufts.edu

Name of College
Boston University

Name of Program
Academic Immersion Program

Academic / Career Interest
Health

Website
https://www.bu.edu/summer/high-school-programs/academic-immersion/medicine.shtml

Application Timeline
Contact Institution for more information.

Eligibility
You need to be entering your junior or senior year. Requirements: online app, one letter of recommendation from science teacher, personal statement, transcript, and $50 application fee

Tuition Fees
Estimated fees:

- Application Fee (non-refundable): $50
- Total Charge: $6,200

Information about the program
AIM's pre-medicine track provides a broad introduction to the field of medicine, combining coursework in related sciences with experiential learning activities and explorations of the various career possibilities that exist within the field. In the mornings, you attend seminars led by Boston University instructors that focus on three core topics: Anatomy and Physiology, Infectious Diseases, and Contemporary Issues in Medicine. In the afternoons, you engage in hands-on learning activities that introduce you to what medical students experience in the early phase of their education.

Contact
(617) 353-1379
summerhs@bu.edu

Name of College
Boston University

Name of Program
Summer Preview

Academic / Career Interest
Science

Website
https://www.bu.edu/summer/high-school-programs/summer-pre-view/

Application Timeline
Up until 2 weeks before the program begins – Consult Institution for more information

Eligibility
You need to be entering your freshman or sophomore year. Requirements: application, personal statement, transcript, and $50 app fee.

Tuition Fees
Estimated fees:

- Application Fee (non-refundable): $50
- Program Fee: $1,430
- Room & Board (residential students): $466
- Lunch (commuter students): $59

Information about the program
For one week this summer, explore fascinating subjects, make new friends, and become familiar with college life at Boston University. The Summer Preview program offers rising ninth and tenth graders a choice of three weeklong, non-credit seminars. It's an ideal opportunity to explore an area of academic interest or become familiar with an entirely new subject. Includes Biology focused program

Contact
(617) 353-1378
summerhs@bu.edu

Name of College
Boston University

Name of Program
Greater Boston Research Opportunities for HS Women

Academic / Career Interest
Science

Website
http://www.bu.edu/lernet/grow/about.html

Application Timeline
Approx. April 15th

Eligibility
Must currently be a junior enrolled in a school in Massachusetts and live within a 30-mile radius of Boston, Must be at least 16, Must have a demonstrated record of achievement in science, You should be taking, or have completed at least one AP course. If your school does not offer AP courses, please note that in your application. Requirements: application, two recommendation letters from STEM teachers, and transcript.

Tuition Fees
Estimated fees: free. Receive a stipend of up to $1500 upon completion of all program requirements.

Information about the program
GROW offers rising high school seniors the opportunity to perform research in a lab at BU for six weeks;

Contact
(774) 606-9367
cyber@bu.edu

Name of College
Boston University

Name of Program
Summer Lab

Academic / Career Interest
Science

Website
http://www.bumc.bu.edu/citylab/summerlab/

Application Timeline
Approx. – Rolling acceptance admissions that Opens in Jan, Close date mid June
Consult Institution for more information

Eligibility
SummerLab is a program for students entering the 10th–12th grades as well as those entering college. Requirements: application (not currently available nor additional details about the application process - will email to get more details)

Tuition Fees
Estimated fees:

- $1,000 for one week
- $1,800 for two weeks
- $416 room and board per student for a double room and for 14-meals per week

Information about the program
Created in 1996, the summer program provides an opportunity for students to develop a deeper understanding of basic techniques and concepts related to DNA science. While working in teams, the students assume the role of a biotechnology company and work together to design and carry out an investigation to solve problems in biotechnology.

Contact
(617) 638-5620
sumlab@bu.edu

Name of College
Boston University

Name of Program
Summer pathways in Science and Engineering

Academic / Career Interest
Science

Website
http://www.bu.edu/lernet/spathways/

Application Timeline
Approx. May 1st

Eligibility
Young women who attend high schools in the greater Boston area, are entering their junior or senior year, show promise and/or interest in science, technology or engineering. Requirements: online app, two STEM letters of recommendation.

Tuition Fees
Estimated fees: $675

Information about the program
Summer Pathways is an opportunity for young women to discover the infinite possibilities that await them in science and engineering fields. Participants arrive on a Friday afternoon, and for the duration of the program, live in a BU dormitory.

Contact
(617) 353-7021
cab@bu.edu

Name of College
Georgia Tech

Name of Program
Chaos Campus

Academic / Career Interest
Science

Website
https://ceismc.gatech.edu/studentprograms/summer-peaks_pro-grams/highschool/h1

Application Timeline
Contact Institution for more information

Eligibility
Rising grades 10-12. Must be local to metro Atlanta area. Program is non-residential. Requirements: online application

Tuition Fees
Estimated fees: $450 + $10 application fee

Information about the program
Chaos may sound like it means complete disorder, but there is a method to the madness! Students in this program will learn the fun physics behind chaos theory including what it means for physical systems to be "chaotic," and how chaotic systems relate to the formation of patterns in nature. During the week, students will conduct many hands-on experiments related to current physics research, including designing their own fractals. Students will also conduct field research at the Georgia Aquarium to observe fundamental principles of physics and math at work on the skin of living creatures. Parents, we promise the class won't get too chaotic!

Contact
(404) 894-0777

Name of College
University of Rochester

Name of Program
Science and Technology Entry Program (STEP)

Academic / Career Interest
Health

Website
https://www.urmc.rochester.edu/education/md/undergradu-ate-programs.aspx

Application Timeline
Approx. April 1st

Eligibility
Must be from Wayne or Monroe County in NY and enrolled full time as a HS student. Program is designated for students from economically disadvantaged or underrepresented backgrounds. Requirements: online application. Additional materials such as transcripts or recommendations may be asked for at a later date.

Tuition Fees
Estimated fees: free

Information about the program
STEP is a New York State funded program for high school students who are economically disadvantaged or from underrepresented backgrounds. The program is designed to stimulate participants' interest in career development opportunities in medicine and the health care professions. STEP students have the opportunity to work directly with physicians, technical staff, certified teachers, medical, and graduate students. Students are exposed to a variety of academic and professional skill development opportunities to enhance their problem solving, critical thinking and test taking skills with an emphasis on active or "hands-on" learning.

Contact
(585) 276-3000

Name of College
University of Rochester

Name of Program
Summer Research Program for HS Juniors

Academic / Career Interest
Science

Website
http://www.lle.rochester.edu/about/education/high_school_program.php

Application Timeline
Approx. March 19th

Eligibility
Must be rising senior in HS, must be local to Rochester area (commuter program). Requirements: application form, letter, essay, transcript, most recent report card, and teacher recommendation must be mailed to scra@lle.rochester.edu

Tuition Fees
Estimated fees: Free. Paid internship.

Information about the program
The Laboratory for Laser Energetics (LLE) at the University of Rochester holds an annual summer research program for Rochester-area high school students who have just completed their junior year. The eight-week program provides an exceptional opportunity for highly motivated students to experience scientific research in a realistic environment. Students who are accepted into the program are assigned to a research project and supervised by a staff scientist at the Laboratory. These projects form an integral part of the research program of the Laboratory and are related to the Laboratory's 60-beam OMEGA laser, one of the world's most powerful fusion lasers, and the OMEGA EP laser, completed in 2008.

Contact
Jean Steve, Program Coordinator
(585) 275-5286

Name of College
Northeastern University

Name of Program
Biosummer Immersion

Academic / Career Interest
Science

Website
https://www.northeastern.edu/precollegeprograms/programs/bioe/

Application Timeline
Contact institution for more information

Eligibility
Current 10th and 11th grade HS students. Requirements: application, transcript, resume, and letter of recommendation.

Tuition Fees
Estimated fees: $5,330

Information about the program
BioE Summer Immersion is an intensive, experiential, and project-based program for talented high school students who want to deepen their understanding of bioengineering and build a toolbox of technical skills to set themselves apart from their peers and gain an edge in the college admissions process.

Contact
(617) 373-2000

Name of College
UC San Diego

Name of Program
Research Scholars

Academic / Career Interest
Science

Website
http://academicconnections.ucsd.edu/research-scholars/index.
html

Application Timeline
Approx. Feb 2nd

Eligibility
10th - 12th grade and have a 3.8 (or above) weighted cumulative GPA. Requirements: Online Academic Connections Research Scholars Application, Transcript, Recommendation Form completed by the student's science teacher, and Research Scholars Essay questions - these are included with the application form.

Tuition Fees
Estimated fees:

- $100 non-refundable application fee
- $4,200 tuition

Information about the program
Research Scholars offers an opportunity for high achieving high school students to work side-by-side on projects with one of about 20 world renown faculty researchers in the academic disciplines such as biochemistry, chemistry, and nanotechnology. Research Scholars work full-time on discovery-based research projects in the lab of one of the mentors.

Contact
(858) 534-2230

Name of College
UC San Diego

Name of Program
BioChemCoRe

Academic / Career Interest
Science

Website
http://biochemcore.ucsd.edu/welcome/

Application Timeline
Approx. March 1st

Eligibility
Must be in 9th - 12th grades. Requirements: Essay describing your-self and why you would like to join this program (1 page max),.

Tuition Fees
Contact institution for more information

Information about the program
BioChemCoRe (formerly known as CompChemBioCAMP) was conceived and initially launched as a program aimed at increasing the retention of talented young women in science. The uniquely multi-faceted approach BioChemCoRe takes to encourage female scientists stems from the belief that a career in research extends be-yond the laboratory. BioChemCoRe considers learning from experi-ence essential to a student's progress and building a strong network crucial for the student's continued success. BioChemCoRe also rec-ognizes the importance of exposure to international perspectives, especially in light of the exponential advancements in communica-tion technology that allow more and more scientists from across the globe to collaborate and synchronize efforts.

Contact
(858) 534-9629
biochemcoreprogram@gmail.com

Name of College
UC San Diego

Name of Program
Summer School for Silicon Nanotechnology (SSSiN)

Academic / Career Interest
Science

Website
http://sailorgroup.ucsd.edu/courses/SummerSchool/

Application Timeline
Approx. May 1st

Eligibility
In HS, preferably taken one year of chemistry and biology, must have a research background or some form of past research work to show. Requirements: resume, personal statement including description of past research or related experiences and a brief Discovery Project proposal, and up to 3 letters of references should be sent to msailor@ucsd.edu.

Tuition Fees
Estimated fees: free

Information about the program
The Summer School for Silicon Nanotechnology (SSSiN) is an intensive, six-week workshop on the synthesis, properties, and applications of porous silicon-based nanomaterials. Based on the book "Porous Silicon in Practice," this hands-on course begins with an intensive training in theory, techniques and laboratory methods of silicon nanotechnology, and concludes with a capstone "Discovery Project"- an independent research project implemented by the student under the mentorship of a current research group member.

Contact
(858) 534-4466

Name of College
University of Florida

Name of Program
Research Immersion in Science and Engineering

Academic / Career Interest
Science

Website
https://www.cpet.ufl.edu/students/rise/

Application Timeline
Approx. March 15th - priority deadline – Consult Institution for more information

Eligibility
Rising Sophomores only. Requirements: Online application form, Two 300-500 word essays, One teacher/mentor endorsement from STEM teacher, and A copy of your current report card.

Tuition Fees
Estimated fees: $900 dollars

Information about the program
Research Immersion in Science and Engineering introduces students in the iterative cycle of innovations in science and engineering. From basic science research to the development of new applications, therapies, and technologies, students learn how research scientists and engineers contribute new knowledge and innovative approaches to tackle societal issues. Students visit active research laboratories and facilities, attend discussions highlighting current research at UF, and participate in hands-on activities and experiments with leading UF research faculty and graduate students. A culminating group project encourages collaborative learning, synthesis of ideas and technologies learned at UF, and the development of new project ideas.

Contact
(352) 392-2310
RISE@cpet.ufl.edu

Name of College
University of Florida

Name of Program
REx — Research Explorations

Academic / Career Interest
Science

Website
https://www.cpet.ufl.edu/students/research-explorations/

Application Timeline
Approx. March 15th - priority deadline

Eligibility
Grades 11 and 12. Requirements: Online application form, Two 300-500 word essays, two teacher/mentor endorsement from STEM teachers (encouraged but at least one must be), and unofficial or official transcript.

Tuition Fees
Estimated fees: $2,400 + $35 application fee

Information about the program
The REx program (Formerly RET and EBR) is an advanced intro-duction to research science. Students can attend one of two tracks, described below. While the specialized components of each track are separate, REx functions as one program with students from both tracks living, dining & socializing together.

Biomedical Track: This program focuses on translational research, from discovery-based research to clinical therapeutics. This pro-gram connects high school students to researchers in interdisciplin-ary biomedical sciences to promote interest in and preparation for bioscience careers.

Contact
(352) 392-2310

Name of College
University of Florida

Name of Program
Florida Youth Institute

Academic / Career Interest
Science

Website
https://www.cpet.ufl.edu/students/florida-youth-institute/

Application Timeline
Approx. first week Jan to March 15th
Consult Institution for more information

Eligibility
Eligibility: students entering grades 11 and 12. Requirements:
Online application form, Two 300-500 word essays, One teacher/
mentor endorsement from STEM teacher, and a copy of your current
report card.

Tuition Fees
Cost: Approx. 350. No application fee and includes housing, tuition,
and dining.

Information about the program
FYI students will learn about and discuss issues pertaining to
Florida agriculture, life sciences, and natural resources. Students
will gain an appreciation for the range of college majors and career
opportunities available in these areas. This program is sponsored
by the College of Agricultural and Life Sciences at the University of
Florida, in partnership with the Florida Department of Agriculture
and Consumer Services.

Contact
(352) 392-2310

Name of College
University of Florida

Name of Program
VolunTEEN Program at UF health

Academic / Career Interest
Health

Website
https://ufhealth.org/volunteen

Application Timeline
Approx. Feb 16th

Eligibility
Must be rising sophomores or older. Requirements: app, essay, interest form, and reference.

Tuition Fees
Estimated fees: Free

Information about the program
UF Health offers high school student ages 14-17 who have completed the 9th grade, an opportunity to volunteer in a variety of areas throughout the hospital. VolunTEENS provide valuable service to staff members and patients while gaining valuable experience.

Contact
(904) 244-4271

Name of College
UC Davis

Name of Program
Coastal Marine Sciences Program

Academic / Career Interest
Science

Website
https://precollege.ucdavis.edu/programs/coastal-marine-sciences

Application Timeline
Sessions I, II, III – Approx. June 6th, July 3rd, July 18th respectively
Consult Institution for more information

Eligibility
Must be Sophomore or Junior in HS. Requirements.

Tuition Fees
Estimated fees:

- Application fee: $80
- Tuition: $5,400
- Housing/dining fee: $1,600
- International service fee: $250 for international students only

Information about the program
Experience the satisfaction and excitement of scientific discovery in the Coastal & Marine Sciences Pre-College Program. You'll spend an exciting week on the UC Davis campus with scientists from the Coastal and Marine Sciences Institute learning about plants, animals and processes that span the California landscape, linking the Sierras to the sea. In the second week, we hit the beach, exploring one of the world's most biologically rich coastal and marine environments—Bodega Bay and the UC Davis Bodega Marine Laboratory and Bodega Marine Reserve.

Contact
(530) 752-1011

Name of College
UC Davis

Name of Program
Veterinary Medicine

Academic / Career Interest
Science

Website
https://precollege.ucdavis.edu/programs/veterinary-science

Application Timeline
Sessions I, II, III – Approx. June 6th, July 3rd, July 18th respectively
Consult Institution for more information

Eligibility
Must be Sophomore or Junior in HS. Requirements.

Tuition Fees
Estimated fees:

- Application fee: $80
- Tuition: $5,400
- Housing/dining fee: $1,600
- International service fee: $250 for international students only

Information about the program
The UC Davis Pre-College Program will introduce you to veterinary medicine, as taught by faculty from the field's top-ranked school in the world. Explore the rewarding veterinary medical profession and gain an understanding of the passion and commitment it requires, learn about the history and evolution of veterinary medicine, work with the extraordinary resources and mentors at the UC Davis School of Veterinary Medicine, and discover the wide-variety potential career paths beyond college—from researcher to practicing veterinarian.

Contact
(530) 752-1011

Name of College
UC Davis

Name of Program
Young Scholars Program

Academic / Career Interest
Science

Website
https://ysp.ucdavis.edu/

Application Timeline
Approx. March 16th

Eligibility
At least 16 years of age in HS. Requirements: Two teacher recommendations submitted through the UCD-YSP teacher recommendation website.

Tuition Fees
Estimated fees:

- $6500
- $200 security deposit (fully refundable)
- $25 application fee

Information about the program
The UC Davis Young Scholars Program (UCD-YSP) strives to engage approximately 40 academically talented high school rising juniors and rising seniors in a variety of research experiences within the areas of biological and natural sciences. Each student will undertake a six-week, long-term, apprentice-level research project in a university laboratory under the mentorship of university researchers. The laboratory experience, involving approximately 85 percent of the program time, will focus on original research including experimental design, data collection, statistical analysis, and communication of results through written and oral means.

Contact
(530) 752-0622

Name of College
University of Wisconsin Madison

Name of Program
CIMSS Student Workshop on Atmospheric, Satellite, and Earth Sciences

Academic / Career Interest
Science

Website
http://cimss.ssec.wisc.edu/studentworkshop/index.html

Application Timeline
Approx. May 11th

Eligibility
Students in grades 9-12th. Requirements: app, short student essay, parent/guardian signature, science teacher signature, as well as a $100 nonrefundable deposit.

Tuition Fees
Estimated fees:

- $400: 1 February - 6 April 2018
- $500: 7 April - 11 May 2018
- $700: After 11 May 2018
- $100: Application Deposit (non-refundable, upon acceptance)

Information about the program
The CIMSS Student Workshop on Atmospheric, Satellite, and Earth Sciences features an exciting five-day agenda in meteorology, astronomy, remote sensing and geology. Participating students stay on campus in lakeside dorms and experience science education, research and technology through hands-on activities, working directly with scientists, graduate students and professors.

Contact
(608) 263-7435

Name of College
Penn State

Name of Program
Forensic Science Camp

Academic / Career Interest
Science

Website
https://berks.psu.edu/forensic-science-camp

Application Timeline
Rolling admission – Approx. closes two weeks prior to camp start date
Consult Institution for more information

Eligibility
Grades 9-12. No prior experience needed. Requirements: online application.

Tuition Fees
Estimated fees:

- Residential: $800
- Commuter: $500

Information about the program
Students will be introduced to the world of forensic science and will take a behind-the-scenes look at crime investigations and uncover a series of "who dunnits" using current forensic techniques. They will use molecular biology to examine DNA left behind at the crime scene and ID the culprit. Participants will have the chance to interact with scientists and investigators as they learn and perform experiments to help solve crimes.

Contact
Cathleen Phillips
(610) 396-6225
cxp57@psu.edu

Name of College
Penn State

Name of Program
Veterinary Science Camp

Academic / Career Interest
Science

Website
https://berks.psu.edu/veterinary-science-camp

Application Timeline
Rolling admission – Approx. closes two weeks prior to camp start date
Consult Institution for more information

Eligibility
Grades 9-12. No prior experience needed. Requirements: online application.

Tuition Fees
Estimated fees:

- Residential: $800
- Commuter: $500

Information about the program
The Veterinary Science Camp combines hands-on experience with live animals by introducing and reviewing the scientific principles of biology, chemistry, and anatomy. Students will take on the role of veterinary assistants under the watchful eye of a veterinarian. Campers will gain firsthand experience with laboratory work, surgery, ultrasound, x-rays, cultures, suturing, and administration of injections. Students will have the opportunity to explore the many different veterinary science career possibilities as they visit a small animal veterinary hospital, a dairy farm and a veterinary emergency hospital.

Contact
Cathleen Phillips
(610) 396-6225
cxp57@psu.edu

Name of College
Penn State

Name of Program
Make it Matter Science Camp

Academic / Career Interest
Science

Website
http://www.sciencecamps.psu.edu/make-it-matter

Application Timeline
Approx. March 19th priority deadline, post March 20th is based on availability
Consult Institution for more information

Eligibility
Students entering grades 9-12. Requirements: application.

Tuition Fees
Estimated fees:

- $365 before March 19th
- $395 after March 19th

Information about the program
This camp is your gateway to the fascinating world of materials science! Materials science researchers have brought us amazing new technologies like flexible screens, nanoscale sensors, and self-folding materials – in this camp you'll explore how researchers take new technologies like these from initial concept all the way to actual implementation. Through visits to labs to meet researchers, demonstrations of cutting-edge tools, and a hands-on challenge to design and prototype your own solution to a pressing societal problem, this camp will bring the research process alive for you and inspire you to think about the world-changing possibilities of science and engineering in whole new ways!

Contact
(814) 865-0083
sciencecamps@science.psu.edu

Name of College
Penn State

Name of Program
Science Leadership

Academic / Career Interest
Science

Website
http://www.sciencecamps.psu.edu/science-leadership

Application Timeline
Approx. March 19th priority deadline, post March 20th is based on availability.
Consult Institution for more information

Eligibility
Students entering grades 9-12. Requirements: application.

Tuition Fees
Estimated fees:

- Before March 19th - $410 (commuter) or $815 (resident)
- After March 19th - $440 (commuter) $845 (resident)

Information about the program
Do you think the world needs more leaders in science? The Science Leadership Camp is designed to prepare participants to successfully build futures that combine science with their desire to make a difference. During this experience, campers will be challenged to think about issues in their communities and articulate a vision for how they can make a difference with their leadership and scientific abilities. They will also learn from the leadership experiences of Penn State science students and faculty, explore cutting-edge scientific research, and engage in activities that will challenge them to think innovatively and creatively.

Contact
(814) 865-0083
sciencecamps@science.psu.edu

Name of College
University of Illinois Urbana Champaign

Name of Program
Global Studies Summer Program - Health

Academic / Career Interest
Health

Website
http://cgs.illinois.edu/activities/2018-global-studies-summer-workshops/global-health/

Application Timeline
Approx. May 18th

Eligibility
Rising sophomores or above. Requirements: online app, transcript, and one teacher recommendation form.

Tuition Fees
Estimated fees:

- Domestic resident - $1,000
- Domestic commuter student - $600
- International resident student - $1,200

Information about the program
This intensive course for motivated high school students offers a college-level interdisciplinary survey of global health. Students will examine and compare intra- and inter-national differences in both disease burden and characteristics, quality, and access to health-care systems to address those burdens. The course will study the intersections of nutrition, taking note of medical, economic, social, epidemiological, and political contributors to healthcare access and quality, and enable students to think critically about the broader implications of health as a human right.

Contact
(217) 265-5186
global-studies@illinois.edu

Name of College
University of Illinois Urbana Champaign

Name of Program
Global Studies Summer Program - Sustainable Futures

Academic / Career Interest
Science

Website
http://cgs.illinois.edu/sustainable-futures-2/

Application Timeline
Approx. May 18th

Eligibility
Rising sophomores or above. Requirements: online app, transcript, and one teacher recommendation form.

Tuition Fees
Estimated fees:

- Domestic resident - $1,000
- Domestic commuter student - $600
- International resident student - $1,200

Information about the program
This intensive course for motivated high school students offers a college-level interdisciplinary foundation in environmental sustainability. The course includes discussions with University faculty and expert practitioners, combining an academic assessment of the fundamental challenges of sustainability with case-study investigations of local practice. Students will engage in research, visit field sites and make team presentations on their findings.

Contact
(217) 265-5186
global-studies@illinois.edu

Name of College
The Ohio State University

Name of Program
Research Internship Program

Academic / Career Interest
Science

Website
https://oardc.osu.edu/research-resources/research-intern-ship-program

Application Timeline
Approx. Feb 28th

Eligibility
Must be a senior in HS and 18 by May 1st. Must be local to OSU (program requires self-transportation and does not provide housing. Students are free to apply for summer housing at the student's expense. Requirements: online app.

Tuition Fees
Estimated fees: free. Students receive a $3,000 dollar stipend.

Information about the program
The summer OARDC Research Internship Program (ORIP) is targeted to provide research experiences for high school students and undergraduates. Students must be 18 years of age by May 1st to participate. The goal of this exclusively faculty-driven program is to substantially expand research opportunities to area students and to significantly enhance their interest in science, technology, engineering, and mathematics by inculcating critical thinking skills through rigorous laboratory and field-based research experiences, seminars, group discussions and symposia.

Contact
Dr. Daral Jackwood
(330) 263-3964
Jackwood.2@osu.edu

Name of College
University of Georgia

Name of Program
Young Scholars Internship Program

Academic / Career Interest
Science

Website
http://www.caes.uga.edu/academics/diversity-affairs/programs/
young-scholars.html

Application Timeline
Approx. Jan 31st

Eligibility
Completion of sophomore year and be 16 years old by program start
date, Completion of at least one high school science course (including a laboratory class), and one semester of algebra, Acceptance
to the University of Georgia for graduating seniors. Requirements:
Completed application form, Campus selection (Athens, Griffin or
Tifton), Short essay questions, Two letters of recommendation from
science or math teachers, and Official school transcript

Tuition Fees
Estimated fees: Free with hourly pay per 40 hours worked

Information about the program
The Young Scholars program at the College of Agricultural and Environmental Sciences (CAES) is a 6-week summer internship program
for talented high school students who show a high aptitude in math
and science related subjects. Selected summer interns work side-by-
side with CAES researchers for six weeks, and are paid a salary for
up to 40 hours of work per week. The students earn money, learn
job responsibility and, most importantly, are introduced to the work
of agricultural scientists.

Contact
Dr. Victoria David, Administrative Director
(706) 542-8826
vdavid@uga.edu

Name of College
University of Texas Austin

Name of Program
Summer High School Research Academy

Academic / Career Interest
Science

Website
https://cns.utexas.edu/tides/k-12/high-school-summer-research-academy

Application Timeline
Approx. April 2nd

Eligibility
Must be 15 years or older and be either a junior or senior. Requirements: Liability Release and Medical Authorization Form, online app, and a teacher recommendation.

Tuition Fees
Estimated fees: $1,600

Information about the program
The Summer High School Research Academy allows high school participants to participate in one of the Research Streams of the Freshman Research Initiative in the College of Natural Sciences. The students will be integrated into the research labs and participate in the ongoing research projects. The participants will see how research works by being directly involved in research projects on the UT-Austin campus. They will learn advanced techniques and interact with students and faculty at UT-Austin. By being involved in research, the students will experience the joy of discovery that is central to being a scientist.

Contact
Dr. Stuart Reichler
utaustinhsra@gmail.com

COLLEGE
CONSULTING
EXPERTS

Pre-Medical Collegiate Programs

Name of College
Stanford University

Name of Program
SIMR

Academic / Career Interest
Medical

Website
http://simr.stanford.edu/

Application Timeline
Approx. February

Eligibility
Students must currently be juniors or seniors.

Tuition Fees
Contact institution for more information.

Information about the program:
The Stanford Institutes of Medicine Summer Research Program (SIMR) is an eight-week program in which high school students from diverse backgrounds are invited to perform basic research with Stanford faculty, postdoctoral fellows, students and researchers on a medically-oriented project. The goals of the program include increasing interest in biological sciences and medicine in high school students, helping students to understand how scientific research is performed, and increasing diversity of students and researchers in the sciences.

Contact
simr-program@stanford.edu

Name of College
Stanford University

Name of Program
SMYSP

Academic / Career Interest
Science and Medicine

Website
http://smysp.stanford.edu/

Application Timeline
Approx. February

Eligibility
The Summer Residential Program is open to low-income and/or underrepresented minority high school sophomores and juniors who live in Northern and Central California.

Tuition Fees
Free

Information about the program:
Stanford Medical Youth Science Program is a five-week residential enrichment program focused on science and medicine that is open to low-income and underrepresented minority high school sophomores and juniors who live in Northern and Central California.

Contact
youth-science@stanford.edu

Name of College
University of Pennsylvania

Name of Program
Penn Medicine Program for HS students

Academic / Career Interest
Health

Website
https://www.jkcp.com/program/penn-medicine-summer-program-for-high-school-students.php

Application Timeline
Approx. March

Eligibility
Juniors and Seniors only

Tuition Fees
Estimated fees: $7,925 + $100 application fee (financial aid is available)

Information about the program
The summer high school medical program curriculum is modeled on actual Penn Medicine first year classes, but redesigned to engage bright high school students who are serious about medical careers. The program exposes you to the basics of medical training while allowing you the opportunity to pursue or discover your passions and interests.

Each morning, students participate in interactive lectures and labs by Penn clinicians on the day's featured topics, including transplant surgery, emergency medicine, cancer, resuscitation science, kidney disease and sports medicine. Afternoons will be devoted to a variety of hands-on, virtual and simulated experiences at Penn's Clinical Simulation Center and other sites.

Contact
(610) 265-9401
Imagine@JKCP.com

Name of College
Yale University

Name of Program
EXPLO Future of Medicine

Academic / Career Interest
Medicine

Website
https://www.explo.org/focus/future-of-medicine/

Application Timeline
Contact institution for more information

Eligibility
Entering grades 10-12

Tuition Fees
Estimated $2,610

Information about the program:
The future of medicine combines talents and specialties that go beyond traditional lab coats and stethoscopes. Take on contemporary case studies and explore career options beyond the hospital, from research and administration to patient care and integrative healthcare. Dig into big data and tailor medical interventions with regard to sociological actors surrounding a particular patient. Interview medical practitioners and pharmaceutical companies about strategies to deal with the opioid epidemic. Practice diagnostic methods with top doctors at a state of the art MRI laboratory that is advancing how we see patients inside and out.

Contact
(781) 762-7400

Name of College
Harvard

Name of Program
MedScience Summer Program

Academic / Career Interest
Health

Website
http://hmsmedscience.org/home/

Application Timeline
Approx. March

Eligibility
Any student who is currently in 9th-12th grade (student must have completed 9th grade before the summer session begins).

Tuition Fees
Contact institution for more information

Information about the program
HMS MEDscience offers an exciting and engaging hands-on experience for young, passionate minds with an interest in the medical sciences, health care, or STEM fields. No textbooks, no homework! The classroom will be an emergency room simulation laboratory on the Harvard Medical School campus where students learn to treat a high-tech "patient" with state-of-the art realistic and medically accurate features.

Contact
(617) 432-7047

Name of College
University of California, Los Angeles

Name of Program
Premed summer college program

Academic / Career Interest
Health

Website
https://www.uclahealth.org/volunteer/pre-med-summer-scholar-westwood

Application Timeline
Approx. March

Eligibility
High school sophomores and juniors at time of application, Must be at least 16 years old by the start of the program,

Requirements: application, essay, program acknowledgement, transcript, and recommendations

Tuition Fees
Estimated fees: $500 + $100 deposit

Information about the program
The Pre-Med Summer Scholar Program is an intense, one-week, primarily educational program incorporating medical guest speakers and hospital-related tours and activities giving the Summer Scholar an involved sense of working within the field of medicine. This is not a "summer camp-like" program and housing accommodations are not included. Last year's curriculum included: Neurosurgeon roundtable, Cardiac surgeon lecture, Internal Medicine resident forum, Oncologist Q&A, School of Medicine and School of Dentistry, Brain Mapping and Robotics Tour, CPR Training, and Volunteer shifts and service. Program is held at Ronald Reagan Medical Center.

Contact
summerscholars@mednet.ucla.edu

Name of College
University of Southern California

Name of Program
Future Physicians Program

Academic / Career Interest
Health

Website
https://summerprograms.usc.edu/programs/4-week/future-physicians/

Application Timeline
Approx. April

Eligibility
Age 16 or older by June. No exceptions.

Tuition Fees
Estimated fees:

- $8,534 for residential
- $6,059 for commuter
- $500 non-refundable deposit
- $60 application fee

Information about the program
This course is for anybody considering being a physician. The focus will be on giving students a real feel for what it is like to be a working doctor: its fulfillments and its challenges. Become immersed in what it is like to live, think, feel, see, behave and be treated as a doctor every day. This is an introduction. This is meant to give students a sense of the real-life factors and current issues to consider as they mull this option over.

Contact
(213) 740-5679
summer@usc.edu

Name of College
University of Southern California

Name of Program
Pre-health program

Academic / Career Interest
Health

Website
https://summerprograms.usc.edu/programs/2-week/kinesiology/

Application Timeline
Approx. April

Eligibility
Students must have completed at least the 9th grade by June and should be pursuing a rigorous high school curriculum to excel in USC Summer Programs.

Tuition Fees
Estimated fees:

- $4,385 for residential
- $3,270 for commuter
- $500 non-refundable deposit
- $60 application fee

Information about the program
In this introduction to kinesiology and movement science course, students learn about major scientific foundations of key domains including exercise physiology, biomechanics, and motor learning. Students discover the integration of movement science and explore career paths including physical therapy, sports performance coaching and training, exercise testing, academic research, and fitness industry consulting.

Contact
(213) 740-5679
summer@usc.edu

Name of College
Wake Forest University

Name of Program
Medicine Immersion Institute

Academic / Career Interest
Health

Website
https://immersion.summer.wfu.edu/institutes/medicine-institute/

Application Timeline
Contact institution for more information

Eligibility
Sophomores, juniors, and seniors in high school w/ good academic standing. Requirements: online application, online recommendation form. No transcript required or formal letter of recommendation.

Tuition Fees
Estimated fees: $2,500

Information about the program
Interested in donning the white coat, but not sure what being a healthcare professional is really like? Gain hands-on experience into the medical field and insight into the many career opportunities available within the various disciplines of medicine. Students visit healthcare facilities in Charlotte and Winston-Salem, participate in simulations and labs, and learn basic skills like taking blood pressure and suturing.

Contact
(336) 758-5000

Name of College
University of Michigan

Name of Program
Michigan Health Sciences Pre-College Exposure Academy

Academic / Career Interest
Health

Website
https://ohei.med.umich.edu/educational-programs/michigan-health-sciences-summer-institute/michigan-health-sciences-pre-college

Application Timeline
Approx. March

Eligibility
Students must be in the 10th or 11th grade at the time of submitting their application, and maintain at least a 3.0 GPA on a 4.0 scale.

Tuition Fees
Estimated fees: FREE

Information about the program
The Michigan Health Sciences Pre-College Exposure Academy (MHSPEA) is an entry-level residential academic enrichment program that brings together highly motivated rising 10th and 11th grade high school students to gain exposure to health professions and what it takes to be successful. MHSPEA is designed for participants who typically come from groups underrepresented in medicine, medically under-served areas or have an interest in combating health disparities. Our goal is transform medicine through development of highly qualified students who want to become future leaders in health science careers.

Contact
oheiprecollegeprograms@umich.edu

Name of College
Brandeis University

Name of Program
Global youth summit on the future of medicine

Academic / Career Interest
Health

Website
http://www.brandeis.edu/precollege/global-youth-summit/index.
html

Application Timeline
Application decisions are rolling

Eligibility
Juniors and seniors. Requirements: submit student and parent/
guardian contact information (name, e-mail, mailing address, etc.)
student academic information (high school GPA and GPA scale) as
well as two essay responses in order to complete the application
process.

Tuition Fees
Estimated fees: $2,980 + $280 deposit required

Information about the program
The Global Youth Summit on the Future of Medicine (GYS) is a prestigious and challenging program for rising high school juniors and
seniors — students with a passion for medicine and science, who
are leaders in their schools and communities.

Contact
(781) 736-8416
youthsummit@brandeis.edu

Name of College
University of Rochester

Name of Program
Precollege program in Hajim Engineering

Academic / Career Interest
Computer Science

Website
https://enrollment.rochester.edu/precollege/

Application Timeline
Approx. March

Eligibility
11th or 12 graders. Requirements: application, 2 short essay responses, transcript, letter of recommendation from a teacher/guidance counselor, and $50 application fee

Tuition Fees
Estimated fees: $4,600

Information about the program
Students can develop their independence, eye for invention, and advanced research and problem-solving skills in the Hajim Engineering program. This hands-on engineering program allows students to investigate topics like biomedical engineering, data science, and audio and music, using the vast resources of the Hajim School of Engineering and Applied Sciences.

Contact
(585) 275-3221
precollege@rochester.edu

Name of College
University of Rochester

Name of Program
Mini medical program

Academic / Career Interest
Health

Website
https://enrollment.rochester.edu/precollege/

Application Timeline
Approx. March

Eligibility
11th or 12 graders. Requirements: application, 2 short essay responses, transcript, letter of recommendation from a teacher/guidance counselor, and $50 application fee.

Tuition Fees
Estimated fees: $4,800

Information about the program
Interested in a career in medicine? This unique and selective program offers research labs, rotations, and service learning. Students will get firsthand experience with the clinical, community service, and public health aspects of medicine, gaining a real taste of the medical school experience.

Contact
(585) 275-3221
precollege@rochester.edu

Name of College
University of Rochester

Name of Program
Rochester Early Medical Scholars (REMS)

Academic / Career Interest
Health

Website
https://enrollment.rochester.edu/professional/rems/#tab1

Application Timeline
Approx. November

Eligibility
Seniors only. Passionate about a career in medicine. Take challenging classes (honors, AP, IB, college-level classes, etc.).

Tuition Fees
Contact institution for more information

Information about the program
REMS is an eight-year BA/BS + MD program for outstanding rising HS seniors who are committed to pursuing a medical career. Established in 1991, it's the most competitive combined-admission program at Rochester. As a REMS student, you're admitted to the University's School of Medicine and Dentistry once you successfully complete your bachelor's degree and pre-med core courses.

Contact
(585) 275-3221

Name of College
University of California, Irvine

Name of Program
Summer Premed program

Academic / Career Interest
Health

Website
https://www.som.uci.edu/summerpremed/summer-premed-program.asp

Application Timeline
Approx. February

Eligibility
Must be 15 to 18 years of age, have a minimum weighted GPA of 3.5, and are interested in the healthcare field. Requirements: online application, transcript, and letter of recommendation.

Tuition Fees
Estimated fees:

- Session I: $2940 (commuter only)
- Session II: $2,700 (commuter only)
- Session III: $4,315 (residential)

Information about the program
The Summer Premed Program is a two-week program dedicated to fostering the interest of high school students toward careers in medicine. This program combines didactic lectures given by distinguished UC Irvine faculty members and hands-on workshops to provide a first-rate exposure to the medical field. All activities are geared toward an "insider's look" at being a medical student.

Contact
(949) 824-6689
summerpremed@uci.edu

Name of College
Pennsylvania State University

Name of Program
Pre-Med Camp

Academic / Career Interest
Health

Website
https://berks.psu.edu/pre-med-camp-0

Application Timeline
Rolling admission - closes two weeks prior to camp start date

Eligibility
Grades 9-12. No prior experience needed. Requirements: online application

Tuition Fees
Estimated fees:

- Residential: $800
- Commuter: $500

Information about the program
Pre-Med camp provides an excellent opportunity for those wishing to explore a career in the medical field. Students will engage in lecture, hands-on lab exercises, demonstrations, and take a field trip tour of a local hospital. Pre-med campers will receive adult, pediatric and AED training to receive their CPR Certificate during their camp experience.

Contact
Cathleen Phillips
(610) 396-6225
cxp57@psu.edu

Name of College
The Ohio State University

Name of Program
MD Camp

Academic / Career Interest
Health

Website
https://medicine.osu.edu/students/diversity/programs/md_camp/
Pages/index.aspx

Application Timeline
Approx. March

Eligibility
Sophomores, juniors, and seniors, overall GPA of at least 3.0/4.0 and
3.3/4.0 STEM GPA. Requirements: online application, transcript, and
two letters of recommendation w/ one being from a STEM teacher

Tuition Fees
Estimated fees: $700

Information about the program
MD Camp, sponsored by the Area Health Education Center is an
intensive, three-week summer day camp providing participants an
experience in the rigors of medical school. It is open to sophomores,
juniors, and seniors who are interested in pursuing careers in the
health professions, including biomedical research. We typically accept students who are considered traditionally underrepresented in
medicine, and traditionally underserved which can include women
and individuals from socio-economic and / or educationally disadvantaged backgrounds.

Contact
mdcamp@osumc.edu

Name of College
University of Connecticut

Name of Program
Health Career "Camp"

Academic / Career Interest
Health

Website
http://www.centralctahec.org/index.php/programs/summer-migrant-farm-workers-program

Application Timeline
Approx. May

Eligibility
Must be in high school. Requirements: application. Applications are given out after emailing Guisela Laureano at glaureano@centralctahec.org.

Tuition Fees
Estimated fees: $50

Information about the program
During this opportunity with the University of Connecticut School of Medicine, high school students will be trained and supervised by Central AHEC staff/chaperone at the UConn Migrant Farm Worker Clinic for one week during the summer. Participants will be exposed to different health care careers (medical, dental, physical therapy, nursing and more!) and by seeing health care students and clinicians "in action" at these clinics providing direct patient care to our target population, migrant and seasonal farm workers (and their dependents!) at farms across Connecticut. The sessions run Tuesday, Wednesday and Thursday evenings at the tobacco farms with Mondays as a full day of orientation and training.

Contact
(860) 231-6250
info@centralctahec.org

Name of College
University of Pennsylvania

Name of Program
Summer Teen Volunteer Program

Academic / Career Interest
Health

Website
https://www.pennmedicine.org/for-patients-and-visitors/
penn-medicine-locations/hospital-of-the-university-of-pennsylva-
nia/volunteering/summer-teen-volunteer-program#tab-4

Application Timeline
Contact institution for more information

Eligibility
Students are mature and willing to adhere to hospital policies and
procedures, interested in helping care for patients by assisting
hospital staff and operations, are 14 years old to 18 years old, have
a professional and positive attitude about your commitment to the
hospital and its patients and visitors.
Requirements: Completion of application, immunization and health
records, health system orientation including competency assessment, Attendance every weekday of the chosen block, enrollment in
an accredited high school, and online purchase of a volunteer jacket
for approximately $25.

Tuition Fees
Estimated fees: FREE

Information about the program
The Summer Teen Program is designed to expose students interested in healthcare access to the operations of a world-class medical center. Volunteers will have a chance to interact with patients,
observe clinicians and support hospital staff.

Contact
(215) 662-2576
teen.volunteer@uphs.upenn.edu

Name of College
St. Louis University

Name of Program
AIMS Medical Workshops

Academic / Career Interest
Health

Website
https://www.slu.edu/medicine/clinics-community/aims/sum-mer-workshops.php

Application Timeline
Approx. June

Eligibility
For medical and surgical workshop - must be a sophomore, junior or senior year of high school. For anatomy 101 - sixth through ninth grades. Requirements: online application + $100 deposit that goes towards tuition.

Tuition Fees
Estimated fees:

- Anatomy 101 - $225
- Medical and Surgical Workshop - $750.
- An additional $700 is charged for overnight housing participants

Information about the program
AIMS summer workshops provide an in-depth look into various fields of medical science and are attended by students from across the country. The AIMS Medical and Surgical Procedures Workshop provides an overview of anatomy and introduction to careers in the health care field. Physicians and professionals from various medical specialties provide programs in their area of expertise using auditorium presentations, hands-on laboratory experiences, group interactions and patient interactions. Students also view several surgical demonstrations on-site.

Contact
Kim Dondanville, Program Coordinator
(314) 977-7379

Name of College
St. Louis University

Name of Program
Summer Scholars Program

Academic / Career Interest
Health

Website
https://www.slu.edu/medicine/medical-education/md/diversity/

Application Timeline
Approx. March

Eligibility
10th - 12th graders, minimum GPA 2.5, must be able to attend all three weeks of the program, and parent and student must attend the orientation. Only students interested in pursuing a career in health will be considered for this program. Requirements: online application, typed essay that explains student's personal interest in the medical profession, one letter of recommendation from a counselor, science or math teacher.

Tuition Fees
Estimated fees: FREE

Information about the program
Summer Scholars is a three-week program for sophomore, junior and senior high school students designed to motivate them to pursue a career in medicine. Activities include participation in practical anatomy workshops, preparing for college, a group research project and more.

Contact
Michael T. Railey, M.D.
(314) 977-8730
Michael.railey@health.slu.edu

Name of College
Stanford University

Name of Program
Stanford Anesthesia Summer Institute

Academic / Career Interest
Health

Website
https://med.stanford.edu/anesthesia/education/SASI.html#important_dates

Application Timeline
Approx. January

Eligibility
Open to junior and senior high-school and undergraduate college students.

Tuition Fees
Estimated fees: $4,000. Scholarships available to students who demonstrate financial need.

Information about the program
Are you a high school or college student with a passion for health care and curiosity about the field of anesthesia, health care technology, science-related careers or medical education? Our two-week summer program is designed for high school and pre-medical undergraduate students interested in pursuing careers in medicine, STEM, medical research and development, or health care design, with a specific focus on medicine, Anesthesiology, Perioperative and Pain Medicine. This summer program will provide clinical observation opportunities, hands-on experience with anesthesia skills, and mentorship from Stanford medical students and faculty to foster career development in the health professions.

Contact
(650) 723-6412

Name of College
Stanford University

Name of Program
High School and Pre-medical Student Stanford Summer Internship

Academic / Career Interest
Health

Website
http://med.stanford.edu/cssec/summer-internship.html#application-faqs

Application Timeline
Approx. January

Eligibility
Must be 16 years of age on the first day of the program.

Tuition Fees
Estimated fees:

- $5,950 + $2,950 for Stanford housing
- $195 for the application fee.

Information about the program
The Cardiothoracic Surgical Skills and Education Center Stanford Summer Internship is designed to educate high school and pre-medical students considering careers in science, medicine, and public health in basic and advanced cardiovascular anatomy and physiology as well as medical and surgical techniques that will be utilized in pre-medical and medical school. This program is open to all students worldwide. This program will provide exposure to the steps towards mastering basic and advance cardiothoracic surgery (e.g., knot tying, dissection, suturing, coronary artery bypass graft, and aortic valve replacements).

Contact
Mikaela Louie
M2louie@stanford.edu

Name of College
Stanford University

Name of Program
Clinical Summer Internship

Academic / Career Interest
Health

Website
http://med.stanford.edu/medcsi.html

Application Timeline
Approx. January

Eligibility
Must be high school juniors and seniors.

Tuition Fees
Estimated fees:

- $95 application fee
- $4,995 tuition
- $2,300 housing

Information about the program
The Stanford Clinical Summer Internship (CSI) is a 2-week program for high school juniors, seniors, and undergraduate pre-med students designed to empower and energize diverse learners as they delve into the art and science of being a doctor, and gain new skills and insights to plan for a career in medicine. The rich and unique curriculum includes hands-on skills sessions, interactive lectures and simulation experiences in primary care, emergency medicine, obstetrics, sports medicine, cardiology, neurology, and surgery, providing the students a glimpse of various specialties. The program is taught by the top-notch Stanford faculty, students and staff. Sessions with current medical students and residents provide an inside knowledge of admission into medical school and the rigors and fulfillment of a life in medicine.

Contact
http://med.stanford.edu/medcsi/contact.html

Name of College
Stanford University

Name of Program
Brain Camp

Academic / Career Interest
Health

Website
https://med.stanford.edu/s-spire/outreach-programs/smash-sum-mer-2018-high-school-outreach-program.html

Application Timeline
Contact institution for more information

Eligibility
Must be in the 9th grade at the time of application, have strong mathematics skills appropriate for your grade level, as determined by your state standardized math test scores, attend a public high school or private high school via scholarship, and reside in the United States within 50 miles* of a SMASH site as determined by your zip code.

Tuition Fees
Estimated fees: FREE

Information about the program
SMASH Academy is a free-of-cost, STEM-intensive college preparation program for underrepresented and low-income high school students. Students admitted to this program will spend 5 weeks at Stanford University, where they will engage in STEM coursework, participate in networking activities, and prepare for the college application process. Students spend 3 consecutive summers in this program to gain support throughout high school and connect with long-lasting mentors. The SMASH Medical Curriculum is comprised of five sessions designed to be interactive and expose the students to a range of healthcare careers. Led by social science researcher Serena Bidwell, our instructors are medical students, residents, faculty, and staff from the Stanford Department of Surgery.

Contact
(650) 723-4000

Name of College
Washington University

Name of Program
Pre-Medical Institute

Academic / Career Interest
Health

Website
https://summerexperiences.wustl.edu/premedical

Application Timeline
Approx. April

Eligibility
Must be a current freshman, sophomore, or junior in high school, and have an academic average of B+ (3.3/4.0) or better. Requirements: online application, three short essays, transcript, teacher Recommendation, and international applicants must send proof of English ability.

Tuition Fees
Estimated fees: $5,585. Scholarship assistance is available to students who demonstrate financial need.

Information about the program
The ever-changing world of medicine is a fast-paced and exciting atmosphere in which to spend the summer. The Pre-Medical Institute is designed to build on students' strong scientific academic foundations and introduce them to topics that they may not otherwise experience before college. Through this research-based program, students are exposed to academic publications, theories, and resources that examine human health and medicine. This institute combines traditional undergraduate curriculum with guest lectures, discussion, field trips, and small group work in order for students to gain valuable academic and career experience.

Contact
(314) 935-4807
summerexperiences@wustl.edu

Name of College
University of California, Berkeley

Name of Program
Medicine & Healthcare @ UC Berkeley Springboard

Academic / Career Interest
Health

Website
https://summerspringboard.com/teen-programs/medicine-health-care-at-berkeley/

Application Timeline
Rolling admissions, first come first served.

Eligibility
Eligibility: must be in high school. Requirements: online application, $365 deposit, and $30 application fee

Tuition Fees
Estimated fees:

- Residential Tuition - $4,998
- Commuter Tuition - $2,590 + $280 for meals (if desired)

Information about the program
Considering a career in medicine? Thinking about being a pre-med major in college? Is the student interested in biology, fascinated with the human body, or want a career helping people? These are big questions that can influence the next four to twelve years of a student's life. Our summer medical program for high school students gives them a 360-degree view of the medical and healthcare field, as well as immersive learning through hands-on projects and simulations. Students learn real world skills in emergency medical care through our hands-on, field-based curriculum. Learning has never been so fun!

Contact
(858) 780-5660
info@summerspringboard.com

Name of College
Columbia University

Name of Program
State Pre-College Enrichment Program (S-PREP)

Academic / Career Interest
Health

Website
https://www.ps.columbia.edu/sprep

Application Timeline
Approx. March

Eligibility
Must be enrolled in 7th - 12th grade, must also be a New York state resident or a permanent resident alien residing in the state.

Tuition Fees
Estimated fees: FREE

Information about the program
The State Pre-College Enrichment Program (S-PREP) is a free high school and college preparatory program designed for students who are seriously interested in pursuing a career in medicine or related STEM fields. The long-range objective of the program is to increase the number of underrepresented minorities in healthcare and STEM professions. The program offers enrichment courses geared towards preparing students for success in math and science. Courses include, but are not limited to the following: Anatomy, Biochemistry, Chemistry, Genetics, Neuroscience, Organic Chemistry, Physics, Physiology, Psychology, Algebra, Geometry, Pre-Calculus, and Calculus. In addition, the program offers PSAT (summer only), SHSAT and SAT (academic year) preparation courses.

Contact
(212) 305-4157
ps@cumc.columbia.edu

Name of College
Dartmouth University

Name of Program
Health Careers Institute at Dartmouth

Academic / Career Interest
Health

Website
https://tdi.dartmouth.edu/health-careers-institute

Application Timeline
Contact institution for more information

Eligibility
Must be a sophomore, junior or senior in high school.

Tuition Fees
Estimated fees:

- New Hampshire students, or those attending school in New Hampshire - $1,700
- Out-of-state tuition for students is $2,550

Information about the program
The Health Careers Institute provides opportunities for high school students from New Hampshire and beyond to explore different areas of health care as a discipline. We do this through experiential and academic endeavors. These experiences include visiting clinical settings such as Dartmouth-Hitchcock Medical Center (DHMC). Additionally, participants have opportunities to converse with health care professionals including physicians, nurses, and research scientists.

Contact
Lillian Emerson, HCID Program Coordinator
(603) 646-1225
Lillian.emerson@dartmouth.edu

Name of College
Notre Dame University

Name of Program
Summer Scholars Program

Academic / Career Interest
Health

Website
http://precollege.nd.edu/courses/global-health/

Application Timeline
Approx. February

Eligibility
Current sophomores and juniors, strong academic standing with solid extracurricular activities, and at least 16 years old.

Tuition Fees
Estimated fees: $3,500 + $50 lab fee

Information about the program
Summer Scholars participants spend two intense weeks in one of 21 exciting programs of study. We keep the classes small and personal attention from Notre Dame faculty high. The coursework is a true preview of college academics—it is both rigorous and rewarding, and students earn one college credit upon the completion of a program track. Students collaborate on coursework outside designated class times, as they would in any college setting. There is also ample time to enjoy the social facets of college life, especially those unique to Notre Dame.

Contact
(574) 631-0990
precoll@nd.edu

Name of College
Rutgers University

Name of Program
SMART (Science Medicine and Related Topics)

Academic / Career Interest
Health

Website
http://njms.rutgers.edu/smart/

Application Timeline
Contact institution for more information

Eligibility
Students in grades 7-12 and are New Jersey residents. Requirements: completed application, teacher's recommendation, transcripts, student essay, parental consent form, and immunization record

Tuition Fees
Estimated fees: $25 non-refundable application fee + $900 per student

Information about the program
SMART is a pre-college enrichment program designed to cultivate students' interest in health science and research, culminating in enhanced competitiveness and expansion of the pool of underrepresented minority students interested in pursuing health-related professions. The program focuses on youth development and academic excellence, provides opportunities to students to gain the knowledge and experiences necessary to maximize their potential for success. During the Summer Academy, we accept students who are rising 7th – 12th graders.

Contact
(973) 972-5245
smartprogram@njms.rutgers.edu

Name of College
University of South Florida

Name of Program
Pre-College Summer Program

Academic / Career Interest
Health

Website
https://www.usf.edu/innovative-education/programs/pre-college/
programs/future-physicians.aspx

Application Timeline
Approx. May

Eligibility
For 11th and 12th grade high school students. Requirements: online
application.

Tuition Fees
Estimated fees:

- Future Physicians, Scientists and Engineers program :
  $1,250
- Advanced Future Physicians, Scientists and Engineers pro-
  gram: $1,550 (Includes trip to Busch Gardens - Physics of
  Roller Coasters)

Information about the program
This academically intensive, residential summer program for students entering grades 11-12 is designed to directly involve students
in hands-on inquiry, discovery, creativity and research across a
broad array of disciplines that impact the human endeavor. Students
will be exposed to basic, clinical and translational research. This
program also offers a unique hands-on experience to go behind-the-
scenes at the Center for Advanced Medical Learning & Simulation
(CAMLS), a virtual patient care and surgery training center.

Contact
(813) 974-3139
InEd-PreCollege@usf.edu

STEM Collegiate Programs

Name of College
Harvard

Name of Program
Harvard Pre-College Program

Academic / Career Interest
Engineering

Website
https://www.summer.harvard.edu/high-school-programs/pre-college-program

Application Timeline
Approx. February

Eligibility
Complete an online application and provide supplemental materials, including:

- The $50 nonrefundable application fee
- Counselor report
- Transcripts with fall grades
- Signed rules and regulations

Tuition Fees
Estimated fees - $4,500

Information about the program:
The Harvard Pre-College Program is an immersive, collaborative, and transformative residential experience. Alongside peers from around the world, students will thrive in a dynamic and supportive academic environment.

Contact
(617) 495-4024
precollege@summer.harvard.edu

Name of College
Carnegie Mellon

Name of Program
AP/EA - Summer Pre-College

Academic / Career Interest
Engineering

Website
https://admission.enrollment.cmu.edu/pages/pre-college-apea

Application Timeline
Approx. April

Eligibility
High School Transcript - Please send an official, recent high school transcript, including as complete a listing as possible of classes and grades.

Tuition Fees
Tuition waivers are available. Resident (2 courses) - $10,283

Information about the program:
The Advanced Placement/Early Admission (AP/EA) Program provides talented, motivated high school students with the unique opportunity to take summer courses offered by Carnegie Mellon. Students earn college credit while working in an academic setting that mirrors the supportive, rigorous environment of the first year of college. Every summer, AP/EA offers close to 40 courses from academic disciplines across the university. Successful AP/EA students leverage their experiences to demonstrate their ability to succeed in college, and have the potential to receive advanced college credit for the coursework from Carnegie Mellon and other institutions.

Contact
(412) 268-2082
admission@andrew.cmu.edu

Name of College
University of Michigan

Name of Program
Michigan Math and Science Scholars

Academic / Career Interest
Math and Science

Website
http://www.math.lsa.umich.edu/mmss/

Application Timeline
Application currently open

Eligibility
Contact institution for more information

Tuition Fees
$100 application fee and $2,150 for one session

Information about the program:
A program designed to introduce high school students to current developments and research in the sciences and to encourage the next generation of researchers to develop and retain a love of mathematics and science.

Contact
(734) 647-4466
mmss@umich.edu

Name of College
University of Pennsylvania

Name of Program
Penn Engineering Summer Academy

Academic / Career Interest
Engineering

Website
https://esap.seas.upenn.edu/about/

Application Timeline
Approx. February

Eligibility
Online application for high school students.

Tuition Fees
Estimated fees - $7,635

Information about the program:
The Engineering Summer Academy at Penn (ESAP) welcomes highly motivated and talented students to explore Engineering at the college level. The Academy's intensive, three-week programs combine sophisticated theory with hands-on practical experience in cutting edge technologies. Work with leading faculty while earning college credit, live on Penn's historic campus, and connect with new friends from around the world.

Contact
(215) 898-0053
esap@seas.upenn.edu

Name of College
Boston University

Name of Program
RISE Internship

Academic / Career Interest
Engineering and science

Website
https://www.bu.edu/summer/high-school-programs/research/
internship/

Application Timeline
Approx. February

Eligibility
We consider applicants who are entering their senior year of high
school and are U.S. citizens or permanent residents.

Tuition Fees
Estimated fees - $7,200

Information about the program:
With hands-on research opportunities in multiple fields, the Research in Science & Engineering (RISE) Internship track provides
students an opportunity to explore in depth the many facets of
university laboratory research. Take some time to peruse the faculty
profiles on the departmental websites of the student's interest
through the links above. Not only will these profiles give you a sense
of the exciting research going on at Boston University, but you will
be able to identify professors whose research interests match your
own.

Contact
(617) 353-1378
rise@bu.edu

Name of College
Columbia University

Name of Program
SHAPE Program

Academic / Career Interest
STEM

Website
https://outreach.engineering.columbia.edu/content/shape-summer-high-school-academic-program-engineers

Application Timeline
Approx. March

Eligibility
Be High School sophomores, juniors, or seniors.

Tuition Fees
Estimated fees - $4,000

Information about the program:
Columbia Engineering Summer High School Academic Program for Engineers (SHAPE) is a selective summer program for high school sophomores, juniors, and seniors. The program is geared toward local students who have demonstrated an interest in science, technology, engineering, and mathematics (STEM). Each 3-week session offers college-level courses in robotics, computer science, electrical and biomedical engineering, which are complemented by electives in research skills and entrepreneurship, labs, and college preparation workshops.

Contact
(646) 745-8422
engineeringoutreach@columbia.edu

Name of College
Cornell University

Name of Program
Cornell Engineering Experience

Academic / Career Interest
STEM

Website
https://www.sce.cornell.edu/sc/programs/index.php?v=184

Application Timeline
Approx. May

Eligibility
Current juniors and seniors encouraged to apply.

Tuition Fees
$4,250-$12,825 depending on which program you choose (two-week to six-week respectively)

Information about the program:
In this six-week program, offered in collaboration with Cornell's distinguished College of Engineering and taught by R. Bruce van Dover, students will enroll in the three-credit course Exploration in Engineering (ENGRG 1060).

Contact
(607) 255-6203
summer_college@cornell.edu

Name of College
Stanford University

Name of Program
High School Summer College

Academic / Career Interest
STEM

Website
https://summer.stanford.edu/program/high-school-high-school-summer-college

Application Timeline
Approx. February

Eligibility
Be a current sophomore, junior, or senior, or a gap year student at the time of application.

Tuition Fees
$14,426 to $17,054 is the estimated range for a student attending Stanford Summer Session taking eight units and living on campus.

Information about the program:
During Stanford University's Summer Quarter, high school students from the United States and around the globe are invited to spend eight or nine weeks living and learning in the heart of Silicon Valley.

Contact
(650) 723-3109

Name of College
Washington University St. Louis

Name of Program
High School Scholars Program

Academic / Career Interest
Math and Science

Website
http://summerexperiences.wustl.edu/scholars

Application Timeline
Approx. April

Eligibility
Be a current sophomore or junior in high school.

Tuition Fees
A $35 application fee is due upon submitting an application. This fee is waived if students apply before February.

Session A or B (five weeks): $8,085
Session C (eight weeks): $10,585

Information about the program:
Through our High School Summer Scholars Program, students have the opportunity to enroll in courses for credit and study alongside undergraduates. Students select from a broad range of stimulating introductory courses in the humanities, math, sciences, and social sciences.

High School Summer Scholars live on campus in one of our top-ranked, air-conditioned residence halls. In addition to coursework, students participate in specialized seminars, academic support groups, and a variety of weekend and evening social events. Learn about life on campus during a Summer Experience.

Contact
(314) 935-4807
summerexperiences@wustl.edu

Name of College
Brown University

Name of Program
Pre-Baccalaureate Program

Academic / Career Interest
Computer Science, Math, Science

Website
https://precollege.brown.edu/prebaccalaureate/

Application Timeline
Approx. April

Eligibility
For current or recently graduated high school seniors.

Tuition Fees
Estimated Fees:
Residential, 2 courses: $11,967
Commuter, 1 course: $4,046
Commuter, 2 courses: $7,992

Information about the program:
The Brown University Pre-Baccalaureate Program is a highly
selective program for college-bound students. Get a head start on
college credit, explore fields of study that may become your major,
and prepare for college success with an introduction to Ivy League
academics.

Contact
(401) 863-7900
precollege@brown.edu

Name of College
New York University

Name of Program
NYU Precollege

Academic / Career Interest
Engineering, Math, Science

Website
http://engineering.nyu.edu/highschoolsummer

Application Timeline
Approx. March

Eligibility
High school sophomores and juniors are eligible to apply to NYU Precollege. Applicants must be in good academic and disciplinary standing as demonstrated in their academic transcript and application.

Tuition Fees
Estimated tuition fees start at $3,000 based upon credits.

Information about the program:
NYU Precollege offers rising high school juniors and seniors the opportunity to experience academic and student life at New York University. This academically rigorous program places high school students in six-week, intensive, college-level courses with current college students and allows them to gain academic credit, which may be applied to a future degree.

Contact
(646) 997-3600

Name of College
Vanderbilt University

Name of Program
Vanderbilt Summer Academy

Academic / Career Interest
Engineering, Math, Science, Computer Science, Health

Website
https://pty.vanderbilt.edu/students/vsa/

Application Timeline
Applications open approx. February (rolling admission)

Eligibility
Students applying to Vanderbilt Summer Academy must submit qualifying documentation at the time of application. To be eligible for VSA, students may either submit ACT, SAT, or PSAT scores or a recent individual ability/achievement test at the 95th percentile and above in one or more subject areas. In lieu of the above mentioned test scores, students may prefer to submit a portfolio for further assessment and review.

Tuition Fees
Contact institution for more information

Information about the program:
This residential academic experience provides qualifying students with a taste of college life. As a VSA student, you will live on campus and take accelerated courses with Vanderbilt professors, lecturers, and graduate students. Outside the classroom, our carefully selected residential staff members supervise the dining and residence halls, plan fun and engaging recreational activities, and help ensure that every VSA student has a fulfilling experience.

Contact
(615) 322-8261
pty.peabody@vanderbilt.edu

Name of College
Texas Tech University

Name of Program
Clark Scholars Program

Academic / Career Interest
Engineering, Math, Science, Computer Science, Health

Website
http://www.depts.ttu.edu/honors/academicsandenrichment/affili-atedandhighschool/clarks/

Application Timeline
Approx. February

Eligibility
Contact institution for more information

Tuition Fees
Free - There is no cost to attend the program. If selected, the student is responsible for his/her transportation to and from the program.

Information about the Program
The Clark Scholar Program is an intensive seven week summer research program for highly qualified high school juniors and seniors. The Program at Texas Tech University helps the Scholars to have hands-on practical research experience with outstanding and experienced faculty.

- The Scholars will receive a $750 tax-free stipend and room and board.
- The Program includes fun activities, weekly seminars and field trips.
- This Program provides opportunities for research in all academic areas in the university.
- International Students are eligible/welcome to apply.
- Student must be 17 years of age by the program start date.

Contact
clark.scholars@ttu.edu

Name of College
Princeton University

Name of Program
Summer Institute for the Gifted (unaffiliated)

Academic / Career Interest
Engineering, Math, Science

Website
https://www.giftedstudy.org/residential/princeton/

Application Timeline
Approx. May

Eligibility
Students applying to the Residential/Commuter Programs must be ages 9-17 by August (students must be ages 13-17 for Princeton University.

Tuition Fees
Estimated cost:
Residential: $5,795.00
Extended Commuter: $4,895.00

Information about the program:
SIG students and staff are usually housed in Whitman College, one of Princeton's six residential colleges. Uniquely situated in the heart of Princeton's campus, Whitman College offers easy access to Dillon Gym, Princeton classrooms, and Nassau Street, which affords students the opportunity to explore Princeton's thriving academic, commercial, and creative community. When not in class, students have the opportunity to explore the Princeton Art Museum, Prospect Gardens, Frist Campus Center, and other cultural venues on campus, in addition to offering academic and communal spaces via its dining hall, lounges and dance studio.

Contact
(866) 303-4744
Sig.Info@GiftedStudy.org

Name of College
Princeton University

Name of Program
WEB Debois Scholars - Summer Institute

Academic / Career Interest
Engineering, Computer Science, Science

Website
http://duboisscholars.org/programs/summer-institute.html

Application Timeline
Contact institution for more information

Eligibility
Student must be a freshman, sophomore or junior in high school.

Tuition Fees
The total cost for residential participants is $6,500.

Information about the program:
The Engineering Academy aims to stimulate interest among participants in careers in Engineering. The curriculum includes integral courses on advanced mathematics and physics principles. These courses also incorporate analytical thinking, and cooperative problem-solving strategies. These engineering geared courses may include: Intro to Engineering, Engineering Computing, and Physics.

Contact
(609) 955-0666
admissions@duboisscholars.org

Name of College
University of Chicago

Name of Program
Pathway Program Molecular Engineering

Academic / Career Interest
Science and Engineering

Website
https://summer.uchicago.edu/course/pathway-program-molecular-engineering-0

Application Timeline
May 1st. Students may apply after this deadline, but will be required to pay an additional $100 rush processing fee. Enrollment is limited to 30. **Apply as early as possible.**

Eligibility
Holistic Application Includes: Personal Profile
Test Scores (if applicable)
Writing Sample and/or supplement (if applicable)
Recommendations
Housing (if applicable)

Tuition Fees
Estimated cost: $5,700. Includes housing, tuition, and meals.

Information about the program:
The Pathway Program in Molecular Engineering will provide an overview of the basic components of engineering – design principles, modeling, and optimization. Students will spend their mornings in lectures and discussions with faculty and researchers at the university and their afternoons completing group-based projects in labs overseen by faculty and TAs. The TAs will also conduct occasional evening tutoring sessions. A computation unit will provide students with the opportunity to use super computers and create models, which will inform their optimization efforts, at the university's Research Computing Center.

Contact
(773) 702-2149
summersession@uchicago.edu

Name of College
Yale University

Name of Program
Yale Summer Session

Academic / Career Interest
Computer Science, Math, Science, Engineering

Website
https://summer.yale.edu/academics/courses-yale

Application Timeline
Approx. May

Eligibility
Requirements: must be juniors.

Tuition Fees
Estimated cost: Tuition is $4,045 for 1 credit course. Science labs are half tuition. $75 application fee. Housing Estimated cost: 5 weeks - $3435 and 10 weeks is $6870. Residential fees include meals and student activity costs.

Information about the program:
Yale Summer Session combines the resources of a world-class university with the close-knit community of a liberal arts college. In our small classes, Summer Session students work closely with world-renowned faculty; they also have access to the vast array of resources on campus, including the libraries, galleries and a gym. Our diverse student body comes from across the U.S. and around the world. Courses include STEM selections for pre-college students such as introductory CS and Electrical Engineering.

Contact
(203) 432-2430

Name of College
Yale University

Name of Program
Pathways Summer Scholars Program

Academic / Career Interest
Science and Health

Website
https://pathwayssummerscholars.yale.edu/

Application Timeline
Approx. February

Eligibility
Student must be:

- current 9th, 10th, or 11th grader enrolled in Yale Pathways to Science
- attend a New Haven, West Haven, or Amity Public High School
- demonstrate a strong academic performance in school, especially in math and science
  Note: only seniors in Pathways can apply to the residential component of the program

Requirements: Full application including short-answer questions and essay response (online application strongly preferred). Parent signature pages and teacher recommendation forms are required.

Tuition Fees
Estimated cost: FREE

Information about the program:
Yale Pathways Summer Scholars is a free two-week summer science day program for 100 local high school students in the Yale Pathways to Science program. As part of the program, students have the opportunity to select from a variety of STEM workshops, collaboratively designed and taught by Yale faculty and graduate students.

Contact
(203) 432-2430

Name of College
Columbia University

Name of Program
Columbia Summer Immersion

Academic / Career Interest
Computer Science, Math, Science

Website
https://sps.columbia.edu/highschool/summer-immersion/new-york-city-3-week

Application Timeline
Approx. January - priority deadline

Eligibility
Eligibility: must be at least a junior at the time of applying. To live in dorms, students must be 16 or 15 with a special petition.

Tuition Fees
Estimated cost: $11,064 for total residential cost - housing, meals, tuition included. Course materials like textbooks are not included. For commuters: $5,600. Neither program offers financial aid.

Information about the program:
This is a residential summer program where admitted students may take courses in Engineering as well as other disciplines. Students over the age of 16 will be allowed to reside in the dorms and participate in student activities on and outside of campus in their time outside of classes.

Contact
(212) 854-9889
hsp@columbia.edu

Name of College
Massachusetts Institute of Technology

Name of Program
MITES

Academic / Career Interest
Engineering, Computer Science, Math, Science

Website
https://oeop.mit.edu/programs/mites/program-details

Application Timeline
Approx. Feb 1st.

Eligibility
Eligibility: Must be a HS junior. Strong academic record and is a minority or low income or from a geographic area historically underrepresented at MIT such as rural HS. Requirements: Unsure of specific application requirements as the application portal is now closed for the Summer. Will update after emailing MIT.

Tuition Fees
All costs are covered by MIT

Information about the program:
Minority Introduction to Engineering and Science (MITES) is a rigorous six-week residential academic enrichment program for rising high school seniors – many of whom come from underrepresented or underserved communities – who have a strong academic record and are interested in studying and exploring careers in science and engineering. This national program stresses the value and reward of pursuing advanced technical degrees and careers while developing the skills necessary to achieve success in science and engineering.

Contact
summerapp@mit.edu

Name of College
Rockefeller University

Name of Program
Summer neuroscience program

Academic / Career Interest
Science and Health

Website
https://www.rockefeller.edu/outreach/snp/

Application Timeline
Approx. March

Eligibility
Eligibility: must be 16 years old and enrolled in a NY high school. Must be nominated by a teacher; students can request a teacher nominate them for the program. Requirements: both student and teacher nomination forms must be completed. No required application materials like transcript, test scores required.

Tuition Fees
Estimated cost: FREE

Information about the program:
The Summer Neuroscience Program (SNP) at The Rockefeller University is a two-week course aimed at introducing talented and enthusiastic high school students to the brain. Led by graduate students, the program takes a look at the most current research in neuroscience in an effort to understand how our brain works and how it relates to our daily life. In addition to the series of highly interactive lectures, students present fun and fascinating journal articles to their classmates. Students also visit research laboratories, dissect brains, and design and conduct neuroscience experiments.

Contact
snp@rockefeller.edu

Name of College
Stanford University

Name of Program
Pre Collegiate Summer Institute

Academic / Career Interest
Engineering, Computer Science, Math and Science

Website
https://summerinstitutes.spcs.stanford.edu/about

Application Timeline
Early Deadline: approx. January. Regular Deadline: approx. February

Eligibility
Eligibility: For students ages 13-17 grades 8-11. Admission commit-tee encourages students of color, underrepresented minorities and low income applicants to apply. Requirements: online application, any standardized test scores at the state or national levels including ACT/SAT/PSAT or AP exams, 1-4 recommendations from teachers more relevant for your desired subject area, some courses expect work samples so if the course expects that, applicants must provide it to complete application. Requires a $50 application fee.

Tuition Fees
Estimated cost: $6850 + $50 application fee. This covers everything outside of airfare/transportation and incidental purchases. Finan-cial Aid is available and need based, however merit does play a factor in the decision making process to receive financial aid as well.

Information about the program:
We invite high school students from around the world to discover, study, and explore in small classes with instructors who are experts in their fields and passionate about teaching. Includes courses in STEM. This is a 3 week residential program only for enrichment not course credit.

Contact
precollegiate@stanford.edu

Name of College
Stanford University

Name of Program
RISE Internship

Academic / Career Interest
Engineering, Science and Health

Website
https://oso.stanford.edu/programs/39-rise-summer-intern-ship-program

Application Timeline
Approx. February

Eligibility
Eligibility must be 16 by June.

Tuition Fees
Estimated cost: FREE. Students receive a 2,500 dollar stipend.

Information about the program:
The RISE (Raising Interest in Science and Engineering) Summer Internship Program for HS Students is sponsored by Office of Science Outreach. It's an intensive 7-week summer program for Bay Area students interested in science, engineering, math, computer science, or psychology. Students spend 30 hours a week on campus, working in an active research lab under the guidance of a mentor from the lab, and attending weekly group sessions that include field trips, presentations, hands-on science activities, and lab tours. RISE is designed for bright low-income students and those who will be the first in their family to attend college. We give priority to groups historically under-represented in science and engineering.

Contact
mbruhis@stanford.edu

Name of College
Stanford University

Name of Program
Young Earth Investigators program

Academic / Career Interest
Engineering and Science

Website
https://pangea.stanford.edu/stanford-earth-young-investigators

Application Timeline
Opens approx. Feb 1st, Closes approx. March

Eligibility
Eligibility: Sophomore and older. You must live and attend school in the San Francisco Bay Area, within 25 miles of campus or in San Francisco. No exceptions. Interns must be confident enough to talk to professors. Applicants must live within 25 miles. We want interns to be able to get to campus in less than an hour. We will accept applications from students living in San Francisco, on the peninsula south through San Jose and Los Gatos, and in the East Bay from San Leandro south to Milpitas. Requirements: just the online application and a letter of recommendation. No transcripts/scores/tests required.

Tuition Fees
Estimated cost: FREE. This is an internship.

Information about the program:
At the School of Earth, Energy & Environmental Sciences, students spend the summer working in research laboratories. This program enables graduate students to serve as supervisors, prepares high schools students for college and helps strengthen the connections between Stanford and local high schools. Since 2004, over 250 high school students have worked in research labs in the School of Earth, Energy & Environmental Sciences and learned about the process of science first hand.

Contact
Jennifer Saltzman
saltzman@stanford.edu
(650) 725-2410

Name of College
Stanford University

Name of Program
SIMR

Academic / Career Interest
Science and Health

Website
http://simr.stanford.edu/

Application Timeline
Approx. Mid-December – late February

Eligibility
Eligibility: All of the following requirements must be met (no exceptions):

- Students must currently be juniors or seniors.
- Students must also be 16 years old or older by the start of the program.

Tuition Fees
Estimated cost: $40 application fee. Fee waiver is available for families who make under 80K. It's in the application. The application must be submitted before February due to processing time. Students will receive a $500 stipend and can receive more if their family is under the 80K income cap. Meals, housing, transportation are not provided. Students will need to cover these costs themselves and on campus housing is not offered for this program.

Information about the program:
The Stanford Institutes of Medicine Summer Research Program (SIMR) is an eight-week program in which high school students from diverse backgrounds are invited to perform basic research with Stanford faculty, postdoctoral fellows, students and researchers on a medically-oriented project. The goals of the program include increasing interest in biological sciences and medicine in high school students, helping students to understand how scientific research is performed, and increasing diversity of students and researchers in the sciences.

Contact
simr-program@stanford.edu

Name of College
University of Pennsylvania

Name of Program
UPenn Summer Academies

Academic / Career Interest
Math and Science

Website
https://www.sas.upenn.edu/summer/programs/high-school/academies

Application Timeline
Approx. May 1st

Eligibility
Eligibility:

- 9th - 11th grades. Minimum 3.3 high school GPA

Tuition Fees
Estimated cost: $8,199 for residential, $6,999 for day commuter as well as a $500 dollar lab fee and $75 dollar application fee.

Information about the program:
Academies are subject-intensive three-week programs that fuse sophisticated scientific or social theory with relevant application. The science academies draw upon Penn's cutting-edge technology and resources to provide innovative lab experiences while the social academies draw upon the rich history and diversity of Philadelphia to provide a sociologically comprehensive summer experience. There are 5 Engineering focused academies: Biology Research Academy, Chemistry Research Academy, Experimental Physics Research Academy, Mathematics Academy, and Neuroscience Research Academy

Contact
summer@sas.upenn.edu

Name of College
Duke University

Name of Program
Summer College for HS students

Academic / Career Interest
Math and Science

Website
https://summersession.duke.edu/high-school-students/summer-college-for-high-school-students

Application Timeline
Approx. April

Eligibility
Eligibility: U.S. students in 10th and 11th grades

Tuition Fees
Estimated cost: $8,895 + $50 application fee. Includes housing, dining, tuition, linen pack, transportation from and to Raleigh Durham International Airport and student activities. Does not include airfare cost or campus facilities fee. Limited financial aid available.

Information about the program:
This 4-week credit-bearing program offered by Duke University attracts students who represent the next generation of leaders from around the world. Students will become immersed in an international college experience by enrolling in this élite program designed to provide high school students with an academic and residential environment conducive to collegiate success. This program is not entirely STEM focused however there are specialty areas of focus available for students such as Physics, Mathematics, and Biology for those who wish to pursue STEM.

Contact
summercollege@duke.edu

Name of College
Duke University

Name of Program
Intensive STEM Academy

Academic / Career Interest
Engineering and Science

Website
https://summersession.duke.edu/high-school-students/intensive-stem-academy

Application Timeline
Approx. May 1st

Eligibility
Eligibility: 9th - 12th grade students.

Tuition Fees
Estimated cost:
$2,250 and $500 deposit is required. Covers Course Fee , Housing , Dining, Program-Sponsored Activities, Linen Pack Rental , Ground Transportation to and from Raleigh-Durham International Airport. There is financial aid but it is heavily limited.

Information about the program:
Students will spend the summer alongside the next generation of innovators at Duke University's Intensive STEM Academy and engage with some of the world's top researchers. During this one-week program, students will explore Duke's state-of-the-art laboratories, learn about trailblazing research, and experience the life of an élite researcher. Students currently in grades 9 – 12 are eligible to apply to this prestigious program. Enroll in this program and take what may be a powerful first step in a lifelong pursuit of innovation.

Contact
summeracademy@duke.edu

Name of College
Health Careers Institute at Dartmouth

Name of Program
Sustainable Summer Camp

Academic / Career Interest
Engineering and Science

Website
https://sustainablesummer.org/programs/dartmouth-college-summer-program/

Application Timeline
Priority deadline: approx. January. Regular deadline: April 1st

Eligibility
Eligibility: current 9th, 10th and 11th grade high school students. Requirement: primary application w/ essay demonstrating the reasons for interest and passion in environmental sciences, secondary application which consists of a teacher recommendation letter, an audio response to a question related to sustainability and your response to a thought experiment.

Tuition Fees
Estimated cost: $2895. Includes housing, food, program materials, etc. but doesn't include transportation to and from the program.

Information about the program:
Sustainable Summer's Environmental Leadership Academy at Dartmouth College enables the next generation of environmental leaders to engage in sustainability inquiry and action. This program focuses on environmental engineering as well as entrepreneurship

Contact
See website for contact information

Name of College
John Hopkins University

Name of Program
Discover Hopkins Program

Academic / Career Interest
Science and Health

Website
https://summerprograms.jhu.edu/program/pre-college-students-discover-hopkins/

Application Timeline
Approx. March

Eligibility
Eligibility: must be sophomore, junior, or senior.
Requirements: online application, Writing Sample, Official High School Transcript including Fall grades
One completed teacher recommendation, Parent/Guardian Approval Form

Tuition Fees
Estimated cost: $3800-4200 for residential (depending on the subject selected costs marginally differ). Costs include housing, tuition, and dining. Financial aid is available; financial aid application is on the website. $75 application fee. Upon acceptance, a non-refundable deposit of $500 (commuters), $1250(residential) is required to secure a spot in the program

Information about the program:
Discover Hopkins Programs are intensive programs designed to expose you to topics from different perspectives. For instance, observe top researchers and listen to experts at Johns Hopkins Medical Institutions, as you survey the latest in environmental health. These programs are primarily focused on medical experiences, biology, chemistry, and math.

Contact
summer@jhu.edu

Name of College
Brown University

Name of Program
Summer at Brown

Academic / Career Interest
Computer Science, Engineering, Science, and Health

Website
https://precollege.brown.edu/summeratbrown/

Application Timeline
Rolling admissions up until program start date - penalties for late submissions. No penalty before March.

Eligibility
Eligibility: grades 9-12. Requirements: application, transcript, and essay response. Additional documents such as teacher recommendations may be requested at a later date.

Tuition Fees
Estimated cost: residential - 1-Week Course: $2,709, 2-Week Course: $4,191, 3-Week Course: $5,966, 4-Week Course: $6,764.
Commuter - 1-Week Course: $2,125, 2-Week Course: $3,023, 3-Week Course: $4,214, 4-Week Course: $4,428. Plus additional $50 application fee.

Information about the program:
Summer@Brown offers more than 200 courses that reflect the wide range of Brown University's "open" curriculum - providing students the skills necessary for success in college and guiding them in their exploration of potential majors. Without the pressure of formal grades and credit, students can immerse themselves in subjects they choose and experience the satisfying challenges of college-level academics. This program offers a variety of courses in computer science as well as neuroscience, chemistry and biology.

Contact
(401) 863-7900
precollege@brown.edu

Name of College
Cornell University

Name of Program
Bioinformatics Internship

Academic / Career Interest
Computer Science and Science

Website
https://btiscience.org/education-outreach/internships/?-card#page=PGRPSummerInternships

Application Timeline
Approx. February

Eligibility
Eligibility: must be at least 16 years old enrolled in high school.

Tuition Fees
Estimated cost: FREE. High school students receive a $2,400 stipend but are responsible for their own housing, meals, and transportation.

Information about the program:
At BTI, molecular biologists and computer scientists are working together at the forefront of biological discovery to solve real world problems. With novel technologies, researchers can now access entire genome sequences, and the details of the proteome, transcriptome, and metabolome of many organisms, to better understand biological systems and interactions. Though information-rich, the size and complexity of these data sets pose new challenges for scientists and society. The growing field of bioinformatics addresses these challenges. Bioinformatics interns will focus on data analysis and developing computational tools and resources to store, analyze, and integrate large-scale "omics" data sets. The program offers a unique training in genome research, computer programming, and systems biology.

Contact
(607) 254-1234
contact@btiscience.or

Name of College
Rice University

Name of Program
Summer Session for HS students

Academic / Career Interest
Computer Science, Math and Science

Website
https://summer.rice.edu/programs/highschool

Application Timeline
Contact institution for more information

Eligibility
Eligibility: Must be a junior or senior. Must be from the metro Houston area.
Requirements: Visiting Student Application, Teacher and counselor recommendation attesting to the applicant's ability to pursue a university-level course, Test scores (SAT or ACT); either an official copy or as reported on the high school transcript, Official high school transcript, Application fee of $75.
This must be paid online on the Office of the Registrar Fees website and may be paid by credit card or electronic check.
Proof of meningococcal vaccination record or waiver (Required if under the age of 22).

Tuition Fees
Estimated cost: $1,000 per credit hour. Housing is available at additional cost. Housing application is required.

Information about the program:
Rice Summer Sessions offer the opportunity for highly accomplished high school students to enroll in college-level courses. Students take courses taught by Rice faculty and earn credit that may be applied to their undergraduate degree. High school students will learn alongside current undergraduate students from Rice and other universities. These courses are all STEM courses from Physics to Bio to Chem.

Contact
(713) 348-4999
summercredit@rice.edu

Name of College
Rice University

Name of Program
Tapia STEM Camp

Academic / Career Interest
Engineering, Computer Science, Math and Science

Website
https://tapiacamps.rice.edu/say-stem-camp

Application Timeline
Approx. June 15th

Eligibility
Eligibility: must be grades 10-12.
Requirements: Just application and a few essay responses.

Tuition Fees
Estimated cost: 1,495. Cost includes lodging, food, entertainment, and a field trip. Transportation to and from the camp is not included.

Information about the program:
A 6-day, 5-night residential summer camp at Rice University in Houston, TX covering topics in Math, Physics, Computer Science, Engineering, and Biology.

Contact
Leticia Velazquez, Ph.D.
leti@rice.edu

Name of College
Vanderbilt University

Name of Program
Research Experience for High School Students (REHSS)

Academic / Career Interest
Science and Health

Website
https://www.vanderbilt.edu/cso/rehss/

Application Timeline
Contact institution for more information

Eligibility
Contact institution for more information

Tuition Fees
Estimated cost: FREE

Information about the program:
The Research Experience for High School Students is an intense, 6-week scientific research internship at Vanderbilt University, centering on full immersion in a Vanderbilt University or Vanderbilt University Medical Center research lab. Students engage in an independent research project under the mentorship of a research faculty member at Vanderbilt.

Contact
(615) 322-7140

Name of College
Emory University

Name of Program
Summer Science Academy

Academic / Career Interest
Science and Health

Website
http://med.emory.edu/summercamps/about/index.html

Application Timeline
Approx. May

Eligibility
Must be in 9th or 10th grade.
Requirements: apply online, parental consent form, photo consent release form, copy/proof of health insurance, and deposit of 200 dollars.

Tuition Fees
Estimated cost: $800

Information about the program:
The Summer Science Academy is a science enrichment program for students entering the 9th or 10th grade during the next academic year. There are three sessions, each being two weeks in length. The Program's curriculum consists of a series of lectures, labs, and field experiences for high school students. These "hands on" experiences are designed to heighten students' interest in science, increase their awareness of how science is the foundation of healthcare and careers in health, and introduce and/or reinforce some principles of science. Topics that will be explored but not limited to are: Physics/ Chemistry/ Biology, Human Anatomy, Neuroscience, Human Diseases, and Genetics.

Contact
(404) 727-0016
som-ssa@emory.edu

Name of College
University of California, Berkeley

Name of Program
Pre-college summer program

Academic / Career Interest
Engineering, Computer Science, Math and Science

Website
http://summer.berkeley.edu/precollege-programs/precollege-resi-dential

Application Timeline
Approx. May 1st

Eligibility
Eligibility: Have completed the 10th or 11th grade by the start of summer classes, Have an overall B average (3.0, weighted or unweighted) in all of their high school coursework, 16 years of age by June, Require residential housing. Requirements: application, letter of interest (personal essay), transcript including fall quarter, liability form and code of conduct form must be filled out.

Tuition Fees
Estimated cost: 8 week - Session C : $15,000
6 week - Session D : $13,700. Includes housing, meals, and all other associated costs sans transport to and from the program.

Information about the program:
The Berkeley Pre-College Scholars: Summer Residential Program offers international and domestic high school students the opportunity to live on campus and enjoy the summer at Berkeley. Get involved in Berkeley courses, extracurricular activities and excursions, and workshops. Take advantage of everything campus has to offer, while also earning college credit. This program includes introductory courses in CS, Math, and Neuroscience.

Contact
(510) 642-5611
summer@berkeley.edu

Name of College
UC Berkeley

Name of Program
Academic Talent Development Program

Academic / Career Interest
Computer Science, Math and Science

Website
https://atdp.berkeley.edu/apply/

Application Timeline
Application deadline: Approx. February. Extended deadline - May 30th.

Eligibility
Eligibility: grades 9-11 for secondary school program. Requirements: Application, teacher review form, transcript, copy of SAT/PSAT score report (if available), essay response, letter of interest.

Tuition Fees
Estimated cost: $800-1100 per course for STEM courses, $50 application fee, financial aid is available. Non- residential program.

Information about the program:
ATDP's goal is to select students who will benefit from the challenging course offerings as well as succeed in this fast-paced program. Students are eligible to attend ATDP's Secondary Division once they complete Grade 7 and can return each summer through the completion of Grade 11. Students become ineligible for ATDP when they complete Grade 12. Courses include CS curriculum, Mathematics curriculums, and Natural Sciences Curriculums for STEM focused students.

Contact
(510) 642-8308
atdpoffice@berkeley.edu

Name of College
University of California, Berkeley

Name of Program
SMASH academy

Academic / Career Interest
Engineering, Computer Science, Math and Science

Website
http://old.lpfi.org/programs/smash/

Application Timeline
Opens in Early November

Eligibility
Must be in 9th grade.

Tuition Fees
Estimated cost: FREE

Information about the program:
The Summer Math and Science Honors Academy (SMASH) is a free of cost, STEM-intensive college preparatory program for underrepresented high school students of color. SMASH boasts a rigorous 5-week, 3-year summer, fully residential STEM enrichment program which provides access to STEM coursework and access to mentors, role models, and support networks of students of color. Each summer, SMASH scholars spend five weeks on a college campus immersed in STEM and live among other high-potential, underrepresented (African American, Latino/a, Native American, Southeast Asian or Pacific Islander, low-income, first-in-family to attend college) high school students.

Contact
programs@smash.org

Name of College
University of California, Berkeley

Name of Program
Summerfuel

Academic / Career Interest
Engineering, Computer Science and Science

Website
https://www.summerfuel.com/pre-college/berkeley#main-menu

Application Timeline
Approx. May 15th

Eligibility
Eligibility: grades 9-12.
Requirements: application, transcript, teacher recommendation form, and parent/student agreement form

Tuition Fees
Estimated cost: $7,895. Includes tuition, room, 3 meals per day, use of select campus facilities, included excursions and daily activities, bed linens, pillow and towels, 24-hour residential care and support, staff accompanied airport transfer during specified windows.

Information about the program:
Summerfuel Berkeley inspires high school students to engage intellectually and personally and experience life at the nation's premier public research university. A Summerfuel Pre-College program is designed to reflect a collegiate liberal arts environment and students are strongly encouraged to explore and take ownership of their experience. Courses are small, active and engaging, requiring student involvement. Activities are designed by staff with student input to ensure a very personalized, unique experience. STEM track is available for students and includes hands on workshops in robotics.

Contact
(212) 796-8359
info@summerfuel.com

Name of College
University of Southern California

Name of Program
Intro to Game Design

Academic / Career Interest
Engineering and Computer Science

Website
https://summerprograms.usc.edu/programs/4-week/game-de-sign/

Application Timeline
Approx. April

Eligibility
Eligibility: Must have completed at least the 9th grade.

Tuition Fees
Estimated cost: $8,534 for residential and $6,059 for commuter. $500 deposit non refundable is required to save a seat and a $60 application fee applies on top of that.

Information about the program:
This course will provide students with an overview of the video game production process. Students will gain hands-on experience by developing video games and utilizing various software applications. Upon completion of the course, students will be able to conceptualize, design, develop, implement and integrate current and emerging video game features and technologies.

Contact
(213) 740-5679
summer@usc.edu

Name of College
Carnegie Mellon

Name of Program
National High School Game Academy

Academic / Career Interest
Engineering and Computer Science

Website
https://admission.enrollment.cmu.edu/pages/pre-college-nhsga

Application Timeline
Approx. April 15th

Eligibility
Eligibility: must be at least juniors.

Tuition Fees
Estimated cost: Resident - $9,283
Commuter - $6,882. Some financial aid is available but limited.

Information about the program:
The National High School Game Academy explores the video game industry and the skills needed to be successful in it. The program includes an exciting blend of hands-on exercises combined with traditional lecture and discussion. Students are encouraged to expand their own creative possibilities in a unique blend of left- and right-brain college-level work.
The facts: 230 students apply; 100 students are admitted, and approximately 75 complete the program annually.

Contact
(412) 268-2082
admission@andrew.cmu.edu

Name of College
Carnegie Mellon

Name of Program
Summer Academy for Math and Science

Academic / Career Interest
Engineering, Computer Science, Math and Science

Website
https://admission.enrollment.cmu.edu/pages/access-sams

Application Timeline
Approx. March 1st

Eligibility
Eligibility: must be a high school senior, age 16 or older. Should be either/or some combination of low income, underrepresented minority or group, from rural high school w/ historically low rates of acceptances at top tier institutions, or potential first to go to college. Requirements: application, high school transcript, letter of recommendation from one STEM teacher, resume, essay response, and standardized test scores.

Tuition Fees
Estimated cost: FREE

Information about the program:
The Summer Academy for Math and Science provides rising high school seniors with a strong interest in computer science, engineering and/or the natural sciences, with the opportunity to achieve essential skills necessary to pursue and complete majors in STEM fields. The Summer Academy curriculum includes seminars and highly collaborative hands-on projects, designed and taught by Carnegie Mellon faculty, outstanding teachers and graduate students, carefully chosen due to their commitment to teaching. Upperclass college students also serve as classroom assistants, tutors and mentors.

Contact
(412) 268-2082
admission@andrew.cmu.ed

Name of College
University of Virginia

Name of Program
Summer Session Commuters Program

Academic / Career Interest
Engineering, Computer Science, Math and Science

Website
https://summer.virginia.edu/admission-charlottesville-ar-
ea-high-school-students-commuting-students

Application Timeline
Opens approx. April and closes 5 days before class begins.

Eligibility
Eligibility: juniors and seniors w/ exceptional academic records.
Requirements: application, medical consent forms, terms of understanding form, secondary school report filled out by principal, and
transcript.

Tuition Fees
Estimated cost: $386.00 per credit. This program is only for local
students (non residential program)

Information about the program:
High school commuting students accepted in the summer are
considered visiting undergraduate students and are enrolled in
classes with undergraduate students. Only juniors and seniors with
excellent academic records are eligible to enroll for summer classes.
With the exception of students accepted into the Summer Language
Institute, high school students may take only one class per term.
Students should choose a course offered through the College of
Arts and Sciences in the 1000- to 2000-level for which there are no
prerequisites.

Contact
(434) 924-3371

Name of College
University of Michigan

Name of Program
Computational Biology Camp for High School Students

Academic / Career Interest
Computer Science and Science

Website
http://www.mircore.org/2018-summer-camps/2018-cb-camp/

Application Timeline
Contact institution for more information

Eligibility
Academically motivated current high school students interested
in computers, math, science, and medicine. Must be local to U of M
(commuter program). Bring own laptop and lunch.
Requirements: application, essay submission.

Tuition Fees
Estimated cost: $530

Information about the program:
This camp is for academically motivated current high school and 8th
grade students interested in computer, math, science, and medicine. The camp will focus on the role of genomics in diseases and
symptoms and guide students to perform computational biology
research using patient RNA expression data to identify genes related
to certain diseases. There will be a separate basic genomics session
to accommodate students who have not taken first year high school
biology. Students will have a chance to experience wet-lab experiments.

Contact
(734) 288-8647
info@mircore.org

Name of College
Tufts University

Name of Program
Tufts College Experience

Academic / Career Interest
Computer Science, Math and Science

Website
http://summer.tufts.edu/study-pre-college-courses.asp

Application Timeline
Opens approx. December 1st, closes May 1st

Eligibility
Eligibility: must be in grades 11-12. Requirements: $65 fee, application, 1 letter of recommendation, transcript, and test scores are optional (but encouraged)

Tuition Fees
Estimated cost: 10K. + $65 application fee. deposit is $500. Includes housing, tuition, and meals. Doesn't include transportation to and from program

Information about the program:
Get a taste of what it is like to study at Tufts University and try-out life as a college student! Enroll in Tufts Undergraduate courses and/ or in one of four college-level courses designed specifically for high school students. This program is designed to mirror the Undergraduate experience, allowing highly motivated students to select their own course schedule and mix college-level study with fun activities and the opportunity to build college and life skills. Includes a variety of courses in STEM as well as a coding bootcamp course.

Contact
(617) 981-7008
summer@tufts.edu

Name of College
New York University

Name of Program
ARISE program

Academic / Career Interest
Computer Science, Engineering and Science

Website
http://engineering.nyu.edu/k12stem/arise/

Application Timeline
Approx. March 1st

Eligibility
Eligibility: New York City residents who are completing 10th or 11th grade,

Tuition Fees
Estimated cost: FREE to participate. Transportation and meals are not covered.

Information about the program:
After a successful launch in summer 2013, the NYU Tandon School of Engineering continues to conduct the Applied Research Innovations in Science and Engineering (ARISE) program. This program is for academically strong, current 10th and 11th grade New York City students with a demonstrated interest in science, technology, engineering and math (STEM). This full-time, seven week program includes: college level workshops and seminars, a high level research experience in participating NYU faculty labs, and mentoring in that placement by a graduate or postdoctoral student. In the seminars and workshops, students will be introduced to the scientific method and ethics, data collection and analysis, research practices and lab safety.

Contact
K12.stem@nyu.edu

Name of College
New York University

Name of Program
Summer Program for Automation Robotics and Coding

Academic / Career Interest
Engineering and Computer Science

Website
https://engineering.nyu.edu/research-innovation/k-12-stem-edu-cation/student-programs/sparc#chapter-id-27311

Application Timeline
Rolling admissions w/reply after 2 weeks of submission

Eligibility
Eligibility: Students entering 9th, 10th, 11th or 12th grade in September.

Tuition Fees
Estimated Tuition: $2,000 per two-week session
Program Fee (special events and activities) of $100
Housing is available at an additional cost of $510 for 2 weeks
Meal plan is available at an additional cost of $340 (10 meals/week for two weeks)

Information about the program:
NYU's Summer Program for Automation Robotics and Coding (SPARC) is a two-week, full-day summer program for introducing rising 9th through 12th high school students to the basics of robotics, mechatronics and programming on the NYU Tandon Downtown Brooklyn campus. SPARC is best suited for academically strong students with an interest, but not necessarily experience in robotics.

Contact
(646) 997-3524
K12.stem@nyu.edu

Name of College
University of California, Santa Barbara

Name of Program
Pre-college program

Academic / Career Interest
Computer Science, Math and Science

Website
http://www.summer.ucsb.edu/pre-college/pre-college-programs

Application Timeline
Opens approx. February 1st, closes end of June

Eligibility
Eligibility: must be in high school, Min 3.0/4.0 GPA, Requirements: online application, $200 fee for application, transcript.

Tuition Fees
Estimated cost: $281.00 per unit, $490.50 campus-based fee, $200.00 Summer Application Fee, and $2.50 per unit L&S technology fee

Information about the program:
UCSB Summer Sessions offers a variety of Pre-College programs that provide students with a unique opportunity to earn college credit while in high school. Simultaneously, these programs are designed to help shape students academic, professional, personal, and social development. Our programs will challenge high school students by exposing them to the academic excellence of UCSB while acclimating to the university's social environment. We have programs designed for every type of student. Various math, physics, chemistry, STEM related courses offered.

Contact
See website for contact information

Name of College
University of California, Santa Barbara

Name of Program
Research Mentorship Program

Academic / Career Interest
Engineering, Computer Science, Math and Science

Website
http://www.summer.ucsb.edu/pre-college/research-mentorship-program-rmp

Application Timeline
Opens approx. Dec 15th

Eligibility
Eligibility: Must currently be a high school student in the 10th or 11th grade, Completed a minimum of 12 academic semester courses (or the equivalent in UC a-g requirements), Have a minimum 3.8 GPA weighted in UC a-g requirements, Must attend the program in its entirety. Requirement: online application including emails for 2 recommenders, AP test scores, transcript

Tuition Fees
Estimated cost: $95 Application Fee (non-refundable), $4,500 Commuter Student Tuition, and $10,899 Residential Student Tuition

Information about the program:
The Research Mentorship Program is a competitive, six-week summer program that engages qualified, high-achieving high school students from all over the world in interdisciplinary, hands-on, university-level research. Students will be paired up with a mentor (graduate student, postdoc, or faculty) and choose a research project from a large list of disciplines offered by the program each year.

Contact
(805) 893-2315

Name of College
University of California, Santa Barbara

Name of Program
Science and Engineering Research Academy

Academic / Career Interest
Engineering and Science

Website
http://www.summer.ucsb.edu/pre-college/science-engineering-re-search-academy-sera

Application Timeline
Approx. March 15th

Eligibility
Eligibility: Must currently be a high school student in the 9th, 10th or 11th grade, Have a minimum 3.6 GPA weighted in UC a-g requirements, and must attend the program in its entirety. Requirements: online app including contact info for 3 recommenders, personal statement, official transcript.

Tuition Fees
Estimated cost: $75 Application Fee (non-refundable)
$2,100 Commuter Student Tuition
$8,199 Residential Student Tuition

Information about the program:
The Science & Engineering Research Academy is a dynamic, 4-week residential and commuter summer program that introduces qualified high school students to the research enterprise through project-based, directed research in STEM-related fields. Students will take a 4-unit university course where they choose and develop a research topic specific to the track they select, under the direction of an instructor who is conducting active research in that field.

Contact
(805) 893-2315

Name of College
University of California, Santa Barbara

Name of Program
Early Start Program

Academic / Career Interest
Computer Science, Math and Science

Website
http://www.summer.ucsb.edu/pre-college/early-start-program

Application Timeline
Closes when program fills (Rolling Admissions)

Eligibility
Eligibility: in grades 9-12. Minimum required GPA is 3.3.
Requirements: online application.

Tuition Fees
Estimated cost: $9,299 for 6 week residential and $7,799 for 4 weeks residential

Information about the program:
Students enroll in two UC Santa Barbara courses and live in a residence hall for six-weeks. High school students who are looking to increase their competitiveness when applying to UCs or other top universities in the nation should enroll in this program. By taking two academic courses, ESP provides students the opportunity to explore some of the university's different disciplines and gain valuable college experience. Minimum required GPA is 3.3.

Contact
(805) 893-2315

Name of College
Northeastern University

Name of Program
Young Scholars Program

Academic / Career Interest
Engineering and Science

Website
https://stem.neu.edu/summer/ysp/

Application Timeline
Approx. March 31st

Eligibility
Eligibility: must be permanent Massachusetts residents (this is a non-resident program), Rising Seniors only. Students from any schools (public, private, home schooled, etc) are eligible.
Upon entrance into the program there will be a $150 commitment fee. Requirements: application, teacher recommendations from 2 STEM teachers, transcript (unofficial is ok)

Tuition Fees
Estimated cost: $150

Information about the program:
The Young Scholars Program offers future scientists and engineers a unique opportunity for a hands-on research experience while still in high school. The program is open to Massachusetts residents (within commuter distance) who have completed their junior year of high school (i.e. rising seniors).

Contact
NUStemEd@gmail.com

Name of College
Tulane University

Name of Program
Science Scholars Program

Academic / Career Interest
Engineering, Computer Science and Science

Website
http://www2.tulane.edu/sse/tssp/

Application Timeline
Approx. March 31st

Eligibility
Eligibility: 10th-12th grades. Requirements: application, essay and transcript, the name and email address of the teacher writing your recommendation, and the $25.00 application fee.

Tuition Fees
Estimated cost: $1500 in-state and $1700 out-of-state

Information about the program:
The Tulane Science Scholars Program (TSSP) gives high school students the opportunity to take college-credit courses taught by Tulane faculty in the School of Science and Engineering before high school graduation. The TSSP is a selective program for 10th through 12th grade students who have exceptional talent in the sciences, engineering, and mathematics. A variety of courses in science and engineering are offered each summer and have a workload similar to that of a regular undergraduate course. During the course of a two-week session, students will also attend lunch-n-learns with invited speakers as well as tour many of our science and engineering research labs including the Tulane Makerspace.

Contact
tssp@tulane.edu

Name of College
Tulane University

Name of Program
Summer enrichment institute

Academic / Career Interest
Engineering and Computer Science

Website
https://summer.tulane.edu/pre-college/stem

Application Timeline
Contact institution for more information

Eligibility
Eligibility: 9th-11th graders. Requirements: application, statement of purpose and transcript, the name and email address of the teacher writing your recommendation, and the $25.00 application fee. A $300 deposit is required as well.

Tuition Fees
Estimated cost: Two-week residential program: $2,350
Deposit due upon application: $300 + $25 application fee.

Information about the program:
When it comes to remedying challenges regarding the environment, cybersecurity, and health care, America is in desperate need of more STEM-educated professionals. The Tulane Summer Enrichment Institute in STEM is designed to inspire the future generation to pursue careers and academic disciplines within STEM (Science Technology Engineering and Mathematics) to help tackle some of the biggest challenges facing our world. Our classes and faculty will nurture curiosity, incubate ideas, and provide students with an experience that will help take their college applications to the next level.

Contact
(504) 314-7619
summer@tulane.edu

Name of College
Rensselaer Polytechnic Institute

Name of Program
Current Smart Grid

Academic / Career Interest
Engineering, Science and Computer Science

Website
http://summer.rpi.edu/programs/smart-grid

Application Timeline
Approx. March 31st

Eligibility
Eligibility: 10th, 11th, 12th graders. Requirement: application, two letters of recommendation, and copy of transcript.

Tuition Fees
Estimated cost: FREE thanks to the sponsorship of the NSF CURENT Engineering Research Center.

Information about the program:
This program is sponsored by the National Science Foundation and the Department of Energy, CURENT Engineering Research Center! Learn about how the electric grid is being adapted to incorporate renewable sources such as solar arrays and wind turbine farms. Students will use a simulation tool to explore how the grid responds to loss of equipment and extreme power demands when these problems might lead to blackouts. A market experiment on pricing electricity is also part of the program. In addition students will learn about computer networks and cyber security. Students will work with Rensselaer Polytechnic Institute faculty and graduate students on hands-on activities and go on a tour of the regional New York power grid manufacturing or control facilities.

Contact
(518) 276-6809
SOAPS@rpi.edu

Name of College
Rensselaer Polytechnic Institute

Name of Program
Polymer Chemistry Research Experience

Academic / Career Interest
Engineering and Science

Website
http://summer.rpi.edu/programs/research-polymers

Application Timeline
Approx. March 31st

Eligibility
Eligibility: 10th, 11th, 12th graders. Requirement: application, two letters of recommendation, and copy of transcript.

Tuition Fees
Cost is $850.00 for commuters. There is a $425.00 non-refundable deposit required in order to reserve a spot in the program, once the student is academically accepted. Residential Cost is $1835. This cost includes room and board, program materials, residential events and programs, and any academic related materials.

Information about the program:
The goal of this research week is to provide students with the opportunities to (1) characterize and identify plastic materials using cutting-edge thermal analysis instruments, (2) promote their understanding of the thermal properties of polymers, such as glass transition and melting temperatures, which will be the main consideration to dictate the usage of polymers in modern life and (3) ultimately enhance their awareness of plastic recycling issues. Because different types of plastics do not mix, they have to be separated for the recycling and reuse of the plastic materials.

Contact
(518) 276-6809
SOAPS@rpi.edu

Name of College
Rensselaer Polytechnic Institute

Name of Program
Exploring STEAMM Careers

Academic / Career Interest
Engineering and Science

Website
http://summer.rpi.edu/programs/STEAMM

Application Timeline
Approx. March 31st

Eligibility
Eligibility: 10th, 11th, 12th graders. Requirement: application, two letters of recommendation, and copy of the transcript.

Tuition Fees
Estimated cost: $1300.00 for commuters, $3270.00 for residential. There is a $425.00 non-refundable deposit required in order to reserve a spot in the program, once the student is academically accepted. The cost includes room and board, program materials, residential events and programs, and any academic related materials.

Information about the program:
Students will explore cutting-edge interdisciplinary topics and career paths that integrate disciplines in science, technology, engineering, art, mathematics, and medicine. This is a project-based program that combines hands-on discovery with classroom learning.

Contact
(518) 276-6809
SOAPS@rpi.edu

Name of College
University of California, Irvine

Name of Program
Summer Research Program

Academic / Career Interest
Science and Health

Website
https://www.som.uci.edu/summerpremed/summer-research-program.asp

Application Timeline
Approx. February

Eligibility
Eligibility: must be 16 to 18 years of age, have a minimum weighted GPA of 3.5, and interested in research in the healthcare field. Requirements: Online application, one letter of recommendation, and high school transcript.

Tuition Fees
Estimated cost: $2940 for non-room and board and $4315 for room and board

Information about the program:
Through this innovative program, we inspire premedical students to accelerate healthcare discoveries through state of the art technologies and research. The activities vary from summer to summer depending on the laboratory availabilities and resources. In the past, the students have participated in hands-on research projects involving nanotechnology, microfluidics, neurobiology, immunostaining, and study of coma in animal models.

Contact
(949) 824-6689
summerpremed@uci.edu

Name of College
University of California, Irvine

Name of Program
Online Research Program

Academic / Career Interest
Science and Health

Website
https://www.som.uci.edu/summerpremed/online-research-program.asp

Application Timeline
Admissions are rolling until spots fill.

Eligibility
Eligibility: must be 15 to 18 years of age, have a minimum weighted GPA of 3.5, are interested in research in the healthcare field. Requirements: application, one teacher recommendation, and transcript

Tuition Fees
Estimated cost: $1865.

Information about the program:
The Online Research Program at UC Irvine School of Medicine is a three-week mentored program designed to increase the exposure of high school to research methods. At the completion of the program the students will be able to: understand the core concepts for responsible conduct of research involving human subjects, understand the importance of evidence-based medicine, learn how to critically evaluate the medical literature on a given topic, access the University of California libraries, write an organized research report, and submit an abstract to a national meeting where the student's name will be listed as a co-author.

Contact
(949) 824-6689
summerpremed@uci.edu

Name of College
University of California, San Diego

Name of Program
UC San Diego Academic Connections

Academic / Career Interest
Engineering, Computer Science and Science

Website
http://academicconnections.ucsd.edu/?_
ga=2.143161085.973216637.1529953090-
1590914610.1529953090

Application Timeline
Approx. June 15th

Eligibility
Eligibility: high school students with a 3.3/4.0 or greater GPA.
Requirements: application, teacher recommendation, authorization
forms, medical form, and unofficial transcript.

Tuition Fees
Estimated cost: $100 non-refundable application fee
$4,200 (all inclusive) tuition, course materials, housing, all meals,
activities, SAT Prep course. Transportation to and from UC San Diego is not included.

Information about the program:
In Session I, students choose one of approximately 25, three-week
courses offered. Classes meet five hours a day, with a maximum of
22 students per class, to ensure quality interaction with instructors
and instructional assistants. Academic Connections instructors
are typically UCSD doctoral students who design and instruct the
course. This engaging combination brings freshness and excitement
to the classes. Courses vary however include many STEM focused
courses including Mechanical Engineering and Fluid dynamics.

Contact
(858) 534-2230

Name of College
University of California, San Diego

Name of Program
COSMOS Program

Academic / Career Interest
Engineering, Computer Science and Science

Website
http://jacobsschool.ucsd.edu/cosmos/

Application Timeline
Approx. February

Eligibility
Eligibility: 9th - 12th graders.
Requirements: Completed and submitted online application, recommendation from a math/science teacher, OFFICIAL transcript, $30 application fee (paid online by credit card or check/money order mailed to address above)

Tuition Fees
Estimated cost: California Residents: Tuition is $3,745. Financial aid is available for CA residents only.
Non-California Residents: Tuition is $6,000. No financial aid is available. $200 Non-Refundable Deposit for ALL accepted students and $30 non-refundable application fee.

Information about the program:
The California State Summer School in Mathematics and Science (COSMOS) at UC San Diego is a rigorous, four week residential program for talented and motivated students. COSMOS students attend clusters that are designed to introduce students to STEM subjects not traditionally offered in high school.

Contact
(858) 822-4361
cosmos@ucsd.edu

Name of College
University of Florida

Name of Program
Student Science Training Program

Academic / Career Interest
Engineering, Computer Science, Math, Science, Health

Website
https://www.cpet.ufl.edu/students/sstp/

Application Timeline
Approx. early December - February (rolling admissions until the program ends) No hard cutoff date listed.

Eligibility
Eligibility: Seniors. Requirements: online application, two STEM letters of recommendation, academic record form filled out by guidance counselor, and an official HS transcript.

Tuition Fees
Estimated cost: $4800 + $35 application fee. Includes housing, tuition, program activity costs, campus facilities fee but doesn't include transportation to and from the program nor daily meals.

Information about the program:
The UF-SSTP is a seven week residential research program for selected rising juniors and seniors who are considering medicine, math, computer science, science, or engineering careers. The program emphasis is research participation with a UF faculty research scientist and his or her research team.

Contact
See website for contact information

Name of College
Lehigh University

Name of Program
Summer Engineering Institute

Academic / Career Interest
Engineering, Computer Science, Science

Website
https://www.lehigh.edu/engineering/research/undergraduate/sei/

Application Timeline
Approx. March

Eligibility
Eligibility: Must be at least junior.
Requirements: Students are selected by teachers within the Lehigh University School Study Council (LUSCC) consortium of schools across the states of DE, MD, NJ, NY, OH, PA, or VA. For students interested in this program, reach out to a teacher to find out if your school falls within that consortium and if not, the opportunity to have your school join is through a single applications at https://ed.lehigh.edu/lussc

Tuition Fees
Estimated cost: FREE. 4 weeks residential housing, food, and tuition covered.

Information about the program:
Lehigh University's Summer Engineering Institute (SEI) is a chance for deserving kids to experience the challenge and thrill of science, technology, engineering and math in a cooperative, team-based environment.

Contact
(610) 758-4025

Name of College
University of California, Davis

Name of Program
Shaping the Future of the World's Food Supply

Academic / Career Interest
Engineering, Computer Science, Science

Website
https://precollege.ucdavis.edu/programs/food-agriculture-technology

Application Timeline
Contact institution for more information

Eligibility
Eligibility: Must be Sophomore or Junior in high school.
Requirements: High school transcript, personal statement, short essay responses, two letters of recommendation from teachers of students' choice, optional materials like test scores, academic writing samples, or other materials with a maximum of 3 uploads allowed.

Tuition Fees
Estimated cost: Application fee - $80
Tuition - $5,400
Housing/dining fee - $1,600
International service fee - $250 for international students only

Information about the program:
As the world's population continues to grow, agriculture will increasingly depend on innovative new approaches to farming, food production and environmental stewardship. The UC Davis Pre-College Program in Food & Agriculture Technology lets students explore the future of agriculture and how new technologies, such as unmanned aerial vehicles (drones), robotics and artificial intelligence, can be used to sustainably increase food production to match demand.

Contact
(530) 752-1011

Name of College
University of Miami

Name of Program
Howard Hughes Medical Institute (HHMI) High School Scholars

Academic / Career Interest
Science and Health

Website
https://ugr.miami.edu/programs/community-outreach-programs/
howard-hughes-medical-institute-hhmi-high-school-scholars/index.
html

Application Timeline
Approx. March

Eligibility
Eligibility: Must be attending high school in Miami-Dade County,
must be entering into their senior year in fall 2018, must be at
least 16 years of age by program start date. Requirements: letter of
recommendation from STEM teacher, application, personal essay
questions responses, and transcript.

Tuition Fees
Costs: FREE and includes stipend.

Information about the program:
The HHMI High School Scholars Research Program is an exciting
opportunity for public and private students with a passion for science to gain hands-on research experience. Students work in teams
to conduct biomedical research over the course of seven weeks at
the University of Miami. Placements are available in areas such as
biology, biomedical engineering, neuroscience, ophthalmology, and
other research areas. We make every effort to place students in labs
conducting research that align with students' interests, but we cannot guarantee that placements will be made in students' exact area
of interest.

Contact
(305) 284-4000
hhmi@miami.edu

Name of College
University of Wisconsin Madison

Name of Program
ACCELERATED LEARNING PROGRAM (ALP)

Academic / Career Interest
Engineering, Computer Science, Science

Website
https://wcaty.wisc.edu/alp/?_
ga=2.27321340.1981839210.1530408438-
1189959001.1530408438

Application Timeline
Approx. April 30th

Eligibility
Eligibility: For students finishing grades 9-12, Requirements: application, transcript, standardized test scores, letter of recommendation.

Tuition Fees
Estimated cost: Residential: $2,800, Commuter: $1,900, International: $3,450, and Application Fee: $60 (Non-Refundable)

Information about the program:
The Accelerated Learning Program (ALP) engages talented students from across Wisconsin, the nation, and the world at the prestigious University of Wisconsin–Madison. ALP is an intense, three-week summer camp designed to push students to the next academic level while housing them in an intimate learning environment. Students enroll in a single course for an in-depth experience. Students have the opportunity to work with their school to receive high school credit for each course. STEM courses available for study

Contact
(608) 890-3260
wcaty@wisc.edu

Name of College
University of Wisconsin Madison

Name of Program
Engineering Summer Program

Academic / Career Interest
Engineering, Math, Science

Website
https://www.engr.wisc.edu/academics/student-ser-
vices/diversity-programs/engineering-summer-pro-
gram/?_ga=2.241771330.1981839210.1530408438-
1189959001.1530408438

Application Timeline
Contact institution for more information

Eligibility
Eligibility: be a current sophomore or junior in high school.

Tuition Fees
Estimated cost: FREE. Travel to and from the program is on the
student.

Information about the program:
Engineering Summer Program (ESP) is a fully funded, six-week
residential program for students who will be high school juniors
or seniors in the upcoming school year. The ESP course curriculum
includes math, physics, chemistry, engineering, and technical communications. Other structured programming such as industry site
visits, field trips, guest lectures, workshops, and faculty mentoring
will help students gain a better understanding of the field of engineering and its applications.

Contact
(608) 890-1403
dao@engr.wisc.edu

Name of College
University of Wisconsin Madison

Name of Program
Pharmacy Summer Program

Academic / Career Interest
Science and Health

Website
https://pharmacy.wisc.edu/programs/pharmd/before-you-apply/
high-school-program/?_ga=2.28058748.1981839210.1530408438-
1189959001.1530408438

Application Timeline
Approx. March 30th

Eligibility
Eligibility: either junior or senior in HS, low income/minority/or
first gen and interested in pharmaceutical or health sciences.

Tuition Fees
Estimated cost: FREE. Students are responsible for the transportation costs to and from the program.

Information about the program:
The Pharmacy Summer Program (PSP) is a five-day summer program for high school juniors and seniors interested in learning more
about pharmacy careers and the UW-Madison Doctor of Pharmacy
Program. The Pharmacy Summer Program targets rising high school
juniors and seniors from traditionally underrepresented groups in
the health science fields. Students who identify as African-Amer-
ican/Black, Native American/American Indian, Latino/a, Laotian,
Vietnamese, Hmong, Cambodian are especially encouraged to apply.

Contact
(608) 262-6234

Name of College
University of Wisconsin Madison

Name of Program
Promoting the Computational Science Initiative (ProCSI)

Academic / Career Interest
Engineering and Computer Science

Website
http://outreach.sbel.wisc.edu/ProCSI/?_
ga=2.241249474.1981839210.1530408438-
1189959001.1530408438

Application Timeline
Approx. June 15th

Eligibility
Eligibility: must be in grades 9,10,or 11. Requirements: online
application, one letter of recommendation from teacher, counselor,
mentor, or community leader, school transcript (unofficial), and
an essay addressing the reasons for attending the ProCSI program,
along with career and education goals.

Tuition Fees
Estimated cost: program is FREE.

Information about the program:
A free six day residential program will be held in July on the campus of the University of Wisconsin-Madison to promote a multi-
disciplinary Computational Science Initiative (ProCSI, pronounced
"proxy"). Organized by the members of the Simulation-Based Engineering Lab, in collaboration with the Wisconsin Applied Computing
Center, ProCSI introduces high-school students to the Computational Science discipline. Participants will be shown how the fundamental building blocks they are currently learning in high-school math,
physics, and science classes are connected to advanced concepts in
computer science and engineering that they may encounter at the
University as a student or in the everyday world around them.

Contact
uwprocsi@gmail.com

Name of College
Penn State

Name of Program
STEM Summer Enrichment Program

Academic / Career Interest
Engineering, Computer Science, Science

Website
https://harrisburg.psu.edu/science-engineering-technology/STEM/
summer-STEM-program

Application Timeline
Approx. February

Eligibility
Eligibility: High school students currently in the 10th and 11th grades are invited to apply.
Requirements: completed app form, transcript, and 300-500 word essay on why they would like to attend the STEM enrichment workshop. Applications should be mailed or delivered to: Dr. Ray Bachnak, STEM Summer Enrichment Program School of Science, Engineering & Technology
W-215 Olmsted Building, Penn State Harrisburg, 777 W. Harrisburg Pike, Middletown, PA 17057

Tuition Fees
Estimated cost: FREE. It's a local commuter day program. Transportation to and from the program will not be provided.

Information about the program:
The workshop is designed to improve students' knowledge through hands-on activities in a variety of STEM areas, including: mathematics, computer science, chemistry, biology, civil engineering, mechanical engineering, electrical engineering, and physics.

Contact
(717) 948-4347
hbgstemsep@psu.edu

Name of College
Penn State

Name of Program
Infection!

Academic / Career Interest
Science and Health

Website
http://www.sciencecamps.psu.edu/infection

Application Timeline
Approx. March

Eligibility
Eligibility: Students entering grades 9-12. Requirements: application

Tuition Fees
Estimated cost: before March 19th - $365 (day) $815 (residential) and after March 20th - $395 (day) $845 (residential)

Information about the program:
There is no shortage of new, captivating, often scary things to learn about the world of infectious diseases! Join Penn State disease experts and learn the shocking truths of how parasites and pathogens impact you and all living organisms on the planet! Through hands-on activities, simulations, and visits to real research labs and field sites, campers will get a whirlwind introduction to what we know – and don't know – about infectious diseases. By the end of camp, campers will be challenged to put their new knowledge to the test by solving a mysterious disease outbreak.

Contact
(814) 865-0083
sciencecamps@science.psu.edu

Name of College
University of Illinois Urbana Champaign

Name of Program
Illini Summer Academies

Academic / Career Interest
Science and Engineering

Website
https://4h.extension.illinois.edu/events/4-h-illini-summer-academies

Application Timeline
Approx. May 15th

Eligibility
Eligibility: in high school grades 9-12. Must be a 4-H club member. Open to out of state students however very limited registration slots for them. Requirements: online application.

Tuition Fees
Estimated cost: Ranges from $225 to $500 depending on the program

Information about the program:
This program offers teens the opportunity to explore the University of Illinois campus and many degree programs and careers. Illini Summer Academies is supported through the Illinois 4-H Foundation and intended to serve youth living in Illinois. A limited number of registration slots are available to youth living outside Illinois. Programs include engineering and STEM disciplines from Aerospace and Electrical to Game Design and Cellular Microbiology. Please see the link provided for more program specific descriptions.

Contact
alvarezd@illinois.edu

Name of College
Research Apprenticeship Program

Name of Program
Illini Summer Academies

Academic / Career Interest
Science and Engineering

Website
https://academics.aces.illinois.edu/diversity/research-appren-tice-program

Application Timeline
Approx. March

Eligibility
Eligibility: must be sophomore or junior at time of application sub-mission. Must be from economically disadvantaged area.
Requirements: Counselor recommendation form, Teacher recom-mendation form, High School Transcript (unofficial transcripts are accepted), and online application. Application fee is $50.

Tuition Fees
Estimated cost: program is FREE w/ housing included. Opportunity for monetary rewards at the end of the program for research com-pleted during the program. A $50 application fee is required.

Information about the program:
All students will be participating in a two week session that will involve a number of special hands-on mini-laboratory and science exercises developed to help them understand the application of math and science in various areas in the food, human and environ-mental sciences. A session on math enrichment, micro-computer, writing, and presentation skills will also be offered.

Contact
(217) 333-3380
cacesoap@illinois.edu

Name of College
University of Illinois Urbana Champaign

Name of Program
Discover Bioengineering Camp

Academic / Career Interest
Science and Engineering

Website
https://wyse.engineering.illinois.edu/summer-camps/

Application Timeline
Approx. April 15th

Eligibility
Eligibility: freshman and sophomores. Requirements: application, email for teacher recommender, transcript, and statement of purpose essay.

Tuition Fees
Estimated cost: $50 deposit + $1,000 for all housing, tuition, and meal costs.

Information about the program:
Discover bioengineering is a week-long residential camp that introduces rising freshman and sophomores to the field of Bioengineering. Bioengineering is all about modeling of systems, design of new technologies and devices for low cost, effective medical care. Bioengineers study and understand how complex biological systems work and how to design and construct medical devices, design better therapeutics, and solve big problems facing society.

Contact
(217) 244-3517
wyse@illinois.edu

Name of College
University of Illinois Urbana Champaign

Name of Program
Nuclear, Plasma, and Radiological Engineering

Academic / Career Interest
Science and Engineering

Website
https://wyse.engineering.illinois.edu/summer-camps/

Application Timeline
Approx. April 15th

Eligibility
Eligibility: Juniors and Seniors. Requirements: application, email for teacher recommender, transcript, and statement of purpose essay.

Tuition Fees
Estimated cost: $50 deposit + $1,000 for all housing, tuition, and meal costs.

Information about the program:
The NPRE Program provides campers with the opportunity to explore nuclear, plasma and radiological engineering disciplines through many hands-on projects and demonstrations. Through individual and team activities, participants will investigate the disciplines of nuclear energy; plasma and fusion technologies; and radiological science.

Contact
(217) 244-3517
wyse@illinois.edu

Name of College
University of Illinois Urbana Champaign

Name of Program
GAMES - Bioengineering

Academic / Career Interest
Science and Engineering

Website
http://wie.engineering.illinois.edu/k-12-programs-resources/
gameswyse-camp/camp-tracks/bioengineering/

Application Timeline
Approx. April 15th

Eligibility
Eligibility: 9th through 12 grades, must be a woman. Requirements: application, email for STEM teacher recommender, transcript, and statement of purpose essay.

Tuition Fees
Estimated cost: $50 deposit, $1,000 for all housing, tuition, and meal costs.

Information about the program:
Bioengineers study and understand how complex biological systems work and how to design and construct medical devices, design better therapeutics, and solve big problems facing society. The intended long-term impact is to enrich the educational experience through technical education that uses a more inclusive, holistic view of social science integration that piques interest in STEM disciplines among underrepresented students, and provides a framework for current issues such as healthcare, health disparities, and sustainability.

Contact
(217) 244-3517
wie@illinois.edu

Name of College
University of Illinois Urbana Champaign

Name of Program
Girls Learning About Materials (GLAM)

Academic / Career Interest
Science and Engineering

Website
http://wie.engineering.illinois.edu/k-12-programs-resources/
gameswyse-camp/camp-tracks/girls-learning-about-materi-
als-glam/

Application Timeline
Approx. April 15th

Eligibility
Eligibility: 10th through 12 grades, must be a woman. Requirements: application, email for STEM teacher recommender, transcript, and statement of purpose essay.

Tuition Fees
Estimated cost: $50 deposit, $1,000 for all housing, tuition, and meal
costs.

Information about the program:
Materials science and engineering is all about studying the fundamentals of materials and how they behave in different conditions.
This information is then used to develop new materials and improve all the materials being used today. Campers will get to see
how varied materials science and engineering really is! We will be
exploring topics such as: 3D Printing, Shape Memory Alloys, Bioma-
terials, Non-Newtonian Fluids, Materials Casting, Crystallography,
Polymers—Vacuum Forming, Nucleation and Growth, The Materials
Science of Chocolate, and many more!

Contact
(217) 244-3517
wie@illinois.edu

Name of College
University of Illinois Urbana Champaign

Name of Program
researcHStart

Academic / Career Interest
Science and Health

Website
https://cancer.uchicago.edu/education/pipeline-programs/re-searchstart/
http://cancer.illinois.edu/researchstart/

Application Timeline
Approx. January

Eligibility
Eligibility: High school junior or senior at time of application. Requirements: online application, two STEM teacher recommendations, transcript.

Tuition Fees
Estimated cost: FREE. Includes stipend of $2,000

Information about the program:
ResearcHStart welcomes high school students from the Chicago and Urbana-Champaign areas to explore exciting careers in cancer research. Participants work full time in the laboratories of established cancer researchers, gaining hands-on experience in areas at the forefront of the field: cancer immunology, pharmacogenomics of anticancer agents, bioengineering, experimental cancer therapeutics, cancer disparities, and more. Rigorous research training is complemented by career development and skill-building workshops, a cancer-based faculty lecture series, and a network of faculty and peer mentors dedicated to students' success.

Contact
(773) 702-4678
researcHStart@bsd.uchicago.edu

Name of College
The Ohio State University

Name of Program
Ohio Supercomputer Center Summer Institute

Academic / Career Interest
Engineering, Computer Science, Math, Science

Website
https://www.osc.edu/education/si

Application Timeline
Approx. April

Eligibility
Eligibility: High school students entering their sophomore, junior or senior year. Requirements: Student Information form, a Student Essay, and one Teacher Recommendation.

Tuition Fees
Estimated cost: $1100.

Information about the program:
SI is a two-week residential program that gives gifted high school students entering their sophomore, junior or senior year project-based, hands-on learning. Working in small peer teams, the students use supercomputers for practical applications such as solving complex science and engineering problems, conducting network forensics to catch hackers, studying the spread of the bird flu and designing computer games.

Contact
(614) 292-9248

Name of College
The Ohio State University

Name of Program
Summer STEM Camp

Academic / Career Interest
Engineering, Computer Science, Science

Website
http://osumarion.osu.edu/academics/majors/biology/stem-summer-camp.html

Application Timeline
Contact institution for more information

Eligibility
Eligibility: upcoming freshman, sophomore, or junior in any U.S. high school. Requirements: registration form.

Tuition Fees
Estimated cost: $100.

Information about the program:
The STEM Summer Camp focuses on relevant science and engineering topics, as well as incorporating the arts through video production and editing. Camp attendees will experience four integrated, multidisciplinary projects working directly with Ohio State Marion faculty, undergraduate peer mentors, and local high school teachers. Students will experience a field biology exercise in the Yoder Prairie Nature Center, an 11-acre tall grass prairie at Ohio State Marion. Attendees will combine mechanical and electrical engineering, computer programming, and robotics as they design, build, and write the code to control an electric-powered model Advanced Energy Vehicle (AEV). Students will use state-of-the-art biochemistry techniques to identify a "guilty suspect" via the DNA samples left behind at a mock crime scene.

Contact
MRN-SummerPrograms@osu.edu

Name of College
The Ohio State University

Name of Program
Explorations in Neuroscience Summer Camp

Academic / Career Interest
Science and Health

Website
https://wexnermedical.osu.edu/neurological-institute/depart-ments-and-centers/departments/department-of-neuroscience/out-reach-and-events/explorations-in-neuroscience-summer-camp

Application Timeline
Approx. May

Eligibility
Eligibility: 11th and 12th graders with an interest in the nervous system and a potential career in the biomedical sciences

Tuition Fees
Estimated cost: $735 includes supplies, meals, snacks, t-shirt and other accessories

Information about the program:
The Explorations in Neuroscience Summer Camp is designed for high school juniors and seniors with an interest in learning more about the brain and spinal cord in health and disease. Participants will have the opportunity to interact with faculty and students carrying out neuroscience related research. In addition, they will meet with clinicians from various clinical departments such as Neurology and Neurosurgery. Throughout the course, participants will meet with graduate students in the Neuroscience Graduate Program who will lead discussions and talk about their exciting research.

Contact
(614) 688-5501
Melissa.Stenger@osumc.edu

Name of College
University of Georgia

Name of Program
VetCamp

Academic / Career Interest
Science and Health

Website
https://vet.uga.edu/academic-affairs/vetcamp#application

Application Timeline
Contact institution for more information

Eligibility
Eligibility: current 10th, 11th or 12th grade high school students.
Requirements: online application

Tuition Fees
Estimated cost: $900. It covers lodging, meals, instruction and social activities.

Information about the program:
VetCAMP (Veterinary Career Aptitude and Mentoring Program) will house up to 52 high school students on UGA's campus for seven days. At VetCAMP, students will be involved in various activities aimed at evaluating their skills and competitiveness as future veterinarians, providing mentorship and helping them experience veterinary medicine as an exciting career path.

Contact
vetcamp@uga.edu

Name of College
University of Texas Austin

Name of Program
CODE @ TACC

Academic / Career Interest
Science and Engineering

Website
https://www.tacc.utexas.edu/education/stem-programs/code-at-tacc/designsafe-summer-camp

Application Timeline
Contact institution for more information

Eligibility
Eligibility: sophomores, juniors, and seniors. Requirements: online application

Tuition Fees
Estimated cost: FREE of cost for selected participants. All program expenses (lunch, travel to / from field trips) are paid for by program. Participants are responsible for travel to and from TACC.

Information about the program:
CODE @ TACC DesignSafe CI is an innovative and exciting summer program to exposes students to the nation's civil infrastructure and communities to prevents natural hazard events from becoming societal disasters. Students will foster their talent and creativity by being introduced to the principles of high performance computing and engineering that utilizes cloud computational tools from the natural hazards research community.

Contact
(512) 232-0831
K12@tacc.utexas.edu

Name of College
University of Texas Austin

Name of Program
CREATEatUT

Academic / Career Interest
Science and Engineering

Website
http://www.engr.utexas.edu/wep/k12/createatut

Application Timeline
Contact institution for more information

Eligibility
Eligibility: high school senior student and must be a woman. Requirements: application, supplementary materials.

Tuition Fees
Estimated cost: registration fee is $300 per participant. This fee includes housing, meals, and programming for the entire program.

Information about the program:
CREATEatUT introduces students to a variety of engineering studies and exciting career options, exposes students to female engineering role models through hands-on workshops and engineering sessions facilitated and attended by female engineering students, faculty and industry professionals. CREATEatUT focuses on a different disciplines and/or themes of engineering to provide focused hands-on activities, demonstrations and/or tours, and connections with female STEM role models.

Contact
(512) 471-5650
wep@engr.utexas.edu

Name of College
Case Western Reserve

Name of Program
Pre-college Scholars Program

Academic / Career Interest
Computer Science, Math, Science

Website
https://case.edu/ugstudies/students/non-degree-students/
pre-college-scholars-program

Application Timeline
Approx. March 15th

Eligibility
Eligibility: must live in Ohio, must be in high school. Requirements: must complete registration form, guidance counselor form, course selection form, and submit supplementary materials (official HS and/or college transcripts).

Tuition Fees
Contact institution for more information

Information about the program:
The Pre-College Scholars Program at Case Western Reserve is open to Ohio residents only. Selected Scholars are allowed to enroll in summer courses at Case Western Reserve. Course topics include Math, Science, Programming, and more.

Contact
(216) 368-2928
ccplus@case.edu

Name of College
Wellesley College

Name of Program
Summer Term

Academic / Career Interest
Computer Science, Math, Science

Website
http://www.wellesley.edu/summer/generalinfor

Application Timeline
Approx. May

Eligibility
Eligibility: Wellesley College students, Visiting College Students, US High School Juniors and Seniors, International students, and Professionals. Requirements: Visiting Student Summer Term Form, $50 dollar registration fee, and consent & authorization forms and immunization records for those living on campus during the term.

Tuition Fees
Estimated cost: 0.5 Units - $1,350
1.0 Unit - $2,700
1.25 Units - $3,380
Housing - $150/week
Meal Program - $25/day (Summer Term II only)

Information about the program:
Summer Term features full-credit classes drawn from a sampling of courses taught during the academic year at Wellesley. All current college students as well as college graduates, professionals and commuting high school juniors and seniors in good academic standing are eligible to enroll in this exciting summer program.

Contact
(781) 283-1000

Name of College
US ARMY

Name of Program
UNITE Program

Academic / Career Interest
Computer Science, Math, Science, Engineering

Website
https://www.usaeop.com/program/unite/

Application Timeline
Approx. May

Eligibility
Eligibility: 9th through 12th grade students and must be from groups historically underrepresented and underserved in science, technology, engineering, and mathematics (STEM). Requirements: online application. For more information and general questions email cpettis@alasu.edu, site director for the Alabama site.

Tuition Fees
Contact institution for more information

Information about the program:
Unite is a four-to-six week, pre-collegiate, academic summer program for talented high school students from groups historically underrepresented and underserved in science, technology, engineering, and mathematics (STEM). Funded by the U.S. Army Educational Outreach Program (AEOP) and administered by the Technology Student Association (TSA), the UNITE program is designed to encourage and help prepare students to pursue college-level studies, and ultimately, careers in engineering and related STEM fields.

Contact
https://www.usaeop.com/program/unite/

Name of College
US ARMY

Name of Program
Science and Engineering Apprenticeship Program (SEAP)

Academic / Career Interest
Computer Science, Science, Engineering

Website
https://www.usaeop.com/program/seap/

Application Timeline
Approx. February

Eligibility
Eligibility: varies by location. For Alabama location, must be a senior and at least 18 by the start date. Requirements: online application.

Tuition Fees
Estimated cost: FREE. Commuting students only. Students are required to travel to and from the program site daily. In addition, the program does not supply an allowance for housing, meals or travel reimbursement. Students will receive a stipend but that varies by location

Information about the program:
SEAP matches practicing DoD scientists with talented high school students creating a direct mentor-student relationship that provides students with training that is unparalleled at most high schools. SEAP participants receive first-hand research experience and exposure to Department of Defense laboratories. SEAP fosters desire in its participants to pursue further training and careers in STEM.

Contact
https://www.usaeop.com/program/unite/

Name of College
US ARMY

Name of Program
The High School Apprenticeship Program

Academic / Career Interest
Computer Science, Science, Engineering

Website
https://www.usaeop.com/program/hsap/

Application Timeline
Approx. Feb 28th

Eligibility
Eligibility: Juniors and Seniors only. Requirements: online application.

Tuition Fees
Estimated cost: FREE. Commuting students only. Students are required to travel to and from the program site daily. In addition, the program does not supply an allowance for housing, meals or travel reimbursement. Students will receive $10 per hour for 8 to 10 weeks/up to 300 hours.

Information about the program:
HSAP provides current rising high school juniors and seniors with an authentic science and engineering research experience alongside university researchers sponsored by the Army Research Office. Though this commuter program, students will learn research methods and develop skills in Army critical research areas in a university lab setting, preparing them for the next steps of their educational and professional career.

Contact
https://www.usaeop.com/program/unite/

Name of College
US ARMY

Name of Program
Research & Engineering Apprenticeship Program

Academic / Career Interest
Computer Science, Science, Engineering

Website
https://www.usaeop.com/program/reap/

Application Timeline
Approx. Feb 28th

Eligibility
Eligibility: Must be a U.S. citizen or permanent legal resident.

Tuition Fees
Estimated cost: FREE. Students will receive a $1,500 stipend for minimum of 200 hours. This program is for commuting students only. Students are required to travel to and from the program site daily. In addition, the program does not supply an allowance for housing, meals or travel reimbursement.

Information about the program:
REAP is a summer STEM program that places talented high school students, from groups historically underserved in STEM, in research apprenticeships at area colleges and universities. REAP apprentices work under the direct supervision of a mentor on a hands-on research project. REAP apprentices are exposed to the real world of research, they gain valuable mentorship, and they learn about education and career opportunities in STEM. REAP apprenticeships are 5-8 weeks in length (minimum of 200 hours) and apprentices receive a stipend.

Contact
https://www.usaeop.com/program/unite/

Name of College
University of Alaska Fairbanks

Name of Program
Alaska Summer Research Academy

Academic / Career Interest
Science and Engineering

Website
https://www.uaf.edu/asra/summer-programs/high-school/

Application Timeline
Approx. April 15th

Eligibility
Eligibility: must be in high school. Requirements: online application and high school reference form.

Tuition Fees
Estimated cost: $700. Program is a commuter/day program. If the student is from out of town, it's the responsibility of the student to sort out housing.

Information about the program:
High School ASRA is an intensive, DAY ONLY two-week learning experience for students with an interest in science, technology, engineering and math. Students study one subject (module), work in small teams, and participate in project based learning in a college-like environment. No housing is provided; however, some modules take students off campus for portions of the ASRA experience to engage in field work. Module sizes are small with an average of ten students and two instructors. Our instructors are faculty, graduate students and industry professionals. There are no grades, tests or homework. Modules are designed to be fun and engaging while offering challenging content. Past module subjects include Biomedicine, Veterinary Medicine, Field Geology, GIS, Remotely Operated Vehicles, Civil Engineering, and others.

Contact
Christa Mulder, ASRA Director
cpmulder@alaska.edu

Name of College
Arizona State University

Name of Program
Barrett Summer Scholars

Academic / Career Interest
Science and Engineering

Website
https://eoss.asu.edu/bss

Application Timeline
Approx. March

Eligibility
Eligibility: 8th, 9th, and 10th graders can apply.

Tuition Fees
Estimated cost: rising 9th grade - $700. Rising 10th grade - $1,400.

Information about the program:
The Barrett Summer Scholars (BSS) program provides students with the opportunity to experience college firsthand and prepare for enrollment and success at Arizona State University and Barrett, the Honors College. The program is designed for academically-talented and motivated students entering the 8th, 9th, and 10th grade in fall 2018. Our residential program invites students to live on campus, engage in college-level coursework, and participate in a community of peers from across the state.

Contact
(480) 965-6060
bss@asu.edu

Name of College
Arkansas School for Mathematics, Sciences, and the Arts

Name of Program
NERD C.A.M.P.

Academic / Career Interest
Computer Science and Math

Website
http://asmsa.org/outreach/summer-at-asmsa

Application Timeline
Approx. April 30th

Eligibility
Eligibility: must be sophomores. Requirements: the online application form with biographic and school information, answers to two short essay questions, a current transcript with fall semester grades and a spring semester progress report, any standardized test scores (ACT-ASPIRE, PLAN, PSAT, ACT, SAT, etc.), and a brief letter of recommendation from a teacher, counselor, or principal.

Tuition Fees
Estimated cost: FREE. Includes all camp activities — including tuition, housing, meals and class supplies.

Information about the program:
ASMSA is a place where the state's top students in mathematics and computer science can soar among talented peers. Nerd C.A.M.P. (Computational Analysis, Math and Programming) will help students understand the links between subjects through classes in mobile app development, number theory, and other mathematic principles. We wear the name "nerd" as a badge of pride because being a nerd means getting excited about technology and solving problems. Students should have strong prior experiences in math and an interest in coding.

Contact
(501) 622-5100

Name of College
Arkansas School for Mathematics, Sciences, and the Arts

Name of Program
ENTREPRENEURSHIP AND INNOVATION BOOTCAMP

Academic / Career Interest
Engineering, Computer Science, Science

Website
http://asmsa.org/outreach/summer-at-asmsa

Application Timeline
Approx. April 30th

Eligibility
Eligibility: must be sophomores.

Tuition Fees
Estimated cost: FREE. Includes all camp activities — including tuition, housing, meals and class supplies.

Information about the program:
ASMSA's Entrepreneurship and Innovation Bootcamp is for all innovators, aspiring entrepreneurs, and outside-the-box thinkers! This immersive, hands-on, student-driven learning experience introduces participants to the "lean startup" process, which is the basis of successful business launch programs like the National Science Foundation's i-Corps program. Students explore rapid product development and iteration, identify product/market fit, and business model development. The week culminates with an exciting expo in which attendees prepare and deliver a public pitch of their ideas. Students gain valuable team-building, communication, and critical thinking skills in a supportive and challenging environment. Don't miss out on the fun!

Contact
(501) 622-5100

Name of College
Buck Institute for Aging

Name of Program
High School Summer Scholars

Academic / Career Interest
Engineering and Science

Website
https://www.buckinstitute.org/education/k-12/

Application Timeline
Applications will be available in January

Eligibility
Eligibility: must be in high school and have completed at least one science AP course or equivalent. Requirements: application, resume, cover letter, letter of recommendation (from a teacher or mentor), and transcript.

Tuition Fees
Estimated cost: $2500. Full and partial scholarships are available based on financial need.

Information about the program:
The Buck Institute for Research on Aging provides a seven-week research internship to prepare local high school students for careers in biomedical and geroscience research. With up to 20 research mentors participating, students have the opportunity to explore research involving the aging process and aging-related disease. Through these mentorships, students develop the skills and background necessary to pursue scientific research. Students are encouraged to visit Buck Institute faculty websites to read about the research being conducted at the Buck and to indicate an area of interest when applying for the program.

Contact
(415) 209-2000
info@buckinstitute.org

Name of College
Children's Hospital Oakland Research Institute

Name of Program
Student Research Internship

Academic / Career Interest
Science and Health

Website
http://www.chori.org/Education/Summer_Internship_Program/
summer_research_home.html

Application Timeline
Approx. February

Eligibility
Eligibility: must be in high school and it is recommended to have completed some biology and chemistry. Requirements: online completed application form, Official School Transcript, personal essay responses, Two letters of recommendation (must be signed and written on school letterhead), and Resume.

Tuition Fees
Contact institution for more information

Information about the program:
The CHORI Summer Student Research Program is designed to provide an unsurpassed opportunity for students to immerse themselves in the world of basic and/or clinical research for three months during the summer. The program pairs students with one or two CHORI principal investigators who serve as mentors, guiding the students through the design and testing of their own hypotheses and methodology development. At the end of the summer, students present their research to their peers just as any professional researcher would do.

Contact
summerstudentprogram@chori.org

Name of College
Carlsbad Education Foundation

Name of Program
High School Summer Academy

Academic / Career Interest
Science and Math

Website
https://www.carlsbaded.org/high-school/

Application Timeline
Approx. May

Eligibility
Eligibility: must be entering grades 9 through 12 and live in the San Diego County Area. Requirements: online registration form, and prerequisites must be completed prior to program acceptance as shown by transcript.

Tuition Fees
Estimated cost: $625. Commuter program so transportation must be provided by the student.

Information about the program:
Join our High School Summer Academy program, servicing all North San Diego County students. Receive high school credit for a full year course in six weeks. Courses are designed to provide both in-person and online instruction, so students have the flexibility to enjoy their summer! The program is taught by credentialed teachers and the summer courses are equivalent to a full school year. The courses offered span Geometry, Honors Geometry, College Algebra , Algebra 1 and 2, US History, World History, Spanish 1, 2, 3, and 4, Physics, Biology, Chemistry, PE 1 and 2, Government, and Economics

Contact
(760) 929-1555

Name of College
University of Southern California

Name of Program
Chevron Frontiers of Energy Resources Summer Camp

Academic / Career Interest
Science and Engineering

Website
https://cisoft.usc.edu/chevron-usc-partnership-program/fron-tiers-of-energy-resources-summer-camp/summer-camp-2018/

Application Timeline
Approx. April

Eligibility
Eligibility: high school juniors who are interested in a future in the energy industry. Requirements: sealed teacher recommendation, upload an unofficial transcript, and compose a statement of purpose with their application.

Tuition Fees
Estimated cost: FREE. All costs including housing, meals, and tuition.

Information about the program:
Chevron Corporation has come together with USC's Viterbi School of Engineering collaboratively to host a summer camp for High School Juniors and High School Science and Math Teachers at the University of Southern California in Los Angeles. The Frontiers of Energy Resources Summer Camp offers a preparatory, interactive training program focusing on various energy resources including fossil fuels, solar, biofuel, wind, nuclear energy, and information technologies for energy efficient operations.

Contact
(213) 740-1076
cisoft@vsoe.usc.edu

Name of College
Keck Graduate Institute

Name of Program
Student Research Internships

Academic / Career Interest
Engineering, Science and Health

Website
http://www.kgi.edu/academic-programs/summer-programs/high-school-summer-stem-program/student-internships

Application Timeline
Approx. May

Eligibility
Eligibility: age 16 or older at the start of the program.

Tuition Fees
Estimated cost: FREE. This is an unpaid internship. All housing and transportation needs are to be sorted out by the student.

Information about the program:
During the summer, Keck Graduate Institute offers a limited number of unpaid internship opportunities to exceptionally motivated and academically strong high school students to gain hands-on research experience, and learn about the pursuit of a science or engineering related college education and professional career. High school students work under the supervision of a KGI faculty mentor, initially shadow undergraduate students and other researchers at KGI, and are then able to engage in a small, well-defined research project matched to their skills and knowledge. High school students further are able to participate in SURE program activities such as seminars and workshops.

Contact
909-607-785

Name of College
Colorado Rocky Mountain School

Name of Program
(HS)2 - Summer Program

Academic / Career Interest
Science and Math

Website
http://www.crms.org/hs2/

Application Timeline
Approx. December 15th

Eligibility
Eligibility: Currently in 9th grade in a public high school in the following cities: Denver, CO; Fort Worth TX; New Orleans, LA; or New York, Brooklyn or Bronx, NY.

Tuition Fees
Estimated cost: (HS)2 scholars receive full scholarships to attend the program for three consecutive summers. Students can receive $200 travel stipend to help offset the cost of airline transportation to and from CRMS, airline baggage fees (range between $25-$35 per checked bag), and incidental expenditures for the five weeks.

Information about the program:
During five weeks for three summers, (HS)2 scholars live and learn on the CRMS campus in Carbondale, Colorado. On weekdays, students engage in six hours of academic classes relating to science, math, writing, and college counseling. In the afternoons, they participate in the Active Program, which includes rock climbing, kayaking, and team sports, as well as art classes such as silversmithing, blacksmithing, and music. On weekends, the natural environment surrounding campus inspires exploration.

Contact
(970) 963-2562
info@crms.org

Name of College
Smith College

Name of Program
Summer Science and Engineering Program

Academic / Career Interest
Engineering, Computer Science, Math, Science

Website
https://www.smith.edu/academics/precollege-programs/ssep

Application Timeline
Approx. March 1st

Eligibility
Eligibility: open to women who are in grades 9,10,11,12. Requirements: application, essay, recommendation, transcript, $50 application fee, and financial aid application (if needed).

Tuition Fees
Estimated cost: $5,800.

Information about the program:
The Smith Summer Science and Engineering Program (SSEP) is a four-week residential program for exceptional young women with strong interests in science, engineering and medicine. Each July, select high school students from across the country and abroad come to Smith College to do hands-on research with Smith faculty in the life and physical sciences and in engineering.

Contact
(413) 584-2700

Name of College
Department of Navy Lab

Name of Program
Science and Engineering Apprenticeship Program (SEAP) -

Academic / Career Interest
Engineering and Science

Website
https://seap.asee.org/

Application Timeline
Due in the Fall.

Eligibility
Eligibility: High school students who have completed at least 9th grade, must be 16 years of age or older at the time of application to participate, and applicants must be US citizens. Requirements: online application, unofficial transcript, research interests, personal statement and your recommender's contact information.

Tuition Fees
Estimated cost: Students receive a $3,300 dollar stipend for 8 weeks of work. Housing is not provided however Navy host personnel and lab coordinators may be able to assist you in finding suitable housing.

Information about the program:
The apprentice program is designed to encourage high school students to pursue science and engineering careers; acquaint qualified high school students with the activities of Department of Navy (DoN) laboratories through summer science and engineering research experiences; to provide students with opportunities in and exposure to scientific and engineering practice.

Contact
(202) 649-3833
seap@asee.org

Name of College
State of Georgia

Name of Program
Governor's Honors Program

Academic / Career Interest
Engineering, Computer Science, Math, Science

Website
https://gosa.georgia.gov/governors-honors-program

Application Timeline
Teacher Nomination deadline: approx. November, January for student application deadline

Eligibility
Eligibility: current sophomore or junior.

Tuition Fees
Estimated cost: FREE. Tuition, room, and board are covered under appropriations made by the Georgia General Assembly, so there is no cost to attend GHP.

Information about the program:
The Georgia Governor's Honors Program (GHP) is a residential summer program for gifted and talented high school students who will be rising juniors and seniors during the program. The program offers instruction that is significantly different from the typical high school classroom and that is designed to provide students with academic, cultural, and social enrichment necessary to become the next generation of global critical thinkers, innovators, and leaders. GHP is held in mid-summer (mid-June to mid-July) as a residential educational experience on a college or university campus.

Contact
(800) 436-7442

Name of College
StemWorks Hawaii

Name of Program
Summer internship program

Academic / Career Interest
Engineering, Computer Science, Math, Science

Website
http://stemworkshawaii.org/internships/

Application Timeline
Approx. April 30th

Eligibility
Eligibility: must be in high school (9th-12th), must be enrolled at a Hawaii STEMworks Participating High Schools. Requirements: contact institution for more information

Tuition Fees
Estimated cost: FREE

Information about the program:
The STEMworks™ Summer Internship program prepares students for a STEM career by providing real world opportunities to work with local companies. During the six weeks in the summer, interns use industry standard technologies to develop meaningful projects. MEDB augments their professional experiences with weekly college awareness and employability training websites. Opportunities available for STEMworks™ students on Big Island, Kauai, Maui, Oahu, Molokai, Lanai and Kauai.

Contact
Lalaine Pasion
(808) 875-2341
lalaine@medb.org

Name of College
SpaceTrek

Name of Program
Space Science Camp

Academic / Career Interest
Engineering and Science

Website
http://www.spacetrekky.org/camp

Application Timeline
Approx. April 30th

Eligibility
Eligibility: High school girls who are at least a sophomore and are interested in STEM. Requirements: online application, one teacher recommendation.

Tuition Fees
Estimated cost: $500 fee. Program is residential.

Information about the program:
SpaceTrek is a unique space science camp offered at Morehead State University's state-of-the-art Space Science Center housing a Satellite Development Laboratory, Space Tracking Antennas, Electronic Laboratories and a digital Star Theater for planetarium and LASER shows. SpaceTrek was created in 2012 as a pilot program thanks to a partnership between AAUW Kentucky and Morehead State University.

Contact
Kim Boggs
(606) 922-2705
spacetrekky@gmail.com

Name of College
Joint Science and Technology Institute

Name of Program
Joint Science and Technology Institute for Students (JSTI-HS)

Academic / Career Interest
Engineering, Computer Science, Math, Science

Website
https://orise.orau.gov/jsti/

Application Timeline
Approx. March

Eligibility
Eligibility: Must be a U.S. citizen, must be age 15, and must be entering the 10th, 11th, or 12th grade. Requirements: application, and recommender information.

Tuition Fees
Estimated cost: FREE.

Information about the program:
The Joint Science and Technology Institute for Students (JSTI-HS) is a two-week, fully-funded, residential STEM research program for current high school students in the United States and Department of Defense schools around the world. Students will participate in research projects mentored by Department of Defense research scientists and other subject matter experts.

Contact
Marie Westfall
(865) 576-3425
JSTI@orau.org

Name of College
WPI

Name of Program
Frontiers Summer Program

Academic / Career Interest
Engineering, Computer Science, Math, Science, Health

Website
https://www.wpi.edu/academics/pre-collegiate/summer/
stem-residential/frontiers

Application Timeline
Approx. April 1st

Eligibility
Eligibility: 11th or 12th grades.

Tuition Fees
Estimated cost: $2,995 for session I or II
$4,795 for both sessions

Information about the program:
Frontiers Summer Camp is a residential, on-campus summer program for high school students, Frontiers is celebrating more than 30 years of challenging participants to explore the outer limits of their knowledge in science, technology, engineering, and math (STEM) with current laboratory techniques and exploring unsolved problems across a wide spectrum of disciplines. Frontiers participants will be utilizing state-of-the-art technology and facilities, and enjoy added activities such as evening workshops, field trips, movies, live performances, and tournaments

Contact
(508) 831-5000

Name of College
The Museum of Flight

Name of Program
Montana Aerospace Scholars

Academic / Career Interest
Engineering and Science

Website
http://www.museumofflight.org/Education/Explore-programs/
Montana-Aerospace-Scholars

Application Timeline
Approx. Feb 16th

Eligibility
Eligibility: Rising Junior in HS and resident of Montana. Must have available and reliable internet connection to be in the program. Requirements: online application.

Tuition Fees
Estimated cost: FREE. There is no cost to participate in either phase of the sophomore program.

Information about the program:
Western Aerospace Scholars (WAS) is an online distance learning course and summer experience specifically designed for high school sophomores and juniors interested in science, technology, engineering and math (STEM) fields. The online curriculum is a University of Washington college course focused on NASA's space exploration program as well as topics in earth and space science. If they successfully complete the online curriculum, students are invited to participate in multi-day summer experiences that provide them to the opportunity to work with STEM professionals, NASA scientists, university students and STEM educators.

Contact
(206) 764-5700
info@museumofflight.org

Name of College
US ARMY & UNLV

Name of Program
Army Education Outreach program

Academic / Career Interest
Engineering and Science

Website
http://aeop.asecamps.com/

Application Timeline
Approx. April 1st

Eligibility
Eligibility: must be in high school, must have a minimum 3.0 GPA.
Requirements: online application and official HS transcript.

Tuition Fees
Estimated cost: FREE if accepted. DoD provides full tuition scholarships for 20 students and $100 a week stipends.

Information about the program:
The United States Army has long recognized that a scientifically
and technologically literate citizenry is our nation's best hope for
a secure, rewarding, and successful future. AEOP UNITE is a STEM
Enrichment program, designed to spark student interest in STEM
fields- especially among the undeserved and those in earlier grades
and educators by providing exciting, engaging, interactive, hands-on
STEM experiences. AEOP offers our nation's youth and teachers a
collaborative, cohesive portfolio of opportunities that effectively engage future workforce generations in meaningful, real-world STEM
experiences, competitions, and paid internships.

Contact
(702) 895-3681

Name of College
State of New Jersey

Name of Program
Governor's Science and Engineering Schools

Academic / Career Interest
Engineering, Computer Science, Math, Science

Website
https://www.nj.gov/govschool/

Application Timeline
Approx. January

Eligibility
Eligibility: students must be residents of New Jersey and must have completed their junior year of high school.

Tuition Fees
Estimated cost: the program is tuition-FREE.

Information about the program:
The Governor's School of New Jersey was established in 1983. It is a tuition-free, summer, residential program for high-achieving high school seniors who have an interest in STEM (science, technology, engineering, and mathematics) subjects. Currently, there are two programs: the Governor's School in the Sciences at Drew University and the Governor's School of Engineering & Technology at Rutgers, The State University of New Jersey. The programs are open to students from diverse economic backgrounds who are New Jersey residents and who have completed their junior year in any public or private high school or are home-schooled. The mission of the Governor's School in the Sciences is to broaden students' appreciation and knowledge of science through exposure to a range of scientific topics and scientists.

Contact
(848) 445-4756
lrosen@rci.rutgers@edu

Name of College
CUNY & New York Dept of Education

Name of Program
The STEM Institute

Academic / Career Interest
Engineering, Math, Science

Website
https://stem.ccny.cuny.edu/

Application Timeline
Approx. May

Eligibility
Eligibility: must be minority students in grade 9-11.

Tuition Fees
Estimated cost: FREE. Students who are accepted will receive free textbooks and supplies. Public transportation, breakfast and lunch will be provided free of charge for eligible students, ONLY if funds will be available.

Information about the program:
The STEM Institute prepares students for the greater demands of college-level study and helps them adjust to campus life. It offers academic and tutoring support services designed to help students prepare for these new challenges. STEM is a challenging academic enrichment program to encourage talented Latinos, female, and under-represented minority and disadvantaged high school students currently enrolled in the 9th, 10th, and 11th grades to pursue careers in the field of engineering, computer science, science, business management, entrepreneurs, and mathematics.

Contact
marte@ccny.cuny.edu

Name of College
North Carolina School of Science and Mathematics

Name of Program
The Summer Ventures Program

Academic / Career Interest
Engineering, Computer Science, Math, Science

Website
https://www.ncssm.edu/summerventures

Application Timeline
Approx. January 15th

Eligibility
Eligibility: must be a rising Junior or Senior in high school.
Requirements: official transcript, online application, teacher and
counselor recommendation letters, and Pre-ACT/PLAN scores
required (if student doesn't have them, send in SAT/ACT scores
instead).

Tuition Fees
Estimated cost: FREE. Summer Ventures is a state-funded program
for NC residents with room and board provided.

Information about the program:
Summer Ventures in Science and Mathematics is a no-cost,
state-funded program for academically talented North Carolina students who aspire to careers in science, technology, engineering, and
mathematics. As a rising high school junior or senior, you live on a
college campus for four weeks in the summer and conduct research
around topics of your interest — while enjoying the company of
like-minded peers.

Contact
summerventures@ncssm.edu

Name of College
State of Vermont

Name of Program
Governor's Institutes of Vermont

Academic / Career Interest
Engineering, Computer Science, Math, Science, Health

Website
https://www.giv.org/

Application Timeline
Opens approx. Feb 1st, closing date yet to be announced.

Eligibility
Eligibility: students who have just completed their freshman, sophomore, or junior year of high school.

Tuition Fees
Estimated cost: at full tuition, $1695 for a summer short institute and $2395 for a summer long institute. This program offers tuition assistance for families unable to pay the full amount. See link for program cost per household income bracket: https://www.giv.org/placeholder/tuition/

Information about the program:
The Governor's Institutes of Vermont provides prestigious, fun, accelerated learning residencies on college campuses for highly-motivated Vermont teenagers.

Contact
(802) 865-4GIV
info@giv.org

Name of College
Prepare Rhode Island

Name of Program
Summer Internship Program

Academic / Career Interest
Computer Science, Science, Health

Website
https://www.prepare-ri.org/internships-schools/

Application Timeline
Opens approx. March, closes April 15th. Rolling admissions.

Eligibility
Eligibility: Entering 12th grade, enrolled at a Rhode Island public high school, a minimum of 16 years of age, eligible to work in the United States, and a resident of Rhode Island. Requirements: online application.

Tuition Fees
Estimated cost: FREE. PrepareRI and the Governor's Workforce Board cover the cost of the internship. Students will also earn a competitive wage.

Information about the program:
The PrepareRI Internship Program provides paid summer internships for rising public high school seniors in Rhode Island. An outside intermediary, Skills for Rhode Island's Future, will match students with internship placements based on fit, preparedness, and skill.

Contact
Cali.cornell@ride.ri.gov
Paul.mcconell@ride.ri.gov

Name of College
University of Chicago

Name of Program
Chicago EYES (Educators and Youth Enjoy Science) on Cancer

Academic / Career Interest
Science and Health

Website
https://cancer.uchicago.edu/education/pipeline-programs/eyes/

Application Timeline
Approx. January

Eligibility
Eligibility: High school sophomore, junior or senior.

Tuition Fees
Estimated cost: FREE. Taxable stipend of $2,600 (high school students).

Information about the program:
Chicago EYES on Cancer is a cancer research training program for high school and college students interested in careers in biomedicine. The program also welcomes secondary science educators. For two consecutive summers, participants work full-time in the laboratories of established cancer researchers at the University. Rigorous research training is complemented with a cancer-based lecture series, skill-building workshops, and a network of faculty and peer mentors dedicated to participants' success.

Contact
Megan Mekinda, PhD
(773) 702-4678
EYES@bsd.uchicago.edu

Name of College
Muhlenberg College

Name of Program
Brain Camp

Academic / Career Interest
Science and Health

Website
https://www.muhlenberg.edu/academics/braincamp/

Application Timeline
Approx. April

Eligibility
Eligibility: senior in high school.

Tuition Fees
Estimated cost: FREE. All expenses, including housing, meals, and social activities are included. Brain Camp is funded by a generous gift from The Sentience Foundation.

Information about the program:
Brain Camp is a residential science camp for motivated, energetic high school students who are interested in the wonders of the brain and who will be beginning their senior year in Fall. Over the course of one week, campers will live on campus in supervised student housing, explore the inner workings of the nervous system, participate in hands-on laboratory exercises, work closely with Muhlenberg College neuroscience faculty and students, and direct their own research project.

Contact
(484) 664-3100

Name of College
Cornell University

Name of Program
Cornell Summer College Experience

Academic / Career Interest
Engineering, Computer Science, Math, Science, Health

Website
https://www.sce.cornell.edu/sc/index.php

Application Timeline
Approx. May

Eligibility
Eligibility: Sophomores: must be a current high school student.

Tuition Fees
Estimated cost: Two-week (non-credit) - $4,250, Three-week - $6,310, Five-week - $10,560, Six-week - $12,825.

Information about the program:
Cornell University Summer College - one of the oldest and most prestigious programs of its kind - invites talented high school sophomores, juniors, and seniors to its acclaimed three- and six-week precollege programs. If selected for Summer College, students will join more than 1,200 other motivated high school students from around the world as you live, study, and play on the Cornell campus.

Contact
(607) 255-6203
summer_college@cornell.edu

Name of College
Creighton University

Name of Program
HS-MACA/CPHHE High School Community Research Program

Academic / Career Interest
Science and Health

Website
https://healthsciences.creighton.edu/diversity/research/summer-research-institute

Application Timeline
Approx. March

Eligibility
Eligibility: Must have a 3.0 or better grade point average and sophomore, junior or senior.

Tuition Fees
Estimated cost: Monetary Stipend: $1,200. Program is free. *No housing accommodation is provided nor transportation*

Information about the program:
The HS-MACA/CPHHE Summer Research Institute at Creighton University introduces high school students and college students to research and prepares them for careers in the health sciences through biomedical research and community-based research. Students are paired with either an university faculty member who involves the student in an ongoing research project or with a community organization where the student will design and conduct community-based participatory research along with the site manager.

Contact
cphhe@creighton.edu

Name of College
Rutgers University

Name of Program
Medical Imaging Technology Academy

Academic / Career Interest
Science and Health

Website
https://em.rutgers.edu/ncp/search/ProgramDetails.aspx-?id=475&awesomeBar=Medical%20Imaging%20Technology%20Academy&sdr=home

Application Timeline
Approx. May

Eligibility
Eligibility: high school students ages 16 to 18. Requirements: online application, transcript, and recommendation letter.

Tuition Fees
Estimated cost: Yes - $2,239.00 (one-time)

Information about the program:
Discover how CAT Scan, MRI, and other imaging technologies are used in prevention, diagnosis, and treatment of disease and trauma. Hear from faculty and residents, collaborate on small group exercises and case studies, and take field trips to the medical school and a radiology office to learn first-hand about this exciting and dynamic field.

Contact
(848) 932-7565

Name of College
Albert Nerken School of Engineering at Cooper Union

Name of Program
Summer Stem program

Academic / Career Interest
Engineering, Computer Science, Science

Website
http://cooper.edu/engineering/summer-stem

Application Timeline
Approx. March 2nd

Eligibility
Eligibility: All current high school sophomores or juniors spending the summer in the Greater NYC area.

Tuition Fees
Estimated cost: $3,250, excluding the $50 application fee. Financial aid offered and must fill out need based application.

Information about the program:
The Summer STEM Program is a six-week intensive that immerses current high school sophomores and juniors in hands-on engineering design and problem-solving, thereby placing them on the right track for careers in technological innovation. Projects range broadly and include robotics, digital fabrication, computer programming and app development, biomedical and genetic engineering, improved urban infrastructure, and even racecar design. Faculty and teaching assistants from the departments of civil, chemical, electrical, and mechanical engineering provide students with foundational knowledge and expert guidance to address real-world problems in their respective disciplines of expertise.

Contact
summerSTEM@cooper.edu

Name of College
Rensselaer Polytechnic Institute

Name of Program
Research Experience for HS students program

Academic / Career Interest
Science and Engineering

Website
http://summer.rpi.edu/programs/researchexperience

Application Timeline
Approx. March 31st

Eligibility
Eligibility: Open to 11th and 12th graders. Requirements: application, two letters of recommendation, 1-3 page resume, and copy of student's transcript

Tuition Fees
Estimated cost: $6,000.00

Information about the program:
This is a four week residential program. Rensselaer faculty and Summer@Rensselaer work together to provide select high school students the unique opportunity to conduct research and learn new skills specific to their assigned research group. They will work alongside an assigned faculty mentor, graduate, and undergraduate students on unique research opportunities. The program concludes with a poster session presentation. Because research is so specific in nature, we will not be announcing participating labs until after students have been academically accepted and enroll in program. Students who have successfully completed this program have gone on to apply to various departments at Rensselaer.

Contact
(518) 276-6809
soaps@rpi.edu

Name of College
US ARMY

Name of Program
Gains in the Education of Mathematics and Science (GEMS)

Academic / Career Interest
Science and Engineering

Website
https://www.usaeop.com/program/gems/

Application Timeline
Contact institution for more information

Eligibility
Eligibility: must be between grades 5th -12th. Requirements: online application.

Tuition Fees
Estimated cost: FREE. Students can receive an educational stipend ($100 per week) to offset any cost to the student or family to participate (travel and food).

Information about the program:
Gains in the Education of Mathematics and Science (GEMS) is an Army-sponsored, summer STEM enrichment program for middle and high school students that takes place in participating Army research laboratories and engineering centers. GEMS' mission is to interest young people, who might not otherwise give serious thought to becoming scientists or engineers, in STEM careers early enough that they have the time to attain the appropriate academic training. The program is based on a multi-disciplinary educational curriculum, and is focused on age and grade-appropriate hands-on activities, in areas such as science, engineering, mathematics, computational sciences, computational biology, biomedical sciences, chemistry and biology.

Contact
800-807-9852

COLLEGE
CONSULTING
EXPERTS

**Non-Profit and Government Agency Based
STEM Collegiate Programs**

Name of College
Tuskegee University

Name of Program
AgDiscovery Program

Academic / Career Interest
STEM

Website
https://www.aphis.usda.gov/aphis/ourfocus/civilrights/agdiscovery/ct_agdiscovery_program/!ut/p/z1/04_iUlDg4tKPAFJABpSA0f-pReYllmemJJZn5eYk5-hH6kVFm8Z5GRs6GhiaGPhYm5kYGjiGhAc-4GYWbGzj7m-l5gjQj9IBPw64iA6oAqh1P6kUZFvs6-6fpRBYklG-bqZeWn5-hHJJfGJ6SmZxcn5ZalFlfEFRfnpRYm5-gXZUZEAmXMJ8g!!/

Application Timeline
Approx. March

Eligibility
Must be in high school and at least 15 years of age at the start of the program.

Tuition Fees
Estimated fees: FREE, $200 stipend

Information about the program:
AgDiscovery is a summer outreach program to help teenagers explore careers in plant and animal science, wildlife management, agribusiness, and much more!

The program allows students to live on a college campus and learn about agriculture from university professors, scientists, and administrative professionals who work for the U.S. Government in a variety of fields.

Contact
(202) 799-7020

Name of College
United States Army

Name of Program
Unite Program

Academic / Career Interest
STEM

Website
https://www.usaeop.com/program/unite/

Application Timeline
Approx. May

Eligibility
9th through rising 12th grade students. Must be from groups historically underrepresented and underserved in science, technology, engineering, and mathematics (STEM).

Tuition Fees
Contact institution for more information.

Information about the program:
Unite is a four to six-week, pre-collegiate, academic summer program for talented high school students from groups historically underrepresented and underserved in science, technology, engineering, and mathematics (STEM). Funded by the U.S. Army Educational Outreach Program (AEOP) and administered by the Technology Student Association (TSA), the Unite program is designed to encourage and help prepare students to pursue college-level studies, and ultimately, careers in engineering and related STEM fields.

Contact
cpettis@alasu.edu

Name of College
United State Army

Name of Program
Gains in the Education of Mathematics and Science (GEMS)

Academic / Career Interest
STEM

Website
https://www.usaeop.com/program/gems/

Application Timeline
Contact institution for more information.

Eligibility
Must be between grades 5th -12th

Tuition Fees
Estimated fees: FREE

Information about the program:
Gains in the Education of Mathematics and Science (GEMS) is an Army-sponsored, summer science, technology, engineering, and mathematics (STEM) enrichment program for middle and high school students that takes place in participating Army research laboratories and engineering centers. GEMS' mission is to interest young people, who might not otherwise give serious thought to becoming scientists or engineers, in STEM careers early enough that they have the time to attain the appropriate academic training. The program is based on a multi-disciplinary educational curriculum and is focused on age and grade-appropriate hands-on activities, in areas such as science, engineering, mathematics, computational sciences, computational biology, biomedical sciences, chemistry and biology.

Contact
https://www.usaeop.com/about/contact-us/

Name of College
United States Army

Name of Program
Science and Engineering Apprenticeship Program (SEAP)

Academic / Career Interest
STEM

Website
https://www.usaeop.com/program/seap/

Application Timeline
Approx. February

Eligibility
Varies by location.

Tuition Fees
Estimated fees: FREE

Information about the program:
SEAP matches practicing Department of Defense (DoD) scientists with talented high school students creating a direct mentor-student relationship that provides students with training that is unparalleled at most high schools. SEAP participants receive first-hand research experience and exposure to DoD laboratories. SEAP fosters desire in its participants to pursue further training and careers in science, technology, engineering, math (STEM).

Contact
https://www.usaeop.com/about/contact-us/

Name of College
United States Army

Name of Program
The High School Apprenticeship Program

Academic / Career Interest
STEM

Website
https://www.usaeop.com/program/hsap/

Application Timeline
Approx. February

Eligibility
Rising Juniors and Seniors only.

Tuition Fees
Estimated fees: FREE, students will receive a stipend equivalent to $10 per hour for 8 to 10 weeks/up to 300 hours.

Information about the program:
The High School Apprenticeship Program (HSAP) provides current rising high school juniors and seniors with an authentic science and engineering research experience alongside university researchers sponsored by the Army Research Office. Though this commuter program, students will learn research methods and develop skills in Army critical research areas in a university lab setting, preparing them for the next steps of their educational and professional career.

Contact
https://www.usaeop.com/about/contact-us/

Name of College
United States Army

Name of Program
Research & Engineering Apprenticeship Program (REAP)

Academic / Career Interest
STEM

Website
https://www.usaeop.com/program/reap/

Application Timeline
Approx. February

Eligibility
Varies by location.

Tuition Fees
Estimated fees: FREE, students will receive a $1,500 stipend for minimum of 200 hours.

Information about the program:
REAP is a summer science, technology, engineering, and mathematics (STEM) program that places talented high school students, from groups historically underserved in STEM, in research apprenticeships at area colleges and universities. REAP apprentices work under the direct supervision of a mentor on a hands-on research project. REAP apprentices are exposed to the real world of research, they gain valuable mentorship, and they learn about education and career opportunities in STEM. REAP apprenticeships are 5-8 weeks in length (minimum of 200 hours) and apprentices receive a stipend.

Contact
https://www.usaeop.com/about/contact-us/

Name of College
University of Alaska, Anchorage

Name of Program
Acceleration Academy (Summer)

Academic / Career Interest
STEM

Website
http://www.ansep.net/high-school/acceleration-academy

Application Timeline
Approx. March

Eligibility
Must be a high school student.

Tuition Fees
Estimated fees: free

Information about the program:
The Acceleration Academy (Summer) is designed to develop students academically and socially for college, while creating excitement around STEM (Science, Technology, Engineering and Mathematics) degree programs and careers. Students develop skills that can be used for the rest of their academic careers. The classes are taught by university faculty for college credit. Students can earn high school credit by applying for credit through their school counselor. Students will learn more about career opportunities in STEM fields while getting a jumpstart in pursuing those degrees. Acceleration Academy students are hyper-prepared for college and beyond. The Acceleration Academy will have two 5-week sessions that will be held on the University of Alaska Anchorage (UAA) campus and hosted by ANSEP. Students will be housed on the UAA campus for the duration of the ANSEP Acceleration Academy.

Contact
Michael Ulroan, Regional Director
(907) 352-0451
mikeu@alaska.edu

Name of College
University of Alaska, Fairbanks

Name of Program
Alaska Summer Research Academy

Academic / Career Interest
STEM

Website
https://www.uaf.edu/asra/summer-programs/high-school/

Application Timeline
Approx. April

Eligibility

- Must be in high school
- Requirements: online application and high school reference form.

Tuition Fees
Cost: $700. Program is a commuter/day program. If the student is from out of town, it's the responsibility of the student to sort out housing.

Information about the program:
High School Alaska Summer Research Academy (ASRA) is an intensive, DAY ONLY two-week learning experience for students with an interest in science, technology, engineering and math (STEM). Students study one subject (module), work in small teams, and participate in project based learning in a college-like environment. No housing is provided; however, some modules take students off campus for portions of the ASRA experience to engage in field work. Module sizes are small with an average of ten students and two instructors.

Contact
Christa Mulder, ASRA Director
cpmulder@alaska.edu

Name of College
Arizona State University

Name of Program
Barrett Summer Scholars

Academic / Career Interest
STEM

Website
https://eoss.asu.edu/bss

Application Timeline
Approx. March

Eligibility

- Rising 8th, 9th, and 10th graders can apply.
- Requirements: application, personal essay response, high school transcript, and one letter of recommendation from a teacher.

Tuition Fees
Estimated Fees:

- Rising 9th grade - $700
- Rising 10th grade - $1,400

Information about the program:
The Barrett Summer Scholars (BSS) program provides students with the opportunity to experience college firsthand and prepare for enrollment and success at Arizona State University and Barrett, the Honors College. The program is designed for academically-talented and motivated students entering the 8th, 9th, and 10th grade in fall 2018. The residential program invites students to live on campus, engage in college-level coursework, and participate in a community of peers from across the state.

Contact
(480) 965-6060
bss@asu.edu

Name of College
University of Arizona

Name of Program
Keep Engaging Youth in Science (KEYS) internship

Academic / Career Interest
STEM

Website
https://keys.arizona.edu/

Application Timeline
Approx. December

Eligibility

- High school GPA of at least 3.5 on a 4.0 grading scale
- Arizona resident with U.S. citizenship or legal residency, 16 years or older on the first day of the program
- Prior Chemistry and Biology recommended.

Tuition Fees
Estimated Fees: FREE

Information about the program:
The seven week KEYS Research Internship Program is a unique summer opportunity for motivated Arizona high school students with a strong interest in bioscience, engineering, environmental health, or biostatistics to work side-by-side with top faculty in University of Arizona research labs. After initially training in laboratory techniques and safety, interns will participate in innovative research projects under the guidance of UA faculty and other lab members, including current university students.

Contact
(520) 626-8124
keys@bio5.org

Name of College
Arizona State University

Name of Program
Joaquin Bustoz Math-Science Honors Summer Program

Academic / Career Interest
STEM

Website
https://jbmshp.asu.edu/summer_program

Application Timeline
Approx. February

Eligibility
10th - 12th grades, Sophomores may apply, provided they have completed a minimum of three years of high school mathematics by the end of the academic year prior to start of summer program.

Tuition Fees
Estimated fees: FREE, tuition, room & board, classroom materials, textbooks, and meals are provided.

Information about the program:
The Joaquin Bustoz Math-Science Honors Program is intended for mature and motivated students who are interested in academic careers requiring mathematics, science, or engineering-based coursework and who are typically underrepresented in those fields of study. Selected participants include first-generation college bound students and students representing diverse backgrounds from high schools throughout the State of Arizona, including rural communities and the Navajo Nation.

Participants live on the Arizona State University (ASU) Tempe campus while enrolled in a university level mathematics course for college credit.

Contact
(480) 965-1690
mshp@asu.edu

Name of College
Arkansas School for Mathematics, Sciences, and the Arts

Name of Program
Nerd C.A.M.P.

Academic / Career Interest
STEM

Website
http://asmsa.org/outreach/summer-at-asmsa

Application Timeline
Approx. April

Eligibility
Must be rising sophomores.

Tuition Fees
Estimated Fees: FREE, all camp activities, including tuition, housing, meals and class supplies are free.

Information about the program:
Arkansas School of Mathematics, Sciences, and the Arts (ASMSA) is a place where the state's top students in mathematics and computer science can soar among talented peers. Nerd C.A.M.P. (Computational Analysis, Math and Programming) will help students understand the links between subjects through classes in mobile app development, number theory, and other mathematic principles. The program wears the name "nerd" as a badge of pride because being a nerd means getting excited about technology and solving problems. Students should have strong prior experiences in math and an interest in coding.

Contact
(501) 622-5100

Name of College
Arkansas School for Mathematics, Sciences, and the Arts

Name of Program
Aegis Biomedical Sciences Summer Institute

Academic / Career Interest
STEM

Website
http://asmsa.org/outreach/summer-at-asmsa

Application Timeline
Approx. April

Eligibility
Must be rising sophomores.

Tuition Fees
Estimated fees: FREE, all camp activities including tuition, housing, meals and class supplies are free.

Information about the program:
Calling all future doctors, microbiologists, forensic scientists, biomedical engineers, and other science, technology, engineering, mathematics (STEM) enthusiasts for a once in a lifetime opportunity! Thanks to an AEGIS grant from the Arkansas Department of Education. Arkansas School for Mathematics, Sciences, and the Arts (ASMSA) is excited to offer the ASMSA Biomedical Sciences Summer Institute that will introduce participants to a fascinating range of topics—including forensic crime scene analysis and microbial biochemical identification tests—all while gaining hands-on experience in molecular biology laboratory techniques and scientific literacy and communication skills. Students will isolate their own DNA, collect and assess environmental bacteria for antibiotic resistance, learn about fascinating aspects of protein structure and mutations, and even transform bacteria to make them glow in the dark. Students don't want to miss this!

Contact
(501) 622-5100

Name of College
Arkansas School for Mathematics, Sciences, and the Arts

Name of Program
Entrepreneurship and Innovation Bootcamp

Academic / Career Interest
STEM

Website
http://asmsa.org/outreach/summer-at-asmsa

Application Timeline
Approx. April

Eligibility
Must be rising sophomores.

Tuition Fees
Estimated Fees: FREE. all camp activities including tuition, housing, meals and class supplies are free.

Information about the program:
Arkansas School of Mathematics, Sciences, and the Arts (ASMSA) Entrepreneurship and Innovation Bootcamp is for all innovators, aspiring entrepreneurs, and outside-the-box thinkers! This immersive, hands-on, student-driven learning experience introduces participants to the "lean startup" process, which is the basis of successful business launch programs like the National Science Foundation's i-Corps program. Students explore rapid product development and iteration, identify product/market fit, and business model development. The week culminates with an exciting expo in which attendees prepare and deliver a public pitch of their ideas. Students gain valuable team-building, communication, and critical thinking skills in a supportive and challenging environment. Don't miss out on the fun!

Contact
(501) 622-5100

Name of College
University of Arkansas

Name of Program
Engineering Summer Academy

Academic / Career Interest
STEM

Website
https://engineering-camps.uark.edu/camps/engineering-summer-academy.php

Application Timeline
Contact institution for more information.

Eligibility

- Must be in 10th through 12th grades.
- Requirements: online application, personal essay responses.

Tuition Fees
Estimated fees: $675 for the entire week.
This program fee includes tuition, room and board, lab fees, course materials, recreational program costs, evening entertainment, and field trips.

Information about the program:
The Engineering Summer Academy (ESA) is a one-week residential engineering academy for students who have recently completed 9th, 10th, or 11th grade. This intensive summer academy provides students with the opportunity for in-depth exploration into a concept that crosses engineering disciplines. Each course allows students to participate in hands-on activities in our cutting edge labs, working alongside engineering faculty and current students.

Contact
Amy Warren, Asst. Director, Summer Programs
(479) 575-2562
engrcamp@uark.edu

Name of College
The Yosemite Institute - NatureBridge non-profit

Name of Program
Armstrong Scholars

Academic / Career Interest
STEM

Website
https://naturebridge.org/yosemite/armstrong-scholars

Application Timeline
Approx. April

Eligibility

- Young women, ages 15 to 18.
- Requirements: online application, recommendation form, and medical form.

Tuition Fees
Estimated fees: $150

Information about the program:
This extraordinary program seeks to inspire young women to reach their highest potential, develop a stronger sense of self and community, and explore their personal connection to nature. Participants venture into the backcountry of Yosemite National Park with highly skilled female educators from NatureBridge for an expedition of discovery, leadership, and personal challenge.

Contact
(415) 992-4700
info@naturebridge.org

Name of College
Girls Who Code

Name of Program
Summer Immersion Program

Academic / Career Interest
STEM

Website
https://girlswhocode.com/summer-immersion-programs/

Application Timeline
Approx. March

Eligibility

- Must be in high school and a rising Junior or Senior.
- Requirements: online application.

Tuition Fees
Estimated Fees: FREE, stipends are available for transportation and living costs

Information about the program:
Students learn computer science through real-world projects in art and storytelling, robotics, video games, web sites, apps and more! This camp also brings its students to local area technology companies where they can meet and speak with female engineers at the company and learn what it's like to be a professional computer scientist as a woman in technology.

Contact
international@girlswhocode.com

Name of College
Buck Institute for Aging

Name of Program
High School Summer Scholars

Academic / Career Interest
STEM

Website
https://www.buckinstitute.org/education/k-12/

Application Timeline
Applications will be made available in approx. January.

Eligibility

- Must be in high school and have completed at least one science AP course or equivalent.
- Requirements: application, resume, cover letter, letter of recommendation (from a teacher or mentor), and transcript.

Tuition Fees
Estimated fees: $2,500
Full and partial scholarships are available based on financial need.

Information about the program:
The Buck Institute for Research on Aging provides a seven-week research internship to prepare local high school students for careers in biomedical and geroscience research. With up to 20 research mentors participating, students have the opportunity to explore research involving the aging process and aging-related disease. Through these mentorships, students develop the skills and background necessary to pursue scientific research. Students are encouraged to visit Buck Institute faculty websites to read about the research being conducted at the Buck and to indicate an area of interest when applying for the program.

Contact
(415) 209-2000
info@buckinstitute.org

Name of College
Children's Hospital Oakland Research Institute

Name of Program
Student Research Internship

Academic / Career Interest
STEM

Website
http://www.chori.org/Education/Summer_Internship_Program/
summer_research_home.html

Application Timeline
Approx. February

Eligibility

- Must be in high school and recommended to have completed some biology and chemistry.
- Requirements: online completed application form, official school transcript, personal essay responses, two letters of recommendation (must be signed and written on school letterhead), and resume.

Tuition Fees
Contact institution for more information

Information about the program:
The Children's Hospital Oakland Research Institute (CHORI) Summer Student Research Program is designed to provide an unsurpassed opportunity for students to immerse themselves in the world of basic and/or clinical research for three months during the summer. The program pairs students with one or two CHORI principal investigators who serve as mentors, guiding the students through the design and testing of their own hypotheses and methodology development. At the end of the summer, students present their research to their peers just as any professional researcher would do.

Contact
summerstudentprogram@chori.org

Name of College
City of Hope

Name of Program
Eugene and Ruth Roberts Summer Student Academy

Academic / Career Interest
STEM

Website
https://www.cityofhope.org/education/students-and-youth/summer-student-academy/summer-student-academy-program-overview

Application Timeline
Approx. March

Eligibility
Applicants must be at least 16 years-old before their internship begins.

Tuition Fees
Estimated fees: FREE, students receive $4,000 for completing the 10-week program. Housing and Transportation are not provided.

Information about the program:
The primary goal of the Eugene and Ruth Roberts Summer Student Academy at City of Hope is to provide young people (high school and university students) with an opportunity for a "hands-on" research experience. This program seeks to find students possessing exceptional potential for performing biomedical research. Summer Academy students design and work on their own research projects in areas of their specific interests. City of Hope faculty members act as mentors providing valuable guidance and support, while also encouraging independent thought and exploration. Summer students work closely with post-doctorates, graduate students, and lab personnel of the Irell & Manella Graduate School of Biological Sciences.

Contact
robertsacademy@coh.org

Name of College
Carlsbad Education Foundation

Name of Program
High School Summer Academy

Academic / Career Interest
STEM

Website
https://www.carlsbaded.org/high-school/

Application Timeline
Approx. May

Eligibility

- Must be entering grades 9 through 12 and live in the San Diego County Area.
- Requirements: online registration form, and prerequisites must be completed prior to program acceptance as shown by transcript.

Tuition Fees
Estimated fees: $625. Commuter program so transportation must be provided by student.

Information about the program:
Join our High School Summer Academy program, servicing all North San Diego County students. Receive high school credit for a full year course in six weeks. Courses are designed to provide both in-person and online instruction, so students have the flexibility to enjoy their summer! The program is taught by credentialed teachers and the summer courses are equivalent to a full school year. The courses offered span Geometry, Honors Geometry, College Algebra, Algebra 1 and 2, US History, World History, Spanish 1, 2, 3, and 4, Physics, Biology, Chemistry, PE 1 and 2, Government, and Economics.

Contact
(760) 929-1555

Name of College
University of Southern California

Name of Program
Chevron Frontiers of Energy Resources Summer Camp

Academic / Career Interest
STEM

Website
https://cisoft.usc.edu/chevron-usc-partnership-program/frontiers-of-energy-resources-summer-camp/summer-camp-2018/

Application Timeline
Approx. April

Eligibility

- high school juniors who are interested in a future in the energy industry.
- Requirements: sealed teacher recommendation, upload an unofficial transcript, and compose a statement of purpose with application.

Tuition Fees
Estimated fees: FREE, all costs including housing, meals, and tuition.

Information about the program:
Chevron Corporation has come together with University of Southern California (USC) Viterbi School of Engineering collaboratively to host a summer camp for high school juniors and high school science and math teachers at the USC in Los Angeles. The Frontiers of Energy Resources Summer Camp offers a preparatory, interactive training program focusing on various energy resources including fossil fuels, solar, biofuel, wind, nuclear energy, and information technologies for energy efficient operations.

Contact
(213) 740-1076
cisoft@vsoe.usc.edu

Name of College
Keck Graduate Institute

Name of Program
Student Research Internships

Academic / Career Interest
STEM

Website
http://www.kgi.edu/academic-programs/summer-programs/high-school-summer-stem-program/student-internships

Application Timeline
Approx. May

Eligibility
Age 16 or older at the start of the program.

Tuition Fees
Estimated Fees: FREE, this is an unpaid internship. All housing and transportation needs are to be sorted out by the student.

Information about the program:
During the summer, Keck Graduate Institute (KGI) offers a limited number of unpaid internship opportunities to exceptionally motivated and academically strong high school students to gain hands-on research experience and learn about the pursuit of a science or engineering related college education and professional career. High school students work under the supervision of a KGI faculty mentor, initially shadow undergraduate students and other researchers at KGI, and are then able to engage in a small, well-defined research project matched to their skills and knowledge. High school students further are able to participate in Summer Undergraduate Research Experience (SURE) program activities such as seminars and workshops.

Contact
(909) 607-7855

Name of College
Colorado School of Mines

Name of Program
Engineering Design Summer Camp

Academic / Career Interest
STEM

Website
https://students.csmspace.com/edsc2018.html?20180411

Application Timeline
Open until space closes - program begins approx. June

Eligibility

- Students entering 9th through 12th grade
- Requirement: online registration

Tuition Fees
Estimated fees: $450 - $465. No accommodation or lodging provided.

Information about the program:
These camps, designed for those entering 9th through 12th grade in the fall of 2018, provide exposure to real-world problem solving in a team environment and provide opportunities to learn design skills that are applicable to many fields of engineering. The mission of the camp is to offer high school students an opportunity to participate in a creative challenge as they explore the world of engineering. The goal of the camp is to guide participants through a fun and rewarding hands-on experience of authentic engineering design practices. The expected outcomes of this program address the fundamentals of the engineering design process. This camp aims to provide: challenges of designing and marketing a product, Early exposure to engineering design processes, opportunities to apply basic mathematics and science concepts, importance of team and communications skills, and challenges to step beyond the comfort zone.

Contact
(303) 384-2692
te@mines.edu

Name of College
Northrop Grumman & UCCS

Name of Program
Summer STEM Academy

Academic / Career Interest
STEM

Website
https://lemp.uccs.edu/showcase/stem/

Application Timeline
Approx. April

Eligibility

- any student, entering grades 9 through 12, who is interested in STEM.
- Requirements: application and an essay

Tuition Fees
Estimated Fees: FREE, this is a day camp, no housing provided.

Information about the program:
This innovative program is designed to reach incoming high school students (grades 9-12) at a critical juncture in their academic careers as they begin to plan for college. The week-long event will feature four tracks: robotics, cyber security, drones &CAD, and front-end web design, to highlight STEM subjects and encourage students to delve deeper into STEM exploration. The academy will begin at 8:00 a.m. each day and end promptly at 4:30 p.m., with breakfast, lunch, and snacks provided each day, depending on the schedule. Students will need to bring a water bottle.

Contact
(719) 255-3595

Name of College
Colorado State University

Name of Program
Particle Physics Internship

Academic / Career Interest
STEM

Website
http://projects-web.engr.colostate.edu/accelerator/internships.php

Application Timeline
Approx. March

Eligibility

- Must be in high school.
- Recommended having taken an AP level physics course. Requirements: current transcript and an essay on student's interest in science, engineering, and technology.

Tuition Fees
Estimated fees: FREE, housing is provided. Stipend is $1,000.

Information about the program:
The Electrical and Computer Engineering Department (ECE) at Colorado State University (CSU) is offering a unique opportunity for high school and undergraduate students to participate in a summer internship program. The program and research are centered on particle accelerators and RF devices. Located in beautiful Fort Collins, Colorado, the CSU Accelerator Group will afford interns the chance to learn about this field of engineering and physics, while working side by side with current students in the ECE. Sandra Biedron and Stephen Milton, ECE professors and accomplished researchers in the area of particle accelerators, have instituted this program to expose students to the extensive and exciting applications of this technology.

Contact
Karen.ungerer@colostate.edu

Name of College
Colorado Space Business Roundtable

Name of Program
Aerospace Internship

Academic / Career Interest
STEM

Website
https://www.coloradosbr.org/csbr-summer-internship-program

Application Timeline
Contact institution for more information.

Eligibility

- Colorado Resident, U.S. Citizen, high school student, interested in science, technology, engineering, or mathematics careers.
- Requirements: online application.

Tuition Fees
Estimated Fees: Unpaid internship. Housing is not provided.

Information about the program:
Colorado Space Business Roundtable (CSBR) offers a Colorado Aerospace Internship for rural high school and college students interested in pursuing careers in the aerospace industry. All students pursuing STEM - (Science, Technology, Engineering, and Mathematics) related disciplines are encouraged to apply; however, please note that students from rural locations will be given first priority into the program. If there is still space available, the program will accept students from the Front Range. The Colorado Aerospace Internship will run for two weeks during the summer which gives students ample time to experience what it's like to work in various facets of the aerospace industry.

Contact
Christie Lee
(303) 258-6957
Christie.j.lee@lmco.com

Name of College
ProveIt!

Name of Program
Math Summer Academy

Academic / Career Interest
STEM

Website
https://proveitmath.org/

Application Timeline
Approx. March

Eligibility

- Entering grade 9, 10, 11, or 12, must be at least 14 years old, and currently attending high school in the US or Canada.
- Requirements: online math assessment and online application.

Tuition Fees
Estimated fees: $3,284
Flights are not included in the price, but they provide a free shuttle service from the Denver airport to the campus. The tuition covers dormitory expenses, classroom reservation fees, meals, field trips, and instruction.

Information about the program:
The Purpose of Prove it! Math Academy summer program is to provide an introduction to mathematical proof in a creative, problem-solving context. In a safe, scenic, memorable location, surrounded by like-minded peers and outstanding instructors, our students can reach their full potential. The Prove it! Math Academy curriculum is based on the program's experiences teaching mathematical proof at the undergraduate level, the NSF-funded research project Lurch (a word processor that checks your reasoning), and coaching of proof-oriented mathematics competitions.

Contact
(970) 430-6915
info@proveitmath.org

Name of College
Canada/USA Mathcamp

Name of Program
Mathcamp

Academic / Career Interest
STEM

Website
https://www.mathcamp.org/prospectiveapplicants/theprocess.php

Application Timeline
Approx. March

Eligibility

- Rising 9th grade and above

Tuition Fees
Estimated fees: $4,500
Financial aid is available up to full scholarships.

Information about the program:
Mathcamp is an intensive 5-week-long summer program for mathematically talented high school students. More than just a summer camp, Mathcamp is a vibrant community, made up of a wide variety of people who share a common love of learning and passion for mathematics. At Mathcamp, students can explore undergraduate and even graduate-level topics while building problem-solving skills that will help them in any field they choose to study.

Contact
https://www.mathcamp.org/contact.php

Name of College
Smith College

Name of Program
Summer Science and Engineering Program

Academic / Career Interest
STEM

Website
https://www.smith.edu/academics/precollege-programs/ssep

Application Timeline
Approx. March

Eligibility

- Open to women who are in grades 9,10,11,12.
- Requirements: application, essay, recommendation, transcript, and financial aid application (if needed).

Tuition Fees
Estimated fees: $5,800, plus $50 application fee

Information about the program:
The Smith Summer Science and Engineering Program (SSEP) is a four-week residential program for exceptional young women with strong interests in science, engineering and medicine. Each July, select high school students from across the country and abroad come to Smith College to do hands-on research with Smith faculty in the life and physical sciences and in engineering.

Contact
(413) 584-2700

Name of College
United States Air Force Academy

Name of Program
Society of American Military Engineers (SAME), U.S. Air Force Academy STEM Camp

Academic / Career Interest
STEM

Website
https://www.same.org/Portals/0/same.org/inside_pages/ SAME_Camps/documents/USAFA%20Camp%20Flyer.pd- f?ver=2018-01-24-100320-130

Application Timeline
Approx. April

Eligibility

- Must be at least a sophomore in high school, U.S. citizen, demonstrate proof of medical insurance, minimum 3.2 GPA, physically fit, and have not previously attended a SAME week-long summer Camp.
- Requirements: online application, transcripts.

Tuition Fees
Estimated fees: $580
Students generally pay half the registration fee ($290); the sponsoring SAME Post will pay the remainder of the fee and will work with the student on transportation cost.

Information about the program:
This is a week long, live-in STEM camp, with full emersion in engineering and STEM activities. The Air Force Academy (AFA) provides world class facilities for this program. Campers work as teams of 12 to complete engineering tasks in a competitive environment. Campers are supervised, mentored, coached, lead and guided by young STEM professionals and college students in a STEM major, 24/7.

Contact
Scott Prosuch
(719) 337-0346
sprosuch@earthlink.net

Name of College
The Jackson Laboratory

Name of Program
Summer Student Program

Academic / Career Interest
STEM

Website
https://www.jax.org/education-and-learning/high-school-students-and-undergraduates/learn-earn-and-explore

Application Timeline
Approx. February

Eligibility
Have completed Grade 11 or Grade 12, be at least 16 years old; and be a U.S. citizen or permanent resident.

Tuition Fees
Estimated fees: Students receive a $5,250 stipend. Includes housing and meals.

Information about the program:
The Summer Student Program is designed for students who want to immerse themselves in genetics and genomics research. It emphasizes laboratory discovery, communication of knowledge, and professional growth. Students participate in an ongoing research program with the support of an experienced scientific mentor. They develop an independent project, implement their plan, analyze the data, and report the results. At the end of the summer, they present their findings to researchers, other students, and parents.

Contact
Michael McKernan, Program Director
(207) 288-6806
Michael.mckernan@jax.org

Name of College
Central Area Health Education Center (AHEC)

Name of Program
Health Career "Camp"

Academic / Career Interest
STEM

Website
http://www.centralctahec.org/index.php/programs/summer-migrant-farm-workers-program

Application Timeline
Approx. May

Eligibility

- Must be in high school.
- Requirements: application. Applications are given out after emailing Guisela Laureano at glaureano@centralctahec.org.

Tuition Fees
Estimated fees: $50 (day camp/commuter camp)

Information about the program:
During this opportunity with the University of Connecticut (UConn) School of Medicine, high school students accepted into the program will be trained and supervised by Central AHEC staff/chaperone at the UConn Migrant Farm Worker Clinic for one week during the summer. Participants will be exposed to different health care careers (medical, dental, physical therapy, nursing and more!) and by seeing health care students and clinicians "in action" at these clinics providing direct patient care to our target population, migrant and seasonal farm workers (and their dependents!) at farms across Connecticut. The sessions run Tuesday, Wednesday and Thursday evenings at the tobacco farms with Mondays as a full day of orientation and training.

Contact
(860) 231-6250
info@centralctahec.org

Name of College
Prepare Rhode Island

Name of Program
Prepare Rhode Island (PrepareRI) Internships

Academic / Career Interest
STEM

Website
https://www.prepare-ri.org/internships-schools/

Application Timeline
Approx. March – April, rolling admissions

Eligibility
Entering 12th grade, enrolled at a Rhode Island public high school, a minimum of 16 years of age, eligible to work in the United States, and a resident of Rhode Island.

Tuition Fees
Estimated fees: FREE, PrepareRI and the Governor's Workforce Board cover the cost of the internship. Students will also earn a competitive wage.

Information about the program:
The PrepareRI Internship Program provides paid summer internships for rising public high school seniors in Rhode Island. An outside intermediary, Skills for Rhode Island's Future, will match students with internship placements based on fit, preparedness, and skill.

Contact
Cali.cornell@ride.ri.gov
Paul.mcconell@ride.ri.gov

Name of College
The Governor's Institutes of Vermont

Name of Program
Summer Institutes

Academic / Career Interest
STEM

Website
https://www.giv.org/

Application Timeline
Applications open approx. February

Eligibility
Students who have just completed their freshman, sophomore, or junior year of high school, must be nominated by a teacher from school (students can ask their teacher to nominate them on their behalf) in the subject they're applying for.

Tuition Fees
Estimated fees:

- Short summer institute: $1,695
- Long summer institute: $2,395

Information about the program:
The Governor's Institutes of Vermont provides prestigious, fun, accelerated learning residencies on college campuses for highly-motivated Vermont teenagers. Each Institute is unique, built around a single focus area. But they all share certain similarities: they're all residential, so students live on a college campus and have access to all the resources the college provides, from state-of-the-art labs to studios; they're all hands-on intense bursts of learning and fun, where students and new friends who share their interests explore topics in-depth with leading professionals in the field; and they're a chance to try something new, make lasting memories with new friends, and learn more than imaginable!

Contact
(802) 865-4GIV
info@giv.org

Name of College
The State of Ohio & Ohio State University

Name of Program
Sea Grant Stone Lab Summer Program

Academic / Career Interest
STEM

Website
https://ohioseagrant.osu.edu/education/stonelab

Application Timeline
Approx. March

Eligibility
Sophomore, junior or senior, age 15 or older, GPA of at least 3.0, and have taken biology. Requirements: online application, standardized test scores, and a recommendation letter from a high school biology or science teacher.

Tuition Fees
Estimated fees: costs vary based on unit count and in and out of state residence.

Information about the program:
Stone Laboratory on Gibraltar Island, the South Bass Island Light-house and Aquatic Visitors Center in Put-in-Bay bring hands-on science and education to everyone who visits. Stone Lab offers 25 college-credit science courses each summer, covering biology, geology and natural resources, among other topics.

Contact
(615) 292-8949
ohioseagrant@osu.edu

Name of College
North Carolina School of Science and Mathematics

Name of Program
The Summer Ventures Program

Academic / Career Interest
STEM

Website
https://www.ncssm.edu/summerventures

Application Timeline
Approx. January

Eligibility
Must be a rising Junior or Senior in high school. Requirements: official transcript, online application, teacher and counselor recommendation letters, and Pre-ACT/PLAN scores required (if students don't have them, send in SAT/ACT scores instead).

Tuition Fees
Estimated fees: FREE, Summer Ventures is a state-funded program for North Carolina residents with room and board provided.

Information about the program:
Summer Ventures in Science and Mathematics is a no-cost, state-funded program for academically talented North Carolina students who aspire to careers in science, technology, engineering, and mathematics. As a rising high school junior or senior, students will live on a college campus for four weeks in the summer and conduct research around topics of their interest — while enjoying the company of like-minded peers.

Contact
summerventures@ncssm.edu

Name of College
City College of New York & New York Department of Education

Name of Program
The STEM Institute

Academic / Career Interest
STEM

Website
https://stem.ccny.cuny.edu/

Application Timeline
Approx. May

Eligibility
Must be minority students in grade 9-11. Requirements: online application and official transcript.

Tuition Fees
Estimated fees: FREE

Information about the program:
The STEM Institute prepares students for the greater demands of college-level study and helps them adjust to campus life. It offers academic and tutoring support services designed to help students prepare for these new challenges. STEM is a challenging academic enrichment program to encourage talented Latinos, female, and under-represented minority and disadvantaged high school students currently enrolled in the 9th, 10th, and 11th grades to pursue careers in the field of engineering, computer science, science, business management, entrepreneurs, and mathematics.

Contact
https://stem.ccny.cuny.edu/contact.html

Name of College
New York Math Circle

Name of Program
High School Summer Program

Academic / Career Interest
STEM

Website
https://www.nymathcircle.org/summer

Application Timeline
Approx. April

Eligibility
Must be entering grades 9-12.

Tuition Fees
Estimated fees: FREE

Information about the program:
The Summer High School Math Circle is an academically intensive weekday program for students entering grades 9–12 in the fall that runs for three weeks, five hours a day. A typical day consists of a class in the morning, followed by lunch, and a problem-solving session in the afternoon. Instructors and teaching assistants are very friendly and helpful, and the atmosphere is open and collaborative.

Contact
(646) 706-7647
info@nymathcircle.org

Name of College
State of New Jersey

Name of Program
Governor's Science and Engineering Schools

Academic / Career Interest
STEM

Website
https://www.nj.gov/govschool/

Application Timeline
Approx. January

Eligibility
Students must be residents of New Jersey and must have completed their junior year of high school. Students who are interested should speak with their guidance counselor and STEM teachers to be nominated.

Tuition Fees
Estimated fees: FREE

Information about the program:
The Governor's School of New Jersey was established in 1983. It is a tuition-free, summer, residential program for high-achieving high school seniors who have an interest in STEM (science, technology, engineering, and mathematics) subjects. Currently, there are two programs: the Governor's School in the Sciences at Drew University and the Governor's School of Engineering & Technology at Rutgers, the State University of New Jersey. The programs are open to students from diverse economic backgrounds who are New Jersey residents and who have completed their junior year in any public or private high school or are home-schooled.

Contact
(848) 445-4756
lrosen@rci.rutgers@edu

Name of College
New Hampshire Academy of Science

Name of Program
Summer STEM Program

Academic / Career Interest
STEM

Website
https://www.nhacadsci.org/apply-summer

Application Timeline
Approx. February

Eligibility
A student in grades 7-12 or a graduating senior but preference is given to students who meet the following criteria: show sound academic achievement, exhibit personal and academic responsibility, exhibit curiosity of the natural world, and work well either as an individual or in a team.

Tuition Fees
Estimated fees:

- Tuition: $250
- Non-refundable application fee: $50

Information about the program:
The New Hampshire Academy of Science (NHAS) STEM Lab, located in Lyme New Hampshire is a state-of-the-art laboratory that is equipped with advanced scientific instruments supporting research across the STEM fields. The summer programs are instructed by PhD scientists and engineers. This is a rare opportunity to do authentic hands-on research with professional scientists and engineers. This program operates during the day only. The program does not offer a residence/boarding option.

Contact
https://www.nhacadsci.org/contact/

Name of College
United States Army & University of Nevada, Las Vegas

Name of Program
Army Education Outreach program UNITE

Academic / Career Interest
STEM

Website
http://aeop.asecamps.com/

Application Timeline
Approx. April

Eligibility
Must be in high school (9th-12th), must have a minimum 3.0 GPA.
Requirements: online application and official high school transcript.

Tuition Fees
Estimated fees: FREE, Department of Defense provides full tuition
scholarships for 20 students and $100 a week stipend.

Information about the program:
The United States Army has long recognized that a scientifically
and technologically literate citizenry is our nation's best hope for a
secure, rewarding, and successful future. Army Education Outreach
Program (AEOP) UNITE is a STEM Enrichment program, designed to
spark student interest in STEM fields- especially among the undeserved and those in earlier grades and educators by providing exciting, engaging, interactive, hands-on STEM experiences. AEOP offers
our nation's youth and teachers a collaborative, cohesive portfolio of
opportunities that effectively engage future workforce generations
in meaningful, real-world STEM experiences, competitions, and paid
internships.

Contact
(702) 895-3681

Name of College
Young Nebraska Scientists

Name of Program
Research internship program

Academic / Career Interest
STEM

Website
https://yns.nebraska.edu/research

Application Timeline
Approx. March

Eligibility
Must be 16 years old. Must not have graduated from high school. Must be a Nebraska resident. Must be a U.S. Citizen OR have proof of employment authorization. Requirements: online application and recommendations.

Tuition Fees
Estimated fees: FREE, this is not a residential program however; students will be expected to figure out transportation or housing (if not local) on their own.

- Students will be paid $9 per hour for up to 35 hours per week for up to 8 weeks for bio/chemistry/non-physics-based research.
- Physics positions will be paid $9 per hour for up to 20 hours per week for up to 4 weeks.

Information about the program:
This summer program allows students who are accepted to gain real world STEM research experience with university professors at varying schools in Nebraska. Research Areas include Physics, Plant Science, Agronomy, Biochemistry and more. This is not a residential program however; students will be expected to figure out transportation or housing (if not local) on their own.

Contact
(402) 472-8946
yns@nebraska.edu

Name of College
The Museum of Flight

Name of Program
Montana Aerospace Scholars

Academic / Career Interest
STEM

Website
http://www.museumofflight.org/Education/Explore-programs/
Montana-Aerospace-Scholars

Application Timeline
Approx. February

Eligibility
Rising Junior in high school and resident of Montana. Must have available and reliable internet connection to be in the program. Requirements: online application.

Tuition Fees
Estimated fees: FREE

Information about the program:
A two-part program for high school sophomores and juniors with an online distance learning course and summer experience specifically designed for high school sophomores and juniors interested in science, technology, engineering and math (STEM). The sophomore level program serves as an introduction to the junior course. It is an online course that takes place in the spring of sophomore year and contains the first two lessons of the junior program. The online curriculum is a University of Washington college course focused on NASA's space exploration program as well as topics in earth and space science.

Contact
(206) 764-5700
info@museumofflight.org

Name of College
ASM International Minnesota Chapter

Name of Program
Material Science Camp

Academic / Career Interest
STEM

Website
http://www.mnasm.org/camp/

Application Timeline
Approx. March

Eligibility
Rising junior or seniors, must have basic knowledge of algebra, chemistry, and physics and describe why they want to learn more about engineering and materials science. Requirements: online application and one teacher recommendation

Tuition Fees
Estimated fees: FREE

Information about the program:
The material science camp is a four-day, summer camp utilizing hands-on learning principles of materials engineering. Students will gain a unique science experience under the direction of industry and education based "Materials Mentors". This camp includes a combination of mini-demonstrations, field trips with extensive involvement in laboratory facilities to actively explore materials science & engineering principles.

Contact
MaterialsCamp@mnasm.org

Name of College
Michigan State University

Name of Program
High School Honors Science, Math and Engineering Program

Academic / Career Interest
STEM

Website
http://education.msu.edu/hshsp/program-information/

Application Timeline
Approx. March

Eligibility
Rising junior in high school, in the upper 20 percent of high school classes, and have taken at least 3 years of college preparatory mathematics and 2, or more years of science.

Tuition Fees
Estimated fees: $3,800

Information about the program:
This program is for mature high school juniors with a keen interest in science, math or engineering and the ability to work independently and responsibly. The High School Honors Science, Engineering and Mathematics Program (HSHSP) is a non-credit enrichment program sponsored by the Department of Teacher Education of Michigan State University. Founded in 1958, the HSHSP is the oldest, continuously running program of its kind in the United States. The HSHSP allows its students to undertake detailed, focused investigation of challenging problems and to participate in many dimensions of the research process—opportunities rarely possible in schools.

Contact
Gail Richmond, Director, High School Honors Science / Mathematics / Engineering Program
(517) 432-4854
gailr@msu.edu

Name of College
Joint Institute for Nuclear Astrophysics
Notre Dame University & Michigan State University

Name of Program
Physics of Atomic Nuclei Collaborative Summer Program

Academic / Career Interest
STEM

Website
http://www.jinaweb.org/outreach/PAN/

Application Timeline
Approx. March

Eligibility
Must be at least a sophomore in high school and interested in science and physics. Requirements: online application and teacher recommendation from a STEM teacher.

Tuition Fees
Estimated fees: FREE

Information about the program:
Notre Dame University, Nuclear Science Laboratory: Students will be introduced to the fascinating fields of astrophysics, cosmology, and nuclear science through lectures and tours, perform a series of experiments using state of the art experimental equipment in Notre Dame's Jordan Hall of Science, experience the college atmosphere at a prestigious university, and learn experimental techniques used by the experimental nuclear astrophysics community through the use of various gamma, neutron and charged particle detectors.

Contact
Micha Kilburn
(574) 631-5326
mkilburn@nd.edu

Name of College
Worcester Polytechnic Institute

Name of Program
Frontiers Summer Program

Academic / Career Interest
STEM

Website
https://www.wpi.edu/academics/pre-collegiate/summer/
stem-residential/frontiers

Application Timeline
Approx. April

Eligibility
Rising 11th or 12th grades. Requirements: application, $50 application fee, recommendation form from student's mathematics teacher, science teacher, or guidance counselor, essay response, and official high school transcript.

Tuition Fees
Estimated fees:

- One session: $2,995
- Two sessions: $4,795

Information about the program:
Frontiers Summer Camp is a residential, on-campus summer program for high school students, Frontiers is celebrating more than 30 years of challenging participants to explore the outer limits of their knowledge in science, technology, engineering, and math (STEM) with current laboratory techniques and exploring unsolved problems across a wide spectrum of disciplines. Frontiers participants will be utilizing state-of-the-art technology and facilities, and enjoy added activities such as evening workshops, field trips, movies, live performances, and tournaments. Throughout each session, teens will focus on one STEM discipline and enroll in one humanities workshop of their choice. Learn from WPI professors and graduate students while using experimental, analytical, and computer technology.

Contact
(508) 831-5000

Name of College
Joint Science and Technology Institute

Name of Program
Joint Science and Technology Institute for Students (JSTI-HS)

Academic / Career Interest
STEM

Website
https://orise.orau.gov/jsti/

Application Timeline
Approx. March

Eligibility
Must be a U.S. citizen, must be age 15, and must be entering the 10th, 11th, or 12th grade. Requirements: application, and recommender information.

Tuition Fees
Estimated fees: FREE

Information about the program:
The Joint Science and Technology Institute for Students (JSTI-HS) is a two-week, fully-funded, residential science, technology, engineering, math (STEM) research program for current high school students in the United States and Department of Defense schools around the world. Students will participate in research projects mentored by Department of Defense research scientists and other subject matter experts. The purpose of the program is to inspire and encourage students to pursue careers in STEM fields, increase STEM literacy, and expose students to the importance of STEM through hands-on, relevant research.

Contact
Marie Westfall
(865) 576-3425
JSTI@orau.org

Name of College
MDI Biological Laboratory

Name of Program
High School Student Summer Research Fellowship

Academic / Career Interest
STEM

Website
https://mdibl.org/education/hs-undergrad/hs-applications/

Application Timeline
Approx. February

Eligibility
Must be at least 16, must be nominated by a teacher prior to applying.

Tuition Fees
Estimated fees: FREE, students receive full room, full meal plan, and a stipend.

Information about the program:
The program provides participants hands-on, research training experience within an advanced laboratory that complements current resident research programs. High school students become a summer cohort with each student assigned and supervised by a senior scientist mentor as well as residential life staff. Co-curricular and residential life programs extend our immersion program to help students develop professional skill sets and foster connections within the scientific research community. Summer high school fellows live on campus in a structured and supervised living-learning environment. High School Fellows are provided with on campus dormitory style accommodations, full meal plans in our dining hall, and a stipend. Travel is not funded. Dormitories are supervised by live-in residential advisors.

Contact
(207) 288-3605
mdibl_info@mdibl.org

Name of College
University of Maine, Established Program to Stimulate Competitive Research (EPSCoR), National Science Foundation

Name of Program
High School Research Internship Program

Academic / Career Interest
STEM

Website
https://umaine.edu/epscor/2018/01/02/3623/

Application Timeline
Approx. February

Eligibility
ALL Maine high school students, but preference is given to Juniors. Applicants must be 16 or older. Students must have daily transportation to the University of Maine at Orono. Requirements: online application, copy of student's transcript, and one letter of recommendation.

Tuition Fees
Estimated fees: FREE, students receive a stipend.

Information about the program:
Students are invited to apply to take part in an exciting, paid research internship opportunity to gain real-world experience. Accepted applicants will work with University of Maine (UMaine) faculty, students, and others to learn about sustainable science and aquaculture. The internship includes an orientation on the UMaine campus, participation in science research, an exploration of career options, and the opportunity to be paid while having fun!

Contact
(207) 581-2285
maine.epscor@maine.edu

Name of College
Math Circle, Emory University & Louisiana State University

Name of Program
Math Summer Program

Academic / Career Interest
STEM

Website
https://www.mathcircle.us/summer

Application Timeline
Approx. May

Eligibility
Rising 9th through 12th graders, who have completed algebra and passion for math, not necessarily ability. Requirements: Student Application, pay the $50 application fee.

Tuition Fees
Estimated fees estimated $1,000 - $2,000

Information about the program:
Math Circle Summer Programs give talented high school students a unique introduction to the complex world of college mathematics. At Math Circle, you will participate in hands-on lessons, activities, and games centered around logic and math. Students test their probability skills at the Math Circle casino, face off against the house and see if they can hit the jackpot! They crack codes and unveil a campus-wide mystery in the Cryptography Scavenger Hunt, and more. Students will take two courses: Combinatorics and Number Theory, taught by graduate students and postdoctoral students in mathematics. In addition, students will choose an elective course ranging from coding to statistics. Over the three weeks of Math Circle, students will be exposed to a wide variety of topics in these fields and will gain a solid foundation in university-level mathematics.

Contact
(225) 892-1981
contact@mathcircle.us

Name of College
SpaceTrek, Morehead State University

Name of Program
Space Science Camp

Academic / Career Interest
STEM

Website
http://www.spacetrekky.org/camp

Application Timeline
Approx. April

Eligibility
High school girls who are at least a sophomore and are interested in STEM. Requirements: online application, one teacher recommendation.

Tuition Fees
Estimated fees: $500

Information about the program:
SpaceTrek is a unique space science camp offered at Morehead State University's state-of-the-art Space Science Center housing a Satellite Development Laboratory, Space Tracking Antennas, Electronic Laboratories and a digital Star Theater for planetarium and LASER shows. SpaceTrek was created in 2012 as a pilot program thanks to a partnership between AAUW Kentucky and Morehead State University. This one-week educational experience is designed to expose incoming sophomore, junior and senior high school girls to space science and engineering concepts in fun and exciting ways.

Contact
Kim Boggs
(606) 922-2705
spacetrekky@gmail.com

Name of College
IUPI (Indiana University Purdue University Indianapolis) Physics Department

Name of Program
High School Research Summer Program

Academic / Career Interest
STEM

Website
https://physics.iupui.edu/phys/research/high-school-research-opportunities

Application Timeline
Approx. April

Eligibility
High School juniors and seniors. Requirements: a cover letter and essay, contact information for two science teacher recommenders.

Tuition Fees
Estimated fees: FREE

Information about the program:
Open to high school juniors and seniors (and advanced sophomores), the Summer Research Experience in Physics is an intensive six-week summer research program. Selected students are paired with faculty mentors, and participate in cutting-edge research projects in the IUPUI Department of Physics. At the end of the program, each student must complete a written research report and deliver a presentation to physics faculty and fellow students.

Contact
(317) 274-6900
physics@iupui.edu

Name of College
Purdue University & American Chemical Society Project SEED

Name of Program
High School Summer Research Internship

Academic / Career Interest
STEM

Website
http://www.purdueprojectseed.org/

Application Timeline
Approx. April

Eligibility
Be a high school student, complete 1 year of high school chemistry, and meet the family income requirement. Requirements: general information form, academic achievement form, teacher recommendation, parent & financial information, and official transcript.

Tuition Fees
Contact institution for more information.

Information about the program:
The Purdue Project SEED program aims to offer university-level research experience to high school students interested in science and engineering. In this program, the high school student is teamed with a faculty mentor and a graduate researcher in order to make a true scientific impact during his/her internship. While all research projects are rooted in chemistry, the program has a wide range of participating faculty with interests ranging from biotechnology to flexible solar cells. Furthermore, students are given training regarding safety and career training in order to create a balanced program.

Contact
Professor Corey Thompson
(765) 494-9006
cmthompson@purdue.edu

Name of College
Areteem Institute for Mathematics

Name of Program
Zoom Mathematics Summer Camp

Academic / Career Interest
STEM

Website
https://areteem.org/summer-camps/summer-program-overview

Application Timeline
Approx. February

Eligibility
Must be in grades 6th-12th.

Tuition Fees
Estimated fees:

- Georgetown University: $4,775 - $400 = $4,375 (residential)
- UC San Diego: $4,775 - $400 = $4,375 (residential)
- South Bay Area: $1,700 (day camp only)
- Chicago: $1,900 - $200 = $1,700 (day camp only)
- East Bay Area: $1,900 - $200 = $1,700 (day camp only)

Information about the program:
Math Zoom Summer Camp is Arteem's flagship summer program for gifted and advanced middle school and high school students, it has been running since 2007. Math Zoom Summer Camps are usually hosted on prestigious university campuses. Selected campuses that hosted the Math Zoom Summer Camps include Georgetown University, Yale University, University of Chicago, Rutgers University, Boston College, Rensselaer Polytechnic Institute, the University of California at Los Angeles, University of California at Berkeley, Harvey Mudd College, California Polytechnic University, etc.

Contact
(949) 305-1705
info@areteem.org

Name of College
StemWorks Hawaii

Name of Program
Summer internship program

Academic / Career Interest
STEM

Website
http://stemworkshawaii.org/internships/

Application Timeline
Approx. April

Eligibility
Must be in high school(9th-12th), must be enrolled at a Hawaii STEMworks Participating High Schools.

Tuition Fees
Estimated fees: FREE

Information about the program:
The STEMworks™ Summer Internship program prepares students for a STEM career by providing real world opportunities to work with local companies. During the six weeks in the summer, interns use industry standard technologies to develop meaningful projects. Maui Economic Development Board augments their professional experiences with weekly college awareness and employability training websites. Opportunities available for STEMworks™ students on Big Island, Kauai, Maui, Oahu, Molokai, Lanai and Kauai.

Contact
Lalaine Pasion
(808) 875-2341
lalaine@medb.org

Name of College
State of Georgia, Governor's Office of State Achievement

Name of Program
Governor's Honors Program

Academic / Career Interest
STEM

Website
https://gosa.georgia.gov/governors-honors-program

Application Timeline
Teacher nomination deadline: approx. November
Student application deadline: approx. January

Eligibility
Current sophomores or juniors must have their nomination originate with the subject area teacher.

Tuition Fees
Estimated fees: FREE

Information about the program:
The Georgia Governor's Honors Program (GHP) is a residential summer program for gifted and talented high school students who will be rising juniors and seniors during the program. The program offers instruction that is significantly different from the typical high school classroom and that is designed to provide students with academic, cultural, and social enrichment necessary to become the next generation of global critical thinkers, innovators, and leaders. GHP is held in mid-summer (mid-June to mid-July) as a residential educational experience on a college or university campus. Students attend classes in the mornings and afternoons in specific areas of study, and they participate in a wide variety of social and instructional opportunities every evening. Meals and rooms are provided by the program with the only required and expected costs to the students being travel expenses to and from the interviews, a few basic supplies for classes and dorm rooms, and spending money as desired during the program.

Contact
(800) 436-7442

Name of College
The Smithsonian Institute

Name of Program
Youth Engagement through Science

Academic / Career Interest
STEM

Website
https://qrius.si.edu/teachers/youth-programs/yes-science-intern-ships#/-1/

Application Timeline
Contact institution for more information.

Eligibility
Students enrolled in 9th through 11th grade and live in the Washington, DC, metropolitan region, be a U.S. Citizen, Attend a local high school (public or private) in the Washington, DC, metropolitan region (DC, MD or VA, and Participate in both the summer and fall sessions of the program.

Tuition Fees
Estimated fees: FREE, students receive a stipend of $1,750.

Information about the program:
The Youth Engagement through Science (YES!) internship is a career immersion and science communication program for youth between the ages of 13-19, who are currently enrolled in high school (grades 9-11) in the Washington D.C. region. The YES! program, which runs from June-October, gives interns practical experience through a hands-on science internship with Smithsonian science staff. By participating in the program, teens will also have access to behind-the-scenes tours and field trips, creative studio workshops, college preparatory classes, and the opportunity to create their own TED-type talks.

Contact
(202) 633-4588
youthnmnh@si.edu

Name of College
Sigma

Name of Program
SigmaCamp

Academic / Career Interest
STEM

Website
http://sigmacamp.org/

Application Timeline
Approx. April

Eligibility
Students must be 12-16 years old.

Tuition Fees
Estimated fees: $1,250

Information about the program:
SigmaCamp is a week-long math and science sleepaway camp for students 12-16 years old. SigmaCamp gives campers a unique opportunity to learn math and science from professional scientists. SigmaCamp faculty include leading specialists from Stony Brook University, Brookhaven National Lab and Harvard Medical School. The goal of SigmaCamp is to ignite a spark of interest and curiosity in students. At Sigma, campers spend time around scientists who can give a first-hand account of what real science research is like. SigmaCamp shows them the interdependence of the sciences: Physics, Mathematics, Chemistry, Biology, and Computer Science. SigmaCamp hopes not simply to interest campers with cool facts and exciting demos, but to give them a profound understanding of why and how things work.

Contact
(631) 672-1592
info@sigmacamp.org

Name of College
University of Connecticut

Name of Program
Explore Engineering Program

Academic / Career Interest
STEM

Website
http://edoc.engr.uconn.edu/explore-engineering/

Application Timeline
Approx. June

Eligibility
Sophomore or Junior in high school. Requirements: Online application, teacher recommendation letter (must be on official school letterhead).

Tuition Fees
Estimated fees: $700

Information about the program:
Explore Engineering (E2) is a one-week residential summer program for current high school sophomores and juniors. During this exciting week at the University of Connecticut Storrs Campus participants explore engineering careers by working in small groups with faculty and college students. They will learn what various engineers do in the workplace and see engineering concepts demonstrated. During the evenings, through the YESS Program, students focus on a single engineering discipline by fabricating a discipline-specific device. The week wraps up with demonstrations of items the students created during the week. Examples have included: rudimentary EKG devices, Smart Lego vehicles that can follow a trail, fuel cell and other energy efficient devices, wooden bridges, environmentally friendly processes, and how to resolve differences.

Contact
Velda Alfred-Abney
(860) 486-5536
engr-explore@uconn.edu

Name of College
Department of Navy Lab

Name of Program
Science and Engineering Apprenticeship Program (SEAP)

Academic / Career Interest
STEM

Website
https://seap.asee.org/

Application Timeline
Approx. October

Eligibility
High school students who have completed at least 9th grade, must be 16 years of age or older at the time of application to participate, and applicants must be U.S. citizens. Requirements: online application, unofficial transcript, research interests, personal statement and student's recommender's contact information.

Tuition Fees
Estimated fees: FREE, students receive a $3,300 stipend.

Information about the program:
The apprentice program is designed to encourage high school students to pursue science and engineering careers; acquaint qualified high school students with the activities of Department of Navy (DoN) laboratories through summer science and engineering research experiences; to provide students with opportunities in and exposure to scientific and engineering practice and personnel not available in their school environment; to expose those students to DoN research and engineering activities and goals in a way that encourages a positive image and supportive attitude toward our defense community; and to prepare these students to serve as positive role models for their peers by encouraging other high school students to take more science and math courses.

Contact
(202) 649-3833
seap@asee.org

Name of College
Fairfield University

Name of Program
Summer Scholars Program

Academic / Career Interest
STEM

Website
https://www.fairfield.edu/part-time-and-continuing-studies/academic-sessions/summer-session/high-school-programs/summer-scholars/

Application Timeline
Approx. June

Eligibility
Junior or senior in high school. Must have at least a 3.2 GPA.

Tuition Fees
Estimated fees: $3,410

Information about the program:
Fairfield University Summer Scholars Program is a great way for rising junior and senior high school students to obtain a dynamic college experience during the summer. Students can select from a wide array of courses in the sciences, arts, humanities, or the social sciences. Students in the Summer Scholars Program will take one 3-credit course during the two-week period that will meet Monday through Friday for three hours a day. Students in this program will take classes alongside current college students and are expected to complete approximately five hours of pre-work through an online communication website prior to the beginning of class. This may include discussion boards, papers, or another way that students can demonstrate their knowledge. After the program, students will have truly learned what it's like to experience the academic rigor of college and will be better prepared to handle that transition from high school to college.

Contact
summerscholars@fairfield.edu

College Consulting Experts

Free Program Opportunities Collegiate Programs

List of Government Agencies and Offices related to STEM

National Science Foundation
Department of Commerce, National Oceanic and Atmospheric Organization (NOAA), Office of International Affairs
Department of Commerce, National Institutes of Standards and Technology (NIST), International and Academic Affairs Office
Department of Education (DoEd), International Affairs Office
Department of Energy (DOE), International Programs
Department of Energy (DOE), National Laboratories
Department of Health and Human Services, Center for Disease Control (CDC), Global Health
Department of Health and Human Services, Food & Drug Administration (FDA), International Programs
Department of the Interior, Office of International Affairs (DOI)
Department of State, Bureau of Educational and Cultural Affairs
Department of State, Bureau of Oceans and International Environmental and Scientific Affairs (DOS/OES)
Environmental Protection Agency (EPA), International Programs
Executive Office of the President, Office of Science and Technology Policy (OSTP),
National Aeronautics and Space Administration (NASA), Office of International and Interagency Relations
National Institutes of Health (NIH), Fogarty International Center
Smithsonian Institution, Office of Policy & Analysis: International Programs
Central Intelligence Agency (CIA)
United States Geological Survey (USGS)
United States Agency for International Development (USAID)
United States Department of Agriculture (USDA)
United States Department of Agriculture, Agricultural Research Service (ARS)
National Security Agency (NSA)
United States Department of Defense (USDOD) - https://dodstem.us/stem-programs/internships
United States Forest Service
Defense Advanced Research Projects Agency (DARPA)

Free Program Opportunities

Alabama

AgDiscovery Summer Program
AgriTek/SciTek Summer Institutes
NASA one stop shop Initiative (marshall space center location)
Technology Students Association UNITE program - Alabama State
University of Southern Alabama STEM camp Robotics

Alaska

Juneau Community Foundation
Alaska Native Science and Engineering Program
Pacific Northwest Girls Collaborative Project
Alaska Summer Research Academy

Arizona

Science Foundation Arizona
Freeport-McMoran Foundation
SARSEF: SOUTHERN ARIZONA RESEARCH, SCIENCE AND ENGI-
NEERING FOUNDATION
New Edge Science Academy
Barrett Summer Scholars - ASU
Flinn Foundation - Biosciences
Bio5 Institute KEYS program - University of Arizona
ASU - SCENE program
ASU - Joaquin Bustoz Math-Science Honors Program
Translational Genomics Research Institute
Ecology Project International
Arizona Dream Builder Foundation
American Conservation Experience
Barrow Neurological Institute
Liberty Wildlife Institute
TGen Helios Scholars
Arizona Science Center

Arkansas

Arkansas School for Mathematics, Sciences, and the Arts
University of Arkansas for Medical Sciences
University of Arkansas Engineering Summer Academy
Arkansas Museum of History and Science

California
The Yosemite Institute - Naturebridge non profit
LA Makerspace
DIY Girls
Teens Exploring Technology
Mission Bit
Girl Develop It
Rails Bridge
Hispanic Foundation of Silicon Valley
Iridescent
David E Glover Education and Technology Center
Girls To Women
Streetcode Academy
Norcal STEM Education Foundation
Silicon Valley Education Foundation
Center for Powerful Public Schools
FreeCodeCamp
HacktheHood
CSavvy
GirlsWhoCode Summer Immersion Program
GameHeads Oakland
HackAway
The Hidden Genius Project
Level Playing Field Institute
Buck Institute for Research on Aging
Children's Hospital Oakland Research Institute
Eugene and Ruth Roberts Summer Student Academy
Scripps Research Institute
Pacific Gas & Electric
Carlsbad Educational Foundation
Chevron Frontiers of Energy Summer Camp
Keck Graduate Institute

Colorado

Telluride Association Summer Program
Metropolitan State University of Denver
University of Colorado Boulder
University of Denver
Colorado School of Mines
Colorado Rocky Mountain School
Northrop Grumman & UCCS
Colorado State University Particle Physics Internship
CSBR Aerospace Internship
Girls in STEM Denver
ProveIt! Math Academy
MathCamp
CyberSecurity Camp at Rangeview HS
Silicon STEM Academy
Smith College (SSEP program)
KilroysWorkshop
Frontiers of Science Institute
Technology Students Association UNITE program - UCCS
Society of American Military Engineers - US Air Force STEM Camp

Connecticut

The Jackson Laboratory
University of Connecticut Health
Connecticut Science Center
Central Area Health Education Center
Summer Institutes at the University of Saint Joseph
Fairfield University Summer Scholars Program
Science and Engineering Apprenticeship Program (SEAP) - Department of Navy Lab
Explore Engineering program - UConn
CPEP
University of New Haven Summer Youth Academies
CRISP - Yale
Connecticut STEM Foundation
Connecticut Technical High School System's Pre-Electrical and Applied Electronics Technology
SIGMA camp

Delaware

Delaware Technical Community College - STEM Camps
District of Columbia
The Smithsonian Institute

Florida

Institute for Mathematics and Computer Science (IMACS)

Georgia

Governor's Honors Program

Hawaii

STEMWorks Hawaii Summer Internship program
Gene-ius Day Program in partnership w/ University of Hawaii

Idaho

Boise State University Summer programs
Boise State University STEM research program

Illinois

EXPLO summer programs
Illinois Mathematics and Science Academy
Areteem Institute for Mathematics